Philosophy of Life

Philosophy of Life

as Reflected in
the Bānī of Guru Nānak and Upaniṣads

Kanta Arora

DK
PRINTWORLD
Publishers of Indian Traditions

Cataloging in Publication Data – DK
[Courtesy: D.K. Agencies (P) Ltd. <docinfo@dkagencies.com>]

Arora, Kanta, 1948- **author**.
Philosophy of life : as reflected in the bāṇī of Guru Nānak and Upaniṣads / Kanta Arora.
pages cm
Includes bibliographical references and index.

1. Nānak, Guru, 1469-1538 – Criticism and interpretation. 2. Ādi-Granth – Criticism, interpretation, etc. 3. Upanishads – Criticism, interpretation, etc. 4. Life. 5. Sikh philosophy. 6. Hindu philosophy. I. Title.

LCC BL2017.85.N36A76 2018 | DDC 294.663 23

ISBN: 978-81-246-0945-3
First published in India, 2019

Printed and published by:
D.K. Printworld (P) Ltd.
Regd. Office : "Vedaśrī", F-395, Sudarshan Park
(Metro Station : ESI Hospital) New Delhi - 110015
Phones : (011) 2545 3975, 2546 6019
e-mail : indology@dkprintworld.com
Web : www.dkprintworld.com

Preface

THE seed of my love for the hymns of Guru Nānak was sown in my childhood when I was merely ten-year old. A simple old lady in my neighbourhood used to frequently utter *satnām wāheguru* and to my childish question as to why these words are uttered by the Sikhs, she explained with extreme love by reciting first two lines of *Japjī* called *mūla mantra* and quipped after the word *jap* and advised me to attend to my school work first and try to know further when time comes. Her simple explanation to the word *wāheguru* was that she is appreciating her *guru* and any one may use this word for saying *wāh-wāh* for his/her *guru* and there is only one God and His name is *sat*, that is the only Truth. People who tell that *satnām wāheguru* words are only for believers of Sikhism are ignorant of the truth taught by Guru Nānak. Her simple explanation to my childish question remained ever fresh till I myself had a chance and ability to enjoy the universal contents of *Japjī* and other hymns of Guru Nānak in the later years with a strengthened belief in the Ṛgvedic statement:

ekam sat viprā bahudhā vadanti ।
– ṚV I.164.46

Today I am made to believe that those who widened Hindu–Sikh divides and created worst horror and turmoil in the last quarter of the twentieth century are either ignorant or are not willing to understand the real message of Guru Nānak. I personally consider, believe and call the hymns of Guru Nānak "Divine Songs of Life". These describe vividly many aspects of physical and metaphysical lives of human beings on earth in a most simple and practical way for the common man.

I conducted a serious search for the relevant materials to the topic from the *Śrī Guru Granth Sāhib* and the principal Upaniṣads.

Relevant abstracts from the verses have been included in each chapter with their code indicated in their original scriptures. Text of the original language is given in English with transliteration to enjoy and understand the essence of the verses. Selection of various verses on the same topic from different hymns impresses upon the instructions and teachings repeated time and again by Guru Nānak, in broken pieces to address all sorts of seekers at different times and places. Some longer abstracts from his hymns are included to enable the reader grasp the fragmented essence of his scriptures.

The subject matter is divided into six chapters. First chapter provides brief introduction to Guru Nānak and his hymns, Vedic religion, the Upaniṣads and a general overview describing *bānī* (hymn) of Guru Nānak as a divine song of life. It discloses as to what Guru Nānak spoke about himself and about the experiences of life lived. It illustrates as to how his philosophy of life is Upaniṣadic in origination and portrays his sound knowledge of existing Vedic literature, his love for God, godly people and vision of better worldliness. Second chapter discusses cosmogony or origin of creation as explained by Guru Nānak and the Upaniṣads in the hymn *arbada narbada dhauṅdhūkārā* (*Ādi Granth*, p. 1035) and Nāsadīya Sūkta of the *Ṛgveda* along with the concepts of Universal Soul and individual soul, identity between the two, nature of individual soul and body.

Third chapter explores the mutual relationship among God, man and the world, world struggle and other concepts of great relevance to human life. Both Upaniṣads and hymns of Guru Nānak provide a deep insight and understanding into these concepts. Fourth chapter is divided into three parts. First part explores the role of a true *guru* and homage paid to such a *guru* in the hymns of Guru Nānak and Upaniṣads. Second part highlights the mutual love between God and man, expression of love for God; experience of reciprocal love of God, man's feeling fire of separation and urge for His blessed vision and ecstasy of union with God. Third part explains the concept of grace (*nadara*) as illuminated in the hymns of Guru Nānak and the Upaniṣads.

Fifth chapter discusses the aim of man's life, suggested path for his liberation and his personal experience of divinity. With struggling and suffering in the worldly life and deeply in love and fear of God, one tries to find a way as to how he should conduct himself to be happy in life and face death peacefully. One starts searching for the meaning of his life and the true aim of his human form. One may wonder as to what path one may follow in his endeavour to attain liberation. The Upaniṣads prescribe the path to liberation through knowledge of *Brahman* and realization of oneness of individual soul with the Universal Soul. Guru Nānak accepts the basic doctrine of liberation (*mokṣa*) of the Upaniṣads and prescribes *sahaja pāṭha* (spontaneous concentration of mind) for personal experience of divinity within oneself for liberation.

Sixth chapter illustrates as to how Guru Nānak with his transcendental exposition, sharp skill and argumentative capability, and common poetic language enriched, explained, simplified and modernized various theological concepts of philosophy of life for use and understanding of a common man and the physical and experiential realities of life derived therefrom, which are required to be revisited and endorsed afresh generation after generation to keep pace with the changing priorities of life and get the best for oneself out of the fleeting moments of precious life.

There is a humble message for claimants and custodians of the legacy of Guru Nānak to shun all preachers and practices advocating separation, of any institutionalized religion, on the basis of philosophy of life of Guru Nānak from the universal approach of Upaniṣadic philosophy being attributed to Sikhism and Hinduism. Both are above the boundary walls of any institute of religion and for the benefit of all mankind at large. Any argument and strife for confinement of highest knowledge revealed by the sages, seers and Guru Nānak for separation and division of society and caging it into religions rather than absorbing their essence for better living is sheer ignorance.

The aspirants of unveiling the mask of Ultimate Reality and cosmic laws, searching for the god element and dreamers of creating a robot of human form are in fact only the technicians of

Divine Will to add to the magnificence of this wonderful creation for betterment of human life. The revelations in the hymns of creation in Nāsadīya Sūkta and *arbad narbad dhauṅdhūkarā* still hold good for humanity. Divine Force reveals itself to one whom it chooses.

In the present fast-worldly life of competitions and turmoil, seekers of liberation should waste no time in religious conflicts, arguments, pseudo rituals and penances, but should develop harmony with Divine Will and live a life of righteousness, acquire knowledge, pursue for prosperity of health, wealth and accumulations necessary for their security in life and their spiritual advancement. They should not live a sordid life; they may seek sense pleasures and human love to enjoy life but should not be lost in the smoke of these worldly aspirations and crazy run for unreal attractions.

asato mā sadgamaya;
tamaso mā jyotirgamaya;
mṛtyor mā amṛtam gamaya ।

From the unreal lead me to Real,
From darkness lead me to light;
From death lead me to immortality.
– *Bṛhadāraṇyaka Upaniṣad*

Acknowledgements

I FEEL pleasure in expressing my gratitude to my most loving sisters Padma and Usha, my nephews Rajinder Kumar, Ranjan and Deepak who had always been my active support in meeting my targets.

This work is dedicated to my soulmate, late Shri H.C. Arora whose cherished memory is a continued source of strength and inspiration for me to continue my research work. I am sincerely thankful to my mother-in-law, brothers and sisters-in-law for their continued love and care enabling me to complete this work.

Kanta Arora

Contents

1

Bānī (Hymns) of Guru Nānak and Upaniṣads

Period of Guru Nānak

PHILOSOPHY of any religion/individual work is intensely influenced by the prevailing socio-political and religious atmosphere. Guru Nānak lived in the second half of the fifteenth century and the first half of the sixteenth century. During his life, he travelled hundreds of miles towards the east, west, north and south of India. He also crossed the Indian borders several times and went to other countries of varying cultures in search of truth with his universal message of love for God, man and divine life.

Before the birth of Guru Nānak, India was under the rule of several Muslim dynasties. When Guru Nānak was born, Bahlol Lodhī was the ruler of Delhi. He was succeeded by Sikandar Lodhī who a policy of persecution. Hindu temples were destroyed and mosques were erected on their sites. Guru Nānak was in his teens at that time. After Sikandar, Ibrāhim Lodhī came to the throne. He was a weak *sultān*. Babur defeated him. He established the Mughal rule in India. The horror and tyranny of Babur and his on-slaught of Hindus appear in many verses of Guru Nānak. He called Babur an angel of death and destruction. As the story goes, the military strength of the Hindus was reduced and several efforts were made to eliminate Hinduism. There was a great religious intolerance on the part of the conqueror, and the defeated people suffered heavily.

The society was divided into two parts representing Indian culture by the Hindus and Semitic culture by the Muslims. Muslims being conquerors had the upper hand and were divided into threefolded strata of the upper, the middle and the lower classes. The upper class led an idle and luxurious life. They took lion's share of earnings of poor people. Middle-class people shared their booty, and also led an easy life. Guru Nānak called upper-class people lions and middle-class people as dogs. "The kings are lions, their officials like dogs disturb the resting people. Officials are like nails which make wounds." Muslim society had two main divisions based on their religious practices. Some were Shias and others were Sunnis.

Hindu society had four major castes and had to face Muslim oppression and tyranny. The main religion of India before the advent of Islam was Hinduism which was divided into various cults. Gopal Singh (2005) writes:

> Guru Nānak came to the scene when three currents, viz. Advaitism, Vaiṣṇavism and yogic cult were flowing.[1]

Doctrine of Advaitism popularized by Śaṅkarācārya postulated that while the *jīva* (soul), *jagat* (world) and *Brahman* (God) were one in essence, they appeared distant and individualized through *māyā* (illusion) and *avidyā* (ignorance). If *jīva* (individual soul) was to acquire *jñāna* (knowledge of the real), through suppression of impressions or desire by giving up all worldly activity, the identity of the three would be established. This creed was too intellectual for ordinary minds to grasp and required disciplined life, too hard to endure. If there is no distinction between the individual soul and *Īśvara* to whom is one to pray except to oneself as he does in "I am He (*aham brahmāsmi*) or That are Thou".

Rāmānuja believed in qualified monism or Viśiṣṭādvaita, Nimbārka in Dvaitādvaita (dual–non-dualism), Madhvācārya in dualism and Vallabha in pure non-dualism. Vaiṣṇavism or the cult of Viṣṇu, popularly known as the school of Bhakti, love or worship of the incarnation of Viṣṇu, like Rāma and Kṛṣṇa, was enjoined to the exclusion of Śaṅkara's *jñāna-mārga*. Cult of Bhakti was made very popular all over India by known *bhakta*s like Rāmānuja, Madhvācārya, Rāmānanda, Kabīr, Vallabhācārya and Caitanya who, differing here and there in their metaphysical beliefs, all believed that it was through love and worship of Viṣṇu in any form of his incarnations one's deliverance from the cycle of

---

[1] *Sri Guru Granth Sahib*, pp. xxv-xxvi.

karma and transmigration could be achieved. They set up a ritual so elaborate for worship that the priestly class could not be dispensed with. The Nātha *yogīs*, who find numerous references in the *Guru Granth*, were nomads wearing mendicants' garb and exploiting spiritual and physical discipline to perform miracles. Their creed, being an amalgam of Śaivism, Buddhism, Yoga of Patañjali and Vedāntism, found widespread popularity. They were supposed to live on air, fly like birds in the sky, bury themselves underground and keep alive through the control of breath, become invisible and so on. These attributes made them a natural fascination for common people. Their blessings were therefore eagerly sought by householders and their curse was avoided at any cost. Kabīr, whose name was a household word when Guru Nānak started his preaching, had indeed emphasized before Guru Nānak, some of the spiritual and moral aspects of life which the Guru followed later.

The hymns of Guru Nānak reflect on all such prevailing political, social and religious conditions.

About Guru Nānak

Guru Nānak lived a life of versatility and left behind a rich spiritual heritage for the succeeding generations of mankind. He was born on 15 April 1469. He was born in the direct line of descendants of Kuśa, one of the sons of Lord Rāma.[2] His father Kalyān Chand was a village *paṭwārī* and was known as Mehtā Kālu. As a child he was often seen absorbed in deep meditation. He learnt Sanskrit and Persian. He was married to Sulakhni and had two sons, namely, Sri Chand and Lakṣmī Chand.

Bhāī Gurdās, who scribed the *Ādi Granth*, said in his Vār Pehlī that Guru Nānak led the life of an ascetic at least for a short period.[3] His food was sand and pod of ak, and his bed was spread on stones. He performed great austerities to the supreme satisfaction of God. J.R. Puri in his book *Guru Nanak: His Mystic Teachings*, quoting Dabistan, says that Guru Nānak underwent severe austerities. At

[2] Kohli, 1969, *Philosophy of Guru Nanak*, p. 1.

[3] Komal, 2007, *Bhai Gurdas di Pehli Var*, p. 91.

first he reduced his food, and after some time, he depended upon drinking a little cow milk. After that he lived on ghee and then on water. Of late, he lived on air like those who in Hindustan are called *pavanahārīs* (consumers of air) alone.[4] Bhāī Gurdās further says that the master visited many places of pilgrimage, especially on festival days to see the people performing the rituals related to their orthodox religions without any loving adoration. During these visits he met ascetics, *yogīs*, *siddhas*, *nāthas*, *gurus* and their disciples and searched for true devotees or believers.[5] He also visited Puri and met Caitanya Mahāprabhu. The two together led the congregation in devotional music or *kīrtana* and divine dance. This meeting left a deep impression on Vaiṣṇavaite scholars and its memory lingered for years as is clear from the following invocation:[6]

> Salutation to Guru Nānak who is enlightened and learned in all scriptures and is the *guru* of *gurus*.
>
> – Ram Narayan Mishra, invocation in Baṅgālī commentary on *Dasam Skandha*

Guru Nānak travelled throughout the length and breadth of India and visited religious centres and holy places of Hindus and also visited Arabian countries, Afghanistan, Tibet and Ceylone (Sri Lanka). His journeys are known as *udāsīs* because he travelled like a person who has renounced the world. He put the dress of a pilgrimage, which varied according to the place of his visit and the people he met. On his south journey he "wore wooden sandals, took a stick in his hand, twisted a rope round his head as a turban and on his forehead put a patch and streak".[7] While proceeding to north, he "wore leather on his feet and a fur robe twisted around his body, and on his forehead stamped a saffron *tilaka*".[8] When he went to Mecca, it is said that he "disguised himself in the blue

---

4 Puri, 2004, *Guru Nanak: His Mystic Teachings*, p. 19.

5 Komal, 2007, op. cit., p. 92.

6 Puri, 2004, op. cit., p. 26.

7 Macauliffe, 2009, *The Sikh Religion*, p. 147.

8 Ibid., p. 163.

dress of a Muhammadan pilgrimage, took a *fakīr*'s staff in his hand and a collection of his hymns under his arm. He also carried with him in style of a Mussalman devotee a cup for his ablutions and a carpet whereon to pray."[9]

It can be concluded that he identified himself with the people whom he visited in different places and adopted their garb signifying that change of outer costumes and look is immaterial for a man who lives in Pure Consciousness and remains tuned to the Ultimate Truth.

In the concluding part of his last *udāsī*, he returned to Kartārpur, and according to Bhāī Gurdās, put aside his garments of renunciation.[10] He spent his remaining life (1520-39) at Kartārpur on the banks of River Rāvī and led the life of a teacher of truth in the garb of a devoted householder.[11] At Kartārpur, a watch before day, the *Japjī* and the *Āsā kī Vār* were repeated and then, followed reading and expounding of *guru*'s hymns till a watch and a quarter after the sunrise. This was succeeded singing and reading the *āratī* (*gagana meiṅ thāla*). In the third watch, there was again singing after which in the evening the *sodar* was read. Then all dined together. The repast ended with further singing. After a watch of night had elapsed, the *sohilā* was read, and everyone then, retired. The *guru*, when not engaged in prayer, occupied himself, during the day, in giving instructions to all who sought it. The most important features of this phase were institution of *laṅgara* (community kitchen) and *sevā* (voluntary physical labour). The *laṅgara* symbolized equality and brotherhood.

We generally see facts and fictions interwoven in the life history of saints and prophets which cannot be easily separated. The sources about the life of Guru Nānak are either *janamsākhīs* (biographies) or the places built in his memory. According to S.S. Kohli some people have made the *janamsākhīs* unauthentic by deliberately twisting the existing material or adding some false

---

9 Macauliffe, 2009, p. 174.

10 Komal, 2007, op. cit., p. 95.

11 Puri, 2004, op. cit., p. 34.

and objectionable incidents. However the true personality of the *guru* is reflected in his compositions.[12]

Hymns of Guru Nānak

Guru Nānak began to compose poetry at a very early age. The thoughts expressed in his composition *Patti*, which is considered to be written in a very tender age, are excellent depiction of his ability to describe the nature of God, need for a *guru*, law of *karma* and transmigration, and the way to escape from the cycle of birth and death. We get glimpses of his life's journey from his refusal to wear the sacred thread saying:

> Let kindness be cotton from which the thread of tranquillity is spun, let the continence be the knot and virtue the twist for the sacred thread. – *Ādi Granth,* p. 471

And also from his last uttering while departing from this world:

> Hail the creator, who hath put each one in this world to his task and when the span is run out and the measure is full, the soul departs the body. – Ibid., p. 578

His hymns are beautifully replete with his philosophy of life and reflect his maturity of spiritual development. He called himself "Nānak śayara" or Nānak the poet. He composed and sang his own verses wherever he went. The fifth Guru, Arjan Dev collected these verses from the people while compiling the *Ādi Granth.*

There is no doubt about the authenticity of Guru Nānak compositions included in the *Ādi Granth.*[13] Major works of Guru Nānak are:

1. *Japjī,*
2. *Āsā kī Vār,*
3. *Mājh kī Vār,*
4. *Malār kī Vār,*
5. *Sidh Gosṭẖa,* and

---

[12] Kohli, 1969, op. cit., p. 7.

[13] Ibid., p. 8.

6. *Dakhanī Oṁkār.*

Japjī is considered a short summary of the *Ādi Granth*. It is meant for recitation in the early hours of morning. Besides the *mūla mantra*, it has thirty-eight stanzas called *pauṛīs*. It deals with the everlasting philosophy and is said to have been composed by Guru Nānak in the latter years of his life, when he settled in Kartārpur after his long journeys. Guru Nānak wrote three *vārs* as stated above which are included in the *Ādi Granth*. In the pre-Nānak period, heroic ballads were written by bards and singers of these songs, wherein the actions of the heroes in the battlefield were highly praised. These heroic ballads were called *vārs*. Guru Nānak adopted this style of folk poetry to instill the spirit of moral and spiritual heroism in people. All the *vārs* are set to the music and put under *rāgas* in the *Ādi Granth*. Guru Nānak wrote these three *vārs* in Āsā, Mājh and Malār Rāgas. These *vārs* contain important philosophical points and description of some aspects of contemporary life. The *Sidh Goṣṭha* contains the conversation in poetry of the *siddhas* and *yogīs* on one side, and Guru Nānak and his companions on the other side. The *Dakhanī Oṁkār* expresses his ideas and imaginary thoughts. These major works contain important aspects of human life. Guru Nānak's philosophy of life discussed in the present work is based on these major works.

It is a common belief that prophets/saints/great poets experience sudden insights and express their experiences in most simple way as such there should be no hair-splitting exercise for interpretations of their works. They may not care to build the systems but report insights of thoughts and visions. In ordinary human psychology there are four principal levels of consciousness. The primary level is the immediate experience of individual in the present ongoing moment of the stream of consciousness and is a pure phenomenon before any judgement or any concept but is only pure sensation. In the secondary level, process of awareness, thinking, judging and concept usage comes into action and language and memory commence. In the third level, I-ness and emotional reactions occur and identity with the personal thoughts or emotions is established. In the fourth stage, advanced concepts, cultural, social and ethical considerations, affect the stream of consciousness. Sometimes the experiences of Pure Consciousness are brought down to the lowest levels by the followers, during their interpretations, to suit their own personal whims or fancies to acquire name and fame or supremacy in the world.

I endeavoured to search for the original *bānī* (hymns) of Guru Nānak relevant to my topic from the *Śrī Guru Granth Sāhib* for comparative study with the contents of principal Upaniṣads.

Vedic Religion

During the time of Guru Nānak there were three main religions in India: Hinduism, Jainism and Buddhism. Hinduism is a Vedic religion, and Jainism and Buddhism reject the authority of the Vedas. The Vedas are the basic scriptures of the Hindus and the highest authority in all matters pertaining to religion and philosophy. The four Vedas are the *R̥gveda*, the *Sāmaveda*, the *Yajurveda* and the *Atharvaveda*. Each Veda consists of four parts, i.e. Mantras, Brāhmaṇas, Āraṇyakas and Upaniṣads. The Mantras present the first stage of the Vedic thought wherein prayers are offered to different deities. The Brāhmaṇas contain the formulas of sacrificial rites. The Āraṇyakas are the forest treatises, which give philosophical interpretation of the rituals. The Upaniṣads are the revelations of the spiritual truth. These four parts of Vedas are associated with the four stages of life, that is, Mantras are meant for *brahmacarya*, the Brāhmaṇas for *gr̥hastha*, the Āraṇaykas for *vānaprastha* and the Upaniṣads for *saṁnyāsa*. The first two parts of the Vedas constitute the ritual section, known as *karma-kāṇḍa*. The third part is known as meditation section (*upāsanā-kāṇḍa)*. The fourth and the final part is called knowledge section (*jñāna-kāṇḍa)*.

Guru Nānak was born and brought up in the Hindu fold, as such he said much about the Hindu institutions, precepts and doctrines, rituals and sacraments. Nānak has expressed his views that the scriptures of Hindus and non-Hindus (*kiteb*s) have not been able to know *Brahman* completely, who is without any father, mother, son and brother. Guru Nānak also talked about six *śāstra*s (systems) in his first *vār*. He seems to have met the followers and believers of all these systems during his journeys in India and brought under discussion their theories and doctrines.

Upaniṣads

The root of the word Upaniṣad is *upa* meaning near, *ni* meaning down, *ṣad* meaning to sit. It denotes the gathering of seekers sitting down close to the teacher for learning from him the higher knowledge. *Ṣad* also means to loosen, to attain and to annihilate. Thus the etymological meaning of the word implies humility with which a student should approach a competent teacher for *vidyā* (higher knowledge) to dispel darkness of his ignorance about the self.

Says S. Radhakrishnan in his book *The Principal Upanishads*:

> The Upaniṣads represent a great chapter in the history of spirit. . . .They have survived many changes, religious and secular and helped many generations of men to formulate their views on chief problems of life existence.[14]

Swami Ranganathananda, in his book *The Charm and Power of Upanishads*, says:

> Swami Vivekananda presented Vedānta as a fearless philosophy of life which helps man to frame ideologies for himself combining the intensity of the fanatic with the extensity of the materialist.[15]

Constant summons to man is to wake up and march on. Adapting the powerful words of the *Kaṭha Upaniṣad*: *uttiṣṭhata, jāgrata, prāpya, varaṇa nibodhāt*, he said: "Arise, awake and stop not till the goal is reached".

The Upaniṣads are the works of deep philosophy. They speculate about the nature of *Brahman* (Ultimate Reality) and *ātman* (individual self). According to Swami Nikhilananda, the Upaniṣads advise

> to cultivate a warm love for life, one must enjoy on earth a long life, marriage is compulsory, except for a specified few. One must heighten the powers of senses so that through the enjoyment of material pleasures one may relieve the drabness of everyday existence. However absorption of individuality in *Brahman* is

---

14 Radhakrishnan, 2012, *The Principal Upanishads*, p. 17.

15 Ranganathananda, 2006, *The Charm and Power of Upanishads*, p. 51.

the highest goal.[16]

The Upaniṣadic teachers formulated qualifications for the pupils entitled to study *ātmavidyā* and seekers were subject to severe tests. One of the cardinal disciplines for the knowledge of *ātman* is practical ethical virtues. Self-knowledge is denied to him who has not first got rid of evil thoughts and is not pacified and subdued. They teach regarding *jīvas*, *jagat* and *Īśvara* (living beings, the universe and God), nature and attributes of *Brahman* and its powers of creation, preservation and ultimate destruction. Vedic rituals are observed at the time of birth, marriage, death and other important occasions of life. Liberation through knowledge of *ātman* is to be acquired now and here in this life and not anywhere else, after death.

We find strong women like Maitreyī, a type of spiritual woman fit to be a consort of philosopher Yājñavalkya and Gārgī who is fully equipped in the art of intellectual warfare and dare to make her presence felt where a number of great philosophers are assembled in the court of King Janaka. In the *Chāndogya Upaniṣad* the son, who wished to become a *brahmacārī*, asked his mother about his ancestry. Mother Jābālā tells to her son Satyakāma that she does not know of what ancestry he has, as she was busy with her many (household) duties and attending on guests when she conceived him. Sage Gautama accepts to teach Satyakāma as he considers the truthfulness of the reply of a mother saying that none but a brāhmaṇa would have spoken like this.

The ultimate goal of the Upaniṣads is to show the way to liberation through *jñāna* or unitive knowledge of *Brahman*.

PRINCIPAL UPANIṢADS

The principal Upaniṣads are accepted to be those which Śaṅkarācārya "chose to comment upon. They are ten in number and enumerated in the Indian tradition as follows: *Īśa*, *Kena*, *Kaṭha*, *Praśna*, *Muṇḍaka*, *Māṇḍūkya*, *Taittirīya*, *Aitareya*, *Chāndogya*, and *Bṛhadāraṇyaka*".[17] The present study includes the following principal Upaniṣads only.

---

[16] Swamy Nikhilananda, 2008, *The Upanishads*, p. 60.

[17] Ranganathananda, 2006, op. cit., p. 5.

Īśa Upaniṣad

It contains the central theme of all the Upaniṣads in its opening verse, namely, the spiritual unity and solidarity of all existence. It says that the opening of the truth is covered with a golden disc. This veil must be removed so that the seeker may behold the truth. It refers to both the discipline of action and discipline of knowledge. Life in the world alone leads to one result and meditation to another. They who devote themselves both to life in the world and to meditation overcome death and achieve immortality.[18] The two disciplines should be harmonized. In the heart of all existence of the universe, the Lord, who alone is the Ultimate Reality, resides.

Kena Upaniṣad

It illuminates the nature of knowledge by pointing out the eternal knower behind all acts of knowing and purifies man's concept of Ultimate Reality revealing its character as the eternal self of man and the self of the universe. At whose behest the mind thinks? Who makes the tongue speak, who directs the eye to form and colour and the ear to sound?[19] Self is the ear of the ear, mind of the mind, speech of the speech, breath of the breath and eye of the eye. Him the tongue cannot express, eye cannot see and mind cannot grasp. Flash of light and wink of eye are his power.

Katha Upaniṣad

It holds special attraction for all the students of Upaniṣads for a mixture of poetry, deep mysticism and philosophy expressed therein. It contains the brief sum of Vedānta and its charm is heightened by the dialogue between old Yama, the teacher, and young Naciketā:

> Know that the Self is the rider, body the chariot, intellect the charioteer, mind the reins, senses are horses, roads they tread are the mazes of desires.[20]

---

[18] *Īśa Upaniṣad* 10-11.

[19] *Kena Upaniṣad* 1.1-2.

[20] *Kaṭha Upaniṣad* 1.3.3.

When the mind lacks discrimination and is uncontrolled, his senses are unmanageable, like the restive horses of the charioteer. But if a man has a real understanding for charioteer, and a controlled mind for reins then only he can reach the end of the journey. Senses of a wise man follow mind, mind follows intellect, intellect ego, and ego Self.

> Arise and awake and approach the master. Good is one thing, pleasant is another. Blessed are those who choose the good over the pleasant. Both good and pleasant present themselves to men, and wise after examination of both can distinguish one from another.[21]

Self is without any sound, form, cannot be touched, non-dying, without taste, odourless, without beginning and without end, eternal, not subject to change and beyond any nature.

By what faculty a mystic can realize God? It tells that it is only when the whole moral being is purged of evil that one is able to realize the greatness of God. We have to extract *ātman* courageously from our body as one extracts a blade of grass from the sheath.[22] Types of mystical experiences of forms and hearing of various sounds on the way to realization are also illustrated with a suggestion that *ātman* cannot be realized except by one whom it itself chooses. With the self-realization the knobs of the heart are broken, all the doubts are cleared and solved, and effects of all his actions are annihilated.

PRAŚNA UPANIṢAD

In this Upaniṣad a group of six students questions on various aspects of Vedānta, and answers are given by their teacher, Sage Pippalāda. The practice of austerity, faith and chastity of body and mind are emphasized as special qualifications on the part of pupils seeking deep spiritual knowledge. As spokes join the rim of a wheel, *prāṇa* dividing itself into five parts supports body and upholds it.

---

21 *Kaṭha Upaniṣad* 1.2.2.

22 Ibid. 2.3.17.

MUṆḌAKA UPANIṢAD

It classifies knowledge (*vidyā*) into *para* (higher), *apara* (lower) and describes all sciences, arts, literature, politics and economics including holy Vedas and sacred books as positive knowledge (*apara*). "It proclaims that one knowledge, as *para*, by which the imperishable changeless reality of the one behind the many is realized."[23]

As web comes out of the spider and is withdrawn, as plants grow from soil, hair and nails from the body, so springs the universe from eternal *Brahman*. From him are born hymns, devotional chants, scriptures, sites and division of time.[24]

The Self is not known through the study of scriptures or through subtlety of intellect nor through much of learning, but by one who longs for him. Self reveals his true being to him. Having known the Self, one is filled with joy, blessed with tranquillity of mind and is free from passion.

The sage of the *Muṇḍakopaniṣad*, when he comes to realize the *Brahman*, falls into mystic ruptures and finds *Brahman*, before and behind, right and left, above and below him. Such is the ecstasy of self-realization by personal experience of divinity.

MĀṆḌUKYA UPANIṢAD

The life of a man is divided between waking, dreaming and dreamless sleep but transcending these three states is superconscious vision, called the fourth. First aspect of Self is universal person, the collective symbol of created beings in his physical nature *vaiśvānara*. Second aspect is in his mental nature *taijasa*, enjoyer of subtle impressions in his mind of deeds done in the past. Third aspect is in dreamless sleep (*prajñāna*) wherein he experiences neither strife nor anxiety: he is said to be blissful and an experiencer of bliss. Fourth aspect is the Self. It is pure unitary consciousness, wherein awareness of the world and multiplicity is completely obliterated. It is one without a second.

---

[23] *Muṇḍaka Upaniṣad* 1.1.4-5.

[24] Ibid. 1.1.7.

The word *auṁ* (*oṁ*) is used in this Upaniṣad as the most effective symbol of *Brahman*. It prescribes meditation by means of *oṁ* as a way to realization. By continuous meditation by the symbol *oṁ* man is relieved of his sins by the power of chants, just as snake is relieved of its slough. It contains one of the four *mahāvākyas* of Upaniṣads: *ayam ātma brahma*. This *ātman* (self) of man is *Brahman*.[25]

TAITTIRĪYA UPANIṢAD

It explains *Brahman* in a systematical way as, "that from which all these beings are born, by which after being born, they live, and into which they merge when they cease to be".[26] A man by ignorance identifies oneself with the material sheaths that shroud his true self. Going beyond these he becomes one with *Brahman*. There is a prayer: "Thou art the refuge of those who surrender themselves to thee. Reveal thyself to me, make me thy own, I take refuge in thee", and advises a lay student for right conduct and action, study teachings of scriptures, truthfulness in word, deed and thought. One should have poise and exercise self-control, perform his everyday duty with a cheerful heart and an unattached mind.

Brahman is the Self. From him came ether; out of ether, air, out of air, fire; out of fire, water; out of water, earth; out of earth, vegetation; out of vegetation, food; out of food, the body of man. From unmanifest he created manifest hence he is known as self-existent. By fear of *Brahman* the wind blows, sun shines and gods perform their tasks.

AITAREYA UPANIṢAD

It proclaims the truth of another *mahāvākya*: *prajñānam brahma* (*Brahman* is Pure Consciousness).[27] *Brahman* is the source, sustenance and end of the universe; it partakes in every phase of existence. It walks with the walking man, dreams with the dreamer, sleeps the deep sleep of a dreamless sleeper; but he transcends these three states to become himself. Its true nature is Pure Consciousness.

---

[25] *Māṇḍūkya Upaniṣad* 2.

[26] *Taittirīya Upaniṣad* 3.1.1.

[27] *Aitareya Upaniṣad* 3.1.3.

CHĀNDOGYA UPANIṢAD

It utters a deep spiritual and philosophical thought which is treated as another one of the four *mahāvākyas*. It sings the glory of divinity of man *tat tvam asi* (you are that).[28] This has been repeated nine times. It advises for attaining the knowledge of this divinity of man as a remedy to face the deeper ills of life: *tarati śokam ātmavit* (the knower of *ātman* rises above all sorrow).

Brahman is the source of all appearances, sensations, desires and deeds. But all these are merely names and forms. One must realize the identity between him and the self for knowledge of *Brahman*. The talk between Śvetaketu, proud of his learning, and his father Uddālaka regarding the knowledge by knowing which all things are known is most fascinating. The identity between the individual soul and the Universal Soul is established by illustrations.

The parable of the blindfolded man,[29] in the *Chāndogya Upaniṣad*, signifies the importance of initiation by a spiritual teacher to progress step by step on the path of realization. Only one who develops faith and respect can reflect on the eternal truth. One gains faith and respect for God who approaches a *guru*, only one who struggles to achieve self-control approaches a *guru*, and one who struggles to achieve self-control, finds joy in it.

BṚHADARAṆYAKA UPANIṢAD

It is the longest Upaniṣad. It sums up the theme of all the Upaniṣads, namely, the divinity of man and spiritual solidarity of the whole universe in *Brahman*. It explains another one of the four *mahāvākyas*, namely, *aham brahmāsmi* (I am *Brahman*)[30] besides the *ayam ātma brahma* of the *Māṇḍūkya Upaniṣad*. It characterizes *Brahman* as without any fear and presents its realization by man in this very life as greatest achievement for a state of absolute fearlessness and fullness of delight.

The subtle principal of life is that yarn wherein this life and

---

[28] *Chāndogya Upaniṣad* 6.8.7.

[29] Ibid. 6.14.1.

[30] *Bṛhadāraṇyaka Upaniṣad* 1.4.10.

the next life and all the beings are twisted. When a man dies, his limbs are loosened, for as long as one is alive, these are held together by that thread of life. The seers call it *akṣara*, in which thread of life is woven, warp and weft. That word is *Brahman*. For one cannot achieve anything without word. It resides in the organ of speech and the ether, which is the primary cause of the universe, is its eternal support. The word is knowledge. For a friend and all knowledge, spiritual or otherwise can be known through word only. It is the word through which we gain knowledge of this world and beyond it. The knowledge of all creatures is also known through word. So word is *Brahman*.

What serves as the light for the man, when there is no sun, moon, fire, or sound?[31] The Self is indeed his light, by the light of the Self man sits, moves, does his work, and when his work is done, rests.

When a man is about to die, the subtle body, mounted by the intelligent Self groans like a heavy laden cart groans under its burden. The path of liberation is subtle, hard and long. *Brahman* can be apprehended only as knowledge itself – knowledge that is one with the reality, inseparable from it. For it is beyond all proof, beyond all instruments of thought. So let the wise man live a life and conduct himself in way to attain knowledge of *Brahman*. All arguments are useless and wasteful as no one can know him by arguments only.

Gods, men and *asura*s all are His descendants and the teaching given to each is understood as *da – damayata* (self-control for gods), *da – datta* (charity for men), *da – dayadhavam* (compassion for *asuras*).[32] Be self controlled, be charitable and be compassionate.

These scriptures have dominated the Indian philosophy, religion and life. Guru Nānak's philosophy of life can be traced back to the Upaniṣads. Guru Nānak has mentioned all the four Vedas in his *Āsā kī Vār* (*pauṛī* 13, *śloka* 2). He says that all the four Vedas are truthful, those who study and ruminate them can

---

[31] *Bṛhadāraṇyaka Upaniṣad* 4.3.2-6.

[32] Ibid. 5.2.1-3.

discriminate between good and bad. Those who are humble with love and devotion can obtain the final emancipation.

According to S.S. Kohli, longer poems of Guru Nānak may be called modern Upaniṣads.[33] A great similarity is noted between the *Āsā kī Vār* and the *Kaṭhopaniṣad*, which indicates that Guru Nānak had studied the Upaniṣads minutely. He was deeply steeped into the Upaniṣadic lore.[34] Vallabhācārya and Mahāprabhu Caitanya were his contemporaries. He met them in his journey to the East at Jagannātha Purī.[35] But Guru Nānak had his own way of expression. The similarity of thought at some places in his works and his comments somewhere else show his vast knowledge of the old scriptures. It may also be the result of his discussions with the *paṇḍitas* and other spiritual dignitaries of his time.

A General Overview of Hymns of Guru Nānak and Upaniṣads

As the Upaniṣads are said to be "breath of the eternal" and the *Bhagavadgītā* (The Song of God), I consider the hymns of Guru Nānak "A Unique Song of Divine Life". Contents of some of his hymns have become a common language for all people who happen to read or listen to these. He talked about the life lived, material spans of life, human nature, role of a true *guru* in life, futility of observance of pseudo rituals without any spiritual awakening, fall of social, ethical and religious values in his times, connubial bliss (reflection of married life) with a supremacy of love for God, *guru* and godly life.

A — BĀNĪ (HYMNS) OF GURU NĀNAK, A SONG OF LIFE

(A) GURU NĀNAK SPEAKS ABOUT LIFE LIVED AND REAL EXPERIENCES OF LIFE

pahilai piāri lagā thaṇa dudhi ||
dūjai māi bāpa kī sudhi ||
tījai bhayā bhābhī beba ||

---

[33] Kohli, 1969, op. cit., p. 186.

[34] Ibid.

[35] Puri, 2004, op. cit., p. 26.

cauthai piāri upaṅnī kheḍa ||
paṅjavai khāṇa pīaṇa kī dhātu ||
chivai kāmu na puchai jāti ||
satavai saṅji kīā ghara vāsu ||
aṭhabai krodhu hoā tana nāsu ||
nāvai dhaule ubhe sāha ||
dasavai dadhā hoā suāha ||
gae sigīta pukārī dhāha ||
uḍiā haṁsu dasāe rāha ||
āiā gaiā muiā nāu ||
pichai patali sadihu kāva ||
nānaka manamukhi aṅdhu piāru ||
bājhu gurū ḍubā saṁsāru ||
– *Ādi Granth*, pp. 137-38

A newly-born child first loves the milk of his mother. Then he comes to know of his mother and father. Third, he falls in love for his family members like brothers, sisters-in-law and sisters. Fourth, his desire for play arises. Fifth, he goes in search of food and drink. Sixth, sexual desires arise. He is ready to break respect for social bondages. Seventh, he hankers after wealth and his house. Eighth, his body is eaten up by anger. Ninth, his hair gets grey and gets difficulty in breathing. Tenth, he is cremated and mixes with ashes. His friends bid farewell weeping and crying. Soul, the essence, takes flight and does not know where to go. He comes and goes and his name dies. After his departure, food is served on leaf to men and offered to birds also. The non-believers of God live in ignorance; the world is drowning without the guidance of a true *guru*.

dasa bālataṇi bīsa ravaṇi tīsā kā suṅdaru kahāvai ||
cālīsī pūru hoi pacāsī pagu khisai saṭhī ke boḍhepā āvai ||
satari kā matihīṇu asīhāṅ kā viuhāru na pāvai ||
navai kā sihajāsaṇī mūli na jāṇai apabalu ||
ḍhaṅḍholimu ḍhūḍhimu ḍiṭhu mai nānaka jagu dhūe kā dhavalaharu ||
– Ibid., p. 138

One is a child up to the age of ten. At twentieth year, he is young and at thirty he is considered good looking. Ageing forty, he becomes full of life. At fifty, starts falling and at sixty, old age starts coming. At seventy, his mental faculty reduces, and at eighty, he is unable to do his work. At ninety he lies on bed, and he is unable to understand as to how he has gone weak. After searching and researching for such a very long period, I realized that this world is a large stately smokey residence.

In the above two hymns Guru Nānak gives a picture of the lifespan of a common man. He gives a message that life is transitory and the self-willed persons live in darkness, and customs like feeding the crows after death can in no way propitiate the souls of the dead.

hama ādamī hāṅ ika damī muhalati muhatu na jāṇā ||
nānaku binavai tisai sarevahu jāke jīa parāṇā ||
aṅdhe jīvanā vīcāri dekhi kete ke dinā ||
sāsu māsu sabhu jīu tumārā tū mai kharā piārā ||
nānaku sāiru eva kahatu hai sace paravadagārā ||
....
nānaku binavai so kichu pāīē purabi likhe kā lahaṇā ||
....
jaba lagu dunīā rahīē nānaka kichu suṇīē kichu kahīē ||
bhāli rahe hama rahaṇu na pāiā jīvatiā mari rahīye ||
– *Ādi Granth*, pp. 660-61

The life of human beings is very short. One cannot know the time of his departure from this world. Guru Nānak prayed to serve the Lord who is the master of our soul and body. One is ignorant and cannot see and forecast the remaining days of his life. One's breath, soul and flesh are all His. He is so dear to individual. Nānak, the poet says, O Lord, nothing is given by you, which could be pledged to you.

He explains that we get whatever we are predestined to receive. So long as one is alive in this world, he must hear and utter the name of the Supreme Being. There is no way to remain ever in this world. So one should remain dead while alive.

Guru Nānak says that our life is measured for a short period. We have nothing with us to pledge to him to receive his bounties. Since we are not to stay here, we should die to the Self while we are living.

ika dajhahi ika dabīahi ikanā kute khāhi ||
iki pāṇī vici usaṭīahi iki bhī phiri hasaṇi pāhi ||
nānaka eva na jāpaī kithai jāi samāhi ||
– *Ādi Granth*, p. 648

Some cremate the dead, some bury, and some are food for dogs. Some dead bodies are assigned to water, while others are pulled down into wells. One cannot know where the dead go and into what they dissolve.

These lines explain that the dead may be buried, cremated, thrown to dogs, cast in water or thrown into the well as per rituals of different communities, but it is not known into what they merge or what their ultimate fate is.

kūḍu maṅḍapa kūḍu māḍī kūḍu baisaṇahāru ||
kūḍu suinā kūḍu rupā kūḍu painhaṇahāru ||
kūḍu kāiā kūḍu kapaḍu kūḍu rūpu apāru ||
kūḍu mīā kūḍu bībī khapi hoe khāru ||
kūḍi kūḍai nehu lagā visariā karatāru ||
kisu nāli kīcai dosatī sabhu jagu calaṇahāru ||
– Ibid., p. 468

The palaces, the sky scrapers and all the living beings residing therein are false. The relation of husband–wife is also false, they are to get wasted. The human beings who are all false, love falsehood and forget the Almighty Father. There is no one worth friendship as no one shall always be there with you. Other than the Supreme Being, all else is false.

After counting all the worldly accumulations and relations as false, it is in the last line, the gist of the hymn is given that without the light of God, the world is false. Everyone has to leave this world; so with whom should we be friendly?

rāṇā rāu na ko rahai raṅgu na tuṅgu fakīru ||
vārī āpo āpaṇī koi na baṅdhai dhīra ||
– Ibid., p. 936

All of us have to leave this world. The kings, or the nobles, the rich or the poor no one will remain here for ever. When there is a call of death one has to go and no one can stay back.

rūpai kāmai dosatī bhukhai sādai gaṅḍhu ||
labai mālai ghuli mili micali ūghai sauḍi palaṅghu ||
bhaṅu kai kopu khuāru hoi phakaḍu piṭe aṅdhu ||
cupai caṅgā nānakā viṇu nāvaiṅ muhi gaṅdhu ||
– *Ādi Granth*, p. 1288

Beauty and sexual desires are bound together. Similarly hunger and tasty food are friends. Greed remains in a look for wealth. Sleep will search even a small place for bed. Anger roars and causes ruin, and blindly runs after useless conflicts. It is better to remain silent about all this. O, Nānak, but for the Name, one's tongue throws out only filth.

siṁmala rukhu sarāirā ati dīragha ati mucu ||
oi ji āvahi āsa kari jāhi nirāse kitu ||
phala phike phula baka bake kaṁmi na āvahi pata ||
miṭhatu nīvī nānakā guṇa caṅgiāīā tatu ||
sabhu ko nivai āpa kau parakau nivai na koi ||
dhari tārājū tolīē nivai su ga-urā hoi ||
aparādhī dūṇā nivai jo haṅtā miragāhi ||
sīsi nivāiē kiā thīē jā ridai kusūdhe jāhi ||
– Ibid., p. 470

The *simmal* tree is thick and shoots up like an arrow into the heights. But the birds which come near it with some hope return in disappointment. Its fruits are not tasty, its flowers are foul-smelling and its leaves are of no use. Being humble and sweet is a perfect virtue. One bends to himself but no one bows down to another. While weighing on the balancing machine, the side which goes down is heavier. The evil intentions such as that of a deer hunter make him bow down much more. But nothing can be found by merely lowering the head if the intentions are not pure.

cākaru lagai cākarī je calai khasamai bhāi ||
huramati tisano agalī ohu vajahu bhi dūṇā khāi ||
khasamai kare barābarī phiri gairati aṅdari pāi ||
vajahu gavāe agalā muhe muhi pāṇā khāi ||
jisadā ditā khāvaṇā tisu kahīē sābāsi ||

nānaka hukamu na calaī nāli khasama calai aradāsi ||
– *Ādi Granth*, p. 474

A servant, who bows to the will of his employer, gets respect and his salary is doubled. In case he starts equating himself with his employer, he gets rebukes, punishment and loses his wages. Let us hail him who sustains us. No one can issue orders to the Supreme Being. Only prayers to Him help an individual.

In the above three verses, Guru Nānak talks about human nature and emphasizes the need to be more careful in our relationship with God and performance in our real life. Humility with truth is a real virtue.

bhaṅḍi jaṁmīē bhaṅḍi niṁmīē bhaṅḍi maṅgaṇu vīāhu ||
bhaṅḍahu hovai dosatī bhaṅḍahu calai rāhu ||
bhaṅḍu muā bhaṅḍu bhālīē bhaṅḍi hovai baṅdhānu ||
so kiu ma ṅdā ākhīē jitu jaṁmahi rājāna ||
bhaṅḍahu hī bhaṅḍu ūpajai bhaṅḍai bājhu na koi ||
nānaka bhaṅḍaiṅ bāharā eko saca soi ||
– Ibid., p. 473

A woman gives birth to a man; a man is conceived within a woman's body; he gets engaged and married to a woman. Woman is a friend and a source of future generations to come; when a wife dies, her husband seeks another wife. Man is bound to woman. She cannot be called bad. A woman gives birth to kings, a woman is born from a woman. There is no one without a woman. Only the Supreme Being is sans a woman.

hukamī hovani ākāra hukamu na kahiā jāī ||
hukamī hovani jīa hukami milai vaḍiāī ||
hukamī utamu nīcu hukami likhi dukha sukha pāīahi ||
ikanā hukamī bakhasīsa iki hukamī sadā bhavāīahi ||
– Ibid., p. 1

With the command of the Supreme Being bodies are created. One cannot describe His command. By His command souls come into being. High name and fame comes by His command. He places some very high and others low. By His written destiny, one gets pain and pleasures. There are some who are blessed and forgiven while others go on wandering aimlessly forever.

In these lines Guru Nānak speaks about the Divine Will and the Divine Power of Creation.

karamī āvai kapaḍā nadarī mokhu duāru ॥
– *Ādi Granth*, p. 2

One acquires physical body by the *karma* of past actions. But emancipation is possible only by His Grace.

Guru Nānak explains that past *karmas* bring forth the cycle of birth and death but emancipation comes by His Grace.

dukhu dārū sukhu rogu bhaiā jā sukhu tāmi na hoī ॥
– Ibid., p. 469

Suffering brings great medicine. Pleasure brings disease because in pleasures there is no desire for God.

Guru Nānak explains that man remembers God in suffering, as such it becomes a blessing in disguise.

satigura jevaḍu dātā ko nahī sabhi suṇiahu loka sabāiā ॥
satiguri miliē sacu pāiā jinhī vicahu āpu gavāiā ॥
jini saco sacu bujhāiā ॥
– Ibid., p. 465

Listen O, all People! True *guru* is the biggest giver. When one meets a true *guru*, one finds the Supreme Being. True *guru* removes all filth from within and teaches the path to the truth of truths.

In the above lines Guru Nānak explains the role of a true *guru*.

khaṅḍita nidrā alapa ahāraṁ nānaka tatu bīcāro ॥
– Ibid., p. 939

One should sleep less and eat less; this is the sum total of wisdom.

haku parāiā nānakā usu sūara usu gāi ॥
guru pīru hāmā tā bhare jā muradāru na khāi ॥
– Ibid., p. 141

To grab other's belongings is like eating forbidden animals for the Muslim as well as the Hindu. The *guru* (peer) only stands by those who avoid this practice.

In the above two verses, Guru Nānak advises to eat less and sleep less and avoid grabbing other's share as these hamper progress in the spiritual life.

All the above verses speak of a life lived and experienced.

(B) GURU NĀNAK SPEAKS ABOUT HIMSELF

Guru Nānak did not claim himself to be a prophet. He considered himself to be assigned the task of singing the praises of God by the Almighty Himself. He was drenched to the skin with the perfume of God's nectar.

hau ḍhāḍhī vekāru kārai lāiā ||
rāti dihai kai vāra dhurahu phuramāiā ||
ḍhāḍhī sacai mahali khasami bulāiā ||
sacī siphati sālāha kapaḍā pāia ||
sacā aṁmṛta nāmu bhojanu āiā ||
guramatī khādhā raji tini sukhu pāiā ||
ḍhāḍhī kare pasāu sabadu vajāiā ||
nānaka sacu sālahi purā pāiā ||
– *Ādi Granth*, p. 150

I was a bard without any work. The Supreme Being called me for His service and ordered me to sing His praises at every moment of day and night. My Master called me to His presence in His true mansion. He empowered me to sing His true praise and glory. He offered me the food and drink of the gods. This food has satisfied me. Now this bard resides in the Lord's praise. By singing His praises the perfect Lord is revealed to me.

Here Guru Nānak speaks about his personal experience of divinity through his constant practice of repeating the *name* and singing the praises of the Lord. He maintained his humble identity of being a bard in the Lord's court in many of his hymns.

guramukhi khojata bhae udāsī || *darasana kai tāī bhekha nivāsī* ||
– Ibid., p. 939

I became a wandering person living in seclusion in search of men of God. I have changed my appearance for seeking the blessed vision of God.

khojata khojata aṁmṛtu pīā ॥ *khimā gahī manu sataguri dīā* ॥
....
ghara dara phiri thākī bahutere ॥ *jāti asaṅkha aṅta nahī mere* ॥
kete māta pitā suta dhīā ॥ *kete gura cele phuni hūā* ॥
....
dahadisa ḍhūḍhi gharai mahi pāiā ॥ *melu bhaiā satigurū milāiā* ॥

– *Ādi Granth*, p. 932

By continued searching, I enjoy the Pure Essence. Tolerance has become a way of my life, and I have surrendered my mind to the *satguru*. After my long wanderings to countless doors and homes, I have become weary. I have gone through many incarnations. I had different mother and father, son and daughter in every birth. I found many *gurus* and disciples. After searching thoroughly all ten directions I found the Supreme Being within my own home. I met Him through a true *guru* who guided me to Him.

It is evident from many references in the hymns of Guru Nānak that he was initiated by some *guru* whom he always kept in high esteem. Maybe, he was hesitant to disclose his *guru*'s name.

ḍhaṅḍholata ḍhūḍhata hau phirī ḍhahi ḍhahi pavani karāri ॥
bhāre ḍhahate ḍhahi pae haule nikase pāri ॥

– Ibid., p. 933

After my long search I feel fallen and broken upon the edges of the river of life. Heavily sinned individuals sink down, but those who are light, swim through.

Here Guru Nānak talks about his tiring efforts to achieve his goal.

manu dīā guri āpaṇai pāiā niramala nāu ॥
jini nāmu dīā tisu sevasā tisu balihārai jāu ॥
jo usāre so ḍhāhasī tisu binu avaru na koi ॥
gura parasādī tisu saṁmhalā tā tani dūkhu na hoi ॥

– Ibid., pp. 933-34

After my mind surrendered to the *guru* I received the pure and faultless *nāma*. I am in the service of one who has given me the true *nāma*. I feel obliged to him. Those who rise also fall down. I do not have anyone else except my Lord. With the grace of the *guru*, I get concentrated and then my body does not suffer any more.

Guru Nānak speaks about the grace of his *guru* to whom he surrendered and sought blessings.

tū prabhu sabhi tudhu sevade ika ḍhāḍhī kare pukāra ||
dehi dānu saṅtokhiā sacā nāmu milai ādhāru ||

– *Ādi Granth*, p. 1285

You are the Supreme Lord and everyone serves you. Your humble bard prays to shower your blessings on him and gift him with contentment so that he may get the true name as his support.

jā hau nāhī tā kiā ākhā kihu nāhī kiā hoā ||
kītā karaṇā kahiā kathanā bhariā bhari bhari dhovāṅ ||
āpi na bujhā loka bujhāī aisā āgū hovāṅ ||

– Ibid., p. 140

What should I say about myself, since I am nothing? As He created myself so I am; I do what He makes me do. I utter what he makes me speak. I am filled and overflowing with my sins. I wish only if I could wash them away. I do not know myself what should I teach others. I am like a guide.

Here Guru Nānak is too humble to disclose and admit his spiritual powers.

āiḍai āpi kare jini choḍī jo kichu karaṇā su kari rahiā ||
kare karāe sabha kichu jāṇai nānaka sāira iva kahiā ||

– Ibid., p. 434

The Supreme Lord himself is the creator of the world. Whatever He feels for doing, He is doing. He performs and makes others perform and has knowledge of everything. Nānak the poet, tells this.

In many of his hymns Guru Nānak calls himself as Nānak the *śāyara*.

vaidu bulāiā vaidagī pakaḍi ḍhaṅḍhole bāṅha ||
bholā vaidu na jāṇaī karaka kaleje māhi ||

– Ibid., p. 1279

A physician was asked to come and examine me. He held my arm for feeling the pulse. The ignorant doctor was unaware that the pain was in my heart.

Guru Nānak was burning with the desire to behold the true Lord, and the doctor was searching his body to locate physical ailment for treating him.

bīrā bīrā kari rahī bīra bhae bairāi ||
bīra cale ghari āpaṇai bahiṇa birahi jali jāi ||
– *Ādi Granth*, p. 935

Sister cried out to brother, don't go away. Please stay back. But brother becomes estranged from all and departs for his own path. The sister burns with the agony of separation.

This depicts the agony of a sister (his own sister Nānakī) while separating from her brother who opts to go in search of truth. In all above verses Guru Nānak gives a vivid picture about himself.

(C) GURU NĀNAK SPEAKS ABOUT THE FALLING SOCIAL, RELIGIOUS AND ETHICAL VALUES

kali kātī rāje kāsāī dharamu paṅkha kari uḍariā ||
kūḍu amāvasa sacu caṅdramā dīsai nāhī kaha caḍiā ||
– Ibid., p. 145

It is a dark age of Kali Yuga working as a knife, the kings behave like butchers; *adharma* has spread its wings and flown away. There is total darkness of falsehood; nowhere the moon of truth is seen.

gali mālā tilaku lilāṭaṁ || *dui dhotī basatra kapāṭaṁ* ||
je jāṇasi brahamaṁ karamaṁ || *sabhi phokaṭa nisacau karamaṁ* ||
kahu nānaka nihacau dhiāvai || *viṇu satigura vāṭa na pāvai* ||
– Ibid., p. 470

Preachers of religion wear rosary round the neck, apply the sacred mark on their forehead, place turban on their head, and they wear two clothes round waist. Had they known the true nature of *Brahman*, all these beliefs, outer appearances and rituals are in vain.

These lines explain the outer and inner life of the preachers of his times. Nānak says to meditate with deep faith. Without a true *guru* no one finds the way. One who knows the Self needs no outer appearance.

khurāsāna khasamānā kīā hiṅdusatānu ḍarāiā॥
āpai dosu na deī karatā jasu kari mugalu caḍāiā॥
etī māra paī karalāṇe taiṅ kī daradu na āiā॥
karatā tūṅ sabhanā kā soī॥
je sakatā sakate kau māre tā mani rosu na hoī॥
sakatā sīhu māre pai vagai khasamai sā purasāī॥
– *Ādi Granth*, p. 360

Supreme Lord has protected Khurāsān and brought terror to Hindustan. The Creator avoids taking the blame on Himself and so He sent Mughals as the angels of death. When there is so much suffering, O Lord, you do not feel the intensity of pain. O Lord, you support all, if a strong man attacks another strong man, there is no feeling of any grief. But if a strong tiger attacks a gathering of innocent sheep and kills them then the master is answerable.

This is the most heart-rendering verse of Guru Nānak about the wholesale massacre of Indians by Babur who invaded Punjab for the third time. Guru Nānak was a witness and raised a cry whether the merciful God had no sympathy for the suffering people. He says that if the equals fight one can understand but if a fierce tiger attacks a herd of sheep then the master must own the responsibility. His depiction of the plight of women after this invasion is very vivid in the following lines.

jina siri sohani paṭīā māṅgī pāi saṅdhūru॥
se sira kātī munianhi gala vici āvai dhūḍi॥
mahalā aṅdari hodīā huṇi bahaṇi na milanha hadūri॥
....
jadahu sīā vīāhīā lāḍe sohani pāsi॥
hīḍolī caḍi āīā daṅda khaṅḍa kīte rāsi॥
uparahu pāṇī vārīē jhale jhimakani pāsi॥
iku lakhu lahanhi bahiṭhīā lakhu lahanhi khaḍīā॥
garī chuhāre khāṅdīā māṇanhi sejaḍīā॥
....
dhanu jobanu dui vairī hoe jinhī rakhe raṅgu lāi॥

dūtā no phuramāiā lai cale pati gavāi ॥

....

iki ghari āvahi āpaṇai iki mili mili puchahi sukha ॥
ikanhā ehā likhiā bahi bahi rovahi dukha ॥
jo tisu bhāvai so thīē nānaka kiā mānukha ॥

– *Ādi Granth*, p. 417

Those heads, which wore dressed hair with vermillion in between the parting, were shaved with razors and their mouths filled with earth. They used to live in big houses, but now they cannot even sit close to those houses. The couples looked very graceful when they were married. The brides came in palanquins decorated with ivory. Water was sprayed over them and shining fans were fluttering above them. They were bestowed with large amounts of coins when they sat or stood. They ate dry fruits and comfortably slept in their beds. Their money and beauty have now become their enemy which were the source of enjoyment. The soldiers spoiled them and took them away. Some have come back to their houses and are seeing their relatives who enquire them about their well-being. But there are some who are pre-ordained to sit and cry out in pain. Whatever pleases the Supreme Lord it must come to happen. O Nānak! this is the fate of mankind.

This hymn gives his insight and understanding of the true picture of life lived. He talks about the glory of life lived with their grooms, the ornamental disposition, the love and regards showered upon the newly-wedded couples, the concern and care by the loved ones. But all that changed in no time with the attacks of Babur. He closes with a message that it was all preordained and the will of God has to be endured.

vāini cele nacani gura ॥ *paira halāini pheranhi sira* ॥
uḍi uḍi rāvā jhāṭai pāi ॥ *vekhai loku hasai ghari jāi* ॥

....

nacaṇu kudaṇu mana kā cāu ॥
nānaka jinha mani bhau tinhā mani bhāu ॥

– Ibid., p. 465

The followers play the instruments and their *gurus* perform and act. They play their feet and bend their heads. Their hairs and body become dusty. People laugh by seeing their actions and go home. These jumps and dance are merely mental inclinations. O Nānak! only those whose minds are filled with the fear of God can experience the love for God.

This long hymn is about the dramatic performances of characters like Lord Rāma and Lord Kṛṣṇa. God is not pleased by mimickers of the incarnations of God. Only fear of God instills love for Him.

All the above verses display a picture of falling social, religious and ethical values at his time.

(D) CONNUBIAL BLISS WITH SUPREMACY OF LOVE FOR GOD

muṅdha raiṇi duhelaḍīā jīu nīda na āvai ||
sā dhana dubalīā jīu pira kai hāvai ||
dhana thī-ē dubali kaṅta hāvai keva naiṇī dekhae ||
sīgāra miṭha rase bhoga bhojana sabhu jhūṭhu kitai na lekhae ||
mai mata jobani garabi gālī dudhā thaṇī na āvae ||
nānaka sādhana milai milāī binu pira nīda na āvae ||

– *Ādi Granth*, p. 242

For a bride who gets separated from her spouse, the night becomes painful. She cannot sleep. She gets thin in desire for her groom. Similarly the "soul bride" is suffering in pain for her separation from her Husband Lord. She cherishes as to how she sees the Husband Lord with her eyes? Her make-ups, rich foods, worldly pleasures become useless for her. Her intoxication with the wine of worldly youthful pride has ruined her and her breasts no longer get filled with milk.

morī ruṇa jhuṇa lāiā bhaiṇe sāvaṇu āiā ||
tere muṅdha kaṭāre jevaḍā tini lobhī lobha lobhāiā ||
tere darasana viṭahu khaṅnīē vaṅñā tere nāma viṭahu kurabāṇo ||
jā tū tā mai māṇu kīā hai tudhu binu kehā merā māṇo ||
cūḍā bhaṅnu palaṅgha siu muṅdhe saṇu bāhī saṇu bāhā ||
ete vesa karedīe muṅdhe sahu rāto avarāhā ||

– Ibid., pp. 557-58

The peacocks are singing so sweetly. O sister! the rainy season of Sāvana has come. O God! your beautiful eyes are like a string of charms, attracting and inviting the soul bride. I have reduced myself to pieces for the blessed vision of your *darśana*. I have all appreciation for your name and I take pride in you. I see nothing to be proud of except you. I shall smash my bracelets along with my bed and break my arms along with the arms of my couch. In spite of all my make-ups, My Lord is enjoying with someone else. Those arms which do not lie around the neck of the Husband Lord burn in the agony of separation.

āvahu bhaiṇe gali milaha aṅki saheladīāha॥
mili kai karaha kahāṇīā saṁbhratha kaṅta kīāha॥
....
jāi puchahu sohāgaṇī tusī rāviā kinī guṇī॥
sahaji saṅtokhi sīgārīā miṭhā bolaṇī॥
piru rīsālū tā milai jā gura kā sabadu suṇī॥
– *Ādi Granth*, pp. 17-18

Gather all my dear spiritual friends and seekers. Embrace and hold me close to you. Let us get together and recite talks of our Almighty Lord. Our Lord/Master is all virtuous. We are simply without any virtue. Go and enquire from the pleased bride how she pleased her husband. I was ever content with Him, remained in peace, decorated myself beautifully for Him, and always spoke sweetly to him (she says).

The above hymns provide glimpses of worldly life lived with supremacy of higher love for God. In many of his hymns Guru Nānak compares the connubial bliss (married life) with the bliss of union of individual soul with the Universal Soul.

B — HYMNS OF GURU NĀNAK ARE UPANIṢADIC

Guru Nānak talked about worldly life with the knowledge derived through sense organs and confirmed by evidence based on experience. But at the same time, through his transcendent exposition, he expressed unity of all existence realized through his mental and spiritual discipline. The words may look different than the language of the Upaniṣads to rigid or ignorant minds but the ideas conveyed in respect of many theological concepts remain the same in spirit. He was deeply steeped in Upaniṣadic lore and expressed unity of all existence in Pure Consciousness. In fact, it will not be out of the way to say that Guru Nānak brought the philosophy of life of Upaniṣads from the clutches of highly-learned brāhmaṇas, sages and seers down to the common man through his simplicity of expression, thought and action.

(A) GURU NĀNAK EXPRESSED UNITY OF ALL EXISTENCE IN PURE CONSCIOUSNESS

visamādu nāda visamādu veda ॥
visamādu jīa visamādu bheda ॥
visamādu rūpa visamādu raṅga ॥
visamādu nāge phirahi jaṅta ॥
visamādu pauṇu visamādu pāṇī ॥
....
vekhi viḍāṇu rahiā visamādu ॥
nānaka bujhaṇu pūrai bhāgi ॥
– *Ādi Granth*, pp. 463-64

The sound current of *nāda*, knowledge of Vedas, all beings and species, forms and colours are marvellous. All beings who go wandering naked all around, the air and the water are also wonderful. Beholding the wonders of Supreme Being I feel wonder all around. O Nānak! those who can feel the marvel of all this creation are blessed with perfect understanding.

In this hymn Guru Nānak expresses wonder about sound current, Vedas, all the existence, discriminating spirit within us, eternal divine law, colours, creatures, air, water, fire, all species, all tastes that lure away life, union, separation, hunger, eulogy and presence of mind and concludes that those who understand this wonder are blessed.

kudarati disai kudarati suṇīē kudarati bhau sukha sāru ॥
kudarati pātālī ākāsī kudarati saraba ākāru ॥
kudarati veda purāṇa katebā kudarati saraba vīcāru ॥
kudarati khāṇā pīṇā painhaṇu kudarati saraba piāru ॥
....
kudarati pauṇu pāṇī baisaṅtaru kudarati dharatī khāku ॥
sabha terī kudarati tūṅ kādiru karatā pākī nāī pāku ॥
nānaka hukamai aṅdari vekhai varatai tāko tāku ॥
– Ibid., p. 464

> One sees by His power, one hears by His power, one fears and feels sense of understanding by His power. It is His power by which the entire creation exists. All Vedas and Purāṇas, holy scripts of Jews, Christians and Muslims and the awareness exist by His power. Our actions to eat, drink, dress and love exist by His power. We acquire virtues and vices, honour and dishonour by His power. The air, fire and water, earth and dust all exist by His power. He is the most powerful creator and sustainer and His name is the holiest.

In continuation of the hymn above, Guru Nānak explains in the present hymn that source of all powers to see, hear, wisdom of expression, deliberations, discriminations, etc. is the one creator who is all powerful.

These teachings are in tune with the following verses in the Upaniṣads:

> A question is put as to who prompts the eye, ear and mind to action? By whose command does life make the first move?
>
> – *Kena Upaniṣad* 1.1

> *Brahman* is the ear of the ear, the mind of the mind, speech of the speech, breath of the breath and eye of the eye.
>
> – Ibid. 1.2

> From Him are born the R̥gvedic verses, the *sāman* (chants), the *yajus* (formulas), the rites of initiation, all sacrificial ceremonies and the worlds where the moon purifies and the sun shines.
>
> – *Muṇḍaka Upaniṣad* 2.1.8

oaṁkāri brahmā utapati || *oaṁkāru kīā jini citi* ||
oaṁkāri sail juga bhae || *oaṁkāri beda nirmae* ||
oaṁkāri sabadi udhare || *oaṁkāri guramukhi tare* ||
onama akhara suṇahu bīcāru || *onama akharu tribhavaṇa sāru* ||
suṇi pāḍe kiā likhahu jaṅjālā || *likhu rāma nāma guramukhi gopālā* ||

– *Ādi Granth*, pp. 929-30

The hymn explains that Oṁkāra created Brahmā (gods). Brahmā absorbed the God's name in his mind. Oṁkāra is the creator of the mountains and the *yugas*. Oṁkāra is the creator of the

> Vedas. Oṁkāra is He who through the word sets all free from wandering. Through the word *oṁkāra* hear the communication from the Creator Lord. The word *oṁkāra* is the vitality of the three worlds. O *paṇḍita*! by arguments you create confusion for the meaning of the word. O God's man! pray and write only the Rāma *nāma* and Gopāla.

Here Guru Nānak discusses the meaning of the word *auṁ* with the *paṇḍita* and advises them not to argue and create confusions as this word contains the essence of all the three worlds, meaning the three states of consciousness.

As per the Upaniṣads, the syllable *auṁ* holds within it the essence of three states of consciousness:

> The fourth is that which has no elements, which cannot be spoken of, into which the world is resolved, benign, non-dual.
> ... – *Māṇḍūkya Upaniṣad* 12

aṁtari suṁnaṁ bāhari suṁnaṁ tribhavaṇa suṁnamasuṁnaṁ ॥
cauthe suṁnai jo naru jāṇai tā kau pāpu na puṁnaṁ ॥
– *Ādi Granth*, p. 943

> The Supreme Being is deep within, as well as outside us. The Supreme Being absolutely fills the three worlds. One who has knowledge of Him in the fourth state of consciousness, rises above virtue and vice.

Here Guru Nānak describes that all the three stages of consciousness do not bring any spiritual change. One who knows the fourth, i.e. *turīya*, goes beyond the cycle of virtue and vice.

> *Turīya* is not that which cognizes the internal, not that which cognizes the external, not what cognizes both of them, not a mass of cognition, not cognitive, not non-cognitive. It is unseen, incapable of being spoken of, ungraspable the essence of the knowledge of the one self, that into which the world is resolved, the peaceful, the benign, the non-dual, such they think is the fourth quarter. He is the Self, He is to be known.
> – *Māṇḍūkya Upaniṣad* 7

āpe paṭī kalama āpi upari lekhu bhi tūṁ ॥
eko kahīē nānakā dūjā kāhe kū ॥ – *Ādi Granth*, p. 1291

Supreme Being Himself is the writing tablet, and Himself is the pen. Whatever is written on it is also He Himself. Speak of the One Supreme Being. Nānak! there is none other than Him.

āpe hī karaṇā kīo kala āpe hī tai dhārīē ||
dekhahi kītā āpaṇā dhari kacī pakī sārīē ||
jo āiā so calasī sabhu koī āī vārīē ||
jisa ke jīa parāṇa hahi kiu sāhibu manahu visārīē ||
āpaṇa hathī āpaṇā āpe hī kāju savārīē ||

– *Ādi Granth*, pp. 473-74

God himself created all this creation and He Himself imbued His power into it. Supreme Being overlooks His creation in His own way. Whosoever takes birth is destined to leave this world. Everyone will have his own turn. One should not forget that Being to which we owe both our body and soul. He is our very breath of life. We should work out our own affairs with our own hands.

nānaka aṅta na jāpanhī hari tā ke pārāvāra ||
āpi karāe sākhatī phiri āpi karāe māra ||
ikanhā galī jaṅjīrīā iki turī caḍahi bisīāra ||
āpi karāe kare āpi hau kai siu karī pukāra ||
nānaka karaṇā jini kīā phiri tisa hī karaṇī sāra ||

– Ibid., p. 475

It is not possible to know the Supreme Being's limits. He is without any end or limit. He Himself is the creator and destroyer of His own creation. Few are bound with ropes around their necks, at the same time others ride on many horses. It is He who performs and causes all to perform. We cannot complain against Him. It is only He who is the creator of all and looks after His creation.

āpe bhāṅḍe sājianu āpe pūraṇu dei ||
ikanhī dudhu samāīē iki culhai rahanhi caḍe ||
iki nihālī pai sabanhi iki upari rahina khaḍe ||
tinā savāre nānakā jina kau nadari kare ||

– Ibid., p. 475

He is the designer of this body pitcher and He fills it Himself. He pours milk in some pitchers and some pitchers are always put on fire. Some sleep on comfortable beds while others stand as watchful. It is His graceful gaze on some that they are honoured.

vaḍe kīā vaḍiāīā kichu kahaṇā kahaṇu na jāi ||
– *Ādi Granth*, p. 475

He is too great to be described. No one can describe or say anything about His greatness.

āpīnhai āpu sāji āpu pachāṇiā ||
aṁbaru dharati vichoḍi caṅdoā tāṇiā ||
viṇu thaṁmhā gaganu rahāi sabadu nīsāṇiā ||
sūraju caṅdu upāi joti samāṇiā ||
kīe rāti dinaṅtu coja viḍāṇiā ||
tīratha dharama vīcāra nāvaṇa purabāṇiā ||
tudhu sari avaru na koi ki ākhi vakhāṇiā ||
sacai takhati nivāsu hora āvaṇa jāṇiā ||
– Ibid., p. 1279

The Supreme Lord Himself created Himself. He can Himself understand Himself. He separated the sky and the earth and created the overhead hanging lie down and without any pillars. The sky is supported with the crown of His *śabada*. He created the sun and the moon and filled His light into them. He is the creator of the night and day. His mystic play of acts is marvellous. He is the creator of all the sacred shrines of pilgrimages, where people assemble for contemplation, exercise goodness and take baths for cleaning themselves on certain events. No one else can equal to you. Guru Nānak wonders as to how he can speak and describe Him. The Supreme Being occupies the throne of truth while all other beings rotate and get new bodies for their soul.

tū sacā saciāru jini sacu varatāiā ||
baiṭhā tāḍī lāi kavalu chapāiā ||
brahamai vadā kahāi aṅtu na pāiā ||
na tisu bāpu na māi ki tū jāiā ||
nā tisu rūpu na rekha varana sabāiā ||
nā tisu bhukha piāsa rajā dhāiā ||
– Ibid., p. 1279

Guru Nānak addresses God and says that He is always true. He exercises true justice for all. He sits in the primal heavenly trance like a lotus. He cannot be seen. Even Brahmā the god, who is considered very high, is not aware of the limits of the Supreme Being. He is without father or mother. No one knows about His birth. He is formless and featureless. He is beyond human knowledge. He is without any hunger or thirst.

The last two hymns above portray the essential attributes of *Brahman* as portrayed in the Upaniṣads.

Eternal Self is never born, nor does it die at any time. He sprang from nothing and nothing sprang from him. He is unborn, eternal, abiding and primeval. – *Kaṭha Upaniṣad*, 1.2.18

dunīā dhaṅdhai lāi āpu chapāiā ||
dharamu karāe karama dhurahu phuramāiā ||
– *Ādi Granth*, p. 1280

He puts all in the world to their job, but He remains Himself away from their view. The Supreme Being issued His will that all the *jīvas* must exercise *dharma* and virtue.

asaṅkha mūrakha aṅdha ghora || *asaṅkha cora harāmakhora* ||
....
jo tudhu bhāvai sāī bhalī kāra || *tū sadā salāmati niraṁkāra* ||
– Ibid., p. 4

Whatever pleases Him is the right action on the part of individuals. He is everlasting and without any form. There are numberless fools who are blind and ignorant. There are numberless thieves, evil-doers. Whatever action of all these pleases you is the real good action.

In this hymn Guru Nānak describes the variety of all sorts of sinners, slanderers, wretches, liars, cut-throats, unwise and ignorant, which are beyond all thought; all are created by Him only.

In the *Chāndogya Upaniṣad* 1.2.1 both gods and demons are called the descendants of Prajāpati.

kete ākhahi ākhaṇi pāhi || *kete kahi kahi uṭhi uṭhi jāhi* ||
ete kīte hori karehi || *tā ākhi na sakahi keī kei* ||

jevaḍu bhāvai tevaḍu hoi || *nānaka jāṇai sācā soi* ||

– *Ādi Granth*, p. 6

There are a large number of individuals who talk and try to portray Him. In the past also a large number of people tried to speak and portray Him, a large number of people talked over and again to portray Him and departed from this world. Even if an equal number of people as in the past and present take birth they would not be able to describe Him. He is as great as He wills to be.

In the above lines Guru Nānak tells that the infinite Lord cannot be described.

The self has no touch and no form. It is non-decaying. Similarly it is without any taste. It is everlasting, without any smell, without any beginning and without any end. – *Kaṭha Upaniṣad* 1.3.15

(B) GURU NĀNAK EXPLAINS THE EXISTING VEDIC PHILOSOPHY WITH HIS SUPERB VISION AND SKILL

Guru Nānak speaks about the existing philosophy and concepts of universal religious thoughts accepted and held true by many preachers and practitioners of his time and explains his own philosophy with his own vision and superb argumentative skill.

nānaka meru sarīra kā iku rathu iku rathavāhu ||
jugu jugu pheri vaṭāīahi giānī bujhahi tāhi ||
satajugi rathu saṅtokha kā dharamu agai rathavāhu ||
tretai rathu jatai kā joru agai rathavāhu ||
duāpuri rathu tapai kā satu agai rathavāhu ||
kalajugi rathu agani kā kūḍu agai rathavāhu ||

– *Ādi Granth*, p. 470

Soulful body has a chariot and a charioteer. The wise men know that they change time to time. In the age of Satya Yuga the chariot was satisfaction and religion was its driver. In the Tretā Yuga, the chariot was continence driven by power. In the Dvāpara Yuga, the chariot was austerity and compassion was the driving force. In the Kali Yuga the chariot is of fire and it is driven by falsehood.

Guru Nānak explains his own philosophy that in the different ages, viz. Satya, Tretā, Dvāpara and Kali, the soulful body had contentment, continence, austerity and fire as chariots driven by religion, power, compassion and falsehood respectively.

There is similarity of description of the parable of chariot with the contents of the *Kaṭha Upaniṣad*, wherein Yama explains his views about soul. Yama says:

> Know the self as the lord of the chariot and body as, verily the chariot, know the intellect as the charioteer and the mind as the reins. The senses are the horses, the object of senses the path. He who has the understanding of the driver of the chariot and controls the reins of his mind, he reaches the end of the journey, the supreme abode of the all-pervading.
>
> – *Kaṭha Upaniṣad* 1.3.3-1.3.9

sāma kahai setaṁbaru suāmī saca mahi āchai sāci rahe ॥
sabhu ko saci samāvai ॥ *rigu kahai rahiā bharapūri* ॥
rāma nāmu devā mahi sūru ॥ *nāi laiē parāchata jāhi* ॥
nānaka tau mokhaṁtaru pāhi ॥
juja mahi jori chalī candrāvali kānha kr̥sanu jādamu bhaiā ॥
pārajātu gopī lai āiā bindrābana mahi raṅgu kīā ॥
kaḷi mahi bedu atharabaṇu hūā nāu khudāī alahu bhaiā ॥
nīla basatra le kapaḍe pahire turaka paṭhāṇī amalu kīā ॥
cāre veda hoe saciāra ॥ *paḍahi guṇahi tinha cāra vīcāra* ॥
bhāu bhagati kari nīcu sadāe ॥ *tau nānaka mokhaṁtaru pāe* ॥

– *Ādi Granth*, p. 470

The *Sāmaveda* describes God as dressed in white and *jīva*'s coming and going and all were living in truth. At the time of the *R̥gveda*, Rāma was spread although as Supreme Lord. He was considered to be the highest among the gods, and it was believed that whosoever uttered his name got rid of his sins and was liberated. At the time of the *Yajurveda*, they named the Lord as Kr̥ṣṇa of the Yādava tribe. He led astray Candrāvalī by force to Vr̥ndāvana and brought the Elysian tree (from heavens) for a *gopī* and enjoyed in Vr̥ndāvana. At the time of the *Atharvaveda*, or Kali Age, the name of God became Allāh, who dressed in blue attire and adopted the attributes of Turk and Paṭhān.

The four Vedas proclaim truth. And those who read and reflect on them know what is merit and what is demerit. Nānak says he who is devoted to the Lord in his loving adoration and dwells in humility attains emancipation.

Guru Nānak here talks about the existing religious concepts and different names given or assumed by God. He emphasizes that by the study of Vedas, one is able to distinguish between good and the pleasant. But for liberation one requires loving devotion. The *Kaṭha Upaniṣad* 1.2.23 explains:

> *Ātman* cannot be attained through study of the Vedas, nor through intelligence nor by hearing of sacred books. It is attained by him alone whom it chooses. To such an individual, *Ātman* reveals its own form.

brahamā bisanu mahesu deva upāiā ||
brahame dite beda pūjā lāiā ||
dasa avatārī rāmu rājā āiā ||
daiṅtā māre dhāi hukami sabāiā ||
īsa mahesuru seva tinhī aṅtu na pāiā ||
sacī kīmati pāi takhatu racāiā ||
– *Ādi Granth*, pp. 1279-80

> The Supreme Being created gods Brahmā, Viṣṇu and Śiva. Brahmā was blessed with the Vedas and assigned them to worship Truth. The ten incarnations like Lord Rāma, the king, took birth by His Supreme Will. These destroyed all the demons very soon. Śiva the deity stands in attendance to the Supreme Lord but even he could not know His limits. The Supreme Lord thrones the chair of truth. He knows His own limits.

In this hymn Guru Nānak explains that all the deities were created and assigned jobs by the Supreme Lord. But no one was able to define Him.

dovai taraphā upāi iku varatiā ||
beda bāṇī varatāi aṅdari vādu ghatiā ||
paravirati niravirati hāṭhā dovai vici dharamu phirai raibāriā ||
– Ibid., p. 1280

> The one Supreme Being created both sides and is spread through

> the entire expanse in between. The words of the Vedas were preached, argued and divisions were created. Attachment and detachment are the two sides of it. *Dharma* is the true religion and creates equilibrium.

This is further explained in the next verses:

> *āpe chiñjha pavāi malākhāḍā raciā*॥
> *lathe bhaḍathū pāi guramukhi maciā*॥
> *manamukha māre pachāḍi mūrakha kaciā*॥
> *āpi bhiḍai māre āpi āpi kāraju raciā*॥
> *sabhanā khasamu eku hai guramukhi jāṇīē*॥
> *hukamī likhai siri lekhu viṇu kalama masavāṇīē*॥
>
> – *Ādi Granth*, p. 1280

> The Supreme Being Himself created the show and arranged the spiritual wrestlers for wrestling. They come for arguments with full pomp and show. The lovers of God feel pleased. The untrue and fools get defeated and are overcome. The Supreme Being Himself participates and wrestles. He Himself defeats them in the staged play by Him. The one and only one Supreme Being is the lord and master of all. This is known by all God-loving individuals. The Supreme Lord writes His *hukam* on every forehead without using any pen or ink.

In the two hymns above Guru Nānak talks about the differences and arguments about the contents of Vedas. He says that God created the Vedas and the arguments and made the true religion as a guide for both between the two. He Himself stages the play of wrestling minds and enters the arena with pomp and show and defeats the false and foolish. Only a saint of high intelligence with a universal mind can write this. I bow before Him for His excellent expression and showing true path to the humanity.

> *satiguru sevahi se paravāṇu jinha jotī joti milāī*॥
> *so sāhibu so sevaku tehā jisu bhāṇā manni vasāī*॥
>
> – Ibid., p. 1285

> An individual who gets into the service of true *guru* becomes acceptable to the Supreme Lord. His individual light merges into the Universal Light. Such a devotee grasps the will of the Lord

> in his mind and gets transformed and becomes like the Lord.

The above lines describe the Upaniṣadic concept that one who realizes *Brahman* becomes *Brahman* (*brahmavid, brahmaiva bhavati*).

> He verily who knows the Supreme *Brahman*, becomes *Brahman*.
>
> – *Muṇḍaka Upaniṣad* 3.2.9

> *ekā māī jugati viāī tini cele paravāṇu* ||
> *iku saṁsārī iku bhaṅḍārī iku lāe dībāṇu* ||
> *jiva tisu bhāvai tivai calāvai jiva hovai phuramāṇu* ||
> *ohu vekhai onā nadari na āvai bahutā ehu viḍāṇu* ||
> ....
> *kari kari vekhai sirajaṇahāru* || *nānaka sace kī sācī kāra* ||
>
> – *Ādi Granth*, p. 7

> It is believed that the holy mother conceived and gave birth to the three deities, one who creates, second who sustains the creation and the third who destroys or dissolves. The Supreme Lord allows all things happen according to His pleasure. That is what His heavenly or divine way is. He keeps a watch over all. But none can see Him. It is most wandering. After He creates, the Supreme Being watches and takes care of His creation. The Supreme Being is the Ultimate Truth and His creation is also true.

In these lines, Guru Nānak talks about the three deities, i.e. Brahmā, Viṣṇu and Śiva, considered to be the creator, sustainer and destroyer. The important point he is making is that the creation created by the Truth is also true and He watches over His creation.

> *janami marai trai guṇa hitakāru* || *cāre beda kathahi ākāru* ||
> *tīni avasathā kahahi vakhiānu* || *turīāvasathā satigura te hari jānu* ||
>
> – Ibid., p. 154

> One who is under the spell of the three modes is subject to coming and going. The four Vedas describe the three visible forms only. But the fourth state of consciousness, that is the merger with the Lord, can be learnt only from a true *guru*.

Here again Guru Nānak emphasizes that the knowledge of the *turīya* state of consciousness can only be gained from the preceptor.

cacai cāri veda jini sāje cāre khāṇī cāri jugā ॥
jugu jugu jogī khāṇī bhogī paḍiā paṇḍitu āpi thīā ॥
– *Ādi Granth*, p. 432

> The Supreme Being is the creator of four Vedas, four modes of creation and four ages. But in every age, it is He who has been the *yogī*, the preacher and the learned man.

In these lines, Guru Nānak expresses the unity of Universal Soul and individual soul as expressed in the following lines of the *Muṇḍaka Upaniṣad* 3.1.1:

> The two birds united always and known by the same name closely cling to the same tree. One of them eats the sweet fruit, the other looks on without eating it.

All above hymns confirm that Guru Nānak had a deep knowledge of existing Vedic philosophy and explained it with his own superb vision and insight.

C — Guru Nānak Placed Love for God and Godly Life above All Organized Religions

Guru Nānak never criticized any religion in his hymns but condemned the futile customs, rituals and beliefs introduced by the priests and practitioners of various religions for selfish motives to gain name, fame and money. Guru Nānak knew no boundaries of any religion with a least thought for further division of humanity into a formal separate religion. His exuberance of love for God, godly life and humanity implied all the attributes of his being above all the castes and creeds, social statutes, religious boundaries and requires no special cry or identification for the social, political and religious change. He was the real exponent of fatherhood of God and brotherhood of mankind, and he preached unity of all existence and unity of all knowledge in Pure Consciousness like the Upaniṣads.

The following verses describe as to how love for God and godly life superseded above all for him:

nadīā hovahi dheṇavā suṁma hovahi dudhu ghīu ॥
sagalī dharatī sakara hovai khusī kare nita jīu ॥
parabatu suinā rupā hovai hīre lāla jaḍāu ॥

bhī tūṅ hai sālāhaṇā ākhaṇa lahai na cāu ||
bhāra aṭhāraha mevā hovai garuḍā hoi suāu ||
caṅdu sūraju dui phirade rakhīahi nihacalu hovai thāu ||
bhī tūṅ hai sālāhaṇā ākhaṇa lahai na cāu ||

– *Ādi Granth*, pp. 141-42

If the rivers are converted to cows providing milk, milk and ghee come from the water springs, if the whole earth becomes sweet-like and pleases with its sweetness, if the mountains transform into heaps of gold and silver along with gems and jewels, if all the vegetables become dry fruit, and grass sprouts forth like sweetened rice and if I am empowered to stop the sun and the moon from their appearances, even then I shall appreciate and love you O God! with a strong desire for you. I shall not stop to praise, adore and love you. My praises will not decrease.

These lines describe Guru Nānak's ardent and steep love for God.

tūṅ sacā dātāru nita devahi caḍahi savāiā ||
nānaku maṅgai dānu jo tudhu bhāiā ||

– Ibid., p. 150

The Supreme Father is the true source of all gifts who continues to provide His bounty. He increases His provisions day by day. But Guru Nānak desired that the Supreme Father may provide gifts whatsoever pleases Him.

Here Guru Nānak prays for the gifts of Lord's pleasure.

chia ghara chia gura chia upadesa || *gura guru ēko vesa aneka* ||
jai ghari karate kīrati hoi || *so gharu rākhu vaḍāī tohi* ||
visue casiā ghaḍīā paharā || *thitī vārī māhu bhaiā* ||
suraju eko ruti aneka || *nānaka karate ke kete vesa* ||

– Ibid., p. 357

There are six systems of philosophy with their six teachers and six doctrines. But the teacher of these six teachers is the one Lord who transforms Himself into many forms. That importance lies in it that one should follow the path where one can sing and hear the praises of the Supreme. The seconds, minutes, hours, days, weeks, months and seasons all come into existence from the sun; similarly all forms and all knowledge come from the one Supreme Being.

musalamāṇu kahāvaṇu musakalu jā hoi tā musalamāṇu kahāvai ||
avali auli dīnu kari miṭhā masakalamānā mālu musāvai ||
hoi musalimu dīna muhāṇai maraṇa jīvaṇa kā bharamu cukāvai ||
raba kī rajāi mañne sira upari karatā mañne āpu gavāvai ||
tau nānaka saraba jīā miharaṁmati hāi ta musalamāṇu kahāvai ||

– *Ādi Granth*, p. 141

It is not easy to call one a Muslim. To be a true Muslim, first let him be a strong lover of the religion of the Prophet then let him shed away his attachments to his all worldly possessions. To become a true Muslim, a follower of the belief of Muhammad, let one shed his doubts about death and life. If one submits oneself to the Supreme Father's Will, who is the creator of everything, he will get rid of I-ness and exaggerated estimate of his own ability and importance. And when the all merciful Lord is pleased then one can be called a Muslim.

This shows Guru Nānak's strong appreciation for the basic tenants of other religions.

rāha dovai iku jāṇai soī sijhasī ||
kuphara goa kupharāṇai paiā dajhasī ||
sabha dunīā subahānu saci samāīē ||
sijhai dari dīvāni āpu gavāīē ||

– Ibid., p. 142

One who understands that all the paths of enlightenment lead to only One Supreme Being shall get free from all bondages. One who is truthless shall go to hell and get burnt. All individuals who remain ever attuned to the Supreme Being are blessed souls.

paraṁdae na girāha jara || *darakhata āba āsa kara* ||

– Ibid., p. 144

The birds keep no valuables in their pockets; they keep flying and put all their hopes on trees and water.

These lines describe that nature takes care of every living being and one requires no wealth and accumulations for his basic maintenance.

maṅdā kisai na ākhīē paḍi akharu eho bujhīē ॥
mūrakhai nāli na lujhīē ॥
– *Ādi Granth*, p. 473

Let no one be called bad. One should understand and practise not to indulge in arguments with fools.

Again it is a masterpiece advice by Guru Nānak.

gurā ika dehi bujhāī ॥
sabhaṇā jīā kā iku dātā so mai visari na jāī ॥
– Ibid., p. 2

The *guru* has made me understand this one thing that there is only one Supreme Being who is the creator and provider of all beings. That One Supreme Father should not be ever forgotten.

The above hymns confirm that Guru Nānak's love for God knew no bounds and he respected all godly people without any boundary of organized religions.

D — Guru Nānak: An Advocate of Better Worldliness

Guru Nānak did not tell any fairy tales nor gave promises of heaven, but talked about facing the reality of life through better worldliness and achieve the real goal of life. He advised to shun off the attractions of sensual pleasures and to lead a life of austerity. He himself lived a practical life of an ascetic and a peasant and undertook long journeys in the most difficult conditions to fulfil his quest for Ultimate Truth of life, ending with a message of universal love and unity of all existence. His message was not for a selected few or chosen ones but for all humanity at large.

jīu pāi tanu sājiā rakhiā baṇata baṇāi ॥
akhī dekhai jihavā bolai kaṅnī surati samāi ॥
pairī calai hathī karaṇā ditā painaiṅ khāi ॥
jini raci raciā tisahi na jāṇai aṅdhā aṅdhu kamāi ॥
jā bhajai tā ṭhīkaru hovai ghāḍata ghaḍī na jāi ॥
nānaka gura binu nāhi pati pati viṇu pāri na pāi ॥
....
tudhu āpe jagatu upāi kai tudhu āpe dhaṅdhai lāiā ॥
– Ibid., p. 138

> The Supreme Lord fashioned our body and placed His essence in it. He protects it also. It is that essence which sees with eyes, speaks with tongue, hears with ears and brings forth awareness of mind. It is that essence which walks with feet, works with hands, and wears and eats whatever is given to it. The ignorant man does not know that Supreme Being and acts blindly. When the vessel of body is broken and shattered into pieces, it cannot be reassembled again. There is no saviour other than a *guru*, and no one can get swim over to other side without a saviour. The Supreme Being Himself is the creator of the world and He Himself makes it to function.

Here Guru Nānak explains that this beautiful body and all sense and action organs are God's gift. If the pitcher of this body is broken, it cannot be reassembled. One should not do blind acts, and to know the benefactor, one must have a true *guru* for guidance.

> *nānaka bolaṇu jhakhaṇā dukha chaḍi maṅgīahi sukha*॥
> *sukhu dukhu dui dari kapaḍe pahirahi jāi manukha*॥
> *jithai bolaṇi hārīē tithai caṅgī cupa*॥
>
> – *Ādi Granth*, p. 149

> It is a mere folly to beg for getting exempted from pain and wish for comforts. Pleasures and sufferings are two dresses provided for wearing in the assembly before the Supreme Lord. Where one realizes that he will lose by speaking out, it is better to observe silence.

It is an excellent advice that one should bear all the pains and happiness alike without grumbling. Further, here he is referring to the *prārabdha karma*, due to which a man takes birth and has to undergo sufferings in this life. For such *karma*s it is better to bear sufferings silently as there is no use for crying.

> *haṁsu hetu lobhu kopu cāre nadīā agi*॥
> *pavahi dajhahi nānakā tarīē karamī lagi*॥
>
> – Ibid., p. 147

> Cruel behaviour, worldly attachment, greed and anger are the four rivulets of fire, falling therein one is bruised. Only one who adopts virtue and good deeds is saved.

Guru Nānak counts the evils which have adverse effects on human beings. He advises to observe austerities in life which may save individuals from many evils.

> *kapaḍu rūpu suhāvaṇā chaḍi dunīā aṅdari jāvaṇā* ॥
> *maṅdā caṅgā āpaṇā āpe hī kītā pāvaṇā* ॥
> – *Ādi Granth*, pp. 470-71

> Everyone has to leave this world of beauty and his beautiful body. Everyone receives the rewards for his good and bad actions.

Guru Nānak advises to remember that one has to leave this world and suffer or get rewarded for his every action.

> *sacā alakha abheu haṭhi na patījaī* ॥
> *ika gāvahi rāga parīā rāgi na bhījaī* ॥
> *iki naci naci pūrahi tāla bhagati na kījaī* ॥
> ....
> *lāhā nāmu saṁsāri aṁmṛtu pījaī* ॥
> *hari bhagatī asanehi guramukhi ghījaī* ॥
> – Ibid., p. 1285

> One cannot win the pleasure of God with a rigid approach. The Supreme Being is true, unseen and mysterious. Some try to approach Him with their songs in traditional *rāgas*, some perform dances. But He is not pleased by these songs and dances. One is benefited only by worshipping Him with devotion.

Guru Nānak explains that God cannot be pleased or won through external actions or hard penances without true devotion.

> *rūpī bhukha na utarai jāṅ dekhāṅ tāṅ bhukha* ॥
> *jete rasa sarīra ke tete lagahi dukha* ॥
> – Ibid., p. 1287

> One cannot satisfy his hunger with beauty. When one sees beauty, he hankers after it even more. Every pleasure of body causes pain.

Guru Nānak explains that all the sensual pleasures of the body bring forth sufferings.

rūpai kāmai dosatī bhukhai sādai gaṅḍhu॥
labai mālai ghuli mili micali ūghai sauḍi palaṅghu॥
bhaṅu kai kopu khuāru hoi phakaḍu piṭe aṅdhu॥
cupai caṅgā nānakā viṇu nāvaiṅ muhi gaṅdhu॥

– *Ādi Granth*, p. 1288

There is friendship between beauty and sexual desires. Hunger and tasty food are in common bondage. Greed searches wealth. Anger roars and destructs, ignorant follow useless arguments. It is good not to count all these. Without the name of the Supreme Lord one's tongue utters only filth.

Guru Nānak explains the interrelations between sense organs and human nature and advises that one has to be silently watchful.

rāju mālu rūpu jāti jobanu paṅje ṭhaga॥
enī ṭhagīṅ jogu ṭhagiā kinai na rakhī laja॥

– Ibid., p. 1288

The power to rule, all accumulations, beauty, social status and youth are the five thieves. These thieves rob the world continuously, sparing none.

In these lines Guru Nānak advises us to be careful against the worldly attractions which cause damage to all.

kari ācāru sacu sukhu hoī॥ *nāma vihūṇā mukati kioa hoī*॥

– Ibid., p. 931

One can find peace by a good lifestyle. Without the true *nāma*, one cannot find liberation.

Guru Nānak advocates better wordliness for peace in life along with true love for God's name.

bharīē hathu pairu tanu deha॥ *pāṇī dhotai utarasu kheha*॥
mūta palītī kapaḍu hoi॥ *de sābūṇu laīē ohu dhoi*॥
bharīē mati pāpā kai saṅgi॥ *ohu dhopai nāvai kai raṅgi*॥
puṅnī pāpī ākhaṇu nāhi॥ *kari kari karaṇā likhi lai jāhu*॥
āpe bīji āpe hī khāhu॥

– Ibid., p. 4

When hands, feet and body become filthy, one may wash off the filth with water. If the dress gets dirty and is stained with urine, it can be washed with soap and water. But when the mind gets polluted with sin, only the love for the true Name can clean it. One cannot attain virtue only by talks. Every action performed in repetition is carved upon the intellect. One will reap what one plants.

These lines of Guru Nānak portray a beautiful piece of poetry, philosophy, advice and caution in life.

tīrathu tapu daiā datu dānu ॥ *je ko pāvai tila kā mānu* ॥
suṇiā manniā mani kītā bhāu ॥ *antaragati tīrathi mali nāu* ॥
sabhi guṇa tere mai nāhī koi ॥ *viṇu guṇa kīte bhagati na hoi* ॥

– *Ādi Granth*, p. 4

The rituals, pilgrimages, self-discipline, compassion and charity bring only a nominal spiritual benefit. One should hear, believe and love the true name of the Lord, and take a dip of bath within oneself for spiritual benefits. The Supreme Being is the source of all virtues and individuals have none. Without acquiring virtue, one cannot adopt devotional worship.

Guru Nānak advises that the outer performances and action give very little relief. One has to go within with all love and devotion for real benefit.

mundā santokhu saramu patu jholī dhiāna kī karahi bibhūti ॥
khinthā kālu kuārī kāiā jugati ḍanḍā paratīti ॥
āī panthī sagala jamātī mani jītai jagu jītu ॥

– Ibid., p. 6

Adopt satisfaction as earrings, humility as a begging bowl and the meditation as ashes to apply on body. One should remember death as a gown to wear and adopt the way of purity in the world. The faith in the Supreme Father should be the walking stick. One should consider all the seekers of the Supreme Being as brothers and classmates. Win over your mind and you will win the world.

Guru Nānak advises us to cultivate humility, purity of mind, brotherhood of all mankind and always remember of death. Over all, he declares that one who conquers mind can conquer the world.

janami marai trai guṇa hitakāru || *cāre beda kathahi ākāru* ||
tīni avasathā kahahi vakhiānu || *turīāvasathā satigura te*
hari jānu || – *Ādi Granth*, p. 154

One who lives in the three states of consciousness is subject to birth and death. The four Vedas only speak of the three visible forms. But the fourth state, union with the Lord, is only known through a true *guru*. To progress on the spiritual path, one has to go beyond the control of three *guṇa*s of nature under the guidance of a preceptor. The fourth state of consciousness, i.e. *turīya*, can be attained through guidance of a self-realized preceptor.

cāre kuṅḍā ḍhūḍhīā ko nīmhī maiḍā ||
jo tudhu bhāvai sāhibā tū mai hau taiḍā ||
daru bībhā mai nīmhi ko kai karī salāmu ||
hiko maiḍā tū dhaṇī sācā mukhi nāmu ||
– Ibid., p. 417

I searched in all the four directions but found none as my true relative. I prayed to God that if it pleases Him, "O Lord! you be mine, and I be yours". I find no other place where I should bow my head for worship. You are my only powerful Lord. Your true name is on my tongue.

He concludes that no one other than God is the real friend. So he prays for mutual adoption of individual Nānak with the Universal Truth.

The Upaniṣads also advocate for better worldliness by leading a virtuous life, higher and lower knowledge in persuit of four *puruṣārthas* discussed in section "Principal Upaniṣads" in this Chapter and in Chapter 5.

Conclusion

Guru Nānak was born in a Hindu kṣatriya family, yet was not bound by any particular sect of religious thought or institution of any particular religion. However his approach towards life represents a revolt of a critical kṣatriya mind against the ritualistic mind of a brāhmaṇa. I find his approach in search of Truth very chivalrous like that of a knight full of courtesy, generosity, valour and dexterity. He was essentially a man of God whose love and quest for search of the Ultimate Truth knew no limits. In the pursuit of this search he enjoyed a reach to the state of void meaning, a state where there is no distinction between the object and the subject – the knower and the known. He was ever tuned and one with the divinity or Pure Consciousness and his hymns are a fearless and bold expression of his Experiential Universal Truth. Guru Nānak never considered himself a prophet, incarnation of any god or son of God. He considered himself to be a bard who was assigned to sing Lord's praises in His Court. He explains that he became a wandering recluse in search of men of God. We find deep within that Upaniṣads also stress that without a burning desire and the real urge, a man cannot achieve his goal for self-realization.

The Upaniṣads constitute the knowledge section of the Vedas and are called Vedānta, i.e. the end of the Vedas or final purport of Vedas. No doubt, the Vedic religion went through many transformations from its initial simple and spontaneous expression of man's wonder and admiration for the Divine Power and Divine Will to His worship through symbols and statues and observance of rituals taught by the priestly class following *karma-kāṇḍa* (the works section of the Vedas). The Upaniṣads represent a culmination or final view or the essence of the Vedic philosophy. But the knowledge of the Upaniṣads was beyond the reach of a person of ordinary intelligence due to its mystic contents, language, condensed version and restrictions for its imparting. Thus the real knowledge was confined to a few learned brāhmaṇas, sages and seers only. The priestly class interpreted and practised without any real knowledge and ordinary people were misled who followed them blindly. Guru Nānak was pained to see all this and the arguments and strife between even the learned men (six systems of philosophy) for interpretations. He declared that all knowledge of Vedas is wonderful and all deliberations including that of Purāṇas and other religions exist by the power of One Supreme Being. Thus he advocated unity of all knowledge in Pure Consciousness and invited his entire spiritual sister companions to come, embrace, hug each other and join together to relate stories of one powerful Lord *"āvahu bhaiṅai gal milai"* He explains that there are six streams of philosophy, six guides and six principles but teacher of all these six preachers is One Lord. He further explains that the three stages of consciousness do not bring any spiritual change, but; one who knows the fourth, i.e. *turīya*, goes beyond the cycle of virtue and vice.

Thus the Upaniṣads and Guru Nānak both aim at inspiring and leading the individuals to realize the Ultimate Truth by shedding intellectual slavery to blind faith, superstitions, sectarian beliefs and dogmas. Both stress on inner

realization and to cultivate logic, reason and make sincere efforts through deep contemplation and meditation to achieve a state of mind to get attuned to the divinity. Hymns of Guru Nānak are songs of life for the masses sharing with them the wisdom of all sages and seers of the Upaniṣads in a most simplified, illuminated, argumentative and innovative manner. These contain a clear vision of Guru Nānak that emancipation can be attained by personal experience of divinity and knowledge of the Ultimate Reality by developing discrimination, dispassion, self-control and a strong desire for liberation. He cautions time and again as not to say anyone bad and understand the real words of scriptures and not to argue with fools. We can say that he had a very sound knowledge of the contents of Vedic literature, appreciated it and was under deep lore of philosophy of life explained in the Upaniṣads. Like the Upaniṣads, he expressed unity of all existence and all knowledge in Pure Consciousness and advocated for better worldliness.

Thus Guru Nānak with the poet in him, with his transcendental exposition, sharp skill and argumentative capability brought out many hymns which enriched, explained, simplified and modernized many theological concepts of Upaniṣads for the use and understanding of a common man.

2

Cosmogony or Origin of Creation

MAN spends his lifetime in acquiring knowledge, professional training and accumulating assets and wows (wonders) to find the answer to the questions.

1. Who am I?
2. Where from have I come?
3. Who is my master or creator?

These questions are not new but repeated many times by great masters of religion and philosophy. Sages and scriptures of different time periods envisaged, revealed and answered them in their own way.

Guru Nānak, in the following lines, says:

kahā te āvai kahā ihu jāvai kahā ihu rahai samāī॥
esu sabada ka-u jo arathāvai tisu gura tilu na tamāī॥
kiu tatai avigatai pāvai guramukhi lagai piāro॥
āpe suratā āpe karatā kahu nānaka bīcāro॥
hukame āvai hukame jāvai hukame rahai samāī॥
pūre gura te sācu kamāvai gati miti sabade pāī॥

– *Ādi Granth*, p. 940

In this hymn Guru Nānak shares his wisdom by queries and answers to them. He questions: From what source we come? To which source we merge after death? What is the way to get absorbed in the ultimate source? If one can explain the meaning of this hymn that *guru* should be considered without any greed at all. How can one find the Ultimate Truth? How one becomes godly and gets absorbed in the love for the Lord? He replies that we are born by His command, and will go by His command; we merge with the Ultimate Reality by His command. Guru Nānak has described *Brahman* as *Kartā-Purakha* (the creator) in the *mūla mantra*. He creates, and is both the cause and effect of the origin of the creation.

Hymns of Creation by Guru Nānak

arabada narabada dhauṅdhūkārā ||
dharaṇi na gaganā hukamu apāra ||
nā dinu raini na caṅdu na surajū suṅna samādhi lagāidā ||
khāṇī na bāṇī pauṇa na pāṇī || *opati khapati na āvaṇa jāṇī* ||
khaṅḍa patāla sapata nahī sāgara nadī na nīru vahāidā ||
nā tadi suragu machu paiālā || *dojaku bhisatu nahī khai kālā* ||
naraku suragu nahī jaṁmaṇu maraṇā nā ko āi na jāidā ||
brahamā bisanu mahesu na koī || *avaru na dīsai eko soī* ||
....
āpe āpi upāi vigasai āpe kīmati pāidā ||
– *Ādi Granth*, p. 1035

āpe sāhu āpe vaṇajārā sāce eho bhāidā ||
....
jā tisu bhāṇā tā jagatu upāiā || *bājhu kalā āḍāṇu rahāiā* ||
– Ibid., p. 1036

For countless years, there was only darkness throughout. Earth or sky did not exist, there was no night, moon or sun; there was only infinite Divine Will. God sat in an absolute state of *samādhi*. There was no existence of any creating source or power of speech. No air or water existed. There were no births or deaths. No one came or went away. There was no existence of any country, region, sea, river, or running water. No heaven or hell, earth, or nether regions of the underworld. There were no gods named Brahmā, Viṣṇu and Śiva. There was nothing there except the One "Being" Himself. There were no men of celibacy, or charity, and no one was dwelling in the forests. After counting non-existence of all sorts of forms of creation, the Lord or Being created Himself from Himself and determined His value. The Lord or Being Himself is the custodian and He Himself is the trader. It is all the pleasure of the Will of the Supreme Lord that when He so desired, He created the universe. He himself is the designer and sustainer of His creation. He is the creator of all forms of existence.

suna kalā aparaṁpari dhārī॥ *āpi nirālamu apara apārī*॥
āpe kudarati kari kari dekhai suṅnahu sunu upāidā॥
pauṇu pāṇī suṅna te sāje॥ *sr̥saṭi upāi kāiā gaḍa rāje*॥
agani pāṇī jiu joti tumārī suṅne kalā rahāidā॥
sunahu brahamā bisanu mahesu upāe॥ *suṅne varate juga sabāe*॥
....
suṅnahu khāṇī sunahu bāṇī॥ *suṅnahu upajī suni samāṇī*॥
....
suṅnahu upaje dasa avatārā॥ *sr̥saṭi upāi kīā pāsārā*॥
– *Ādi Granth*, pp. 1037-38

The Infinite Lord assumed His power in the primal void. He Himself remains unattached; He is endless and without any comparison. He Himself applied his power of creation and glances upon his created one's from the void. He is the creator of void and from this primal void He derived air and water. He is the creator of universe and He rules in the fortress of the body. His essence of light exists in the fire, water and souls. His storehouse of power is in the primal void. Brahmā, Viṣṇu and Śiva were created forth from this primal void. The primal void is pervading throughout all the ages. From this primal void came the sun, the moon, the earth, ākāśic ethers. He bears all the weight of their support by exercising His True power. His support cannot be seen.

He triggers his power through the three *guṇas*: *rajas* (motion) *guṇa, tamas* (inertia) *guṇa* and *sattva* (rhythm) *guṇa*. Brahmā uttered through the mouth, the *R̥gveda*, the *Sāmaveda*, the *Yajurveda* and the *Atharvaveda* and entrapped men in the *māyā* of three modes. No one could assess His worth. Everyone utters what He desires us to utter. He brings forward the pains of birth and death and egoism Himself. He blesses with grace through His mercy to attain the fourth state of consciousness and path to liberation. The creation through four sources and of speeking power came forth from the primal void. The primal void is the source of all creation and all creation rests in the void. The ten incarnations came from the Universal Self. After creating the universe He made all the expanse.

sāce te pavanā bhaiā pavanai te jalu hoi॥

jala te tribhavaṇu sājiā ghaṭi ghaṭi joti samoi ॥
– *Ādi Granth*, p. 19

The air came from the Supreme Being, and water sprang from air. From water the three worlds were created by Him. In each and every heart only His light pervades.

Here Guru Nānak says that from primal void came the air which further transformed into water. This is more near to the present understanding: hydrogen + oxygen = H_2O = water. Gas (symbol H) without colour, taste or smell combines with oxygen to form water.

bhani bhani ghaḍīē ghaḍi ghaḍi bhajai ḍhāhi usārai usare ḍhāhai ॥
sara bhari sokhai bhī bhari pokhai samaratha veparavahai ॥
– Ibid., p. 935

Supreme Being creates and recreates his creations at His own will. He makes what He has demolished and destroys what He has made. He makes the pool he created dry and fills the dried one again. He is Almighty and without any dependence.

kavaṇu su velā vakhatu kavaṇu kavaṇa thiti kavaṇu vāru ॥
kavaṇi si rutī māhu kavaṇu jitu hoā ākāru ॥
vela na pāīā paṅḍatī ji hovai lekhu purāṇu ॥
vakhatu na paio kādīā ji likhani lekhu kurāṇu ॥
thiti vāru nā jogī jāṇai ruti māhu nā koī ॥
jā karata siruṭhī kau sāje āpe jāṇai soī ॥
....
lekhā hoi ta likhīē lekhai hoi viṇāmu ॥

– Ibid., pp. 4-5

Guru Nānak further questions and explains about time, moment, day, date, season, month as to when the universe was created? He explains that no *paṇḍita*s or other preachers of religion can find it even if it is written in the Purāṇas. The *qāẓī*s who study Korān also do not know it. Neither the *yogī*'s know the date or time of its origination. The Supreme Being who created this creation only knows it. If one tries to assess account for this, one is sure to exhaust and go away from life before he comes to any conclusion.

pavaṇu gurū pāṇī pitā mātā dharati mahatu ॥

> *divasu rāti dui dāī dāiā khelai sagala jagatu* ||
> – *Ādi Granth*, p. 8

In this concluding *śloka* of *Japjī*, Guru Nānak talks about the play of gross elements. He explains that the air is the instructing *guru*, the water is the male partner, and the earth is the female partner. *Mahat*[1] (consciousness) joins them. The days and nights are the male and female nurses. In this way the world plays on.

Hymn of Creation (Ṛgveda X.129.1-7)

The preceding simplified expression of the origin of creation by Guru Nānak can be compared with the Nāsadīya Sūkta of *Ṛgveda* wherein the *ṛṣi* of yore has conveyed similar thoughts about the Divine Will:

> *nāsadāsinno sadāsīttadānīṁ ṅasīdrajo no vyomā paro yat* |
> *kimāvrīvaḥ kuha kasya śarmannambhaḥ kimāsīdgahanaṁ gabhīram* ||1||
>
> . . .
>
> *iyaṁ visṛṣṭiryata ābabhūva yadi vā dadhe yadi vā na* |
> *āo asyādhyakkṣaḥ parame vyomantso aṅga veda yadi vā na veda* ||7||

1. *Non-being then existed not nor being:*
   There was no air, nor sky that is beyond it.
   What was concealed? Wherein and in whose protection?
   And was there deep unfathomable water?

2. *Death then existed not nor life immortal;*
   Of neither night nor day was any token.
   By its inherent force the One breathed windless;
   No other thing than that beyond existed.

3. *Darkness there was at first by darkness hidden;*
   Without distinctive marks, this all was water.
   That which, becoming, by the void was covered,

---

[1] *Mahat* in Sanskrit means stretched out, expansive, hence great. However in Sāṁkhya, it means cosmic intelligence or the first product of the cosmic substance.

That One by force of heat came into being.

4. *Desire entered the One in the beginning;*
 It was the earliest seed, of thought the product.
 The sages searching in their hearts with wisdom,
 Found out the bond of being in the non-being.

5. *Their ray extended light across the darkness;*
 But was the One above or was it under?
 Creative force was there, and fertile power;
 Below was energy, above was impulse.

6. *Who knows for certain? Who shall here declare it?*
 Whence was it born, and whence came this creation?
 The gods were born after this world's creation:
 Then who can know from whence it has arisen?

7. *None knoweth whence creation has arisen;*
 And whether he has or has not produced it;
 He who surveys it in the highest heaven,
 He only knows, or haply he may know not.

– *Ṛgveda*, X.129.1-7, tr. A.A. Macdonell[2]

The above hymn starts with a note that in the beginning nothing existed, neither Being nor non-being. There was no air, no sky and there was no knowledge as to what was concealed and where and under whose protection. There was no life or death, no night or day. There was complete darkness hidden by darkness, this was all water that one by force of heat came into being. First desire sprouted forth earliest which produced thought. The sages who searched in their hearts with wisdom, found the bond of Being in the non-being. It ends with, no one can declare whence the creation came, as gods were born after the world's creation. None knows when the creation arose, whether it was produced by Him or not. Only the Supreme Lord who watches it in the uppermost heaven may or even may not know it.

The Puruṣa Sūkta[3] of *Ṛgveda* X.90.1-3 explains:

---

[2] Nikhilananda, 2008, *The Upanishads*, p. 19.

[3] Ibid., p. 17.

> The world is created by dismembering (dividing into pieces) the cosmic giant *Puruṣa* – the primeval man. This *Puruṣa* had innumerable heads, innumerable eyes and innumerable feet. He pervaded the earth from all sides and spread ten figures breadth beyond. The *Puruṣa* is all that has been and that is to be. It is the Lord or ruler of immortality. So mighty is his greatness and greater than this is *Puruṣa*. All creatures are one-fourth of him and three-fourth eternal lives are in heaven.

The *Muṇḍaka Upaniṣad* 1.1.7 explains that as the web sprouts forth of the spider and is withdrawn, as plants grow from soil, hair and nails from body, like that the universe sprouts forth from the eternal *Brahman*.

The *Chāndogya Upaniṣad* 3.13.7-8 also explains that all this, what we see is eternal *Brahman*. The whole universe comes forth from it, lives its life in it and dissolves into it.

Aitareya Upaniṣad also asserts that in the beginning all this verily was *Ātman* only, one without a second:

> *ātmā va idameka evāgra āsīnnanyatkiñcana misat* | *sa ikṣata lokānnu sṛjā iti* |
>
> The self, verily, was (all) this, one only, in the beginning. There was nothing else that winked. He thought Himself let me now create the worlds. – 1.1.1
>
> *sa imāṁllokānasṛjata ambho maricīrmaramāpo 'do 'mbhaḥ pareṇa divaṁ dyauḥ pratiṣṭhā, antarikṣaṁ marīcayaḥ, pṛthivī maro yā adhastāttā āpaḥ* ||
>
> He created these worlds: *ambhaḥ* (the world of water bearing clouds), *marīci* (the world of the solar rays), *māra* (the world of mortals) and *āp* (the world of waters). You is the *ambhaḥ*, above heaven, heaven is its support. The *marīcis* are the mid-region. *Māra* is the earth. What is underneath is *āp*. – 1.1.2
>
> *sa īkṣateme nu lokā lokapālānnu sṛja iti* | *so 'dbhya eva puruṣaṁ samuddhṛtyāmūrchayat* ||
>
> He thought Himself "here now are the worlds. Let me now create world guardians. Right from the waters, He drew forth the person (in the form of a lump) and gave Him a shape". – 1.1.3

Says Radhakrishnan:

> He created these worlds, water, light rays, death and the waters. This water is above the heaven. The heaven is its support. The light rays are the atmosphere. Death is the earth. What is beneath, they are the waters.[4]

> The Upaniṣads assume that the naturalistic theory of evolution cannot be accepted. The world is not to be viewed as an automatic development without any intelligent course or intelligent aim. Matter, life, mind, intelligence are different forms of existence with their specific characteristics and modes of action each acting on the other but not derived from each other. Life is not the mechanical resultant of the antecedent coordination of material forces, but it is what is called an emergent. The life emerges when the material conditions are available which permit life to organize itself in matter. It cannot be produced by lifeless particles. It is essentially the instrument of the Supreme Being. The world is not the result of meaningless chance. There is a purpose working itself out through the ages. We cannot miss the primordiality of the Supreme.[5]

brahmaiva idam agra āsīt, ekam eva.....

Verily, this world was all *Brahman* in the beginning. The action of the Supreme continues in the world. – *BṛUp* 1.4.10-11

taṁ hovāca । yato vā imāni bhūtāni jāyante । yena jātāni jīvanti,
yatprayantyabhisaṁviśanti । tadvijijñāsasva । tadbrahmeti ।
– *Taittirīya Upaniṣad* 3.1.1

That verily from which these beings are born, that by which they live, that into which when dead, they enter. That seeks to know.

The Upaniṣads affirm that *Brahman* is the ground and support of all existence that from which all things originate, and after their origination, they exist, and into which they merge when they get dissolved.

Great similarity of thought and expression is noticed between the Vedic revelations and the teaching of Guru Nānak about

---

4 Radhakrishnan, 2012, *The Principal Upanishads*, p. 515.

5 Ibid., pp. 57-60.

cosmogony or origin of the creation.

Universal Soul and Individual Soul

Ātman, through *māyā*, has projected material forms from itself and then entered into them as their living self – *anena jīvena ātmanā anupraviśya*. *Brahman* (Universal Soul) is the ground and support of all existence. Individual soul (*ātman*) is the fundamental law of individual awareness. By knowing the individual self, the distinction between the two diminishes and oneness between the two gets identified.

The contrast between the two is made vivid in the following text:

> *dvā suparṇā sayujā sakhāyā samānaṁ vṛkṣaṁ pariṣasvajate* ।
> *tayoranyaḥ pippalaṁ svādvattyanaśnannanyo bhicākaśīti.* ॥
>
> *samāne vṛkṣe puruṣo nimagno 'nīśayā śocati muhyamānaḥ* ।
> *juṣṭaṁ yadā pasyatyanyamiśamasya mahimānamiti vītaśokaḥ* ॥
>
> – *Muṇḍaka Upaniṣad* 3.1.1-2
>
> Two birds (the individual self and the Supreme Self) joined together always and are known by the same name. They closely hold tight to the same tree. One of them eats the sweet fruit and the other looks on without eating. Seated on the same tree *jīva* groans confused by its own inability. But on seeing the other, the Supreme Lord, worshipped by all, and His glory, *jīva* gets relief from grief.

Ātman has been used in the Vedānta philosophy to denote both the individual being and the Supreme Being. Individual being has been expressed by *ātman*, soul and self (with small letter); the Supreme Being, by *Ātman*, Soul and Self (with capital letter).

The Upaniṣads explain that the individual soul, with desires, ego and mind, enjoys the fruit of actions which is limited and insignificant. But when it sheds itself from its temporary transformations, it wins immortality. Then it is recognized as identical with the infinitely great Supreme Soul. It is neither a woman, nor a man, nor a neuter. It takes the form with whatever body it takes. *Jīva* gets rebirth at various places and in various forms in accordance with its deeds. But even while it is subjected to all the limitations and sufferings of the relative world, *Ātman* does not lose its perfect nature even in the slightest degree. *Jīva* compelled by its good or bad fruits of actions enters into good or bad births and follows ups and downs and roams about in various forms. He himself becomes bewildered overcome by the *guṇas* and in the delusion he develops a sense,"This is I", "This is mine" and fetters by his own action as a bird in the nest. But one's everlasting Self remains free.

According to Guru Nānak, the *ātman* (*puruṣa*) or soul (self) is one with the *Brahman*. The individual soul within the self and the Universal Soul both are identical. If individual self is known, the Highest Self is also realized. Just as the soul is related to the body, the Highest Self is related to the universe. Individual soul and the body both belong to and are part of *Brahman*. Because of its individuality, the soul appears to be different from *Brahman*, though it is part and parcel of *Brahman*. Both matter and individual soul are real constituents of *Brahman*'s nature. He writes:

jīu piṅḍu sabhu tisadā de khājai ākhi gavāīe ||
– *Ādi Granth*, p. 465

> You are both our body and soul so it is meaningless to ask for individual sustenance.

According to Guru Nānak, while the soul is *puruṣa*, *Brahman* is *kartā purakha, akala purakha, ādi purakha, nirañjana purakha, sat purakha*. *Brahman* is the internal ruler of *puruṣas*. The individual soul has its limitations, and due to these limitations, it cannot understand *Brahman* fully. Individuality is caused by soul's association with mind and intellect.

UNIVERSAL SOUL

The sacred formula or the basic principle of all the hymns of Guru Nānak revolves around his expression that the source and end of all existence is One and only One. Call it a Truth as it is truth. There are innumerable names to that Truth which in fact specify His powers or qualities. Guru Nānak used many current and ancient names of God in his compositions, e.g. Madhusūdana, Murāri, Dāmodara, Hari, Dīna Dayāla and Rāma, but never attached any significance to these names. These names are only for understanding or for the convenience of the seekers. He considered the different names of God as only outward symbol and mode of contact with the Supreme Soul. The most important names according to him are, Oṁkāra and Sat, which convey the unity of *Brahman* and its two aspects, i.e. the unmanifested (*nirguṇa*) and manifested (*saguṇa*) *Brahman*.

The opening lines of the *Japjī* of Guru Nānak are called *mūla mantra*. The *Śrī Guru Granth Sāhib* also opens with these lines. The following lines describe the nature of *Brahman* (Universal Soul) as a divine principle:

Ika Oṁkāra	– The one Oṁkara (manifested as well as unmanifested *Brahman*)
Sat Nāma	– His name is Truth
Kartā Purakha	– A *Puruṣa* who creates
Nirbhau	– He is fearless
Nirvaira	– He is without any enmity
Akāla Mūrata	– A being whom death cannot assail
Ajūnī	– He is not born
Saibham	– He is self-existent
Gura Prasāda	– With the grace of *guru* (preceptor)
Japa	– Utter his name
Āda Saca	– He was Truth in the beginning
Jugāda Saca	– He was Truth in the beginning of the ages
Hai bhi Saca	– He is Truth in the present
Nānaka hosī bhī saca	– and He shall be True in future

– Mūla Mantra, *Japjī*

There is one God whose name is Truth. He is the creator, without any fear and enmity, immortal, unborn, self-existent. He can be realized with the grace of a *guru* by repeating His name. The Truth existed in the beginning; the Truth was in the beginning of ages (primal age). The Truth is prevailing now also and the Truth will prevail always.

thāpiā na jāi kītā na hoī ॥ āpe āpi nirañjanu soī ॥
– *Ādi Granth,* p. 2

The Truth cannot be physically identified, nor created. The Pure One exists by Himself.

These lines further describe the attributes of *Brahman*.

sahasa tava naina nana naina hai tohi ॥
kau sahasa mūrati nanā eka tohī ॥
sahasa pada bimala nana eka pada gañdha ॥
binu sahasa tava gañdha iva calata mohī ॥
sabha mahi joti joti hai soi ॥
tisa kai cānaṇi sabha mahi cānaṇu hoi ॥
– Ibid., p. 663

Virāṭ Puruṣa! your eyes and forms are innumerable yet you have no eye and not a single form for projection. Similarly you have innumerable lotus feet and noses, yet no identified feet or nose. I am astonished with your play. Your divine light exists in everyone which shines within everyone.

In these lines Guru Nānak describes the Universal Soul as the sum total of the individual souls.

āpe rasīā āpi rasu āpe rāvaṇahāru ॥
āpe hovai colaḍā āpe seja bhatāru ॥
rañgi ratā merā sāhibu ravi rahiā bharapūri ॥
....
kaulu tū hai kavīā tū hai āpe vekhi vigasu ॥
– Ibid., p. 23

Supreme Being Himself is enjoyment and He Himself enjoys His creation. He Himself is the emotion and feeling in all. God Himself acts as the bride in her gown and He is also the bridegroom on the bed. God is filled with love and pervades everywhere. God is the blooming flower of the day and He is the water lily of the night. He Himself looks to all and springs forth in bliss.

These lines portray the oneness of the Universal Soul and the individual soul. The Universal Soul is both the cause and the effect of each being.

alakha apāra agaṁma agocara nā tisu kālu na karamā ||
jāti ajāti ajonī saṁbhau nā tisu bhāu na bharamā ||
....
nā tisu rūpa varanu nahī rekhiā sācai sabadi nīsāṇu ||
nā tisu māta pitā suta baṅdhapa nā tisu kāmu na nārī ||
akula niraṅjana apara paraṁparu sagalī joti tumārī ||
ghaṭa ghaṭa aṅtari brahamu lukāiā ghaṭi ghaṭi joti sabāī ||
– *Ādi Granth*, p. 597

He is unknowable, infinite, cannot be approached, and imperishable. He is out of the scope of death or *karma*. He has no caste, He is not born, self-illumined and free of doubt and desire. He reveals Himself through unstruck melody. He is without mother, father, sons or relatives. He has no ancestors. He is pure and faultless. He is without any limit and endless. His light is spread throughout.

This hymn further contains the attributes of the Universal Soul with a message that there is only one light which shines in everybody. It has no mother or father or brother, it is self-existent and without any desire and bondages.

suṅna maṅḍala iku jogī vaise || *nāri na purakhu kahahu koū kaise* ||
tr̥bhavaṇa joti rahe liva lāī || *surinara nātha sace saraṇāī* ||
ānanda mūlu anātha adhārī || *guramukhi bhagati sahaji bīcārī* ||
– Ibid., p. 685

The primal Lord sits within the heavenly abode in the deepest *samādhi*. He is not male and he is not female. He cannot be described. The saints and *yoga* masters search for Him in the holy places silently. The Supreme Being is full of bliss and He supports all the helpless. The God-loving individuals worship and meditate upon Him.

This hymn explains the nature of *Brahman* and Its quality of being, *sat, cit, ānanda*.

ākhaṇi aukhā sunaṇi aukhā ākhi na jāpī ākhi ||
iki ākhi ākhahi sabadu bhākhahi aradha uradha dinu rāti ||
je kihu hoi ta kihu disai jāpai rūpa na jāti ||

sabhi kāraṇa karatā kare ghaṭa aughaṭa ghaṭa thāpi॥
ākhaṇi aukhā nānakā ākhi na jāpai ākhi॥
– *Ādi Granth*, p. 1239

One cannot utter Him, one cannot listen to Him. He cannot be uttered by voice. Some try to utter Him with speech and chant some words in low and high pitch, day and night. He would have been visible if He had any form. One cannot see His form and state. The Supreme Being performs all actions. He resides in all hearts whether high or low. It is not easy to chant Him, one cannot chant Him by mouth.

Universal Soul cannot be described by chanting. It is also not visible. It performs all the actions, yet cannot be seen. It is established deep within one's heart.

jaha dekhā taha dīna daiālā॥ *āi na jāī prabhu kirapālā*॥
jīā aṅdari jugati samāī rahio nirālamu rāiā॥
jagu tisa kī chāiā jisu bāpu na māiā॥
nā tisu bhaiṇa na bharau kamāiā॥
– Ibid., p. 1038

I look all around and find the Lord who is kind to the humble. God is kind. He does not take birth or death. He is spread throughout in all beings in His mystic way. The Supreme Being remains unattatched. This world is His image. He is without any parents. He has adopted no sister or brother.

Here again Guru Nānak wonders about the mystery of Universal Soul which is the part of every existence yet is detached from every action.

nānaka niraguṇi guṇu kare guṇavaṅtiā guṇu de॥
tehā koi na sujhaī ji tisu guṇu koi kare॥
– Ibid., p. 2

Guru Nānak explains that God blesses all with virtue but no one can bestow virtue on Him.

This is a wonderful expression for God's greatness that we derive all our energy of being virtuous and worthy from Him, yet we cannot know whether there is anyone who can bestow some virtues in return to his bounty.

INDIVIDUAL SOUL

God resides in soul and soul abides in God. Ego comes in the way, and obstacle for realization is the false sense of individualization from Universal Reality. The ego manifests itself as duality and love for the impermanent world. Nothing is permanent in this world and our existence in this world is bound with our kārmic account. The moment our account is settled we all are bound to leave this world.

In the following verses Guru Nānak talks about how an individual is misled by the ego of I-ness and how he indulges and leads a life of futility, controlled by sensory pleasures:

> *dūjī māiā jagata cita vāsu* || *kāma krodha ahaṁkāra bināsu* ||
> *dūjā kauṇu kahā nahī koī* || *sabha mahi eku nirañjanu soī* ||
> *dūjī duramati ākhai doi* || *āvai jāi mari dūjā hoi* ||
> *dharaṇi gagani naha dekhau doi* || *nārī purakha sabāī loi* ||
> *ravi sasi dekhau dīpaka ujiālā* || *saraba niraṅtari prītamu bālā* ||
>
> – *Ādi Granth*, p. 223

> The people of the world, under the influence of *māyā*, dwell in duality of consciousness . They are finished in their desire for sex, high temper and I-ness. There is no one to be called the second, as there is only one Truth. The one perfect Lord is spread among all. Those who call for the second are under the effect of duality. They are subject to births and deaths. I do not see any second in the earth and sky other than the One and the only One. Among all the women and men only His light is shining. Both the sun and the moon derive light from Him. My ever-youthful Beloved lives among all.

In this hymn Guru Nānak explains that those who love duality, waste away their life. The unseen cannot be seen. Since He cannot be seen, He cannot be described. It is only through the *guru* that He can be realized and the fire of desires quenched. If one knows this he is attuned to the Truth which is the One and the only One.

> *ghara hī muṅdhi videsi piru nita jhūre saṁmhālē* ||
> *miladiā ḍhila na hovaī je nīati rāsi kare* ||
>
> – Ibid., p. 594

> Individual soul is like a bride at home in this world. The husband Lord is away from her. Soul bride lives in His rememberance and feels the agony of His absence. If she gets rid of duality, she shall meet Him without delay.

In these lines Guru Nānak uses the metaphor of a bride at home, whose spouse has gone afar. She is sad at heart and wriggles in pain due to her desire for him. He gives a hope that if she is earnest and cherishes with a right mind she can meet him instantly. Here he explains that individual soul suffers the pangs of separation due to duality. If one is sincere and remains attuned to God, one can feel satiated.

THE RELATIONSHIP OF INDIVIDUAL SOUL
AND UNIVERSAL SOUL

> *sāgara mahi būṅda būṅda mahi sāgaru kavaṇu bujhai bidh jāṇaī* ||
> *utabhuja calata āpi kari cīnai āpe tatu pachāṇaī* ||
> ....
> *dina mahi raiṇi raiṇi mahi dinīaru usana sīta bidhi soī* ||
> ....
> *purakha mahi nāri nāri mahi purakhā būjhahu brahama giānī* ||
> *dhuni mahi dhiānu dhiāna mahi jāniā guramukhi akatha kahānī* ||
> *mana mahi joti joti mahi manūā paṅca mile gura bhāī* ||
> *nānaka tina kai sada balihārī jina eka sabadi liva lāī* ||
>
> – *Ādi Granth*, pp. 878-79

> The mutual relationship between the individual soul and Universal Soul is like a little fall of drop from the ocean and the ocean lies in the drop. One who can understand this is a wise man. The Supreme Being Himself acts the wonderful play of the world. He Himself through deep consideration understands its trueself. The night resides in the dawn, and dawn resides in the sunset. Likewise position is true of the hot and cold. No one has the knowledge of His state and limit. The female, born from the sperm of male, gives birth to female and the male is born from the female. One should understand it. Melody contains meditation and the knowledge is contained in the meditation. Being a Guramukha one should utter the unspoken word. There is His light in the mind and individual mind is in His light. The

guru binds the five senses together. like good brothers.

Guru Nānak says that the relationship between the individual soul and the Universal Soul is like the relation between a drop of water and the ocean.

ātama mahi rāmu rāma mahi ātamu cīnasi gura bīcārā ||
aṁmṛta bāṇī sabadi pachāṇī dukha kāṭai hau mārā ||
– *Ādi Granth*, p. 1153

The Supreme Being is in the soul. And the soul rests in the Lord. This can be realized through the teachings of the *guru*. With the *guru*'s *bānī* one can realize the word of the *śabada* which clears egoism and dispels sorrow.

In this hymn Guru Nānak emphasizes that God or Universal Soul and individual souls are one only. When I-ness is shed with the knowledge from the *guru*'s word, the nectar flows from within. Individuals get afflicted by dualism and thereby suffer.

sabhanī ghaṭī sahu vasai saha binu ghaṭu na koi ||
nānaka te sohāgaṇī jinhā guramukhi paragaṭu hoi ||
– Ibid., p. 1412

The Universal Soul resides within each heart. No heart can function without that. The godly individuals are pleased noble soul brides to whom the Lord is revealed.

Here Guru Nānak asks individuals to follow the path of Guramukha, who are self-realized to enjoy the happy and virtuous union of the soul bride with God.

ghaṭi ghaṭi gupatā guramukhi mukatā ||
aṅtari bāhari sabadi su jugatā ||
– Ibid., p. 939

The Supreme Being resides in each and every heart. The Guramukha gets liberated. One is united, inwardly and outwardly, through the *śabada*.

He, who is hidden in each heart, is unmanifested. He is united with the word form within and without.

eku acāru raṅgu iku rūpu || *pauṇa pāṇī aganī asarūpu* ||

eko bhavaru bhavai tihu loi॥ eko būjhai sūjhai pati hoi॥
– *Ādi Granth*, p. 930

The one God prevails in all acts, colours and formations. The one soul roams in all the three worlds. He who understands and realizes this is honoured. One God is in all ways, forms and colours. It is He who works through air, water and fire. One should gather wisdom and abide in the state of equipoise.

jetā sabadu surati dhuni tetī jetā rūpu kāiā terī॥
tūṅ āpe rasanā āpe basanā avaru na dūjā kahau māī॥
sāhibu merā eko hai॥ eko hai bhāī eko hai॥
āpe māre āpe choḍai āpe levai dei॥
āpe vekhai āpe vigasai āpe nadari karei॥
jo kichu karaṇā so kari rahiā avaru na karaṇā jāī॥
jaisā varatai taiso kahīē sabha terī vaḍiāī॥
kali kalavālī māiā madu mīṭhā manu matavālā pīvatu rahai॥
āpe rūpa kare bahu bhāṅtiṅ nānaku bapuḍā eva kahai॥
– Ibid., p. 350

As much as the musical vibrations in our mind, so much is melody of God's sound. God's body is as vast as the form of this universe. He Himself is tongue and He Himself is the nose. Do not speak of any other. The Supreme Being and the Master is One. All sisters and brothers of destiny, He is the One and the Only One. He is the One alone. He Himself kills, emancipates and He Himself gives and takes. He Himself beholds and rejoices and bestows His grace. Whatever He is to do, that is what He is doing. No one else can do anything. The Dark Age of Kali Yuga is the bottle of intoxication *māyā* is the sweet the intoxicant and the intoxicated mind continues to drink it. The Supreme Being Himself assumes all sorts of forms.

Here Guru Nānak unfolds the mystery of music and sound within individuals. He exclaims that size of God's body is the size of this universe. He is the tongue that tastes, nose that smells, eye that sees, there is nothing other than Him in me. It is mind under delusion which makes us think as if we are different from Him.

jaha jaha dekhā taha joti tumārī terā rūpu kinehā॥
ikatu rūpi phirahi parachannā koi na kisahī jehā॥

aṅḍaja jeraja utabhuja setaja tere kīte jaṅtā ||
eku purabu mai terā dekhiā tū sabhanā māhi ravaṅtā ||
– *Ādi Granth*, p. 596

> Wherever I looked, I saw His light. He has one form which cannot be seen. There is none like Him. All the living forms whether born of eggs, womb, earth or sweat are created by Him. I find his one glory that He is spread all through and penetrates in all.

Here Guru Nānak addresses God as Kanhaiya and expresses wonder at the play of the true Lord. The Lord pervades earth, water, interspace and wherever we can see. He has one form which is hidden from the eye. From Him are the egg born, the foetus born, the sweat born, the earth born and all types of creatures. No one is like another. The same Universal Soul extends as protoplasm. This is the expression of unity in all existence.

His simple way of poetic and vivid expression of unity of individual soul with Universal Soul can be compared with the philosophical and precise teachings of the Upaniṣads to the seekers of truth.

The Upaniṣads explain that *Brahman*, the ground and support of all creation, can be known through knowledge of *ātman* which is the inner self of man. The *Chāndogya Upaniṣad* explains that this whole universe is *Brahman*. Each soul within every individual is *Brahman*. The reflection of an individual seen in the eye is *ātman*, i.e. *Brahman*. God is unattached to the world and man but He pierces into man and lives along with him. He is the inner most element of man's very life.

The Upaniṣads explain that individuals experience three natural states, viz. waking, dream state and deep sleep. The self (*ātman*) is understood to be the fourth which is not new but is something that remains after attributes of the first three states are obliterated. Absolute *Brahman* manifests itself in three forms, i.e. *jāgrat* (*viśva*), *svapna* (*taijasa*) and *suṣupti* (*prajñā*). It is called *viśva*, when it has consciousness of the outside, *taijasa* when it has consciousness of inside, and called *prajñā* when it is concentrated. In waking state, one enjoys gross objects and is aware of external objects. In dream state one is conscious of internal objects and enjoys the subtle objects. In deep sleep one has no desires for any object nor he gets any dream. This is a state in which one is a mass of consciousness, full of bliss. He is master of all and knows of all and controls the inner self of individual. In *turīya* state one is not conscious of the inner (subjective) world, nor of the outer (objective) world. Neither that in which one is conscious of both, nor that which is mass of consciousness. It is not simple consciousness, nor is unconsciousness. It is all peace and bliss and free from duality. It is cessation of all phenomena.

One uses the gross body to experience the gross world, subtle body to experience the subtle world, and the causal body to experience the causal world. *Ātman* is one without a second. When associated with the three *upādhi*s, it is given three different names. Free from any *upādhi*, it is *Brahman*, the Absolute. This is the description of microcosm or individual soul. The same is true of the macrocosm or totality of souls. As is the individual soul, so is the universe. *Brahman* functions in three states, in association with three *upādhi*s, and is known by three technical names. With reference to the gross *upādhi*, *Brahman* is called Virāṭ; with reference to the subtle *upādhi*, Hiraṇyagarbha or Prajāpati; and with reference to the causal *upādhi*, *sūtrātmā* or *prāṇa*.

The Upaniṣads explain that the Lord, when associated with the *upādhi* of the causal bodies, is called *sūtrātmā*, which means literally the "Thread soul", that is to say, the thread-like substance that joins together all the different individuals – men, gods, animals and inorganic beings. God pervades everywhere in all its creation like the protoplasmic substance with minute threads, passing through the cell walls, which unites the cells in a living organism. As is the individual soul, the same is true of the macrocosm. All living beings respond in more or less the same manner to the outside world and experience the same sensations because their individual minds are controlled by the Cosmic Mind.

A living body consists of innumerable cells. Each cell has a distinctive life and purpose of its own. Whatever is necessary for its growth, it extracts from its immediate environment. The aim is ultimate nutrition and building of the body of which each individual cell forms a small but necessary and distinct unit. Gross living body is the aggregate of its living cells and the aggregate of all individual causal bodies is *sūtrātmā* or Cosmic *Prāṇa* (consciousness).

The Upaniṣads also explain that *Nirguṇa-Brahman* cannot be explained by any suggestive symbol, quality or attribute. No one can describe Him in words. A knower cannot be known. Self is the subject, it cannot be known. Whatever can be known is an object. It can be understood only as knowledge, which cannot be separated from the Ultimate Reality. Though unknown and unknowable, *Brahman* is yet the eternal "knower of knowing". It is also the goal of all knowledge. The impossibility of knowing *Brahman* by human senses has been expressed through employing the formula of negation: *neti, neti* (not this, not this). Vedānta philosophy often describes *Brahman* by the term *Saccidānanda* composed of three words: *sat* meaning the Ultimate Reality which is the Truth and not subjected to change; *cit* meaning intelligence, consciousness or knowledge; *ānanda* meaning permanent bliss.

The Upaniṣads explain that when *Brahman* becomes conditioned by the *upādhi* of *māyā* and shrinks, as it were, because of that *māyā*, it is called *Saguṇa-Brahman*. *Saguṇa Brahman* is the personal god. When *Brahman* imposes on Itself a limit, thus it manifests as god, soul and world. *Saguṇa-Brahman* is also known as creator, preservator and destructor. But *Nirguṇa-Brahman* and *Saguṇa-Brahman* are not two separate identities. The sea is the same, whether it is peaceful or agitated. *Māyā* has no independent reality; it is a part of *Brahman* as the power of *Brahman*, just as essence of fire's burning cannot be conceived different from fire.

Different views are held on the matter as to what is the relationship of the individual self (*jīva*) with the Universal Soul. Śaṅkara held a view that the Universal Self is exactly alike the individual self. Rāmānuja believed that the individual self is forever one with and also different from the Universal Self. But according to Madhva, the individual self is ever different from the Universal Self.

The four sentences in the Vedas, called *mahāvākyas*, convey the purport of the Upaniṣads as an identity between the individual soul and the Universal Soul.

i. *Prajñānam brahma* (Consciousness is *Brahman*): *Prajñānam* is unoccupied awareness in Pure Consciousness. It is unoccupied from the process of cognition, thought, cognition related and created experience, senses or their retrieval (*Aitareya Upaniṣad* 3.1.3 of *Ṛgveda*).

ii. *Ayam ātma brahma* (this individual self is *Brahman*): The identity between *Brahman* and *ātmā* is established (*Māṇḍūkya Upaniṣad* 2 of the *Atharvaveda*).

iii. *Tat tvam asi* (Thou art That): Meaning, the individual self and the Universal Self are the same. The Self and Pure Consciousness are same in nature, content, structure, form (function) and presence. This self-consciousness is superimposed over Pure Consciousness. Pure Consciousness flows continuously, unlike self-consciousness which is transitory (*Chāndogya Upaniṣad* 6.8.7 of *Sāmaveda*).

iv. *Aham brahmāsmi* (I am *Brahman*): *Jīva* realizes his own nature and denotes the real identity of "I". "I" is not a body or a person or a thought, but Pure Consciousness. "I" is the impersonal seer which is the source of mental energy, and guide and witness to transformation of mental energy as mental functions but unaffected by them and transcending both mental functions and their cessation (*Bṛhadāraṇyaka Upaniṣad* 1.4.10 of the *Yajurveda*).

The *Chāndogya Upaniṣad* establishes oneness of the self and *Brahman* by most practically illustrated examples. Some are quoted from the sixth chapter:

(a) Take a fruit of the banyan tree and cut it open. There are extremely small seeds in it. Break open a tiny seed, you will not see any thing in it yet the essence of a big tree is in that seed. The Univesal Soul or Self is that basic essence in which all things exist.

(b) Take a fistful of salt and put it into the water. All the water tastes salty yet it is not visible. Likewise the subtle essence of salt, the *Brahman* is dissolved in this body right to the tips of fingers. When it functions in the living body, it is called *prāṇa*, when one speaks it is called organ of speech, when one sees, it is the eye, when it hears, it is the ear, when it thinks, it is the mind. Thus it is one consciousness which gets the different names according to its functions.

(c) Friends get around the man with fatal illness and ask "do you know me ...". He recogonizes them till his speech is dissolved in his mind, mind in *prāṇa*, *prāṇa* in vital heat and vital heat in the Supreme Being. But when his speech is dissolved in his mind, mind in *prāṇa*, *prāṇa* in vital heat, and vital heat in the Supreme Being, then he does not recognize them.

The *Aitareya Upaniṣad* establishes that all creatures in dreamless sleep or death merge into one existence. They are unaware of their past or present state because of ignorance. They know nothing that they have merged with Him from whom they came. The being may be a tiger or a bear, or gnat or mosquito, they remain same after a dreamless sleep.

Thus Upaniṣads advocate unity of all existence in Pure Consciousness. Guru Nānak also maintains in all his hymns that there is only one Supreme Power which is both a source material and efficient source of all existence. The same light shimmers in each organic and inorganic being.

NATURE OF INDIVIDUAL SOUL AND BODY

In the preceding part of this chapter we have discussed the unity of the individual soul with the Universal Soul. In this part of the chapter the nature of individual soul and body is undertaken in the light of hymns of Guru Nānak and the Upaniṣads. Guru Nānak advocated oneness of the individual soul and the Universal Soul like Advaita but disagreed to that the world is an illusionary appearance.

The Upaniṣads explain that the individual man is unison with five elements: *anna*, *prāṇa*, *manas*, *vijñāna* and *ānanda*. The life and matter consist of the gross physical body (*sthula śarīra*), mind and life make the subtle body (*sūkṣma śarīra*), intelligence is the causal body (*kāraṇa śarīra*) and the *ātman*.

Guru Nānak also addresses the human body:

> You think you are immortal and do not realize that this world is a mere sport that is why you are humiliated into ashes on earth. You indulge in greed, falsehood and make a show of yourself and you carry the heavy burden of your deeds. One day you will blow up like dust on earth. Only good deeds done by you will remain with the soul. You shall not get this opportunity again, so do not waste it in slanders, gossips or gazing at others' wives. When the essence (soul) leaves the body, one remains behind like left-over woman.

He further explains:

> The soul and body are from Him. The main vices connected with the body are cruelty towards others, the act of accumulation of wealth, the theft of others wealth and sexual pleasures. When the body is careless about the real objective of its birth in this world and passes night in sleeps and day in enjoyments, the most precious opportunity in this birth is wasted.

Guru Nānak talks about the nature of body and the individual soul in many of his hymns:

NATURE OF BODY

māta pitā saṁjogi upāe rakatu biṁdu mili piṁḍu kare ||
aṁtari garabha uradhi liva lāgī so prabhu sāre dāti kare ||
....
cari padāratha lai jagi janamiā siva sakatī ghari vāsu dhare ||
lāgī bhūkha māiā magu johai mukati padārathu mohi khare ||
karaṇa palāva kare nahī pāvai ita uta ḍhūḍhata thāki pare ||
kāmi krodhi ahaṁkāri viāpe kūḍa kuṭuṁba siha priti kare ||
khāvai bhogai suṇi suṇi dekhai pahiri dikhāvai kāla ghare ||
....
jetā mohu haumai kari bhūle merī merī karate chīni khare ||
tanu dhanu binasai sahasai sahasā phiri pachutāvai mukhi dhūri pare ||
biradhi bhaiā jobanu tanu khisiā kaphu kaṁṭhu birūdho nainahu nīru ḍhare ||
....

surati gaī kālī hū dhaule kisai na bhāvai rakhio ghare||
bisarata nāma aise dokha lāgahi jamu māri samāre naraki khare||
– *Ādi Granth*, pp. 1013-14

The union of mother and father forms the foetus. Within the mother's womb, it lies upside down ever attuned to God. He is kind to nourish it. One takes birth to achieve the four objectives of life. Hunger drives him to the path of *māyā*'s riches. He gets attached to his kith and kin and loses liberation. One cries and wails to achieve success for the fulfilment of his desires. In search of these he wanders hither and thither and gets tired. Sexual desire, anger and egoism lead him to develop false relations with the world. He indulges in eating, enjoying dressing up to show off this worth. He is driven to more and more attachments and egoism and gets confused. He cries out *merā merā* and loses out further. His body and wealth do not standby him, and he lives ever in doubts and starts regretting. Lamenting and regretting, he faces the dust of his deeds falling on him. He gets older, his body and youth are wasted away. His voice is choked with phlegm and water comes out of his eyes. His mind flickers and his hair go white from black and no one is willing to share his home with him. These are the woes which stick to him but he under the spell of *māyā* does not cherish God. The hangman of death hurts him and pulls him to hell.

In this hymn Guru Nānak describes the pre-natal position of man who stands on his head attuned to the Lord who looks after him. He takes birth to attain four objectives of life, i.e. *dharma*, *artha*, *kāma* and *mokṣa*. But he gets entrapped in the path and is afflicted with lust, ego and starts loving his illusionary kinsmen and sensory pleasures. He cries and wails in pursuit of possessing worldly objects. His body wears out with time and the soul, burdened with the weight of his deeds, is dragged out. This shows the transitory nature of a man's body and its given lifespan.

mā kī rakatu pitā bidu dhārā|| *mūrati sūrati kari apārā*||
joti dāti jetī sabha terī tū karatā sabha ṭhāī he||
– Ibid., p. 1022

Human form is of utmost beauty which is formed with the combination of the blood of mother and sperm of father with the blessings of the Lord.

Here Guru Nānak appreciates and expresses wonder for the body which is designed beautifully in mother's womb. The Lord creates it and puts His own light within all and also showers His blessings.

pauṇai pāṇī aganī kā melu ।। *cañcala capala budhi kā khelu* ।।
nau daravāje dasavā duāru ।। *bujhu re giānī ehu bīcāru* ।।
kathatā bakatā sunatā soī ।। *āpu bīcāre su giānī hoī* ।।
deṁhi māṭī bolai pauṇu ।। *bujhu re giānī mūā hai kauṇu* ।।
mūī surati bādu ahaṁkāru ।। *ohu na mūā jo dekhaṇahāru* ।।
– *Ādi Granth*, p. 152

The union of air, water and fire creates body. In it the wavering intellect plays. It has nine doors and then there is a tenth gate. It is the Lord within it that speaks, teaches and listens. One who concentrates and examines his own self is wise. The body is ashes, the wind is speaker in it. Only senses, contradictions and duality die, but the One who is the seer does not die.

Here Guru Nānak describes body as a play thing of the restless intellect. If the nine doors of body are closed, the tenth gate is opened. He describes body as a mere dust and breath as mere wind which speaks. Who dies? The ego and strife die, but the self which is the seer does not die.

agani pāṇī bolai bhaḍa vāu ।। *jihavā iṁdrī eku suāu* ।।
disaṭi vikārī nāhī bhau bhāu ।। *āpu māre tā pāe nāu* ।।
subadi marai phiri maraṇu na hoi ।। *binu mūe kiu pūrā hoī* ।।
parapañci viāpi rahiā manu doi ।। *thiru nārāiṇu kare su hoi* ।।
– Ibid., p. 153

Inside the body, fire and water join together and speak in fury. The tongue and sensual organs are inclined to their tastes. The eyes look upon evil and forget the love for and fear of God. One obtains name only by shedding ego. One who dies in *śabada* shall be free from further death. No one can be perfect without such a death. The mind is entangled in deceit and duality. Whatever the Supreme Being does that comes to happen.

Guru Nānak further states that it is water and fire which join together and speak in all its fury in human life. The tongue and other sensual organs search for their own tastes in life. The eyes view evil and mind does not fear Lord. Thus if one does not get rid of ego and controls his mind and senses, he cannot merge with Him and enjoy the permanent bliss.

taravaru kāiā paṅkhi manu taravari paṅkhī pañca ॥
tatu cugahi mili eka se tina kau phāsa na rañca ॥
uḍahi ta begula begule tākahi coga ghaṇī ॥
paṅkha tuṭe phāhī paḍī avaguṇi bhīḍa baṇī ॥
binu sāce kiu chūṭīē hari guṇa karami maṇī ॥
āpi chaḍāe chūṭīē vaḍā āpi dhaṇī ॥

– *Ādi Granth*, p. 934

The body is a tree and the mind is the bird. There are five senses in this tree. These five knowing faculties peck the element of reality by uniting with the Supreme Being. They do not fall into any trap. But the others who fly fast on seeing worldly food, their wings are clipped and they fall in the trap and face disaster. One cannot find release without good deeds. They get released by the Divine Will. He is the greatest.

In this hymn Guru Nānak compares the body to a tree and the mind, along with five sensory faculties, to birds. As long as these are attuned or united with the Supreme Soul they enjoy His essence. But those who fly away being attracted by worldly desires, their wings are clipped and they fall in the trap of sin. Without the grace of True Lord they cannot be emancipated.

pañca baila gaḍīā deha dhārī ॥ *rāmakalā nibahai pati sārī* ॥
dhara tūṭī gāḍī sira bhāri ॥ *lakarī bikhari jarī mañjha bhāri* ॥

– Ibid., p. 879

The wagon of the body is driven around by five bulls of the senses with God's power. But when the axle of God's support is withdrawn it gets broken down. It breaks and becomes like a bundle of logs.

In these lines Guru Nānak gives a pictorial description of the body to as a wagon run by the five knowing faculties driven by the Lord's power. If the axle (*prāṇa*) breaks, the wagon crashes and becomes a pile of wood.

suṅñī deha ḍarāvaṇi jā jīu vicahu jāi॥
bhāhi balaṅdī vijhavī dhū-u na nikasiu kāi॥
paṅce ruṅne dukhi bhare binase dūjai bhāi॥
mūḍe rāmu japahu guṇa sāri॥
haumai mamatā mohaṇī sabha muṭhī ahaṁkāri॥
....
tanu jali bali māṭī bhaiā manu māiā mohi manūru॥
augaṇa phiri lāgū bhae kūri vajāvai tūru॥
binu sabadai bharamāīē dubidhā ḍobe pūru॥
....
tanu sūcā so ākhīē jisu mahi sācā nāu॥
bhai saci rātī dehurī jihavā sacu suāu॥
sacī nadari nihālīē bahuḍi na pāvai tāu॥

– *Ādi Granth*, p. 19

> The body without soul becomes dreadful. The life ends when the soul goes out from within and the breath ceases to spit the smoke. All of one's five sense organs then cry that they are beguiled by duality. O fool! gather nothing but good and meditate on Rāma. Ego and avarice are enticing, so all are deceived. The body is burnt to ashes and mind is rusted due to its love of *māyā*. These vices become enemies and falsehood blows sirens of attack. Many have been drowned by their love for duality. With ignorance of *śabada* people get into the web of life and death.
>
> The body becomes pure when the True Name resides in it. One who is fearful of the Supreme Lord and who speaks truth rises to the bliss of ecstasy when the Supreme Being showers His grace. Such a person gets rid of rebirth.

In this hymn Guru Nānak portrays the picture of one's body after the soul leaves it. When the soul departs from the body, it becomes a dreadful carcass. When the fire of the body leaves and smoke of the breath ceases, the five sense organs cry and realize that they are duped by the duality. So he advises to meditate on Rāma and burn the fire of duality and desires. By the Lord's name all ego, attachments, envy, anger and strife end. The body in which the True Name dwells, there is fear of God, truthfulness on tongue and actions, and is blessed to enjoy grace of the Lord.

aṁmṛta kāiā rahai sukhālī bājī ihu saṁsāro ||
labu lobhu mucu kūḍu kamāvahi bahutu uṭhāvahi bhāro ||
tūṅ kāiā mai ruladī dekhī jiu dhara upari chāro ||
– *Ādi Granth*, p. 154

With purity of the body one lives in comfort. This world is a stage for drama. When one acts in greed and desire for undue riches his body is burdened and crushes like earthly dust.

Here Guru Nānak says that as long as the body is attuned to the grace of the Lord it lives in comfort. But when it indulges in vices like greed, anger and falsehood it becomes oppressed with heavy burden and suffers. He warns the body that it will be wasted like dust on earth and may not get another chance.

suṇi mana mitra piāriā milu velā hai eha ||
jaba lagu jobani sāsu hai tabalagu ihu tanu deha ||
binu guṇa kāmi na āvaī ḍhahi ḍherī tanu kheha ||
mere mana lai lāhā ghari jāhi ||
....
hari japi jīare chuṭīē guramukhi cīnai āpu ||
tanu manu gura pahi veciā manu dīā siru nāli ||
tribhavaṇu khoji ḍhaṅḍholiā guramukhi khoji nihāli ||
– Ibid., p. 20

Listen, my darling mind and friend: This life is the right chance to meet the Supreme Being. Offer your youthful breaths and body to Him. The body without virtue is useless and shall be crushed into a pile of dust. So earn some virtue before you are called back. Meditate on the name of the Supreme Being and try to know thyself so that you are liberated and saved. I have sold out myself with my mind and soul to my *guru*. I have surrendered my mind and head as well. I searched for Him throughout the three worlds. It is the *guru* through whom we attain our union with the Lord.

In this hymn Guru Nānak cautions and advises individuals to take the advantage from this body while it breathes young. Before one returns to his home one should unite with the Lord, otherwise life will be like return of dust to dust. So, body is the medium for the individual to unite with the Supreme Being.

jaha dekhā taha ravi rahe siva sakatī kā melu ||
trihu guṇa baṅdhī dehurī jo āiā jagi so khelu ||
vijogī dukhi vichuḍe manamukhi lahahi na melu ||
manu bairāgī ghari vasai saca bhai rātā hoi ||
giāna mahārasu bhogavai bāhuḍi bhūkha na hoi ||
nānaka ihu manu māri milu bhi phiri dukhu na hoi ||
– *Ādi Granth*, p. 21

> Guru Nānak expresses that wherever I look, I see the union of spirit and energy (Śiva-Śakti means conscious *Puruṣa* and unconscious matter) in the creation. Our body is bound by the three modes. Whosoever comes into the world plays within their limits. The self-willed persons get separated from the Supreme Being and remain in trouble. If the wandering mind comes home and dyes itself red in the fear of the Lord and feeds itself on higher wisdom, it hungers no more. Subdue thy ego, therefore, O Nānak! and unite with thy Lord and you will grieve no more.

In this hymn Guru Nānak speaks about the union of spirit and matter, and the body which is subjected to the play of three modes of nature. The individual plays in his limits. One has to control ego and wandering mind to unite with the Supreme Will of the Lord.

kācī gāgari deha duhelī upajai binasai dukhu pāī ||
ihu jagu sāgaru dutaru kiu tarīē binu hari gura pāri na pāī ||
– Ibid., p. 355

> The body is a pitcher of clay. It goes through the pain of birth and death. How can one cross this dreadful sea of this world? It cannot be crossed without a true *guru*.

In this hymn Guru Nānak talks about the nature of body and compares it to an earthen pitcher which is bound to be broken and remains in pain due to worldly sufferings and sorrows.

manu maigalu sākatu Devānā ||
banakhaṇḍi māiā mohi hairānā ||
....
ihu manu karamā ihu manu dharamā ||
ihu manu paṅca tatu te janamā ||
sākatu lobhī ihu manu mūḍa ||

guramukhi nāmu japai manu rūḍā॥
– *Ādi Granth*, p. 415

> The mind commits its deeds both of evil and righteousness. The individual mind is an outcome of the five elements. It is unwise, spoilt and lusty. Only with the utterings of the name of the Lord it can convert to be a Guramukha.

In this hymn Guru Nānak compares the mind with an elephant which gets intoxicated and wild by its power. Even though it knows that death is hovering over its head, it wanders in the woods under illusion. This mind controls the individual's good and bad deeds. The Lord Himself makes us meet a true *guru* who can show us the path to practise righteousness.

eka nagarī paṅca cora basīale barajata corī dhāvai॥
trihadasa māla rakhai jo nānaka mokha mukati so pāvai॥
– Ibid., p. 503

> In the body, which is a village in itself, five thieves of passions live. They still go on stealing even after being warned. He who takes care of his belongings from the three modes of action and ten senses gets liberated and emancipated.

It is an interesting expression that the body is one, and five thieves, i.e. lust, wrath, greed, attachment and ego abide in it. In spite of individual's occasional warnings these go on committing the thefts. Only one who keeps one's soul free from the three modes and ten sense organs is saved.

kāiā kāgadu manu paravāṇā॥ *sira ke lekha na paḍai iāṇā*॥
daragaha ghaḍīahi tīne lekha॥ *khoṭā kāṁmi na āvai vekhu*॥
nānaka je vici rupā hoi॥ – Ibid., p. 662

> It is the mind that controls body and writes the inscription upon it. The mind in its ignorance cannot read the writ of his destiny. In the court of the Supreme Being counterfeit coins become worthless. Only if there is some contents of virtue they get recognition.

Here Guru Nānak describes the body, mind and Truth. He says that on the paper of this body, the mind is the writ. The *qāẓī* utters falsehood and so eats dirt, the brāhmaṇa slays life and then baths at the pilgrimages, the blind *yogī* does not know the way. It is in the Lord's court that writ inscribed in these three minds is forced open. The false ones are exposed and the one who carries some silver is honoured.

All these verses emphasize the need for true devotion and earnest effort of the soul and body to know the True Lord.

NATURE OF INDIVIDUAL SOUL

bimala majhāri basasi niramala jala padamani jāvala re ||
padamani jāvala jala rasa saṅgati saṅga dokha nahī re ||
dādara tū kabahi na jānasi re ||
bhakhasi sibālu basasi niramala jala aṁmr̥tu na lakhasi re ||
basu jala nita na vasata alīala mera cacā guna re ||
caṅda kumudanī dūrahu nivasasi anabhau kārani re ||
aṁmr̥ta khaṇḍu dūdhi madhu sañcasi tū bana cātura re ||
apanā āpu tū kabahu na choḍasi pisana priti jiu re ||
paṅdita saṅgi vasahi jana mūrakha āgama sāsa sune ||
apanā āpu tū kabahu na choḍasi suāna pūchi jiu re ||
iki pākhaṅḍī nāmi na rācahi iki hari hari caraṇī re ||
pūrabi likhiā pāvasi nānaka rasanā nāmu japi re ||
– *Ādi Granth*, p. 990

In the clear waters, both the lotus and filmy layer of impurities exist. The water gets mixed with worthless materials but lotus remains high and dry. A frog eats the dirt, while lotus stands high and dry. Individuals get struck with dirty water of life, but the bumblebee is attracted to the fragrance from a far away place and gets intoxicated with essence. The lotus bends intuitively towards the moon. Individuals feel themselves as wise to live in the water. They cannot control their attractions to the filth like a flea which loves dirty blood. One may live in the company of wise men, and religious scholars, and listening to Vedas and Śāstras but cannot overpower their internal inclinations like the bended tail of a dog. Some live in their vanity and do not dissolve with the True Name of the Supreme Being. But a few get absorbed in Har Har, i.e. the lotus feet of the Supreme Being. Everyone gets what he is destined to get. O Nānak! utter the true *nāma* of the Supreme Father!

In this hymn Guru Nānak skilfully portrays the nature of the individual soul and the body. Out of the clear water sprouts the lotus and the film (*jāla*s). The lotus lives high and dry and detached. The frog catches only the dirt and discards the nectar. It lives in water but cannot love the essence as compared to the bumblebee which with a love for the essence gets attracted and enjoys the flower. A tick does not enjoy the milk with sugar and honey and only sucks the blood from the cattle. One may live with the wise and study scriptures but does not shed the ego like a dog who cannot straighten his crooked tail. Similarly hypocrites cannot merge with *nāma*, while some who utter the Hari's name with tender devotion get absorbed in Him.

dhanu jobanu aru phulaḍā nāṭhīaḍe dina cāri ||
pabaṇi kere pata jiu ḍhali ḍhuli jurimaṇahāra ||
raṅgu māṇi lai piāriā jā jobanu nauhulā ||
dina thoḍaḍe thake bhaiā purāṇā colā ||
sajaṇa mere raṅgule jāi sute jīrāṇi ||
hambhī vaññā ḍummaṇī rovā jhīṇī bāṇi ||
kī na suṇehī gorīe āpaṇa kannī soi ||
lagī āvahi sāhurai nita na peīā hoi ||
nānaka sutī peīe jāṇu viratī sanni ||
guṇā gavāī ganṭhaḍī avagaṇa calī banni ||
– *Ādi Granth*, p. 23

Money, the good looks of youth and flowers are very short-lived. These are destined to dry out and vanish in a short time. One may feel happy for a while but soon they start getting weary and old. My playmates and friends of young age have left for the onwards journey and I am also destined to trudge that path. Hear the call from beyond and get ready to pack up. You cannot stay here forever thus are destined to leave this world. If you sleepover carelessly and forget this you will come to grief. So gather all your virtues and good deeds to carry with you to the Supreme Lord.

In this hymn Guru Nānak addresses the soul and reminds that body will wither away and you will also become weary and the time to go will approach fast. So take the advantage; you enjoy your Lord in this body. You have to return to your own home and do not sleepover here otherwise you have to carry the burden of your deeds and demerits along with.

machulī jālu na jāṇiā saru khārā asagāhu ||
ati siāṇī sohaṇī kiu kītī vesāhu ||
kīte kāraṇī pākaḍī kālu na ṭalai sirāhu ||
bhāī re iu siri jāṇahu kālu ||
jiu machī tiu māṇasā pavai aciṅtā jālu ||
....
mani jūṭhai tani jūṭhi hai jihavā jūṭhī hoi ||
mukhi jhūṭhai jhūṭhu bolaṇā kiukari sūcā hoi ||
binu abha sabada na māṅjīē sāce te sacu hoi ||
– *Ādi Granth*, pp. 55-56

Human beings cannot assess the net of *māyā* and get entrapped in the world attractions. They trust in the looks of this world and act blindly and are entangled in the worldly net. They forget that death hovers over them and is ready to overpower them. People, like a fish in the deep waters getting entrapped by the noose of the fisherman, cannot understand the worldly traps.

If one's mind gets perverted, his body and tongue also get perverted. They start uttering falsehoods and it is difficult to purify their thought and action. It is only the holy water of the *śabada* that they can get themselves cleansed. One can experience truth only from the True Lord.

In this hymn also Guru Nānak addresses the individual soul and calls it a fish which otherwise is so clever and beautiful but is unaware of the net in the deep salty sea. That is why it trusted its eyes and got trapped by its own deeds and folly into the cycle of birth and death. He calls upon all the siblings of this destiny to be aware of the near coming of death. The impure mind perverts the body and tongue also. He further reminds the soul bride that her spouse will enjoy her virtue of love and peace only. When the spouse is away the soul bride grieves in separation like a fish out of water and cries for mercy. She finds the pleasure of her spouse only if the Lord wills and favours His grace.

tr̥sanā māiā mohaṇī suta baṅdhapa ghara nāri ॥
dhani jobani jagu ṭhagiā labi lobhi ahaṁkāri ॥
moha ṭhagaulī hau muī sā varatai saṁsāri ॥
....
āsā aṅdari jaṁmiā āsā rasa kasa khāi ॥
āsā baṅdhi calāīē muhe muhi coṭā khāi ॥

– *Ādi Granth*, p. 61

The enticing worldly desires lead people to emotions and attachments with their kids, relations, friends, spouses, etc. The world is misled and exploited by wealth, youthfulness, desires and duality. The disease of emotions has ruined the whole world. I also feel stung by it.

Here Guru Nānak describes the trap of *māyā* through emotions, greed, youthfulness, riches and ego that enshrine the body and soul, and beguile it.

pāpu puṁnu bīja kī poṭa ॥ *kāmu krodhu jīa mahi coṭa* ॥
nāmu visāri cale mani khoṭa ॥

– Ibid., p. 152

The seeds of bad and good *karma* are tied together. Sexual attractions and bad temperaments inflict wounds on the soul. The perverted minds forget the *nāma* and depart from this world.

In these lines Guru Nānak explains that individual is born out of his desires. His vices of sexual desire, anger and ego keep him trapped till he leaves this world. Forgetting his Lord one carries with him the burden of his deeds.

avari paṅca hama eka janā kiu rākhau ghara bāru manā ॥
mārahi lūṭahi nīta nīta kisu āgai karī pukāra janā ॥

– Ibid., p. 155

There are five vices. But individual is one alone. How can one protect his body and soul? These vices overpower and injure the individuals.

In these lines Guru Nānak talks of soul being alone against the five most enticing vices, i.e. lust, wrath, greed, attachment and ego. These five oppress and beguile. How to save oneself from these?

He further explains that the Lord created the temple of this body with nine doors and the seeker soul resides within it. The body takes pleasures in the false plays leisurely. Five thieves rob it of and demolish the temple. The lone soul gets the deathly grip by her neck, and chained by Yama, who whips it with the rod, drags it out. Now the five thieves are taken to their heels.

dūjī duramati aṅnī bolī II *kāma krodha kī kacī colī* II
ghari varu sahaju na jāṇai chohari binu pira nīda na pāī he II
aṅtāri agani jale bhaḍakāre II *manamukhu take kuṅḍā cāre* II
– *Ādi Granth*, p. 1022

One gets blind and deaf in duality and due to perverted mind. One gets attracted towards sexual desires and bad temperament. The Supreme Being is the master at home within his heart, but one is not aware of Him. One cannot be at rest without his Lord. The fire of separation from Him is lit within self. The self-willed persons search Him all around in the four directions.

In this hymn Guru Nānak explains that the soul bride under the spell of duality shrouds like a dumb and blind woman who wears the clothes of lust and wrath. The Lord is within her home but she does not know Him and cannot sleep in peace with Him. The fire of desire for Him burns in her but due to ego she cannot feel the essence and looks bewildered all around. The peace and glory rest in the hands of the Lord and *manamukhas* cannot enjoy these till they get protected by a *guru* who leads them on the right path.

kāiā nagaru nagara gaḍa aṅdari II *sācā vāsā puri gaganaṅdari* II
asathiru thānu sadā niramāilu āpe āpu upāidā II
aṅdari koṭa chaje haṭa nāle II *āpe levai vasatu samāle* II
bajara kapāṭa jaḍe jaḍi jāṇai gura sabadī kholāidā II
bhītari koṭa guphā ghara jāī II *nau ghara thāpe hukami rajāī* II
dasavai purakhu alekhu apārī āpe alakhu lakhāidā II
pauṇa pāṇī aganī ika vāsā II
– Ibid., p. 1033

This body is a village and there is a fortress within this village. The Supreme Being has a dwelling place in this fort. The residing unit of the Supreme Being is at the tenth gate. God Himself

> created it. There are many natural super powers here under the protection and care of the Lord. The doors of the tenth gate are hard and heavy. These are closed and locked and can be opened only with the *guru*'s word. In the home there is a cave which is the home of the Self. God designed the nine gates of this house by His Will. At the tenth gate, the Supreme Being resides. The body of air, water and fire is the residing place of the Lord who stages all dramas and plays.

Guru Nānak in this hymn points towards the abode of the Lord in the individual body. He compares the body to a village and mind to a fortress. The Lord has His permanent abode in the cave of the heart. He further explains that the Lord exercises all His plays from within the fortress of this body.

> *maraṇi na mūratu puchiā puchī thiti na vāru* ॥
> *ikanī ladiā iki ladi cale ikanī badhe bhāra* ॥
> ....
> *nānaka ḍherī ḍhahi paī miṭī saṅdā kāṭu* ॥
> *bhītari coru bahāliā khoṭu ve jīā khoṭu* ॥
>
> – *Ādi Granth*, p. 1244

> The time, date or day of the week for an individual's death is uncertain. Some are on the way and some have left. Some are destined for punishments and some are rewarded. The body of dust is reduced again to dust. The fortress of the body gets shattered.

In these lines Guru Nānak tells that death has no date and time. It comes uninvited. Some have already left, some have bundled up their belongings and some are on the way. They will leave all their beauteous mansions behind and the body which is made of dust will return to dust. They will carry with them the impressions of their good and bad deeds.

> *bhāṅḍā dhovai kauṇu ji kacā sājiā* ॥ *dhātū paṅji ralāi kūḍā pājiā* ॥
> *bhāṅḍā āṇagu rāsi jāṅ tisu bhāvasī* ॥ *parama joti jāgāi vājā vāvasī* ॥
>
> – Ibid., p. 1411

> No one can wash the unbaked pot of clay. This body pot is made of five elements with a false cover over it. It is the pleasure of the Lord as to how it is to be maintained. His light shines within it and there is heavenly pure music within it.

Guru Nānak wonders as to who can wash a mud vessel! He compares the body with a mud vessel created by the Lord by putting five elements together. The Lord wishes that the sublime light burns within it and the unstuck melody vibrates and rings within it.

All the above verses explain that the individual soul is immaculate but the worldly attractions make it dusty.

The essence of the above hymns of Guru Nānak can be traced in the Upaniṣads' portrayal of nature of the body and individual soul as under.

Bṛhadāraṇyaka Upaniṣad

sa vā ayaṁ puruṣo jāyamānaḥ śarīramabhisaṁpadyamānaḥ pāpmabhiḥ saṁsṛsa utkrāman, mriyamāṇaḥ pāpmano vijahāti ||
– 4.3.8

That person (individual self), when he is born, that is to say, when he assumes a body, is joined with evils, when he dies, that is to say, leaves body, he discards those evils. The individual becomes connected with the evil at birth and leaves all the evils behind at death.

tadyathā 'naḥ susamāhitamutsarjadyāyādevamevāyaṁ śārīram atmā prājñenātmanānvārūḍha utsarjanyāti, yatraitadūrdhvocchavāsī bhavati
– 4.3.35

Just as a heavily loaded cart moves creaking, the self in the body mounted by the self of intelligence moves creaking, when one is breathing with difficulty (i.e. when he is about to expire).

sa yatrāyamaṇimānaṁ nyeti, jarayā vopatapatāvāṇimānaṁ nigaccati, tadyathāmraṁ vaudumbaraṁ vā pippalaṁa vā bandhanātpramucyato evamevāyaṁ puruṣa ebhyo 'aṅgebhyaḥ saṁpramucya punaḥ pratinyāyaṁ pratiyonyādravati prāṇāyaiva ||
– 4.3.36

As a fruit releases itself from the bond of the tree by getting detached from the stalk, when this body gets to thinness individual gets himself free of all his organs and comes back as he had come to this place from which he started.

yadā sarve pramucyante kāmạ ye 'sya hṛdi śritāḥ। atha martyo 'mṛto bhavatyatra brahma samaśnuta iti॥ tadyathā hinireva-yanīvalmīkemṛtāpratyastāśayītaivam evedaṁ śarīraṁ śete-athāyamaśariro 'mṛtaḥ prāṇo brahmaiva, teja eva, so 'haṁ bhagavate sahasraṁdadāmīti hovāca janako vaidehaḥ॥

– *Bṛhadāranyaka Upaniṣad* 4.4.7

The body is called slough of the soul. After all the desires of an individual get exhausted the mortal becomes the immortal. One can realize *Brahman* in this very body. Like a snake cast off its slough, the soul leaves behind the body. This disembodied *Brahman* is the immortal life and is the light indeed.

ātmānaṁ cedvijānīyādayamasmīti pūruṣaḥ kimicchankasya kāmāya śarīramanusaṁjvaret॥ – 4.4.12

A person who realizes the self as "I am this" and does not wish and desire anything more, he will not suffer in the body. one can realize the self only through his body.

TAITTIRĪYA UPANIṢAD

It describes five sheaths arranged one inside another, constituting the various bodily frames enveloping the soul (2.1.1):

1. *annamaya kośa* (the sheath of food forming the *sthūla śarīra* or gross frame),
2. *prāṇamaya kośa* (the sheath of vital breath),
3. *manomaya kośa* (the sheath of mind),
4. *vijñānamaya kośa* (the sheath of intellect), these three (2-4) form the *sūkṣma śarīra* (the subtle frame), and
5. *ānandamaya kośa* (the sheath of bliss), forming the *kāraṇa śarīra* (causal frame).

These are the five sheaths in which the self is manifested.

The first of them consists of food. Other sheaths consist of *prāṇa* (life), *manas* (instinctive consciousness), *vijñāna* (intelligence) and *ānanda* (bliss). The five principles of matter, life consciousness, thought and bliss are found in the world of non-ego. *Anna* (food) is radiant, the *virāj* is that which is perceptible by the senses, life consciousness and intelligence constitute the subtle self, the *sūtrātman* and bliss is the causal sheath.

KAṬHA UPANIṢAD

This Upaniṣad describes the individual self and body as under:

> *puramekādaśadvāramajasyavakracetasaḥ*
> *anuṣṭhāya na socati vimuktaśca vimucyate* ।
> *etad vai tat* ।। – 2.2.1

> There is a city of eleven gates (belonging to) the unborn, uncrooked intelligence. By ruling these one does not grieve and being freed is freed in deed. This verily is that.

> *agniryathaiko bhuvanaṁ praviṣṭo*
> *rūpaṁ rūpaṁ pratirūpo babhūva* ।
> *ekastatha sarvabhūtāntarātmā*
> *rūpaṁ rūpaṁ pratirūpo bahiś ca* ।। – 2.2.9-10

> As one fire entering into this world changes its look in accordance with burning object, the self within all individuals takes the shape of body into which it enters and it exists outside also. As one air adopts different shapes in accordance with the object it enters into, the self within all beings adopts the shape of body into which it enters and also exists outside.

> *aṅguṣṭhamātraḥ puruṣo'ntarātmā sadā janānāṁ hṛdaye sanniviṣṭaḥ* । *taṁ svāccharīrāt pravṛhenmuñjādiveṣikāṁ dhairyeṇa tam vidyācchukramamṛtaṁ taṁ vidyācchukramamṛtamiti* ।।
> – 2.3.17

> The inner self person, sized equal to a thumb, ever resides in the hearts of individuals. Individual should separate it from the body very carefully as one separates a tender stalk from a blade of grass. That self is bright and immortal.

PRAŚNA UPANIṢAD

It suggests that the individual souls reside in the Universal Soul in their subtle condition before they get embodiment or gross condition.

> *sa prāṇamasṛjata prāṇācchraddhāṁ*
> *khaṁ vāyurjyotirāpaḥ pṛthivīndriyaṁ,*
> *mano 'nnam, annādvīryam*
> *tapo mantraḥ karmalokā, lokeṣu ca nāma ca*
> – 6.5.4

Supreme Being created life from life, faith, ether, air, light, water, earth, sense organ, mind and food, vital vigour, austerity, hymns, works, world and in the world's name. Name suggests individuation. The souls exist in the world in Universal Soul in subtle condition, before they acquire embodiment or gross condition.

All the parts of the individual body are well established with the individual soul as spokes in the centre of the wheel. After the soul leaves the body, a living being is reduced to corpse.

CHĀNDOGYA UPANIṢAD

This Upaniṣad also brings forth clear-cut understanding on the relation between the body and the soul.

> *atha yadidamasminbrahmapure daharaṁ puṇḍarīkaṁ veśma*
> *daharo 'sminnantarākāśá tasminyadantas tadanveṣṭavyaṁ*
> *tadvāva vijijñāsitavyam iti* ॥ – 8.1.1

The body is the residing place of the *Brahman*. The body is compared to a royal city. As the royal city is protected by many officers of the king, the body is protected by the various sense organs, the mind, etc. They work for the benefit of the soul. The heart is compared to the royal palace. Its shape is that of the lotus bud. Though *Brahman* pervades the entire body, its presence is specially felt in the heart. The individual is the replica of the universe. Whatever exists in the world also exists in the individual soul.

aśarīro vāyurabhraṁ vidyut stanayitnuraśarīrāṇyetani
thadyathaitānyamuṣmādakāśātsamutthāya paraṁ jyotirupa-

saṁpadya svena rūpeṇābhiniṣpadyante ||

evamevaiṣa samprasādo 'smaccharīrātsamutthāya paraṁ jyotirupasampadya svena rupeṇābhiniṣpadyate, sa uttamaḥ puruṣaḥ, sa tatra paryeti, jakṣatkrīḍanramamāṇaḥ stribhirvā yānairvājñātibhirvā nopajanaṁ smarannidaṁ śarīraṁ sa yathā prayogya ācaraṇe yukta evamevāyamasmiñcharīre prāṇo yuktaḥ | – *Chāndogya Upniṣad* 8.12.2-3

The embodied soul, who in essence is non-different from the serene being, remains merged in the body during the state of ignorance, as wind or cloud merged in *ākāśa*. In that state he regards himself as born or dead, happy or miserable. Then being instructed by a teacher about his true nature, he rises from the body, as the wind or cloud rises in *ākāśa*, reaches the highest light (knowledge of the self) and recognizes his true nature, that is to say, relinquishes the notion that body is the self. The laughing, rejoicing, etc. are all mental, created by the mere will of the self. The self gets enjoyment as a spectator of all these pleasures. It remains far off from pleasure or pain.

Body without soul or self is just a heap of bones. A man must not treat his father, mother, sister, etc. roughly. If he does so, he is condemned by all. But after the *prāṇa* has left them, their bodies become corpses, may be struck with spears, as is done to a burning body on the pyre.

MUṆḌAKA UPANIṢAD

It explains that the individual self-reflected in the mind, identifies itself with pleasure and pain, anger, love and other states of mind.

arā iva rathanābhau saṁhatā yatra nāḍyaḥ
sa eso 'ntaś carate bahudhā jāyamānaḥ |
omityevaṁ dhyāyatha ātmānaṁ, svasti
vaḥ pārāya tamasaḥ parastat || – 2.2.6

He moves about becoming manifold within the heart, where the arteries meet, like the spokes fastened in the nave of a chariot wheel. Meditate on *ātman* as *oṁ*. You may cross beyond the sea of darkness.

The material body is analysed into five sheaths by the seers of the

Upaniṣads. *Ātman* is considered unattached to these sheaths. The body is described as a city of *Brahman*. The nine gates of the body are described as the eyes, ears, nostrils, the mouth and organs of evacuation and generation. Two additional gates are the navel and aperture at the top of the head. The body, without the soul, is absolutely valueless and is a mere corpse. What is the use in enjoying the physical pleasures of the body, which is afflicted by the evil of hate, greediness, fear, anger, jealousy, separation from loved ones, unity with the unwanted, and the feeling of pains of being hungry, thirsty, aged, death, illness, grief and other evils. The heart has received much attention. It is considered as the resting place of *prāṇa*s, the senses and the mind. It is the abode of the *Brahman*.

Conclusion

The hymn of creation in *R̥gveda* (X.129) and the hymns of creation by Guru Nānak *arbad narbad dhauṅdhūkāra* contain similar thoughts regarding the pre-creation state of void or non-being, transformation of non-being into being, Divine Will for expansion, non-ability for description or declaration as to how and when the creation came into being, birth of all gods after the creation. Thus the Upaniṣads establish oneness of the individual self and *Brahman* in many illustrative ways. The four *mahāvākya*s – *prajñānam brahma, ayam ātma brahma, tat tvam asi, aham brahmāsmi* – carry a universal message of oneness of the individual soul and the Universal Soul. The essence of burning cannot be different from fire or waves of the agitated sea cannot be different from the sea. However there are different views as to what is the relationship of the individual souls with the Universal Soul. Śaṅkarācārya believes that the Universal Self and the individual self are identical but due to ignorance or veil of *māyā* one considers the individual self as different from the Universal Self. Rāmānuja believed that individual self is identical with the Universal Self and is also different. Madhvācārya holds that the individual self is eternally different from the Universal Self.

Guru Nānak avoids all strifes and controversies of beliefs and holds simplified Upaniṣadic view and explains that *sāgara meiṅ būnda būnda meiṅ sāgara* (a drop of ocean is not a different ocean), as night wraps the day and day wraps the night (*dina meiṅ raina raina meiṅ dinīar*), as female is born from the sperm of male and male is born from the female a (*purakha meiṅ nāra nāra meiṅ purakha*) such is the relation of the individual soul with the Universal Soul. *Ātama meiṅ rāma, rāma meiṅ ātama* can be realized through the teachings of a *guru*. That very cosmic Universal Soul dwells in every heart (*sabnī ghaṭī saho vasai*). It is hidden in every heart. Only one soul wanders through all three worlds (*aiko bhavar bhavai tihu lo-ai*) and He Himself assumes all sorts of forms.

There is a very close resemblance or similarity of the concept of individual soul and body expressed in the hymns of Guru Nānak and the Upaniṣads. The human body is called a city with a fort (heart) within it as a dwelling unit of the Lord. The concept of nine doors is also similar to the tenth gate (aperture at the top) in the human body, an escape route for the soul is to the higher levels of consciousness. The soul is immaculate and the body is nothing without the soul. The body without the soul is only a heap of bones and dust. The transitory nature of the body, a need for making best of its use for salvation, is impressed upon by both.

3

God, Man and the World

MAN has to face and experience the misery of *roga, soga, mauta* and *adhūrī kāmanā* (disease, distress, death and unfulfilled desires) in life. At the same time he experiences wonderful moments of beauty, love and bliss amongst all the bright and beautiful things of the world. A man may laugh or weep away the events and ordeals of life yet he feels there is someone before whom all become helpless and who solves the complexity of all problems. Man looks towards the sky or falls on earth in his tender expression of thankfulness or dismay before someone whom he has never seen yet always feels Him. The vast display of His bounty is before him and he gets attracted towards it and tries to enjoy and seek rest with it. But he finds a strong attraction and attachment to it. The happiness becomes a further cause of his distress when he finds it to be transitory.

Mutual Relationship between God, Man and the World

Mutual relationship between God, man and the world is very aptly described in the following lines:

> *taṁ hovāca yato vā imāni bhūtāni jāyante* । *yena jātāni jīvanti* । *yatprayantyabhisaṁviśanti* । *tadvijijñāsasva* । *tad brahmeti* । *sa tapo 'tapyata sa tapastaptvā* ।। – *Taittirīya Upaniṣad* 3.1.1
>
> That verily, from which all beings are born, by which when are born they live and that into which they enter when they depart. Seek to know that. That is *Brahman.*

Both the material cause and the intelligence cause of all existence are one and the only one which is the Ultimate Reality. After they come into existence all depend on Him for their maintenance and strength of life. When their time comes to end, they ultimately enter into Him.

yathorṇanābhiḥ sṛjate gṛhaṇte ca
yathā pṛthivyāmoṣadhayaḥ sambhavanti ||
yathā sataḥ puruṣātkeśalomāni
tathākṣarātsaṁbhavatīha viśvam ||
– *Muṇḍaka Upaniṣad* 1.1.7

A spider brings out and takes back its thread, plants grow on the earth, the hair grow on the head and the body of a living person. In a similar manner, everything originates from the imperishable Lord.

It is not suggested that the world is an illusionary or deceptive appearance of *Brahman*. These convey a message that *Brahman* is the sole source and outcome of all creations.

Guru Nānak expresses in many of his hymns the mutual relationship between God, man and the world very vividly.

RELATION BETWEEN GOD AND MAN

tū darīāu dānā bīnā mai mchulī kaise aṁtu lahā ||
jaha jaha dekhā taha taha tū hai tujha te nikasī phūṭi marā ||
na jāṇā meu na jāṇā jālī || *jā dukhu lāgai tā tujhai samālī* ||
tū bharapūri jāniā mai dūrī || *jo kachu kari su terai hadūrī* ||
....
nānaku eka kahai aradāsī || *jīu piṁḍu sabhu terai pāsī* ||
– *Ādi Granth*, p. 25

The Supreme Being holds the power of all knowledge and all feelings. Individual is just a fish who cannot find His limit. Wherever one looks He is there. There is no life outside Him. No one knows the fisherman or his net. But when the pain comes, everyone calls upon Him. He is present everywhere. One thinks He is far away. Whatever one does he does in His presence. Whatever He gives, that is what everyone eats. There is no other door unto man can go. Guru Nānak prays to declare that his body and soul both belong to the Supreme Father who Himself is near; who Himself is far away; who Himself is in-between.

Here Guru Nānak calls God a river of all wisdom, meaning all intelligence, and man as a fish in that river flow which cannot understand the vastness of the flow of wisdom. He further explains that God is felt all around yet no one can explain anything about His appearance and His plan of action. Whenever the pain comes everyone looks towards Him for help, guidance and mercy. There is no life without Him. He is not only near, but at a far away distance also, as well as in-between the two. The body and the soul both are His creation and He deals with His creation as He wills.

sabhe kaṅta sahelīā sagalīā karahi sīgārū ||
gaṇata gaṇāvaṇi āīā sūhā vesu vikārū ||
pākhaṅḍi premu na paīē khoṭā pāju khuārū ||
hari jīu iu piru rāvai nāri ||

– *Ādi Granth*, p. 54

All the individuals are the brides of One all-powerful Lord; all prepare themselves for seeking His pleasure. But when they are tested for their reality, their appearances are found belied. The love for the Supreme God cannot be attained by false appearances. In fact, it causes damages. The Supreme Lord enjoys that bride whom He likes and showers His grace.

In this hymn Guru Nānak calls all beings as brides of the Lord. Everyone bedecks for the pleasure of Him. But He is not pleased with the red robes, self pride or self beauty, meaning the outside false show does not please Him. He enjoys His creation and only the true brides get honours and His grace.

jiu gāī kau goilī rākhahi kari sārā ||
ahinisi pālahi rākhi lehi ātama sukhu dhārā ||
....
kiā lai āiā le jāi kiā phāsahi jama jālā ||
ḍolu badhā kasi jevarī ākāsi patālā ||

– Ibid., p. 228

As the dairy master takes care of his cows and safeguards his cows, the Supreme Lord looks after us and safeguards us all the time of day and night. He blesses our souls with peace. Individuals come and go with empty hands. They are hooked by a pin-like pitcher tied with a rope in the well. Individuals are drawn up and then lowered down to all the regions of the universe.

It is a beautiful description of mutual relationship between God and man. God cares for His creation day out and day in, like a herdsman who protects his cows and tends them. Man is not independent of God. He is bound by the rope like a bucket in the well. He is pulled up and down to the upper and nether regions.

bābā āiā hai uṭhi calaṇā ihu jagu jhūṭhu pasārovā ॥
....
kūḍi labi jāṅ thāi na pāsī agai lahai na ṭhāo ॥
aṅtari āu na baisahu kahīē jiu suṅñai ghari kāo ॥
jaṁmaṇu maraṇu vaḍā vechoḍā binasai jagu sabāe ॥
labi dhaṅdhai māiā jagatu bhulāiā kālu khaḍā rūāe ॥
– *Ādi Granth*, pp. 581-82

Everyone who has come to life will rise up and leave this false show of the world. One can find his true home by serving the Supreme Lord. If one practises falsehood and greed one can find no place of permanent peace. Such a person is like a crow in an abandoned house. He is caught in the rotation of birth and death and gets separated from the Supreme Being for a prolonged period. He is lost in greed, worldly attachments and the death hovers over his head and makes him cry.

In this hymn Guru Nānak reminds us that this world is smoky and one can find the true home only by service to the True Lord. The falsehood cannot bring peace and rest in this world as well give refuse in the next world. The death hovers over every head and worldly entanglements are deceptions and trap us in the cycle of life and death and keep us away from the True Lord.

maṁmai mohu maraṇu madhusūdanu maraṇu bhaiā taba cetaviā ।
kāiā bhītari avaro paḍiā maṁmā akharu vīsariā ॥
– Ibid., p. 434

One dies in emotional attachments. He only thinks of the Supreme Lord when he dies. As long as there is life and body, he studies other things, but does not remember to read the letter *m* which stands for *maraṇā* (death).

Here Guru Nānak cautions that attached to the world, man neither remembers God nor death and only when sees the death nearby, he is reminded of Madhusūdana, meaning God. He cherishes everything in the world but forgets the name of God.

> *rosu na kījai aṁmṛtu pījai rahaṇu nahī saṁsāre* ||
> *rāje rāi raṅka nahī rahaṇā āi jāi juga cāre* ||
> *rahaṇa kahaṇa te rahai na koi kisu pahi karau binaṁtī* ||
> *eku sabadu rāma nāma nirodharu guru devai pati matī* ||
> – *Ādi Granth*, p. 931

One should not be angry with the Supreme Lord. Absorb His essence within you. One will not be there in this world always. The rulers and paupers all have to leave this place. Every one behaves as if he will stay here for ever. People will come and go in all ages. So why to be angry with Him? One should develop and enjoy living harmony with Him by seeking His essence.

> *kītā kahā kare mani mānu* || *devaṇahāre kai hathi dānu* ||
> *bhāvai dei na deī soi* || *kīte kai kahiē kiā hoi* ||
> – Ibid., p. 25

One should not feel pride in one's mind for anything as all the powers of gift are in God's hands. It is His pleasure to give or not to give anything to anyone. Nothing can be done against His orders.

Guru Nānak advises not to practise cleverness of mind before God, who can give or take away whatever He gives in a moment. The best approach in life is to develop living harmony with His will.

Mutual relationship between God and man as illustrated by Guru Nānak can also be traced in the Upaniṣads.

> *tadetatsatyaṁ yathā sudīptātpāvakādvisphuliṅgāḥ sahasraśaḥ prabhavante sarūpāḥ* | *tathākṣarāvividhāḥ saumya bhāvāḥ prajāyante tatra caivāpiyanti* || – *Muṇḍaka Upaniṣad* 2.1.1

The truth is that burning fire produces similar type of sparks in plenty. Similarly innumerable species issue from and return to the immutable and they return thitherto.

Here it has been illustrated that innumerable sparks coming from the fire are like fire itself. Similarly all beings issue forth from Him and return to Him. Ultimately there is one and the only one God, who is known by many names and is the controller of all existence.

> *sa yathā śakuniḥ sūtreṇa prabaddho diśaṁ diśaṁ*
> *patitvānyatrāyatanamalabdhvā bandhanam ...*
> *prāṇa-bandhanaṁ hi saumya, mana iti* ||
> – *Chāndogya Upaniṣad* 6.8.2

Just as a bird tied by a string (to the hand of the bird catcher) first flies in every direction, and (then) finding no rest anywhere, settles down at a place where it is bound, so also the mind (i.e. the individual soul reflected in the mind) after flying in every direction and finding no rest anywhere, settles down in *prāṇa* (i.e. Pure Being), for the mind (individual soul) is fastened to *prāṇa* (Pure Being).

All individual beings are fastened with the string of *prāṇa*. Man's very existence depends on Him. Guru Nānak compares man as a bucket of water tied with a string in a well which is lowered and raised up continuously.

Relation between God and the World (Creation)

The Upaniṣads explain that the world stands as part of God and it is pervaded by Him. The world is steeped in God. God dwells in each and every heart. All dwell in the word *oṁ*.

> *etaddhyevākṣaraṁ brahma etaddhyevākṣaraṁ param* |
> *etaddhyevakṣaraṁ jñātvā, yo yadicchati tasya tat* ||
> – *Kaṭha Upaniṣad* 1.2.16

This syllable (*oṁ*) is verily the everlasting spirit. It is the highest end. Knowing this very syllable whatever a person desires will indeed be his.

Guru Nānak in this hymns describes the relationship between God and world as under:

> *sace tere khaṇḍa sace brahamaṇḍa* || *sace tere lo-a sace ākāra* ||
> ....
> *nānaka sacu dhiāini sacu* || *jo mari jaṁmai su kacu nikacu* ||
> – *Ādi Granth*, p. 463

O Lord! all your worlds, planets and creation are true. All of your work and its plans and rulings of your court are true. Those who meditate on the Supreme Being are also true. Those who undergo the cycle of birth and death are false.

In this hymn Guru Nānak says that all the worlds, universes, regions and all His plays dwell on His truth, and are true. Only that what is born to die is false and vain. The message is that all the creations which dwell on the Truth are also true; as such the world is not an illusion, but a reality and but transitory and dwells on the Divine Will.

hai bhī hosī jāi na jāsī racanā jini racāī ||
raṅgī raṅgī bhātī jinasī māiā jini upāī ||
kari kari dekhai kītā apaṇā jiu tis dī vaḍiāī ||
jo tisu bhāvai soī karasī phiri hukamu na karaṇā jāī ||

– *Ādi Granth*, pp. 347-48

The Supreme Being, the creator of all existence, is there, and shall remain there always as the Ultimate Truth; He shall not go away even after dissolution of all this creation. He is the creator, the sphere of *māyā*, filled with various colours and spicies. After He created everything He Himself keeps watch over it as per His pleasure. He is free for His actions and no one can issue any order to Him.

Here again it is explained that the world with all its illusions, colours and variety is created by God. God shall not depart from the demolition of the world. After creating the world, He looks after it also. The existence and survival of the world are based on the pure will of God and no one can command Him on the subject.

nā ohu marai na hovai sogu || *deṅdā rahai na cūkai bhogu* ||
guṇu eho horu nāhī koi || *nā ko hoā nā ko hoi* ||

....

jini dinu kari kai kītī rāti || *khasamu visārahi te kamajāti* ||

– Ibid., p. 349

The Ultimate Truth is beyond death, so there is no cause for mourning. He continues his supply for the all and his stores do not get exhausted. No one else is like Him. No one is as glorious and virtuous as Him. Neither there had been nor there does anyone like Him. He created day and night. Those who forget

> the Supreme Being are wicked and worth hatred. He Himself functions and puts up all to function. He hears our grievances. Why should one listen to the world when it is He who is the creator and doer?

In this hymn Guru Nānak says that Truth is not subject to death so there is nothing to mourn. He stores are never exhausted even though God's continues to give this world non-stop. There is no reason to submit to the world as the source of all virtues and worldly gifts is one and the only one God. No one else is like Him who can create and give the bounty.

> *ghaḍīā sabhe gopīā pahar kaṅnha gopāla* ॥
> *gahaṇe pauṇu pāṇī baisaṅtaru caṅdu sūraju avatāra* ॥
> *sagalī dharatī mālu dhanu varataṇi saraba jaṅjāla* ॥
> *nānaka musai giāna vihūṇī khāi gaiā jama kālu* ॥
>
> – *Ādi Granth*, p. 465

> All hours of the day are like *gopīs*. The quarters of the day are like Kṛṣṇa. The wind, water and fire are their ornaments. They all dance around sun and moon, assuming forms. Without higher knowledge one wastes life and the messenger of death overpowers him.

This is a beautiful depiction of the running of hours, quarters of time, and the wind, water and fire in the world. It looks like the popular dance of Lord Kṛṣṇa playing with the milkmaids. All the resources, wealth and property of the visible world are nothing but God's play.

> *khakhai khuṅdakāru sāha ālamu kari kharīdi jini kharacu dīā* ॥
> *baṅdhani jā kai sabhu jagu bādhiā avarī kā nahī hukamu paiā* ॥
>
> – Ibid., p. 432

> *jhajhai jhūri marahu kiā prāṇī jo kichu deṇā su de rahiā* ॥
> *de de vekha hukamu calāe jiu jīā kā rijaku paiā* ॥
>
> ....
>
> *tatai tārū bhavajalu hoā tā kā aṅtu na pāiā* ॥
> *nā taranā tulahā hama būḍasi tāri lehi tāraṇa rāiā* ॥
>
> ....
>
> *papai pātisāhu paramesaru vekhaṇa kau parapaṅcu kīā* ॥

dekhai būjhai sabha kichu jāṇai aṅtari bāhari ravi rahiā ||
– *Ādi Granth*, p. 433

The Supreme Being acts as a king who provides everything for our living. His command prevails everywhere and no one can command like Him.... Human beings should not get anxious; whatsoever the Master has to provide, He shall keep on providing. He continues to give, and keeps his watch over us.

The world is a terrible ocean and so deep that its far end cannot be assessed. There is no boat or raft with me, I feel drowned. Let Him save me.

The Supreme King who is beyond human knowledge is the creator of the world and keeps a watch over it. He is the seer and knower of all existence both from inward and outward. He pervades all over.

In the above hymn known as Pātti Likhī or "the poem of alphabet", Guru Nānak speaks of the mutual relationship between God and the world. He says God is the king of the universe and he yokes everyone into His service and feeds all in the world. The whole world is under His sway and there is none another whose command can run. Whatever He has to give, He gives according to His writ and sustains and oversees the whole world. Everyone in this world has to pass away after a brief time so why should one practise guile and gamble away the life. It is better to seek refuge in the Lord. The sea of the material existence is immeasurable. One cannot find its limits. The whole world is bound in Him. The chains of death have chained it. Only those who serve and find *guru*'s grace are saved. The transcendent God created the whole world to be a witness to His creation. He sees all, knows all and pervades both within and without.

bābā nāṅgaḍā āiā jaga mahi dukhu sukhu lekhu likhāiā ||
likhiaḍā sāhā nā ṭalai jehaḍā purabi kamāiā ||
bahi sācai likhiā aṁmr̥tu bikhiā jitu lāiā titu lāgā ||
kāmaṇiārī kāmaṇa pāe bahuraṅgī gali tāgā ||
hochī mati bhaiā manu hochā guḍu sā makhī khāiā ||
....

bābā rovahu je kisai rovaṇā jānīaḍā baṅdhi paṭhāiā hai॥
– *Ādi Granth*, p. 582

We come into the world clothless and go through pains and pleasures as per our destiny. Our destiny of previous actions cannot be overruled. Our past *karma* follows us. The *māyā* works as charmer and puts multi-coloured world before us. Because of ignorance one eats the fly along with the sweets. When the death approaches, the near relations cry and weep. There is an advice that one should not weep and mourn the death of an individual. One must weep for the beloved soul which is bound and driven off. One should love the virtues of God and weep in the fear of God. No one can die with the dead.

In this hymn Guru Nānak speaks about a stark reality that human beings come naked and go back naked and all the worldly accumulations are left behind at a call from God. Whatever we get, we are predestined for it and whatever we do in this world shall be judged by Him. All the worldly relations who weep and mourn one's death today have to go from this world in the same way.

pauṇa pāṇī aganī ika vāsā॥ *āpe kīto khelu tamāsā*॥
baladi jali nivarai kirapā te āpe jalanidhi pāidā॥
dharati upāi dhari dharamasālā॥ *upapati paralau āpi nirālā*॥
pavaṇai khelu kīā sabha thāī kalā khiṅci ḍhāhāidā॥
– Ibid., p. 1033

The body is consisted of air, water and fire, and is the abode of the Lord. The Supreme Lord Himself stages a wonderful drama. It is His power that water extinguishes the burning fire but He keeps it (fire) in the water of ocean. The place of *dharma* was created on earth. He creates, destructs but Himself is not attached to His creation. He acts in the play of breathing everywhere. If He withdraws His power all get crumbled.

Here Guru Nānak speaks about the mystery of the world created by Him. God gives the power to water to put out the fire, and He stores fire in the watery ocean. Strange are the ways of God and the world created by Him. He created the world and its beings, yet He remains unattached to them. God plays as breath for everything.

Withdrawing His power of breath, He lets all to crumble down.

Mutual relationship between God and the world in the hymns of Guru Nānak can be compared with the following verses from the Upaniṣads:

iśāvāsyamidaṁ sarvaṁ yatkiñca jagatyāṁ jagat ।
tena tyaktena bhuñjīthā mā gṛdhaḥ kasya sviddhanam ॥
– *Īśa Upaniṣad* 1

It may be known that whatsoever is moving here in this ongoing world is wraped in God. Therefore one should search for pleasure in renunciation; one should not wish to get what does not belong to him.

This world is not separate from God. God pervades all over. One should seek to enjoy it through *tyāga* of self will. Forget the ownership relation with the world. If we realize that the world in which we live is not our permanent place, we can better enjoy life without getting attached to it.

yasmindyauḥ pṛthivī cāntarikṣaotaṁ manaḥ saha
prāṇaiśca sarvaiḥ ।
tamevaikam jānatha ātmānamanyā vāco vimuñcathā-
amṛtasyaiṣa setuḥ ॥
– *Muṇḍaka Upaniṣad* 2.2.5

In Him are woven heaven and earth, and the space between, and the mind with all the sense organs. Know that non-dual *Ātman* alone and give up all other talk. He is the bridge to immortality.

God, you may call Him by any name, is the ultimate rhythm in all existence. All the earth and heavens, space and mind are interwoven in it. He places the fire in an ocean of water and manages the whole show of running this play of all existence. He Himself is the bridge and Himself the space to immortality.

sa yathorṇanābhistantunoccareyathāgneḥ kṣudrā visphuliṅgā vyuccarantyevamevāsmādātmanaḥ sarve prāṇāḥ, sarve lokāḥ sarve devāḥ sarvāṇi bhūtāni vyuccaranti atasyopaniṣatsyasya satyamiti prāṇā vai satyaṁ teṣāmeṣa satyam ॥
– *Bṛhadāraṇyaka Upaniṣad* 2.1.20

> As a spider glides along the thread, as small sparks come forth from the fire, from this Self comes forth all breaths, all words, all divinities and all beings. Its secret meaning is the Truth of the Truth.

All worlds, all breaths, all divinities are forms of the Ultimate Reality only. Nothing exists outside it.

RELATION BETWEEN MAN AND THE WORLD

Guru Nānak explains the relationship between man and the world in his hymns as under:

> *titu saravaraḍai bhaīle nivāsā pāṇī pāvaku tinahi kīā* ||
> *paṅkaju moha pagu nahī cālai hama dekhā taha ḍūbīale* ||
>
> – *Ādi Granth*, p. 12

> Guru Nānak explains that people have made their homes in a pool where the water is as hot as fire. They cannot move themselves freely due to the mud of their emotional entanglements under their feet. I have seen them drowning there.

> *tr̥sanā māiā mohaṇī suta baṅdhapa ghara nārī* ||
> *dhani jobani jagu ṭhagiā labi lobhi ahaṁkāri* ||
> *moha ṭhagaulī hau muī sā varatai saṁsāri* ||
>
> – Ibid., p. 61

> The strong desire for the worldly life makes people attached with emotion to their kids, relations, friends and spouses. The riches of the world, youth, greed and egotism are a deceit and plunder of individuals. The emotional attachment destroys the whole world.

In the above hymns, Guru Nānak describes the world as a pool of hot desires and mud of attachments where the man abides, and warns that he has seen many who have drowned in the worldly desires and emotional attachments and destroyed their lives uselessly.

> *dūṅgaru dekhi ḍarāvaṇo peīaḍai ḍarīāsu* ||
> *ūcau parabatu gākhaḍo nā pauḍī titu tāsu* ||
> *guramukhi aṅtari jāṇiā guri melī tarīāsu* ||
> ....

dara ghara mahalā sohaṇe pake koṭa hajāra ||

....

sabha jaga mahi dohī pherīē binu nāvai siri kālu ||

....

putā dekhi vigasīē nārī seja bhatāra ||
coā caṅdanu lāīē kāpaḍu rūpu sīgāru ||
khehu kheha ralāīē choḍi calai ghara bāru ||

– *Ādi Granth*, p. 63

> The outside world looks terrible to me. Equally the path to the high mountain within my body frightens me. There are no steps to reach up to it. I found this mountain within me through *guru* and feel safe to cross over it. The abode of the Truth within is beautiful. People build concrete and beautiful houses on earth. They possess elephants, saddled horses and host a number of people therein. But nothing of these possessions can be carried along with oneself in the end. The unwise spend their life to accumulate all these and leave the world. I wandered over all lands and found that nothing is equal to the name of the Lord. A man gets joy in seeing his kids and takes pleasure in bed with his wife. He sprays scented oils and wears clothes to look beautiful. In fact, these are all dust and shall mingle with dust and he will go from this world leaving behind all his possessions.

In this hymn Guru Nānak explains the mutual relationship between God, man and the world. He says that height of God's mountain frightens him on the one hand and on the other hand the world appears dreadful. Mounting on the height to God is very hard and there are no steps up to it and mountain within the man's inner self can be found through a *guru* who can save the individual. On the other hand, the lashing sea of the material world is fearful. All the worldly accumulations are to be left behind. Nothing shall go with man when the body crumbles and the breath stops. In the world a man feels happy to see his children and wife. He applies perfumes, wears best of clothes to make a show of his beauty and possessions and takes pride in being a king, a chief or a renowned leader and burns in ego. In such a way the egotists drown in the sea of agony in pursuit of these pleasures and waste away their life.

mukāmu kari ghari baisaṇa nita calaṇai kī dhokha॥
mukāmu tā paru jāṇīē jā rahai nihacalu loka॥
dunīā kaisi mukāme॥ – *Ādi Granth*, p. 64

Individuals have made this world as their home and each day their anxiety to leave it increases. What type of home this world is? It would have been a true home if we could stay for ever.

In continuation to the above hymn, Guru Nānak explains that our stay in the world is as if in a transit camp. The more we get involved in the worldly possessions, more is the agony of leaving it behind. These lines explain another physical reality of this life.

jaise goili goilī taise saṁsārā॥
kūḍu kamāvahi ādamī bāṅdhahi gharabārā॥
jāgahu jāgahu sūtiho caliā vaṇajārā॥
nīta nīta ghara bāṅdhīahi je rahaṇā hoī॥
– Ibid., p. 418

Individuals are in this world for a very short time like a shepherd in a field. But they build their houses in this world as if they are to be here forever. Guru Nānak warns individuals to wake up from their slumber and see the others who are leaving this world with none of their belongings.

In this hymn Guru Nānak compares the man to a shepherd and the world to a pasture. The man stays in the world for a short time like a shepherd in a green pasture. Yet the man commits falsehood and tries to establish his home here. He gives a clarion call to the mankind to wake up and realize the truth of life. He advises not to wail for the dead and care for the present only. One should take a lesson from the dead that they did not carry their accumulations along with them while leaving this world. Similarly the man may care for the present and earn something which he can carry along with him to the life after. These lines explain yet another physical reality of human life.

cale calaṇahāra vāṭa vaṭāiā॥
dhaṅdhu piṭe saṁsāru sacu na bhāiā॥
....
moiā kau kiā rovahu roi na jāṇahū॥

rovahu sacu salāhi hukamu pachāṇahu ।।
hukamī vajahu likhāi āiā jāṇīē ।।
lāhā palai pāi hukamu siñāṇīē ।।
– *Ādi Granth*, p. 419

The life is like a walk from one end of the road to another end. Individuals travel and get entangled with this worldly relations on the way to another end but they forget their end of life. Some cry for the dead, but they are ignorant as to how to weep. They should weep and praise for the Lord and realize His will. His birth here is blessed who recognizes the command of the Supreme Being and lives according to it. He gets the true profit from this life.

In this hymn Guru Nānak laments the way of life adopted by men. A man shuttles from one end of the road to another in search of God and is entangled in the worldly pursuits. If he leaves his sense of attachment with the world and falsehood of life, he can reach his home within. He should not weep for the dead but wail for himself and abide by the Lord's command.

tūṅ suṇi haraṇā kāliā kī vāḍīē rātā rāma ।।
bikhu phalu mīṭhā cāri din phiri hovai tātā rāma ।।
phiri hoi tātā kharā mātā nāma binu paratā pae ।।
oha jeva sāira dei lahari bijula jivai camkae ।।
....
saṁsāru māiā mohu mīṭhā aṅti bharamu cukāiā ।।
– Ibid., pp. 438-39

This world is a garden full of passionate attractions and attachments. It gives birth to fruits of sin tasting sweet for some time and turns bitter and sour very soon. That fruit which intoxicates one for a short while becomes a source of painful suffering without *nāma*. All sensual pleasures and flashes of comforts of this world are temporary and vanish like the waves of sea, leaving behind a trail of pains and suffering. Those who wander around such pleasures in this garden of passions meet a terrible end. I enquired from my true *guru* to understand all this about the fate of bubblebee which gets much integrated with the just blossomed flowers in the garden. Let this stranger traveller not fall into the entanglements of this passionate orchard. A fish tearfully gets separated from water when the fisherman casts his net, so also the individuals who fall into the net of *māyā* go lamenting from this world.

In the above hymn, Guru Nānak advises not to be entangled with the conflicts of the world and run after the things which seem to be pleasant but not good and may bring more suffering.

vāhu khasama tū vāhu jini raci racanā hama kīe॥
sāgara lahari samuṅda sara veli varasa varāhu॥
āpi khaḍovahi āpi kari āpīṇai āpāhu॥
guramukhi sevā thāi pavai unamani tatu kamāhu॥
masakati lahahu majūriyā maṅgi maṅgi khasama darāhu॥
nānaka pura dara veparavāha tau pari ūnā nāhi ko sacā veparavāhu॥

– *Ādi Granth*, p. 788

Wahoo! O my Master! you are wonderful and great. You are the creator of all this creation including me. We are related to you like waves to oceans, and as rains to plants. You stand yourself amongst all of your creation. You approve the selfless service of the God-loving people who live in heavenly peace ever attuned to the Supreme Being. They are paid salary for their work of staying to beg at the door of Supreme Being. The Lord's treasurer is overflowing with His gifts and no one who approaches His door goes empty handed.

This is one of the most exciting expressions of Guru Nānak for the bounty of provisions made by God for the men which is overflowing. He says that God is great and wonderful. He made the entire creation, provided all required for life. He Himself stands amidst His creation. He entrusted the service of being selfless to the Guramukhas who remain blessed with peace and with the essence of reality.

ujala motī sohaṇe ratanā nāli juḍaṅni॥
tina jaru vairī nānakā ji buḍhe thīi maraṅni॥

– Ibid., p. 788

Youthful teeth sparkle like pearls. Eyes shine like jewels. Getting old spoils all brightness. These get wasted with growing age. This explains that the physical beauty of an individual will go away with age.

dui dīve caudaha haṭa nāle || *jete jīa tete vaṇjāre* ||
khulhe haṭa hoā vāpāru || *jo pahucai so calaṇahāru* ||

– *Ādi Granth*, p. 789

Guru Nānak explains that the sun and moon work as two lamps for providing light to the universe. All individuals are like traders in this universe. They trade day in and day out. Whosoever comes here will go back. The *dharma* is the judge who approves of judgement for right and wrong. Individuals who earn the profit of *nāma* here get accepted and approved in the court of God. They return home cheerfully and are honoured by Him.

Here Guru Nānak describes the world in which the sun and moon are two lamps that light all the fourteen spheres of the universe. All the living beings are customers. The God's stores ever remain open and the trade goes on. Dharmarāja is the broker who approves as to what kind of profit one is carrying with him. When one reaches back Home, his victory is acclaimed on the basis of his personal account.

jiu āiā tiu jāvahi baure jiu janame tiu maraṇu bhaiā ||
jiu rasa bhoga kīe tetā dukhu lāgai nāmu visāri bhavajali paiā ||
tanu dhanu dekhata garabi gaiā ||

....

khina mahi vesa karahi naṭūā jiu moha pāpa mahi galatu gaiā ||

....

dekhi kuṭaṁbu māiā gr̥ha maṅdaru sākatu jaṅjāli parāli paiā ||
jā āe tā tinahi paṭhāe cāle tinai bulāi laiā ||

– Ibid., pp. 906-07

One goes away from this world as he comes. But a fool does not understand that he is born to die. One gets pleasures to enjoy and pain to suffer. One who forgets the *nāma* falls deep into the terrible world ocean. One looks towards his body and wealth and feels so proud. In a minute one changes various costumes like a juggler. Thus he gets entrapped in personal and emotional attachment and sin. When he looks towards his family, wealth, household and mansions, he gets entrapped in useless worldly affairs. One comes to this world when He sends him and goes back from this world when He calls him back.

In this hymn Guru Nānak talks about the world and the life lived by man. He explains that one will go back from this world in the form in which he came to this world. While in this world one becomes proud, seeing his beauty and riches. He does not practise truth, chastity, self-control nor continence and makes himself a ghost in different costumes and appearances. Without one's companionship with the saints and self-discipline, one's life is wasted. One commit sins, changes dresses like a juggler, when he sees ease and riches coming, he gets elated; the wealth and family attractions entangle him. One does all this but forget the true *nāma* of the Lord. Whenever there is a call from Him one will go back, but the Lord is merciful and forgives all.

nānaka dunīā bhasu raṅgu bhasū hū bhasu kheha ॥
bhaso bhasu kamāvaṇī bhī bhasu bharīē deha ॥
jā jīu vicahu kaḍhīē bhasū bhariā jāi ॥
agai lekhai maṅgiē hāra dasūṇī pāi ॥

– *Ādi Granth*, p. 1240

All enjoyments of this world are dusty. These are the dusty heaps of ashes. Those who live in these pleasures earn dust and get mixed with these ashes. The soul and body separate, soul too is found covered with dust of individual's *karma*. When he goes from this world and his accounts are settled in the court of the Lord, he receives ten times more dust.

In these lines Guru Nānak compares the worldly pleasures with dust. If one deals with dust, he can earn only dust. The body is also dust and when soul flies away one rolls in dust. When the man is asked about his account of deeds hereafter, he is greeted with tenfold of dust.

sūraja caḍa vijogi sabhasai ghaṭai ārajā ॥
tanu manu ratā bhogi koi hārai ko jiṇai ॥
sabhu ko bhariā phūki ākhaṇi kahaṇi na thaṁmhīē ॥
nānaka vekhai āpi phūka kaḍhāe ḍhahi pavai ॥

– Ibid., p. 1244

> With every sunrise and sunset the life of an individual rolls out. In the mental and physical pleasures; one loses and another wins. All get aired up with false notions and start talking non-stop. O Nānak! the Supreme Being observes all and when He withdraws air out of this body, as in a balloon the body crumbles and falls down.

It is a poetic cry for the loss of life in a wasteful manner. Guru Nānak says, as the sun rises and then sets, a day of life of a man is gone by. As the body and mind indulge in pleasures, there is loss for one and success for another. Each individual gets elated with ego and talks high. But God sees and hears all and when He punctures the air in a balloon, meaning deprives man of his breath, he falls flat.

kāgada koṭu ihu jagu hai bapuro raṅgani cihana caturāī॥
nānī sī būṅda pavanu pati khovai janami marai khinu tāīṅi॥
nadī upakaṅṭhi jaise gharu paravaru sarapani gharu ghara māhī॥
ulaṭī nadī kahāṅ gharu taravaru sarapani ḍasai dūjā mana māṅhī॥
gāraḍu gura giānu dhiānu gura bacanī bikhiā guramati jārī॥
mana tana heṅva bhae sacu pāiā hari kī bhagati nirārī॥
– *Ādi Granth*, p. 1274

> This terrific world is like a fort of paper of colour and form, and clever tricks. A tiny droppings or a harsh blow of wind spoils its shine immediately and ends its life. It is in a deep hole on a tree near a river wherein a serpent lives. When the river overflows, snake bites like duality in the mind. *Guru*'s spiritual wisdom and meditation work like a miracle and all vice and corruption get burnt away.

In this hymn Guru Nānak explains the relationship between the man of duality and the world. He considers the world as a fortress of paper which is cleverly coloured and formed. But a puff of wind or a little drop of water can make it fall flat. He gives an example that there is a tree on the bank of a river. A snake lives in its trunk. What will happen if the river overflows? The snake of duality will come out of its hiding and bite the man. River is the world, mind is the house and duality is the serpent.

nānaka dunīā kaisī hoī ।। *sālaku mitu na rahio koi* ।।
bhāī baṅdhī hetu cukāiā ।। *dunīā kāraṇi dīnu gavāiā* ।।
hai hai kari kai ohi kareni ।। *galā piṭani siu khoheni* ।।
nāu laini aru karani samāi ।। – *Ādi Granth*, p. 1410

Nānak wonders as to what has gone wrong with the world. One cannot find a friend or a guide. Love is lost among brothers and relatives. In worldly pursuits people lose their faith. There is crying, weeping and wailing all around. Individuals slap others and pull other's hair as their tools. Individuals, who chant the name of God, shall be saved.

Here, Guru Nānak laments that there is no friend and no guide in the world. All brothers and other relations have abandoned love. Should I abandon even my faith for this world? Men wail and cry to bemoan the dead. They strike their cheeks and pluck their hair. But it would have been better if they cherish the Lord's name and practise it too.

udo sāhai kiā nīsānī toṭi na āvai aṅnī ।।
udosīa ghare hī vuṭhī kuḍiīṅ raṅnī dhaṅmmī ।।
satī raṅnī ghare siāpā rovani kūḍī kaṅmmī ।।
jo leva so devai nāhī khaṭe daṅmma sahaṅmmī ।।
– Ibid., p. 1412

The progress of individuals is measured by their storage of food that never get empty. Happiness resides where there are too many women all around. They indulge in shouting and crying for nothing. Whatever a man takes from others he does not give back to them. For increase in one's earnings everyone gets restless and feels troublesome.

This is a satire on a so-called successful man of the world. This is the sign of an overflowing man that he has abundant and never ending food grains, his house is full of wives, daughters and women. Every woman shouts and cries over small things. Abundance of wives makes the home a bedlam. One grabs other's share. Man is uneasy, but is seeking to earn more and more.

raji na koī jīviā pahuci na caliā koī ।।
giānī jīvai sadā sadā suratī hī pati hoī ।।

saraphai saraphai sadā sadā evai gaī vihāi ||
nānaka kisa no ākhīe viṇu puchiā hī lai jāi ||
– *Ādi Granth*, p. 1412

One cannot live for such a period to fulfil all his desires. Only the wise and men of spirit live forever. They get honour for their advanced awareness. Life trickles away slowly. The "destined to die persons" try to hold it back. O Nānak! there is no one to whom we may complain about it. Death takes one's life away without anyone's asking.

These lines of Guru Nānak sum up the play of a man's worldly life. No one lives enough to fulfil all his wishes in this world. Only the wise man lives eternally and is honoured. He cherishes God in his consciousness. Life passes bit by bit and no one can hold it back. God Himself takes life even before one knows.

The gist of the contents in the above hymns of Guru Nānak is comparable with the following verses of Upaniṣads.

kurvanneveha karmāṇi jijīviṣecchataṁ samāḥ |
evaṁ tvayi nānyatheto 'sti na karma lipyate nare ||
– *Īśa Upaniṣad* 2

Always performing works here, one should wish to live a hundred years. If you thus live like a man, there is no way other than this by which *karma* (deed) does not adhere to you.

When one acts merging his individuality with the Universal Cause and dedicates all his actions to God, the action does not bind him.

The Upaniṣads advocate a life of action for the human beings with the ultimate aim of getting out of rotation of coming and going through the knowledge of the Self.

vedamanūcyācāryo … deva pitṛkāryābhyāṁ na
mātṛdevo bhava…tāni sevitavyāni …
no itarāṇi | *ye ke cāsmacchreyāṁso brāhmaṇāḥ …*
– *Taittirīya Upaniṣad* 1.11.1-3

After teaching Vedas, teacher advises the pupil:

Be truthful. Exercise *dharma*. Continue your daily reading. With a pleasing gift brought for the teacher, enter family life and see that the line of offspring is not cut off. Severe not from the truth. Severe not from *dharma*. Forget not personal welfare. Forget not prosperity. Forget not the study and teaching of the Vedas.

Do not omit your duties to gods and manes. Treat your mother as God. Treat your father as God. Treat your teacher as God. Treat your guest as God. Whatever deeds are faultless, these are to be performed, not others. Whatever good works have been performed by us, those should be performed by you, not others.

vedāntavijñānasuniścitārthāḥ saṁnyāsayogādyatayaḥ. . .
parimucyanti sarve || – *Muṇḍaka Upaniṣad* 3.2.6

The ascetics who have ascertained well the meaning of the Vedānta knowledge, who have purified their nature through the path of renunciation, they (dwelling) in the worlds of the Brahmā, at the end of time, being one with the immortal are liberated.

The Upaniṣads stress the need for good deeds and a pleasant life balanced with knowledge and meditation.

Mutual relationship between God, man and the world had been a subject of varied thoughts and opinions in Vedānta. There are three principal schools of thought among the Vedāntins. Their views on the relationship between God, man and the world differ.

Dvaita (dualistic) school of Madhvācārya believes that God creates and rules the universe. He is separate from nature and human soul. God is eternal, nature and all souls are also eternal. Nature and souls are subject to manifestation and changes, but God remains the same. God has human attributes. He is merciful, just and powerful. One can approach Him and pray to Him. One can love Him and He returns love. In nutshell, He is human but higher than man infinitely. He has no bad qualities like man. He is the custodian of innumerable, virtuous qualities.

Viśiṣṭādvaita (special non-dualistic) school of Śrī Rāmānujācārya states that effect is never different from the cause. The effect is only the reproduction of cause in another form. If the universe is the effect and God the cause, it must be God Himself. They believe that God is both the efficient cause and the material cause of the universe. He Himself is the creator, and Himself the material out of which the whole nature is projected. Thus according to this school the whole universe is God Himself.

Advaita (non-dualistic) school of Śrī Śaṅkarācārya declares that God is both the material cause and the efficient cause of the universe. He is both the creator and the created. He Himself is this universe, that what people see as universe does not really exist. What we see around us is mere self hypnotism (*avidyā*). The moment one realizes the Truth, the illusion disappears and he feels illuminated and one with Him.

The Upaniṣads describe both the *Nirguṇa-Brahman* and the *Saguṇa-Brahman*. The *Nirguṇa-Brahman* is described with negation of all attributes and relations. It is beyond time, space and undescribable in words yet it is the very essence of every thing. The *Saguṇa-Brahman* is a personal god, a manifestation of *Brahman* as god, soul and the world. Creation, preservation and destruction are the activities of the *Saguṇa-Brahman*. Thus The *Saguṇa-Brahman* is known respectively as Brahmā, Viṣṇu and Rudra or Śiva. These form the *trimūrti*, (trinity) of Upaniṣads. But the *Nirguṇa-Brahman* and the *Saguṇa-Brahman* are not two realities as the sea is the same whether peaceful (unmanifested) or agitated (manifested). But Guru Nānak held the view in all his hymns that there is *ika oṁkāra* meaning only one God manifested as well as unmanifested.

Both Guru Nānak and the Upaniṣads portray a man to be *aṁśa* (drop) of the Supreme Lord. The very existence of the individual body and soul is His Divine Will. Man has no existence outside Him. He enjoys His creation and takes care of it. Guru Nānak explains that man is separated from God due to individual's *karma* and the ultimate goal of human life is to strive to attain reunion with Him for everlasting peace.

The Upaniṣads explain that the whole world is enveloped by Him. He is the creator of all whatsoever moves or stands apart here. Nothing exists outside Him. He has created it by His ownself and when He withdraws His power the whole creation crumbles. Guru Nānak also expresses same belief and further explains that the world is not an illusion but real even though it is transitory.

It is true as it has been created by the True Lord Himself by His own Divine Will.

Guru Nānak and the Upaniṣads alike describe the aim of human life to get out of the cycle of births and deaths by living a life of virtuous action. The life in this world is transitory and one has to leave this world and go in the form in which he had come. One should cherish and struggle to get a knowledge of the self, live a life of virtue and get freed from many births and deaths.

Divine Will, Fear of God and Free Will

Guru Nānak advocated the supremacy of Divine Will and fear of God in individual life and a freedom of choice between the good and the pleasant. He frequently refers to God's will, His mercy and His fear in his hymns.

DIVINE WILL (HUKAM-DHARMAN)

Guru Nānak advises us to lead a life with fear of God and accept the will of God as a guiding star in his hymns.

hukamī hovani ākāra hukamu na kahiā jāī॥
hukamī hovani jia hukami milai vaḍiāī॥
hukamī utamu nīcu hukami likhi dukha sukha pāīahi॥
ikanā hukamī bakhasīsa iki hukamī sadā bhavāīahi॥
hukamai aṅduri subhu ko bāhari hukama na koi॥
nānaka hukamai je bujhai ta haumai kahai na koi॥
– *Ādi Granth*, p. 1

Souls come into being by the command of the Supreme Lord. Glory and greatness are also achieved by His command. His command places individuals at high or low positions. Both pain and pleasure are received as per His written command. It is He who blesses some and forgives them as per His will while others remain wandering aimlessly forever by His command.

Guru Nānak says that all forms are created by His will. One cannot describe His will. All the streams of life flow by His will and individuals are placed in the high or low levels of consciousness according to His will. The Divine Will prevails all over and controls all existence. Those who realize the Divine Will the feeling of I-ness is no more in them.

tā kau bighanu na lāgaī cālai hukami rajāī ॥
hukami rajāī jo calai so pavai khajānai ॥
khoṭe ṭhavara na pāinī rale jūṭhānai ॥
nita nita kharā samālīe sacu saudā pāīē ॥
khoṭe nadari na āvanī le agani jalāīē ॥
– *Ādi Granth*, p. 421

Those who follow the command of the Supreme Being do not suffer in life and are accepted by the Lord's treasurer. The counterfeits cannot find any place even if they get mixed with the true ones, these shall get separated. The genuine coins are stored for ever. The true traders are purchased. The counterfeit coins are seized and cast into the fire again.

In this hymn Guru Nānak compares the self-willed persons to counterfeit coins which are put again in the fire for casting. Meaning they continue to suffer by birth and death.

hukamai aṅdari nimmiā piāre hukamai udara majhārī ॥
hukamai aṅdari jammiā piāre ūdhau sira kai bhārī ॥
....
hukame bamni calāīē piāre manamukhi lahai sajāi ॥
hukame sabadi pachāṇīē piāre daragaha paidhā jāi ॥
....
hukamu siñāpai sāha kā piāre sacu milai vaḍiāī hoī ॥
– Ibid., p. 636

One is conceived and grows in the womb by the command of the God's will. One's head comes out first and lower body afterwards. It is Lord's will that one is bound to this world and dragged away from it. The self-willed persons go through their punishment here. With Lord's will one realizes the world and one goes to the Supreme Being and gets honour. The accounts of some individual's get settled here, while others suffer due to duality. Under His command only some go on roaming in birth and death cycles due to their sins and go on suffering.

In these lines Guru Nānak explains that by Lord's will one is conceived, thrives in the womb standing on one's head and takes birth. He submits to the will of the Lord. In His will one comes to the world and passes out of it. By His will he suffers for his ego and by His will he realizes the word.

hukame āvai hukame jāvai hukame rahai samāī ||
pūre gura te sācu kamāvai gati miti sabade pāī ||
– *Ādi Granth*, p. 940

We come and go by His *hukam*. By His command we get merged in Him. It is through the grace of *guru* that one lives in truth. It is *guru*'s word through which the state of dignity is achieved.

guramukhi hoi su hukamu pachāṇai mānai hukamu samāidā ||
hukame āiā hukami samāiā || *hukame dīsai jagatu upāiā* ||
hukame suragu machu paiālā hukame kalā rahāidā ||
hukame dharati dhaula siri bhāraṁ ||
hukame pauṇa pāṇī gaiṇāraṁ ||
....
āpi nāthu nathīṅ sabha jā kī bakhase mukati karāidā ||
– Ibid., pp. 1036-37

By Divine Will one comes to this world, lives here and gets merged into Him. By His will the world came into existence.... The Lord brought all this under His control by His own will. Whomsoever He forgives he gets liberated. One who becomes godly comes to realize His command and surrendering thereto, he merges in the Lord.

In this hymn Guru Nānak says that after establishing the creation, God has put all His creation under Him.

sacu kahahu sacai ghari rahaṇā ||
jīvata marahu bhavajalu jagu taraṇā ||
guru bohithu guru beḍī tulahā
mana hari japi pāri laṅghāiā ||
haumai mamatā lobha bināsanu ||
nau dara mukate dasavai āsanu ||
– Ibid., p. 1040

One has to be truthful and always stay in the state of truth. For crossing the deadly world ocean one should remain dead while he lives. The *guru* acts as the boat or the ship or the raft and by

> concentrating on the name of God in mind one will be carried to the other side of the world. By the elimination of one's ego, possessive nature and strong desires, one gets liberated from the nine gates and attains a place at the tenth gate.

> *hukami rajāī sākhatī daragaha sacu kabūlu* ||
> *sāhibu lekhā maṅgasī dunīā dekhi na bhūlu* ||
> – *Ādi Granth*, p. 1090

> Only truthful individuals are welcome in the court of the True Lord. He shall ask you to furnish your account, so do not get attracted to and involved in this flimsy world.

The message is very clear that one should submit to the will of God and follow the way of truth.

> *sabhe suratī joga sabhi sabhe beda purāṇa* ||
> *sabhe karaṇe tapa sabhi sabhe gīta giāna* ||
> *sabhe budhī sudhi sabhi sabhi tīratha sabhi thāna* ||
> ....
> *hukami calāe āpaṇai karamī vahai kalāma* ||
> *nānaka sacā saci nāi sacu sabhā dībānu* ||
> – Ibid., p. 1141

> The Supreme Lord has established all higher understanding, all spiritual knowledge, all action powers, all types of *yoga*, all sacred shrines of pilgrimages ... according to His *hukam*. He has full command upon all of them and accounts for all their acts. The Lord is the Ultimate Truth. His name, congregation and court are also true.

This is a very appreciating piece of acknowledgement of unity of all religious thought of all religions, all scriptures, all intelligence and all religious places as the outcome of the Divine Will. Only a true saint of the status of Guru Nānak could express such a universal solidarity.

FEAR OF GOD (ṚTA), FREE WILL

Vedic texts refer to *ṛta* as order of the universe or truth. *Ṛta* is the law which governs the world. It can be understood in three ways: (i) the physical order of the universe, (ii) the moral law pervading the world, and (iii) the order of the sacrifices. The dawn breaks out in the morning according to *ṛta*, the sun is the bright show of *ṛta*. The year is the wheel of *ṛta* with twelve spokes (months). The river's flow obeys the rule of *ṛta*. *Ṛta* is the cosmic order and the universal moral order. *Ṛta* is truth. It commands positive action. It signifies righteousness. Its opposite, *unṛta*, is falsehood.

Guru Nānak speaks of the Divine Will and fear of God very frequently in his hymns. His concept of *hukam* (Divine Will) is comparable with the stern and permanent laws (*ṛta*) of *prakṛti*. He advises mankind to know, recognize and follow the Divine Will and develop a fear for it. Once the fear of God's will is adopted it will make one fearless of all fears of the world which are unreal.

One will develop a free will for life to follow the desired aim of his life.

Guru Nānak explains the fear of God in operation of His stern laws in the following hymns:

> *bhai vici pavaṇu vahai sada vāu* ॥ *bhai vici cālahi lakha darīāū* ॥
> *bhai vici agani kaḍhai vegāri* ॥ *bhai vici dharatī dabī bhāri* ॥
> *bhai vici iṅdu phirai sira bhāri* ॥ *bhai vici rājā dharama duāru* ॥
> *bhai vici sūraju bhai vici caṅdu* ॥ *koha karoḍī calata na aṅtu* ॥
> *bhai vici sidha budha sura nātha* ॥ *bhai vici āḍāne ākāsa* ॥
> ....
> *sagaliā bhau likhiā siri lekhu* ॥ *nānaka nirabhau niraṅkāru*
> *sacu eku* ॥
> – *Ādi Granth*, p. 464

> In the divine fear, the wind blows. In the divine fear thousands of rivers flow, fire is forced to labour, the earth is crumbled under its own burden, the clouds move in the sky. The righteous *dharma* stands at his door. In the divine fear, the sun and moon shine, and these planets travel miles after miles without end. In the fear of God, the *siddha*, the *buddha*, the demi-gods and *yogīs* exist. In the divine fear, the ākāśic ethers stretch across the sky, the warriors and most powerful heroes exist and innumerable individuals come and go. God has written His divine fear upon all foreheads. Only formless Lord, the True One is Fearless.

> *siri dhari calīē sahīē bhāru* ॥ *nadarī karamī gura bīcāru* ॥
> *bhai binu koi na laṅghasi pāri* ॥ *bhai bhau rākhiā bhāi savāri* ॥

bhai tani agani bhakhai bhai nāli ||
bhai bhau ghaḍīē sabadi savāri ||
....
budhī bājī upajai cāu || *sahasa siāṇapa pavai na tāu* ||
– *Ādi Granth*, p. 151

One should keep the fear of God on one's mind and accept its weight. Blessed with the grace of the Supreme Being, concentrate on the instructions of *guru*. In the absence of divine fear, one cannot cross over the world sea. The divine the fear instills love for the God. The divine fear increases with increase of love for God. Through this increase of God's love, one is blessed with the world. Whatever is done or thought without the awe and the fear of God is useless. The wishes for the worldly enjoyments crop up in the mind but fear of God cannot be generated with cleverness or tricky ways. One has to harvest love and fear for God.

ḍari dharu ghari ḍaru ḍari ḍaru jāi ||
so ḍaru kehā jitu ḍari ḍaru pāi ||
tudhu binu dūjī nāhī jāi || *jo kichu varatai sabha terī rajāi* ||
ḍarīē je ḍaru hovai horu || *ḍari ḍari ḍaraṇā mana kā soru* ||
na jīu marai na ḍūbai tarai || *jini kichu kīā so kichu karai* ||
– Ibid., p. 151

One should have always fear of God in one's heart. When one develops fear of God, all his worldly fears run away. There is no fear which can eliminate all other fears of the world except the fear of God. Guru Nānak says that he has no other support for his rest except the love for and fear of God. All happens as per His command and there is nothing to fear. One should fear if he feels the fear of anything except the fear of God. The fear of worldly affairs of life holds one in confused emotion and one gets entangled in the world. Individual soul neither dies nor drowns, nor swims across.

Through the above hymns Guru Nānak teaches us that it is only the God or the Ultimate Truth which is without any fear and all His creation runs due to fear of Him. The burden of fear of him has to be born by all. In living a life fear of him will make the individual free from all the worldly fears. He will be able to follow the right path and achieve his goal of life.

Guru Nānak stresses the need to follow the Divine Will, develop and bear the fear of God (*ṛta*), i.e. stern laws of universe and attain free will by way of getting fearless.

The Upaniṣads also teach that the universe is governed by the order (*ṛta*), a divine force to which all individuals and gods are subjected to.

> *yadidaṁ kiṅ ca jagatsarvaṁ prāṇa ejati niḥsṛtam* ।
> *mahadbhayaṁ vajramudyataṁ ya etadviduramṛtas te bhavanti* ॥
> – *Kaṭha Upaniṣad* 2.3.2

> The whole world, whatever here exists, springs and moves in life. It is the great fear, like the upraised thunderbolt. They who know that become immortal.

Awe and fear of God originate from *Brahman*. *Brahman* has been described as a great terror-like thunderbolt.

> *bhayādasyagnistapati bhayāttapti sūryaḥ* ।
> *bhayādindraśca vāyuśca, mṛtyurdhāvati pañcamaḥ* ॥
> – Ibid. 2.3.3

> Due to fear of *Brahman* fire burns, sun gives light, the gods, the wind and death catch speed. Everything moves with his vibration.

From the terror of *Brahman*, fire burns, from His terror the sun shines and from His terror the gods and death run for work. *Brahman* is the source and sustenance of the universe. There is no mechanical process of evolution. *Brahman* controls all processes of source and sustenance of this universe.

> *asadvā idamagra āśit* । *tato vai sadajayatu . . . atha tasya bhayaṁ bhavati* । *tattveva bhayaṁ viduṣo manvanasya* । *tad apy eṣa śloko bhavati* ॥
> – *Taittirīya Upaniṣad* 2.7.1

> From the fear of *Brahman*, the wind blows; from the fear of it, the sun rises; from the fear of it, Agni and Indra and death, the fifth, run.

Brahman is bliss. It is a self-made flavour or essence. By getting to this flavour one becomes blissful. When one gets a fearless support from the invisible and all powerful Lord, all his personal fears disappear and he becomes fearless to face the world.

> *saṅkalpo vāva manaso bhuyān yadā vai saṅkalpayate 'tha manasyati. . .* ||
>
> *sa yaḥ saṅkalpaṁ brahmetyupāste kḷptānvai sa lokān dhruvān dhruvaḥ* ||
>
> – *Chāndogya Upaniṣad* 7.4.1, 3

> Will is assuredly greater than mind. For when one wills then one reflects, one utters speech and then one utters it in name. The sacred hymns are included in name and sacred works in the sacred hymns. He who meditates on will as *Brahman*, he verily obtains the worlds he has willed.

As far as will goes, so far is he independent.

The hymns of Guru Nānak portray the concept of fear of God and Divine law (*hukam*) regulating and governing the creation in a similar way to the contents of Upaniṣads. Guru Nānak gives a clarion call to bear the burden of fear of God and follow the Divine Will. This will make one fearless of all worldly fears and help him develop a free will to follow and achieve success in life.

Stages of Life and Haume (I-ness)

STAGES OF LIFE

Guru Nānak describes various stages of life he lived in his hymns.

> *pahilai paharai raṇi kai vaṇajāriā mitrā hukami paiā garabhāsi* ||
> *uradha tapu aṅtari kare vaṇajāriā mitrā khasama setī aradāsi* ||
> ....
> *kahu nānaka prāṇī pahilai paharai hukami paiā garabhāsi* ||
> *dūjai paharai raiṇi kai vaṇajāriā mitrā visari gaiā dhiānu* ||
> ....
> *jini raci raciā tisahi na jāṇai mana bhītari dhari giānu* ||
> *kahu nānaka prāṇī dūjai paharai visari gaiā dhiānu* ||
> *tījai paharai raiṇi kai vaṇajāriā mitrā dhana jobana siu citu* ||
> *hari kā nāmu na cetahī vaṇajāriā mitrā badhā chuṭahi jitu* ||
> ....

kahu nānaka tījai paharai prāṇī dhana jobana siu citu॥
cauthai paharai raiṇi kai vaṇajāriā mitrā lāvī āiā khetu॥
....
kahu nānaka prāṇī cauthai paharai lāvī luṇiā khetu॥
– *Ādi Granth*, pp. 74-75

In the first stage of life, one gets into the womb. He remains upside down and exercises penance within the womb and prays to the Lord and Master. One utters prayers to his Lord, meditates lying upside down, showers love and respect for God. He comes to this world all naked, with a writ on his forehead as how shall he live his life.

In the second stage of life, one forgets meditation. He plays in the hands of relatives all around like Kṛṣṇa in the house of Yaśodā. The proud mother declares him as her son. Her mind cannot realize that nothing belongs to her. No one will be his forever in the end. He gets unaware of the creator of this universe and provider of all spiritual wisdom and forgets meditation.

In the third stage of life, his attention is concentrated on money and youthfulness. He forgets the name of the Lord which released him from the bondage. One becomes engrossed with *māyā* all around him. He enjoys his riches and gets intoxicated in his youthhood. He wastes away his life uselessly. One does not act in goodness and *dharma* and does not get friendly with good thoughts and deeds.

In the fourth stage of life, the harsh hangman of death approaches and catches him and sends him to the other world. None understands the mystery of where one is gone. Everyone is unaware of the mystery of the death man who sieges him and takes him away. All weep and wail for him. In a blink of eye one becomes a stranger. One obtains exactly what one has longed for. So in the fourth watch of the night, O mortal, the reaper God harvests his field. These stages of life are a physical reality.

pahilai paharai raiṇi kai vaṇajāriā mitrā bālaka budhi acetu॥
khīru pīē khelāīē vaṇajāriā mitrā māta pitā sut hetu॥
māta pitā suta nehu ghanerā māiā mohu sabāī॥
....

dūjai paharai raiṇi kai vaṇajāriā mitrā bhari jobani maimati ||
ahinisi kāmi viāpiā vaṇajāriā mitrā aṅdhule nāmu na citi ||
....
tijai paharai raiṇi kai vaṇajāriā mitrā sari haṁsa ulathaḍe āi ||
jobanu ghaṭai jarūā jiṇai vaṇajāriā mitrā āṅva ghaṭai dinu jāi ||
....
cauthai paharai raiṇi kai vaṇajāriā mitrā biradhi bhaiā tanu khīṇu ||
akhī aṅdhu na dīsaī vaṇajāriā mitrā kaṅnī suṇai na vaiṇa ||
....
khaḍu pakī kuḍi bhajai binasai āi calai kiā māṇu ||

– *Ādi Granth*, pp. 75-76

In the first stage the innocent mind has a child-like understanding. The child drinks milk and is fondled so gently and loved by his father and mother. The father and mother love the child so much and get entrapped in the *māyā* of emotional attachment. By destiny of the virtuous actions of the past individual child has come and now should start performing to make his future. One can liberate, only by the name of the Lord. Rememberance of Lord is the remedy to save oneself from all evils.

In the second stage, the individual is entangled with youthhood and beauty. He remains busy in sexual desires. His awareness is blind to the *nāma*. Rāma *nāma* gets out of his heart and he hankers after all other tastes. One loses spiritual intellect, concentration and discipline. He is caught in false practices. Visiting holy places, fasting, bathing at shrines, doing acts of piety, etc. are not enough. Salvation is attained only by loving devotional worship; all other actions lead one to duality.

In the third stage white hair appears upon the surface of the head. Youth runs out and old age wins the ground. As time goes on one's days are limited. At last moment he repents for his follies. When the messenger of death lays his trap, one is carried away from this world. One who used to keep all his things safe and secure for oneself, in an instant, has to leave all behind.

In the fourth stage, one's body grows old and weak and eyes go dim, tongue is unable to taste and one starts living only with

> the help of others. When the crop of life comes to its maturity, it twists, breaks and perishes. One should not be proud of a thing which comes and goes. Without any virtue within, can one find peace?

The above two hymns of Guru Nānak need to be read together. While the one describes the physical development the other describes the mental development in the four phases of life. He calls man a merchant for a night in this world who has come to settle his account in this world to enable him free from the cycle of birth and death. He has divided life into four stages. The first stage explains the prenatal stage when a man is conceived and stays head side down in the mother's womb doing penance and praying to God with his mind fixed on Him. Immediately after birth he sucks milk, is fondled by his parents and others and gets connected to the attachments of *māyā*. His child mind is unconscious. He has come to this world by his past good fortune and to do deeds for his future.

In the second stage, he dances in the hands of his loved ones who feel proud in saying that he is their child and mother and father love their son immensely. But in the later stages, he finds that all these attachments are *māyā*. One is intoxicated by the wine of ripe beauty. All other tastes are sweet but the Lord's name slips and does not come into his heart. So in the second stage he forgets God and comes under the spell of duality.

In the third stage of life, mind is fixed on beauty and riches. One loses head lured by *māyā*. The white hair dawn on one's head, the youth wears out and age wins and one's days are numbered. One accumulates riches and wants to keep all his accumulations with him but forgets that in an instant these will go out of his hands.

In the fourth stage one's crop of life is ready to be plucked. His body is shattered. Eyesight and hearing get weak. One's taste, activity and power are lost. How can one remain peaceful without any virtue? So when the life is ripe it breaks with a click and is destroyed. One cannot be proud of coming and going from this world. When Yama comes and drags one away no one knows where one is gone. Others' wailing over one's death is false and in an instant one becomes a stranger and disappears from this world.

So in the first stage, without the love for the Lord one is drowned for one's love of duality. Second stage is wasted without the art of concentration, doing continence and performing acts of fasting, cleansing one's body in holy dips which cannot emancipate an individual. In the third stage, when one's wisdom departs, and one starts repenting for his evil deeds, one tries to fix his mind on the Lord. In the fourth stage one tries to know the word through his *guru*. He who goes the way of the good and continence is not hurt and gets free from the cycle of birth and death. *Māyā* and death cannot snare him as he swims across the sea of fear with love and devotion. He is merged in the Great Peace. Nānak says that man is saved by truth and through truth he receives honour in the court of God.

Guru Nānak talked about the life lived, wherein he explains mental and physical stages, divided into four, in the above hymns, yet as seen in the first chapter he divides life's journey into nine and ten stages and men's involvement in the world during these stages.

According to Vedic traditions, however, the life time of a man is divided into four stages, namely, *brahmacarya*, *gārhasthya*, *vānaprastha* and *saṁnyāsa*. The first stage is devoted to study and second to the household duties in accordance with the teachings and knowledge acquired from the *guru*. The third, when the hair turned grey, the householder assigns the household duties to the children and retires with his wife to the forests. The final, fourth, stage is culminated with a strictly regulated life, having totally renounced the world and become a wandering monk free from desires and attachments and absorbed in contemplation of *Brahman*. He no longer needs to worship God by means of material articles or even mental symbols. It is for him that the Upaniṣads (which are mostly the concluding portions of the Āraṇyakas) were generally intended.

HAUME (I-NESS)

Guru Nānak speaks of I-ness in his verses as under:

haumai karatiā naha sukhu hoi ।। *manamati jhūṭhī sacā soi* ।।
sagala bigūte bhāvai doi ।। *so kamāvai dhuri likhiā hoi* ।।
aisā jagu dekhiā jūārī ।। *sabhi sukha māgai nāmu bisārī* ।।
....
binu dekhe kahaṇā birathā jāi ।। *guramukhi dīsai sahaji subhāi* ।।
sevā surati eka liva lāi ।।
....
tr̥sanā agani sabadi bujhāe ।। *dūjā bharamu sahaji subhāe* ।।
– *Ādi Granth*, p. 222

One cannot be at peace while acting in ego. The intelligence of mind is false. The Supreme Being is the only Truth. One who loves duality gets crushing defeat. People behave as they are pre-destined. The world is a gamble house. All pray here for peace. But they do not remember the Name of the Lord. No one can see the Almighty. As such He cannot be described. All His descriptions are vague without seeing Him. Those who love God see Him with quick insight within the self, so one should develop that faculty.

haumai karata bhekhī nahī jāniā ।।
guramukhi bhagati virale manu māniā ।।
hau hau karata nahī acu pāīe ।।
haumai jāi parama padu pāīe ।।
....
haumai bandhana bandhi bhavāvai ।।
nānaka rāma bhagati sukhu pāvai ।।
– Ibid., pp. 226-27

When one acts in egotism he cannot approach the Lord even if he wears any sort of religious robes. Only a few seekers of God are able to surrender their minds in the devotional worship. Egotism creates entanglements and leads one to wander all around and get lost. O Nānak! one can attain peace only with devotional worship of the Supreme Being.

Guru Nānak in the above two hymns stresses that if I-ness does not die, the task remains unfulfilled. The mind remains in the grip of duality and evil intent. Only Lord is true. Men seek for pleasures and forget the Lord's name. Through the *guru*'s instruction one is able to enshrine the name of the Lord in his heart, and through the true word, one sings His praises and the fire of his worldly desires is pacified. Within everyone lives the God Himself.

dubidhā duramati adhulī kāra ||
manamukhi bharamai majhi gubāra ||
manu aṅdhulā aṅdhulī mati lāgai ||
gura karaṇī binu bharamu na bhāgai ||
– *Ādi Granth*, p. 1190

One acts blindly when one is in the grip of duality and evil thought. The self-willed persons wander all around and get lost in darkness. The blind man intends to follow the advice of the blind only. Unless one takes refuge in the *guru*'s path his doubts never get cleared.

haumai karī tāṅ tū nahī tū hovahi hau nāhi ||
būjhahu giānī būjhaṇā eha akatha kathā mana māhi ||
– Ibid., pp. 1092-93

When one acts in egotism, then he does not feel the essence of God. Whenever one feels the essence of God he gets rid of all ego. Spiritually enlightened people try to understand that the unspoken word is in the mind.

Guru Nānak explains that when one feels oneness with the Lord, I-ness vanishes, but as long as one feels the sense of I-ness, he cannot realize God.

jiu āraṇi lohā pāi bhaṅni ghaḍāīē ||
tiu sākatu jonī pāi bhavai bhavaīē ||
binu būjhai sabhu dukhu dukhu kamāvaṇā ||
haumai āvai jāi bharami bhulāvaṇā ||
– Ibid., p. 752

As iron is heated in a machine to melt and to get redesigned, the Godless material of individuals is reshaped and forced to wander in circulation. Without true knowledge about the cause of suffering one goes on accumulating more sufferings. One goes on wandering in ego under the spell of doubts and confusion.

In these lines Guru Nānak reminds that individuals are subject to the cycle of coming and going in this world and wander in various forms till they get emancipation.

brahamai garabu kīā nahī jāniā ॥ *beda kī bipati padī pachutāniā* ॥
jaha prabha simare tahī manu māniā ॥
aisā garabu burā saṁsārai ॥ *jisu guru milai tisu garabu nivārai* ॥
– *Adi Granth*, p. 224

Brahmā the deity acted in pride and could not understand the entrapping nature of *māyā*. But when he suffered due to the pain of loss of memory of the Vedas he writhed in repentance. The mind can be won only through remembering the Supreme Lord in meditation. The pride and feeling of duality create horrible experiences. It is a true *guru* who leads one to eliminate and shed off the evil of false pride.

prathame brahamā kālai ghari āiā ॥ *brahama kamalu paiāli na pāiā* ॥
āgiā nahī līnī bharami bhulāiā ॥ *jo upajai so kāli saṁghāriā* ॥
....
māiā mohe devī sabhi devā ॥ *kālu na choḍai binu gura kī sevā* ॥
– Ibid., p. 227

God Brahmā entered the house of death with an idea to get the limits of the Supreme Being. He entered into lotus and searched all the nether regions. But he could not find the end of it. He did not take permission from the Supreme Being for his act and was led by the duality. Whatever is created shall be destroyed by death. All the gods and goddesses also get lured by *māyā*. The cycle of life and death cannot be foregone without service to the *guru*.

In both the above hymns Guru Nānak explains with example of old texts that even the personal gods are not spared by delusion. It is in the event of utmost painful conditions that individuals realize the falsehood of their I-ness and their limitations against the infinity and vastness of the Ultimate Reality.

hau vici āiā hau vici gaiā ॥ *hau vici jiṁmiā hau vici muā* ॥
....
haumai kari kari jaṅta upāiā ॥
haumai būjhai tā daru sūjhai ॥ *giāna vihūṇā kathi kathi lūjhai* ॥

nānaka hukamī likhīē lekhu || *jehā vekhahi tehā vekhu* ||
– *Ādi Granth*, p. 466

Some individuals take birth in egotism; they live life in egotism and die in egotism. One can understand the true nature of the Supreme Lord by understanding the empire of ego. Without higher knowledge one tends to argue and argue. Nānak says that one feels and understands exactly same what is in his mind.

In this hymn Guru Nānak explains that when we do any deed, good or bad, for either fear of punishment, or desire for reward and glory, it further binds us with ego or the I-ness and cannot lead us to emancipation. If one can blot out the ego within, one will realize the gate to deliverance. But without this wisdom, one only rattles and fights worldly duality in vain. We should try to see ourselves as God sees us. We are destined only through God's will.

eko eku kahai sabhu koī haumai garabu viāpai ||
aṅtari bāhari eku pachāṇai iu gharu mahalu siñāpa ||
– Ibid., p. 930

Everyone utters that there is only one God. But they get entangled in egotism and pride. One should realize that the only one God is both inside and outside and in-between. The place of his presence is within the house of one's heart.

Here Guru Nānak explains that people do believe that there is one and only one God but do not realize that He is within as well as outside and in-between also. He has His abode in our heart. It is man's sheer ego that his I-ness dominates his mind.

tatu na cīnai manamukhu jali jāi || *duramati vichuḍi coṭā khāi* ||
mānai hūkamu sabhe guṇa giāna || *nānaka daragaha pāvai mānu* ||
– Ibid., p. 944

The self-willed individuals do not understand the basic element of truth and get blown into dust. One gets separated from the Lord and suffers due to one's evil mindedness. If he accepts the Lord's command he will feel blessed of all virtues and spiritual wisdom.

traiguṇa meṭa sabadu vasāe tā mani cūkai ahaṁkāro ||

aṅtari bāhari eko jāṇai tā hari nāmi lagai piāro॥
– *Ādi Granth*, p. 944

By eliminating the three qualities, one gets hold of the *śabada* within and then his mind gets rid of ego. When he knows that there is only one Lord inside and outside, then he falls in love with the name of the Lord.

kitu kitu bidhi jagu upajai purakhā kitu kitu dukhi binasi jāī॥
haumai vici jagu upajai purakhā nāmi visariē dukhu pāī॥
guramukhi hovai su giānu tatu bīcārai haumai sabadi jalāe॥
– Ibid., p. 946

This world came into existence by the feeling of I-ness or dualism. When one forgets the Lord he suffers and goes dead. One who loves God concentrates on Him and acquires the love, and His essence gets rid of duality. Duality leads one to wander in incarnations. One can attain this state of mind by adhering to *śabada* within oneself.

The above three hymns further explain that by raising oneself above the three qualities of *māyā* and states of consciousness, one should go within and take refuge in *śabada* so that one is able to control the mind.

dūjī duramati aṅnī bolī॥ *kāma krodha kī kucī colī*॥
ghari varu sahaju na jāṇai॥ *chohari binu pira nīda na pāī hai*॥
aṅtari agani jale bhaḍakāre॥ *manamukhu take kuṅdā cāre*॥
– Ibid., p. 1022

Duality and evil mind make the soul bride blind and deaf. She wears the clothes of the physical desires and anger. Her husband resides in her own heart but she cannot recognize Him. She feels the pain of separation and cannot sleep. *Manamukhas* look around all the ways but cannot understand it.

bhari jobani mai mata peīaḍai ghari pāhuṇī balirāma jīu॥
mailī avagaṇa citi binu gura guṇa na samāvanī balirāma jīū॥
guṇa sāra na jāṇī bharami bhulāṇī jobanu bādi gavāiā॥
varu gharu daru darasanu nahī jātā pira kā sahaju na bhāiā॥
– Ibid., p. 763

> Youthhood intoxicates one, and one does not understand that he is only like a guest at his parent's home (world). His consciousness gets spoilt with shortcomings and mistakes; without the guidance of a *guru* one cannot attain virtue. One who does not know the value of virtue is subject to doubtfulness. One wastes away his youth in vain. If one does not know the Supreme Lord, His heavenly abode or experiences the bliss of His holi glimpses, one cannot get the pleasure of heavenly peace.

In the above hymns Guru Nānak describes the agony of a man under the spell of dualism, who realizes and feels the separation from God as very painful. His condition is like a bride who feels the agony of separation from her husband as unbearable.

> *hau muā mai māriā pauṇu vahai darīāu* ||
> *tr̥sanā thakī nānakā jā manu ratā nāi* ||
> – *Ādi Granth*, p. 1091

> Man dies internally because of his ego. The sense of I-ness finishes one completely. The breath goes on flowing like a river to keep one alive. But one's desires come to end only when one comes under the spell of *nāma*.

Guru Nānak believes that all creation is but the God Himself. There is nothing other than Him. However when one develops the sense of ego and the seed of I-ness sprouts in him, he is misled and falls into the trap of *māyā*. I-ness takes an individual away from God.

This expression in his hymns is aptly comparable with the following lines from the Upaniṣads:

> *yatra hi dvaitamiva bhavati taditara itaraṁ jighrati taditaraitaraṁ paśyati taditara itaraṁ śr̥ṇoti taditara itaraṁabhivadati taditara itaraṁ manute taditara itaraṁ vijānāti yatra vā asya sarvamātmaivābhūttatkena kaṁ jighrettatkena kaṁ paśyettatkena kaṁ śr̥ṇuyāttatkena kamabhivadettat kena kaṁ manvīta, tatkena kaṁ vijānīyādyenedaṁ sarvaṁ vijānāti taṁ kena vijānīyadvijñātāramare kena vijānīyāditi* ||
> – *Br̥hadāraṇyaka Upaniṣad* 2.4.14

> For where there is duality as it were, there one smells another, there one sees another, there one hears another, there one speaks

> another, there one thinks another, there one understands another. Where, verily, everything has become the self, then by what and whom should one smell, then by what and whom should one see, then by what and whom should one hear, then by what and whom should one speak, then by what and by whom one should understand? By what should one know that by which all this is known? By what my dear, should one know the knower?

This is a concluding conversation between Yājñavalkya and Maitreyī about the two forms of reality and the Absolute Self. One is formed and another is formless, the mortal and immortal, the moving and unmoving, the actual (existent) and the true (being). This has been illustrated like this: if we put a spoon of salt into water it gets dissolved into water. We cannot take it back but every drop of water tastes salty.

Unlike the Vedic traditions wherein the life period is divided into four stages of learning (*brahmacarya*), household duties (*gṛhastha*), retirement from active life (*vānaprastha*) and life of renunciation (*saṁnyāsa*), Guru Nānak explains the four stages of physical and psychological development of individuals as traditional practical life being followed. He also portrays the ten stages of life of an individual in actual life and his involvement with the world at different levels. He emphasizes the need for developing a right approach in every stage of life which helps one to lead to his final aim of finding an everlasting peace and union with God.

The Upaniṣads teach that a learned man finds all beings in Self and Self in all beings. The thought of duality or I-ness takes a man away from the Ultimate Reality. Man suffers in feeling himself to be other than Self. Where there is I-ness there is no God and where there is God there cannot be the ego of I-ness. Guru Nānak also emphasizes time and again in his hymns that I-ness takes an individual away from God. Self-willed persons wander in this world and get lost. When the seed of I-ness sprouts he develops ego and falls into the trap of *māyā*. One who comes, lives and goes in ego of I-ness cannot be liberated from the rotation in births and deaths. When the mind is imbued with *nāma*, one's all other desires are exhausted and one inclines to be one with God.

The World Struggle and Suffering in the World

Guru Nānak describes the suffering in the world in many of his hymns:

> *cāri padāratha lai jagi janamiā siva sakati ghari vāsu dhare* ||
> *lāgī bhūkha māiā magu johai mukati padārathu mohi khare* ||
> *karaṇa palāva kare nahī pāvai ita uta ḍhūḍhata thāki pare* ||
> *kāmi krodhi ahaṁkāri viāpe kūḍa kuṭaṁba siha prīti kare* ||
> *khāvai bhogai suṇi suṇi dekhai pahiri dikhāvai kāla ghare* ||
> ....
> *jetā mohu haumai kari bhūle merī merī karate chīni khare* ||
>
> – *Ādi Granth*, p. 1014

One takes birth to attain four great objectives of life. But the spirit gets attached to the world of *māyā*. One's hunger for the worldly things leads him to the path of *māyā*'s riches and his emotional entanglements take away his possessions of liberation. He weeps and cries for these unreal things but is unable to get all what he desires. He hankers in all directions and gets tired. With strong sexual desires, bad temper and egotism, he gets attracted to relatives. He indulges in eating and enjoying, listening and watching, and dressings up to show off his possessions. Under the deep spell of egotism and attachments he cries out "mine, mine" and starts getting away from himself. When his body becomes weak and wealth diminishes, he becomes sceptic and cynical. In the long run he laments and regrets and crashes into dust.

In this hymn Guru Nānak says that man is born for attaining the four (*dharma, artha, kāma* and *mokṣa*) of life, but he takes to the path of illusion. He binds himself to the enjoyments and attachments in the world forgetting that he has to go back. He weeps, cries and runs after the world and gets tired. But his ego does not let him rest and he is caught in the web of false illusions and evil pursuits and suffers without the guidance of a *guru*'s word.

> *janame kau bājahi vādhāe* || *sohilaḍe agiānī gāe* ||
> *jo janamai tisu sarapara maraṇā kiratu paiā siri sāhā he* ||
> *saṅjogu vijogu merai prabhi kīe* || *sr̥saṭi upāi dukhā sukha dīe* ||
>
> – Ibid., p. 1032

> At the time of birth, people convey happiness and congratulations. They celebrate the birth with singing songs of joy. One forgets that whosoever takes birth is destined to die by the writ of one's previous actions written upon one's forehead by the Supreme Being. Unions and separations were the work of the Almighty. While creating this universe He poured both pain and pleasure into it.

In the above lines Guru Nānak says that there are many festivities when one is born. Unwise people sing the songs of joy forgetting that one who is born is to die also. God has given pleasure and pain, union and separation together and one should remain detached.

nā bhaiṇā bharajāīā nā se sasuḍīāha ||
sacā sāku na tuṭaī guru mele sahīāha ||
balihārī gura āpaṇe sada balihārai jāu ||
gura binu etā bhavi thakī guri piru melimu ditamu milāi ||
phuphī nānī māsīā dera jeṭhānaḍīāha ||
ābani vaññani nā rahani pūra bhare pahīāha ||
māme tai māmāṇīā bhāira bāpa na māu ||
sātha laḍe tina nāṭhīā bhīḍa ghaṇī darīāu ||
sācau raṅgi raṅgāvalo sakhī hamāro kaṅtu ||

– *Ādi Granth*, p. 1015

> None of the worldly relations like sisters, sisters-in-law, brothers and other relations shall remain forever. All these shall get rolled up. It is only the relation with the Supreme Being that is everlasting and shall never come to end. It is created by the Lord Himself. My entire sister-soul brides of the Lord should understand it. Guru Nānak further explains that one wanders all around without a *guru* and gets tired; when one finds a *guru* he unites the individual in the union with the Supreme Being. The worldly relations of aunts and uncles, grand parents and sisters-in-law, etc. they come and go; they are like passengers catching the same boat for a moment. They cannot be everlasting. The boat gets filled with a large number of passengers at the bank of a river. The Supreme Being has a deep colour of the Truth . . . .

Guru Nānak emphasizes that none of the worldly relations will last longer with us. All are bound for separation as and when their turn comes. Only God, the True Lord, shall always be with you. All seasons are blessed when one loves God. The love of God makes one forget every illusionary world relations.

dukha vici jaṁmaṇu dukhi maraṇu dukhi varataṇu saṁsāri ||
dukhu dukhu agai ākhīē paḍhi paḍhi karahi pukāra ||
dukha kīā paṅḍā khulhīā sukhu na nikalio koi ||
dukha vici jīu jalāiā dukhīā calīā roi ||
nānaka siphatī ratiā manu tanu hariā hoi ||
dukha kīā agī mārīahi bhī dukhu dārū hoi ||

– *Ādi Granth*, p. 1240

An individual who takes birth in pain and remains in pain while living his life, dies in pain. For him there is pain and only pain even after he goes to other world. Such an individual ever remains in pain and goes on crying. The pain gets released in packages; peace does not come out. Such a soul emerges in pain and departs crying and wailing. But if one gets filled with the love of God and praises the Supreme Being, his mind and body blossom forth and he gets a new enthusiasm in life. Some individuals die in the fear of suffering but suffering is also a remedy if it is for the right spiritual cause.

In this hymn Guru Nānak explains as to how pain is part of the very existence of human life. The birth, life, death and in between all these there is pain. Man gets of pain and becomes rejuvenated only in the company of the true Lord.

dukhu vichoḍā iku dukhu bhūkha ||
iku dukhu sakata vāra jamadūta ||
eku dukhu rogu lagai tani dhāi || *vaida na bhole dārū lāi* ||
daradu hovai dukhu rahai sarīra || *aisā dārū lagai na bīra* ||
khasamu visāri kīe rasa bhoga || *tāṅ tani uṭhi khaloe roga* ||
mana aṅdhe kau milai sajāi ||
....
caṅdana kā phalu caṅdana vāsu || *māṇasa kā phalu ghaṭa mahi sāsu* ||
sāsi gaiē kāiā ḍhali pāi || *tā kai pāchai koi na khāi* ||
kaṅcana kāiā niramala haṁsu || *jisu mahi nāmu niraṅjana aṁsu* ||

dūkha roga sabhi gaiā gavāi || *nānaka chūṭasi sācai nāi* ||
– *Ādi Granth*, p. 1256

> There is pain of separation, there is pain of hunger, yet there is a different pain: of mighty hangman of death. There is pain from the diseases which eat up this body. Even if a doctor provides medicines pain continues and body suffers. Individuals enjoy the pleasures of senses and diseases crop up in the body. This is a punishment to the ignorant individuals. The sandalwood is valued for its good flavour; importance of human body ends with the stop of breathing. As the breath is taken back, the body gets crushed into dust. After that there is no need for food, etc. The human body is valuable and the soul in it is stainless and pure. If, even, a tiny spark of the heavenly *nāma* is lighted within it, suffering and pain shall get vanished. An individual is protected by the true *nāma*. . . .

In this hymn Guru Nānak speaks of conditions in which one feels pains. The separation from our loved ones is painful. Poverty and hunger are yet another cause of pain. One does not get what he desires and getting what he is afraid of is also painful. The disease consumes one's body, and in spite of medicines given to him, he continues to suffer. This is also painful. The most fearful is the pain of death which engulfs one without any schedule or intimation. He emphasizes that the sensual pleasures bring disease to the body. As the sandalwood is valued for its fragrance, the body is valued as long as there is life in it. The body crumbles down when the breath is taken away. The body is golden with immaculate soul in it. A tiny particle of immaculate *nāma* within the body can get rid of all pains and diseases.

lakha siu prīti hovai lakha jīvaṇu kiā khusīā kiā cāu ||
vichuḍiā visu hoi vichoḍā eka ghaḍī mahi jāi ||
je sau varhiā miṭhā khājai bhi phiri kauḍā khāi ||
miṭhā khādhā citi na āvai kauḍataṇu dhāi jāi ||
miṭhā kauḍā dovai roga || *nānaka aṅti vigute bhoga* ||
....
kāpaḍu kāṭhu raṅgāiā rāṅgi || *ghara gaca kīte bāge bāga* ||
....

je phiri miṭhā peḍai pāi ।। *tau kauḍataṇa cūkasi māi* ।।
nānaka gurasukhi pāvai soi ।। *jisa no prāpati likhiā hoi* ।।
– *Ādi Granth*, p. 1243

One may fall in love with a number of relations and live for a long period, but what kind of pleasure these relations can give him, when he is sure to be destined to separate from them. Even if he eats sweets for a very long period, he has to taste the bitter items also in life. One cannot always enjoy only sweet things. The moment one tastes bitter he forgets all sweets and bitterness prevails for a long time. So both the sweet and bitter are not good tastes and may cause suffering. Individuals finish themselves by their involvements and worry for short-lived affairs. They get best dresses and furniture of different colours to decorate their houses and paint their houses beautifully white. They go on playing their games for pleasure and show off. When they have to appear before the Supreme Lord, they shall falter. O Nānak! the men of God are blessed to receive what they are predestined to receive.

Here Guru Nānak talks of strifes in life. One may love innumerable persons or relations in life, but should not forget that all of them shall stand separated at one or another time. One may enjoy the sweets as much as one can, yet has to taste the bitter in life. Both sweet and bitter are causes of disease. Similarly all the possessions of worldly value are like tasting the bitter mistaking it as sweet. One should not strive for worldly accumulations and emotional attachments with the worldly relations as these bring bitter taste in the end and make the life more painful.

māiā mohi sagala jagu chāiā ।। *kāmaṇi dekhi kāmi lobhāiā* ।।
suta kañcana siu hetu vadhāiā ।। *sabhu kichu apanā iku rāmu parāiā* ।।
aisā jāpu japau japamālī ।। *dukha sukha parahari bhagati nirālī* ।।
– Ibid., p. 1342

Māyā has spread its wings all over the world. People are engrossed in emotional attachment. Men are getting sexually excited by the evil beauty of women. Individuals are attracted to accumulate gold and wealth by all means and they are getting more and more attached to their family. One considers wealth and family as his safety but has forgotten to own God as the most near benefactor. One should meditate and chant such a true name that may raise him above pleasure and pain of this world and engage him in devotional worship of the Lord.

In this hymn Guru Nānak tells that the canopy of desires is spread all over the world. Everyone is deeply inflicted and stung with lust, gold, riches and emotional attachment to sons and thinks all these are his own. Yet one does not own God. He advises to meditate on and chant His name as the only way out to raise above the condition of pain and pleasure.

sahaṁsara dāna de indru roāiā॥ *parasarāmu rovai ghari āiā*॥
ajai su rovai bhīkhiā khāī॥ *aisī daragaha milai sajāī*॥
rovai rāmu nikālā bhaiā॥ *sītā lakhamaṇu vichuḍi gaiā*॥
rovai dahasiru laṅka gavāī॥ *jini sītā ādī ḍaurū vāī*॥
rovai pāṇḍava bhae majūra॥ *jina kai suāmī rahata hadūrī*॥
rovai janamejā khui gaiā॥ *ekī kāraṇi pāpī bhaiā*॥
rovahi sekha masāika pīra॥ *aṅti kāli matu lāgai bhīḍa*॥
rovahi rāje kaṅna paḍāī॥ *ghari ghari māgahi bhikhiā jāī*॥
rovahi kirapana saṅcahi dhanu jāī॥ *paṅḍita rovahi giānu gavāī*॥
bālī rovai nāhi bhatārū॥ *nānaka dukhīā sabhu saṁsārū*॥
maṅne nāu soī jiṇi jāī॥ *aurī karama na lekhai lāī*॥

– *Adi Granth*, pp. 953-54

The men of name and fame suffer in life. Indra cried in shame, when branded with thousands of marks of disgrace. Paraśurāma came back home weeping. Ajai was offered manure to eat which he had given in charity and he wept. Rāma cried on being sent to forests and was separated from Lakṣmaṇa and Sītā. Ten-headed Rāvaṇa who stole Sītā wept when he lost Lanka. Pāṇḍavas were made slaves and wept even though they once lived in the presence of Lord. Janamejaya wept when he lost his way and became sinner for one mistake.

The *sheikhs*, *pīrs* and spiritual leaders weep at end when they get pain and suffering. The miser weeps when he has to leave behind the wealth he has accumulated. The *paṇḍitas* weep when their knowledge and learning is gone. The young woman weeps on losing her spouse. Nānak says that everyone in this world suffers. One who has faith in God and practises the true name gets out of suffering.

gotamu tapā ahaliā isatrī tisu dekhi iṅdru lubhāiā॥
sahasa sarīra cihana bhaga hūe tā mani pachotāiā॥
koī jāṇi na bhūlai bhāī॥
so bhūlai jisu āpi bhulāe būjhai jisai bujhāī॥
tini harīcaṅdi pṛthamī pati rājai kāgadi kīma na pāī॥
avagaṇu jāṇai ta puṅna kare kiu kiu nekhāsi bikāī॥
karau aḍhāī dharatī māṅgī bāvana rūpi bahānai॥
kiu paiāli jāi kiu chalīē je bali rūpu pachānai॥
rājā janamejā de matīṅ baraji biāsi paḍhāiā॥
tinhi kari jaga aṭhāraha ghāe kiratu na calai calāiā॥
gaṇata na gaṇīṅ hukamu pachāṇā bolī bhāi subhāī॥
– *Ādi Granth*, pp. 1343-44

Guru Nānak, quoting eight events from the historically known characters, explains the effect of *karma* upon an individual leading him to suffer in this world. The above two hymns of Guru Nānak need to be read together as these contain the two aspects of suffering with illustrations by quoting well-known characters and the conclusion of his thoughts. The first hymn concludes with a most popular message being chanted as a household quote:

nānaka dukhīā sabhu saṁsāru।

Everyone in this world is drowned in sorrows and pain. He gives examples of well-known characters who suffered in spite of their all worldly possessions and power due to their ego. In the second hymn he is more philosophical and speaks from the higher platform of consciousness for conclusion that one does not knowingly commit mistakes for which one has to suffer. In spite of all knowledge and virtue; one is entrapped into commit mistakes and suffer.

In both the above hymns he refers to same historical characters of the stories with a message and moral value explained below:

Indra cried in shame: Indra the senior god, on seeing the beauty of Ahilyā, wife of Gautama, developed lust in his mind for her. Disguised as the *ṛṣi* in his absence, he managed to sneak into her bed. When the *ṛṣi* came back, he found Indra with his wife, he cursed him with thousands of marks of disgrace on his body for this evil. So Indra cried and wept and did not return to his Indrapurī for a long time.

According to a legend narrated in the *Mahābhārata*, King Kārtavīrya Arjuna, destroyed Ṛṣi Jamadagni's hermitage and captured the calf of Kāmadhenu. To retreive the calf, Paraśurāma, the youngest son of Jamadagni, a brāhmaṇa warrior, killed King Kārtavīrya Arjuna, whose sons, in turn, killed Jamadagni. Stricken by grief and anger, Paraśurāma killed the king's sons and warriors, and destroyed the entire kṣatriya race twenty-one times and saw his father's resurrection by the divine grace. Thus he himself left the world in great agony.

King Ajai cried and wept: King Ajai was considered to be a great and bountiful king. One day after distributing alms he went to his stable. A *mahātmā* came asking for alms. But the king told him that he came late after he distributed all alms for the day. However the *mahātmā* insisted the king to offer him anything. The king became impatient and noticed some horse dung nearby. He took a handful of it and put it in the begging bowl of the *mahātmā*. After some time, the king was out on hunting in the forest, he came across a *sādhu* sitting in deep meditation. The king asked him for some water. He was told to go inside the hut for a drink. When the king entered his hut he found a large stake of horse dung. He was surprised that there was no horse nearby then where did this dung come from. He was told by the *sādhu* that handful of dung as alms was given to him by King Ajai which grew day by day. The king was shocked and asked for its disposal. The story goes on. In the last, a very small portion was left. He was advised to get the dung dried and mix it with sugar and then eat a little every day, otherwise the dung heap will continue to grow day by day. So he was made to eat what he had given as alms.

Lord Rāma wept: Lord Rāma wept and cried in pain when Rāvaṇa took away his wife Sītā by deceit. He wept in pain when Lakṣmaṇa, his brother, went unconscious during their fight with Rāvaṇa.

The ten-headed Rāvaṇa wept in agony: Rāvaṇa kidnapped Sītā. But when he lost Laṅkā he was agonized and wept in pain.

Pāṇḍavas wept: Pāṇḍavas, the five brave sons of King Pāṇḍu, were made slaves and wept when they lost everything in gambling even though they lived a life in Lord's fear and God was always present with them.

King Janamejaya wept: Ṛṣi Vyāsa foretold the King Janamejaya that he will face disaster and he should try to escape it using his wisdom and intelligence and should avoid three things.

1. Do not buy a horse and ride on it to the east direction.
2. If you do so, do not bring the woman whom you meet on the way to your home and marry her.
3. If you do so, do not perform *yajña* at her request.

The king was enticed by a beautiful horse being sold by a trader. Thinking that this will be a prestigious possession and he can avoid riding it to the east, he purchased it. The moment he tried to ride it the horse ran and he lost the direction and went into a deep forest. He met there a woman crying in pain as she had lost her way home and approached him to save her from the wild animals and take her away from that place. He brought her home and attracted by her beauty and innocence, he fell in love with and married her. After some time she persuaded him to perform *yajña* and offer food to the brāhmaṇas. After the *yajña* and serving food to all the brāhmaṇas she told the king that all brāhmaṇas were looking at her beauty with evil intention. He got furious and took out his sword and killed all the brāhmaṇas present there. The effect of past *karma* cannot be eradicated and it must be settled.

aṅdhule kī mati aṅdhalī bolī āi gaiā dukhu tāhā he॥
dukha mahi janamai dukha mahi maraṇā॥
dūkhu na miṭai binu gura kī saraṇā॥
dūkhī upajai dūkhī binasai kiā lai āiā lai jāhā he॥

– *Ādi Granth*, p. 1033

> An ignorant man thinks and speaks in ignorance. Without the higher knowledge, one suffers the pain of coming and going. Such an individual takes birth in pain and dies in pain. He cannot get rid of pain unless he meets a *guru* who shows him the right path. He should understand that he did not bring anything along with him to this world, nor he shall be able to carry anything along with him when he is called back.

In these lines Guru Nānak explains that man in his darkness due to lack of knowledge acts blindly and falls into the trap of births and deaths. *Guru* is the dispeller of darkness who can show him the way.

saṁsāru bhavajalu kiu tarai ||
guramukhi nāmu nirañjanu pāīē aphario bhāru aphāru ṭarāī ||
– *Ādi Granth*, p. 1013

> One can be carried away across the troubling sea of this world. Only heavenly name of the Supreme Being obtained from true *guru* can eliminate all the sins of an individual who is aired up with false ego.

Guru Nānak gives a hope that this terrible world ocean can be crossed under the guidance of a true *guru* who can unite the individual with the True Lord.

The Upaniṣads describe that man suffers for his own deeds and desires, who weaves the net of *karma* around himself and falls into the trap of the cycle of birth and death. If life is a struggle and suffering, then how to get out of it? What is the hope for the mankind?

The following verse from the *Muṇḍaka Upaniṣad* explains that the desires are the cause of rebirth and suffering. By living a life of virtue and perfect life all the desires can be vanished to clear the way for getting out of the cycle of birth and death.

kāmānyaḥ kāmayate manyamānaḥ
sa kāmabhirjāyate tatra tatra |
paryāptakāmasya kr̥tātmanastu
ihaiva sarve pravilīyanti kāmāḥ ||
– *Muṇḍaka Upaniṣad* 3.2.2

> One who is under the spell of desires continues to think about them. His thinking of strong desires puts him in the cycle of rebirths. But one who gets rid of all his desires by way of self-realization and becomes peaceful he can attain this position even here on earth in this life.

All the above references to the old mythical/historical stories included in the two hymns of Guru Nānak describe how a man is enticed by his ego, false honour, anger, lust, wish to grab other's share and predestined deeds to suffer agony and pain in life. Each of the episodes included in these hymns gives a moral lesson making it an interesting reading. Irrespective of the status, power and intelligence everyone has to suffer the pain to settle his accounts of past or present deeds. There is suffering all around due to his own *karma*, but when one is imbued with Lord's praises one gets rejuvenated. The Upaniṣads also stress that one who lives a perfect life can eliminate all his desires in this life itself by Self-realization and end all the sufferings.

4

God's Love and Grace in Life

A CHILD'S birth in a family is one of a wonderful experience. People celebrate it beating the drums, distributing sweets, throwing parties, and everyone is very keen to carry the newborn into arms thinking what he has brought to the world. No one knows anything about his past or future life. What does his first cry denote? Does he cry for his separation from someone known to or dear to him? Does he feel as if he has been hurled down the drain with closed eyes into a new world? What is this world before him? Is it real or unreal? As he grows up and finds many attractions of the world around him, he is fascinated and is entrapped in their enjoyment. In spite of all attractions of the world sometimes he weeps and cries to see someone whom he has never seen but feels His presence everywhere and considers that his real love and benefactor is someone else than the worldly relations. He finds no meaning in the daily routine and feels unsatisfied. He gropes in darkness and cries for help. Who can show him the way out of the darkness around him?

Individual's love and attraction for God experiences reciprocal love and grace of God. God cares for His creation and makes the individuals feel for His bounty. It is only because of the love of the all merciful for mankind that He established aperture and the way to God-realization within the human body. There is the need for a true *guru* who may dispel all darkness and show him the way to the higher regions within him.

Role of Guru

Guru has been given a very high status and pivotal role in the spiritual progress of an individual. The parable of a blind man in the *Kaṭha Upaniṣad* considers a teacher as being as essential as a remover of a bandage of a blindfolded man who wishes to find his way home. We have our real home in the abode of *sat* (being). We are bound by our worldly desires which make our eyes blind. When we meet a man who has got rid of all these bondages and has realized Self, he opens our bandage of ignorance from our eyes and makes us believe that this world is not our home and we belong to eternity. Our stay in this world is short and temporary and by meaningful living we can unite with our Lord.

There is a small but popular story about Alexander the Great. He was once asked: "Why do you show greater respect and reverence to your instructor than to your father?" He answered: "My father brought me down from heaven to earth but my teacher raised me from the earth to heaven". Father gives a perishable existence, but from his spiritual teacher one obtains life eternal. A true *guru* is sometimes placed above the personal deity because it is he who makes one feel the presence of his deity.

The Upaniṣads are vehicles of spiritual illumination. Role of a teacher is highlighted at every step. These prescribe the instructions for both the seekers and the teacher as to how the wisdom and experiences of the seers are to be communicated. Some references from the principal Upaniṣads are quoted below:

parīkṣya lokānkarmacitānbrāhmaṇo nirvedamāyānnāstyakṛtaḥ kṛtena ।
tadvijñānārthaṁ sa gurumevābhigacchetsamitpāṇiḥ śrotriyaṁ brahmaniṣṭham ॥
– *Muṇḍaka Upaniṣad* 1.2.12

Having scrutinized the worlds won by works, let a seeker arrive at non-attachment. The world that is not made is not won by what is done. For the sake of his knowledge, let him approach a teacher who is learned in the scriptures and established in *Brahman*.

tasmai sa vidvānupasannāya samyak praśāntacittāya samanvitaya ।
yenākṣaraṁ puruṣaṁ veda satyaṁ provāca tāṁ tattvato brahmavidyām ॥
– Ibid. 1.2.13

A teacher, who knows about *Brahman*, should teach the

knowledge of *Brahman* to the seeker who approaches him in a proper way, whose mind is tranquil and peaceful.

te tamarcayantastvaṁ hi naḥ pitā yo 'smākamavidyāyāḥ paraṁ pāraṁ tārayasīiti namaḥ paramaṛṣibhyo namaḥ parama-ṛṣibhyaḥ || – *Praśna Upaniṣad* 6.8

They (pupils) appreciated him (the teacher) and said that he is the real father to them who will take them to the other side of the ignorance. They repeatedly offered their salutations to the supreme seers.

The teacher who helps us to know the truth is the spiritual father as compared to the physical father (*śarīra mātram janayati*).

śravaṇāyāpi bahubhiryo na labhyah śṛṇvanto 'pi bahavo yaṁ na vidyuḥ |
āścaryo vaktā kuśalo 'sya labdhaścaryo jñātā kuśalānuśiṣṭaḥ ||
na narenāvareṇa prokta eṣa suvijñeyo bahudhā cintyāmānaḥ |
ananyaprokte gatiryatra nāstyaṇīyānhyatarkyamaṇupramāṇāt ||
naiṣā tarkeṇa matirāpaneyā proktānyenaiva sujñānāya preṣṭhā |
yāṁ tvamāpaḥ satyadhṛtirbatāsi tvādṛṅno bhūyānnaciketaḥ praṣṭā || –*Kaṭha Upaniṣad* 1.2.7-9

He who cannot be even heard by many, whom many, even hearing, do not know, wondrous is he who can teach (Him) and skilful is he who finds (Him) and wondrous is he who knows, even when instructed by the wise.

Taught by an inferior man He cannot be truly understood, as He is thought of many ways. Unless taught by one who knows Him as himself, there is no going thither for it is inconceivable, being subtler than the subtle.

Not by reasoning is this apprehension attainable, but dearest taught by another, it is well understood. Thou hast obtained it, holding fast to truth. Many we find Naciketā, an enquirer like thee.

yathā saumya puruṣaṁ gandhārebhyo 'bhinaddhākṣamānīya taṁ tat 'tijane visṛjetsa yathā tatra prāṅvodaṅvādharāṅvā pratyaṅvā pradhmāyītābhinaddhākṣa ānīto 'bhinaddhākṣo visṛṣṭaḥ || – *Chāndogya Upaniṣad* 6.14.1

> My dear, one might lead a person away from the Gāndhāras with his eyes bandaged and abandon him in a place where there are no human beings. Just as that person would shout towards the east or north or south or west, I have been led here with my eyes bandaged, I have been left here with my eyes bandaged.

In these lines Śvetaketu's father (Āruṇi Uddālaka) explains to him the need for a teacher through illustration of a blind man searching for the way.

> *tasya yathābhinahanaṁ pramucya prabrūyādetāṁ diśaṁ gandhārā etaṁ diśaṁ vrajeti sa grāmādgrāmaṁ pṛcchan paṇḍito medhāvī gandhārānevopasaṁpadyetaivamevehācāryavān puruṣo veda tasya tāvadeva ciraṁ yāvanna vimokṣye 'tha saṁpatsya iti* ||
>
> – Ibid. 6.14.2

> And as, if one released his bondage and told him, in that direction are the Gāndhāras, go in that direction; thereupon being informed and capable of judgement, he would be asking his way from village to village and arrive at Gāndhāra; in exactly the same manner does one here who has a teacher know, "I shall remain here only as long as I shall not be released (from ignorance). Then I shall reach perfection".

> *sa yathādrairdhāgnerabhyāhitātpṛthagdhūmā viniścaranty-evaṁ vā ar 'sya mahato bhūtasya niḥśvasitametadyadṛgvedo yajurvedaḥ sāmavedo 'tharvāṅgirasa itihāsaḥ purāṇam vidyā upaniṣadaḥ ślokāḥ sūtrānyanuvyākhyānāni vyākhyānāny-asyaivaitāni sarvāṇi niḥśvasitāni* ||
>
> – *Bṛhadāraṇyaka Upaniṣad* 2.4.10

> As from a lighted fire laid with damp fuel, various (clouds of) smoke issue forth, even so my dear, the *Ṛgveda*, the *Yajurveda*, the *Sāmaveda*, the *Atharvāṅgirasa*, history, ancient lore, sciences, Upaniṣads, verses, aphorisms, explanations and commentaries, from this, indeed, breathed forth.

In the following lines Yājñavalkya explains to his wife Maitreyī that the indwelling essence of all, that is *Ātman*, needs to be realized through hearing, reflection and meditation.

ātmā vā are draṣṭavyaḥ śrotavyo mantavyo nididhyāsitavyo maitreyātma vā are darśanena śravaṇena matyā vijñānenedaṁ sarvaṁ viditam ||
– *Bṛhadāraṇyaka Upaniṣad* 2.4.5

O Maitreyī, it is the Self that should be realized, should be heard of, reflected and meditated upon. By realization of the Self, my dear, through hearing, reflection and meditation, all this is known.

Thus time of the seeker is divided into threefold, i.e. hearing of scriptures, reflection on their meaning and practise meditation. A Self-realized guide is a must for the first two steps before making personal efforts to lead one to the goal of Self-realization.

Guru Nānak also laid stress for the need of a true *guru* without whom ignorance cannot be dispelled. His hymns portray a very vivid picture for the requirement of a *guru*. He declares again and again that there is no salvation without a true *guru*. He advises that when a *guru* is found one should run after him with full devotion for his spiritual progress. Whatever one may try, he cannot attain salvation without a *guru*. He equally advises the seekers to devote themselves to the service of the *guru*. His hymns explain how by serving his *guru* one is attuned to the Lord and progresses in his spiritual journey.

Guru Nānak pays rich tributes to a true *guru* and describes how he was benefited from service to his *guru*. The selected hymns have been divided into three parts for facilitation in depicting his declarations about the need for a *guru*, serving the true *guru*, homage's or tributes paid to a true *guru*.

(A) NO SALVATION WITHOUT A TRUE GURU

bana mahi bhūlī je phirā binu gura būjha na pāu ||
nāvahu bhūlī je phirā phiri phiri āvau jāu ||
puchahu jāi padhāūā cale cākara hoi ||
....
aisa satiguru je milai tā sahaje lae milāi ||
kasi kasavaṭī lāīē parakhe hitu citu lāi ||
....

suṇi mana bhūle bāvare gura kī caraṇī lāgu ||
hari japi nāmu dhiāi tū jamu ḍarapai dukha bhāgu ||
– *Ādi Granth*, p. 57

If one loses his way and wanders in the forests, he cannot find the way out without a *guru*. If he forgets the name of the Supreme Being and roams bewildered here and there, he shall remain rotating in reincarnations. One should follow and learn from the travellers on this path as to how one may walk as a slave. If one finds such a *guru* who can lead to that path then the Lord can be approached with ease. He brings individuals to his touchstone to test our faith. Listen, O confused and lost mind, hold the feet of a *guru* with strong belief. Utter and concentrate on the name of God, fear of death will go away and all your pains shall disappear.

In this hymn Guru Nānak compares this world to a forest where one finds it difficult to know the right path. There is the need of a guide who has gone through the path and can lead one to the right direction. He says that if one meets such a *guru*, his way to God-realization becomes easy as the *guru* brings the individual to the point of touchstone where his intuitive powers develop. He advises the individual to catch hold of the feet of the *guru* earnestly and follow him by uttering the name of the Lord and meditate.

bharamai bhāhi na vijhavai je bhavai disaṅtara desū ||
aṅtari mailu na utarai dhṛgu jīvaṇu dhṛgu vesū ||
horu kitai bhagati na hovaī binu satigura ke upadesa ||
– Ibid., p. 22

The burning doubts do not disappear by roaming in stranger places and forests. One should clean oneself from within, otherwise individual life shall get polluted. Without the guidance and the teaching of a true *guru* one cannot find any other way for devotional worship.

Guru Nānak emphasizes that there is no other way than to go through a Self-realized *guru* for God-realization. The fire of doubts is extinguished and the inner self is cleaned, Only with a *guru*'s word.

satiguri agai aradāsi kari sājanu dei milāī ||
sājani miliē sukhu pāiā jamadūta mue bikhu khāī ||
nāvai aṅdari hau vasāṁ nāu vasai mani āī ||
bājhu gurū gubāru hai binu sabadai būjha na pāī ||
guramatī paragāsu hoi saci rahai liva lāī ||
tithai kālu na saṅcarai jotī joti samāī ||

– *Ādi Granth*, p. 55

One should offer humble prayer to his true *guru* for uniting him with the noble Supreme Being. One can find peace only by realizing the Supreme Lord. The messenger of death shall get poisoned and one's fear for death will go away. Guru Nānak always lived deep within himself with the name of the Lord. Without an adept *guru* there is total ignorance all around. One cannot develop knowledge of *śabada* without a true *guru*. Through the teachings of the *guru* one shall gain this knowledge and gets absorbed in the love of the True Lord. Death does not reach there and your light gets absorbed in His light.

In this hymn Guru Nānak says that one's mind is illuminated and tuned to the Truth by *guru*'s wisdom. Without a *guru* there is all darkness and the *guru* is the dispeller of that darkness.

gura saraṇi na āīē brahamu na pāīē ||
bharami bhulāīē janami mari āīē ||
jamadari bādhau marai bikāru || *nā ridai nāmu na sabadu acāru* ||
....
gura kai bhāṇai karama kamāvai || *nānaku sāce sāci samāvai* ||

– Ibid., pp. 904-05

God (*Brahman*) cannot be found without getting into the protection of a *guru*. Due to worldly attachments and doubts one is bound to take birth again and again. He remains tied and entangled with the hook of death in the absence of knowledge of the true *nāma* and *śabada*. One who acts as per the advice of a *guru* earns the true name and gets absorbed in it.

binu gura karama na chuṭasī kahi suṇi ākhi vakhāṇu ||
sabhi guṇavaṅtī ākhīahi mai guṇu nāhī koi ||
hari varu nāri suhāvaṇī mai bhāvai prabhu soi ||

nānaka sabadi milāvaḍā nā vichoḍā hoi॥

– *Ādi Granth*, p. 56

Without the guidance of a *guru* one is not released from the bondage of *karma* even though one may utter, hear, discuss and explain anything. All preachers claim to be virtuous but they are none at all. The soul bride gets happy with her Lord only. Its everlasting union with the Lord is attained through *śabada*.

In this hymn Guru Nānak says that there may be a large number of *paṇḍitas*, preachers or persons trading in knowledge and learning, but all of them are not Self-realized persons and virtuous. It is a word of caution.

kiu gura binu trikuṭī chuṭasī sahaji miliē sukhu hoi॥
nijaghari mahalu pachānīē naari kare malu dhoi॥
binu gura mailu na utarai binu hari kiu ghara vāsu॥
aiko sabadu vīcārīē avara tiāgai āsa॥

– Ibid., p. 18

One cannot go beyond the three states of consciousness without the help of a *guru*. One attains this position with the help of deep insight of a *guru*. An individual reaches his home within and feels God's presence within the self when the Lord showers His glance of grace. Without *guru*'s help an individual's pollution is not removed and without the grace of God one cannot reach one's home within. So one should concentrate on *guru*'s words and leave all else.

In this hymn it is explained that it is the wisdom of a true *guru* which helps one to be risen up from the three conditions of consciousness by inner cleaning and removal of all pollution within one self.

binu satigura kinai na pāio binu satigura kinai na pāiā॥
satigura vici āpu rakhionu kari paragaṭu ākhi suṇāiā॥
satigura miliē sadā mukatu hai jini vicahu mohu cukāiā॥
utamu ehu bīcāru hai jini sace siu citu lāiā॥
jagajīvanu dāta pāiā॥

– Ibid., p. 466

No one can reach the Supreme Lord without the help of a true *guru*. The essence of God is placed within a true *guru*. The *guru* declares and reveals Him. By meeting a true *guru*, one obtains liberation from all attachments. One who developes love for the Lord thinks high and attains Him.

In this hymn there is a cry of soul repeating again and again that no one can realize the truth without the aid of a true *guru*. God speaks and reveals Himself through a true *guru*.

hau sutī piru jāgaṇā kisa kau pūchau jāi ||
satiguri melī bhai vasī nānaka premu sakhāi ||
– *Ādi Granth*, p. 54

While individuals sleep, the Supreme Lord remains awake. Who is to blame? The true *guru* united Guru Nānak with the Supreme Lord who remained in Lord's company always with fear for Him.

This is a beautiful explanation of a mind which is sleeping with closed eyes. How can it seek advice? The Lord is always awake and bountiful but the mind remains with the three conditions of nature and does not fear God.

mana re rāmu japahu sukhu hoi ||
binu gura premu na pāīē sabadi milai raṅgu hoi ||
gura sevā sukhu pāīē hari varu sahaji sīgāru ||
saci māṇe pira sejaḍī gūḍā hetu piāru ||
– Ibid., p. 58

Let an individual utter the name of Rāma for his peace. One cannot find God without the love of *guru*. True happiness is found only when one is united with the *śabada*. By serving the *guru* one attains the path to Truth and the soul bride finds true happiness in the company of the Lord.

In this hymn Guru Nānak stresses that peace is found by doing service to the *guru* and happiness is found in the *śabada*. An individual attains the experience of God's company in love and devotion.

aṅnu na khāhi dehī dukhu dījai ||
binu gura giāna tr̥pati nahī thījai ||
....
satigura pūchi saṅgati jana kījai ||

manu hari rācai nahī janami marījai ||
– *Ādi Granth*, p. 905

One who leaves food troubles his body. Without the guide's insight and blessing one cannot feel satiated. One should follow the *guru* and godly people to become one with God and to avoid further birth and death.

Guru Nānak advises that by torturing the body with hunger and other penances God is not met. It is in the company of His humble servants and *guru* that one is benefited.

pūre gura te nāmu pāiā jāi || *joga jugati saci rahai samāi* ||

....

binu gura bharamai āvai jāi || *binu gura ghāla na pavaī thāi* ||
binu gura manūā ati ḍolāi || *binu gura tr̥pati nahī bikhu khāi* ||
binu gura bisīaru ḍasai mari vāṭa || *nānaka gura binu ghāṭe ghāṭa* ||
– Ibid., pp. 941-42

One acquires *nāma* from a true *guru*. By observing *yoga* one remains attuned to truth. Without the *guru* one roams in incarnations and cycle of death. Without the aid of a *guru* one remains unsteady and is not satiated. Without the guidance of a *guru* one comes under the evil spell of *māyā* and gets stung by death. O Nānak, without a *guru* one gets lost from all sides.

Here Guru Nānak teaches that there is all loss after loss without a *guru*. One is liable to the poisonous effect of the veil of *māyā*, and one remains always dissatisfied and unsteady.

kubudhi miṭai gura sabadu bicārī | *satiguru bheṭai moksha duāra* ||
– Ibid., p. 944

By contemplating upon the word of the *guru*, evil thoughts are cleared. By meeting the *guru*, the door to salvation is found.

binu satigura seve jogu na hoī ||
binu satigura bheṭe mukati na koī ||
binu satigura bheṭe nāmu pāiā na jāi ||
binu satigura bheṭe mahā dukhu pāi ||
binu satigura bheṭe mahā garabi gubāri ||
nānaka binu gura muā janamu hāri ||
– Ibid., p. 946

> Without service to the true Guru, one cannot attain *yoga*, liberation or find true name and one suffers in terrible pain, and there is only deep darkness of ego and pride. Thus one dies and loses the chance of this life.

In this hymn all the negative effects one has to face without a *guru* are counted.

> *guri miliē sukhu pāīē agani marai guṇa māhi* ||
> *mana re ahinisi hariguṇa sāri* ||
> *jina khinu palu nāmu na vīsarai te jana virale saṁsāri* ||
> *jotī joti milāīē suratī surati saṅjogu* ||
> *hiṁsā haumai gatu gae nāhī sahasā sogu* ||
>
> – *Ādi Granth*, p. 21

> One can find peace within oneself after meeting a true *guru*. The fire of dualism is cooled down and one finds the treasure of virtues within. So utter the name of the *guru* both by day and night. There are only a few people who are attuned to His name by day and night. When one's light becomes one with the light of the Supreme Being, and one's deep insight gets joined with the Universal Consciousness, one's cruelty, violence and egotism disappear, one sets him free from the cycle of pain and suffering.

This hymn counts the benefits of peace and removal of all individual evils in the company of a *guru* on the way to the final goal of life, that is, merger with the Truth and getting out of the cycle of sufferings in this world.

> *manu kuñcaru kāiā udiānai* ||
> *guru aṅkasu sacu sabadu nīsānai* ||
>
> – Ibid., p. 221

> The mind works as a wild elephant in the forest and it is *guru* who works as a controlling stick for it.

It is again a beautiful expression comparing mind with a wild elephant and a *guru* as a stick to control it.

> *satiguru seve so jogī hoi* || *bhai raci rahai su nirabhau hoi* ||
>
> – Ibid., p. 223

> One who serves a true *guru* is a *yogī*. One who remains ever

replete in the fear of God becomes fearless.

satiguru milai andherā jāi || *nānaka haumai meṭi samāi* ||
– *Ādi Granth*, p. 939

A true *guru* removes darkness, and by shedding I-ness one becomes one with God. The *guru* is the dispeller of darkness, a help for eradicating egotism and paves the way for one's emancipation.

(B) SERVING THE TRUE GURU

satigura pichai bhaji pavahi ehā karaṇī sāru ||
satiguru khoṭiahu khare kare sabadi savāraṇahāru ||
sacī daragaha mannīani gura kai prema piāri ||
– Ibid., p. 143

Run fast to follow and worship the *guru*; this should be the gist of all your actions in life. A true *guru* changes the counterfeited coins into genuine ones. He initiates into his word and leads individuals to *śabada*. Loving and respecting the *guru* is recognized in the court of Lord.

Guru Nānak in this hymn advises that the pure deed of an individual is to follow the true *guru* who turns the impure ones to pure ones. The love for one's *guru* is also acknowledged in the true court.

sacā sabadu sālāhi saci samāīe ||
viṇu satiguru seve nāhī sukhi nivāsu phiri phiri āīe ||
....
satiguru sevi nisangu bharamu cukaīe ||
satiguru ākhai kāra su kāra kamāīe ||
satiguru hoi daiālu ta nāmu dhiāīe ||
lāhā bhagati su sāru guramukhi pāīe ||
– Ibid., pp. 144-45

By practising *śabada* one becomes one with the true Lord. One is unable to attain peace without following the *guru*. One falls in the trap of taking birth again and again without doing service to the *guru*. One should do what his *guru* directs him to do. When the *guru* pleases, one will be able to meditate; so take this advantage and meditate.

Here Guru Nānak explains that without doing service to the *guru*, there is no peace, and one comes and goes. One should be fearless in serving the *guru*. All doubts shall get removed. Practise that which the true *guru* advises to practise. With the mercy of his *guru* one is able to contemplate and meditate. One profits highly with devotional worship. Only a *guramukha* can attain this position.

binu dama ke saudā nahī hāṭa ||
binu bohitha sāgara nahī vāṭa ||
binu guru seve ghāṭe ghāṭi ||
tisa kau vāhu vāhu ji vāṭa dikhāvai ||
tisa kau vāhu vāhu ji sabadu saṇāvai ||
tisa kau vāhu vāhu ji meli milāvai ||
vāhu vāhu tisa kau jisa kā ihu jīu ||
– *Ādi Granth*, p. 226

As one needs money to buy articles from a store, he requires a boat to cross over an ocean. *Guru* is required at every stage of spiritual advancement and without him one is always at loss. Appreciate the *guru* who shows us the way, who leads us to *śabada* and makes us one with the Supreme Lord. Hail him as he is the one who is the keeper of one's soul.

Guru Nānak explains that as money is needed for purchases from any store, a boat is required to ferry across the sea, so does one need the *guru*, otherwise one will be a loser for ever. Guru Nānak greets again and again the true *guru* who shows the path, recites the word and unites one with the Lord.

gura parasādī būjhi le tau hoi niberā ||
ghari ghari nāmu nirañjanā so ṭhākuru merā ||
binu gura sabada na chūṭīē dekhahu vīcārā ||
je lakha karama kamāvahī binu gura aṅdhiārā ||
aṅdhe akalī bāhare kiā tina siu kahīē ||
binu gura paṅthu na sūjhaī kitu bidhi nirabahīē ||
– Ibid., p. 229

With *guru*'s grace, one understands that in each and every heart there is the same name of the supreme being, who is my lord

> and master. Then one's account is settled. Think and realize that without the *guru*'s word, no one gets freedom for salvation. Even though one may go through innumerable rituals, without the *guru* there is total darkness. No one can advise a man, unwilling to come out of darkness. Without the *guru* one cannot see the step forward.

Here Guru Nānak advises to seek the *guru*'s grace, see and reflect on it without which there cannot be any salvation. Performance of any type of rituals cannot dispel the darkness. *Guru* is the dispeller of darkness.

> *guramati sācī hujati dūri*॥ *bahutu siāṇapa lāgai dhūri*॥
> *lāgī mailu miṭai saca nāi*॥ *guraparasādi rahai liva lāi*॥
> ....
> *guraparasādī hari rasu pāiā nāmu padārathu naunidhi pāī*॥
> – *Ādi Granth*, pp. 352-53
>
> Arguments end with the proper lessons of the *guru*. If one tries to be over-smart he gets more layers of dirt. The dirt of entanglements goes away by the gracious name of God. With the grace of *guru* one is attuned to the love for God. Nānak prays to God to keep him ever under His grace. He discloses that with the grace of his *guru*, he attained the *hara rasa* (pure essence). He received all nine treasures of virtue through the blessings of *nāma*.

This is a beautiful expression and prayer of Guru Nānak to remain ever attached to the *guru* for getting his grace. When one receives the true instructions from the *guru*, one's doubts get cleared. One's cleverness which causes dust of sins settles down and one gets attuned to God. Only with *guru*'s grace, one obtains the essence of the Lord and loses oneself.

> *gura pūre te gati miti pāī*॥
> *ihu saṁsāru bikhu vata ati bhaujalu gurasabadī hari pāri laṅghāī*॥
> ....
> *nivi nivi pāi lagau gura apune ātama rāmu nihāriā*॥
> *karata bīcāru hiradai hari raviā hiradai dekhi bīcāriā*॥
> *bolahu rāmu kare nisatārā*॥
> *guraparasādi ratanu hari lābhai miṭai agiānu hoi ujīārā*॥

....
satiguru milai ta haumai tūṭai tā ko lekhai pāī ॥
– *Ādi Granth*, p. 353

The *guru* leads one on the way to salvation. This world is a horrible stream of entanglements. The word of the *guru* helps one to cross over this turbulent sea. I repeatedly bow before the *guru* and touch his feet because it is he through whom I have seen the Lord Divine within myself. One's ignorance goes only when he gets enlightened. His entire ego runs away when he meets a *guru* and he gets to the Self within.

Again, this is a heart-rendering prayer of Guru Nānak. By falling to his *guru*'s feet that it is through him only that he realized the Divine Self within and saw the Lord.

āpu vīcārai su parakhe hīrā ॥ *eka dr̥saṭi tāre gura pūrā* ॥
gura mānai mana te manu dhīrā ॥ *aisā sāhu sarāphī karai* ॥
sācī nadari eka liva tarai ॥
– Ibid., p. 413

One who reflects his own self, he can realize his gist. With a single glance of a perfect *guru* one is saved. With the pleasure of *guru*, one's own mind gets comforted itself. *Guru* is the storehouse of wisdom who puts one to test. With his graceful glance he blesses one, and with the love of Supreme Being, one gets saved.

Here Guru Nānak explains that one, who reflects on oneself, realizes God's essence and a perfect *guru* saves him with his glance. On whom his *guru* is pleased, his mind gets tranquillized. The *guru* tests him with his touchstone and casts his grace and attunes him to the Lord.

guru seve so ṭhākura jānai ॥ *dūkhu miṭai sacu sabadi pachānai* ॥
rāmu japahu merī sakhī sakhainī ॥
satiguru sevi dekhahu prabhu nainī ॥
– Ibid., p. 416

One who serves the *guru* comes to know God and all his pains are eliminated. He recognizes *śabada* within and meditates upon the Supreme Being. Let it be known to all my friends that one will be able to see God through the eyes of his *guru*.

In these lines Guru Nānak advises one to serve his true *guru* and by serving the *guru* one can see the Lord with own eyes.

janami marai bharamāīē hari nāmu na levai ||
tākī kīmati nā pavai binu gura kī sevai ||
jehī seva karāīē karaṇī bhī sāī ||
āpi kare kisu ākhīē vekhai vaḍiāī ||
gura kī sevā so kare jisu āpi karāe ||
nānaka siru de chūṭīē daragaha pati pāe ||
– *Ādi Granth*, pp. 420-21

One never recognizes his own value without serving the *guru*. He keeps wandering through birth and death and never realizes the *nāma*. We act whatever God makes us to act. Only one who gets inspired from the *guru* can serve his *guru*. O Nānak, one gets salvation only if one offers his mind completely to the *guru*.

Here Guru Nānak explains that one does not realize his value without a true *guru*. A true *guru* himself inspires one for doing his service. It is by complete submission of individual's mind to the *guru* that one gets salvation and honours before God.

balihārī gura āpaṇe diuhāḍī sadavāra ||
jini māṇasa te devate kīe karata na lāgī vāra ||
....
nānaka gurū na cetanī mani āpaṇai suceta ||
chuṭe tila būāḍa jiu suṅñe aṅdari kheta ||
khetai aṅdari chuṭiā kahu nānaka sau nāha ||
phalīahi phulīahi bapuḍe bhī tana vici suāha ||
– Ibid., pp. 462-63

I appreciate my *guru* many times a day. He can convert men into angels in no time. Nānak says that if one does not search for the *guru* and thinks himself very clever and wise he will be left behind in this world like a residue of sesame left after harvesting a field. He will get abandoned in the field and these unlucky ones shall never bear flower and fruit, and get filled with ashes.

In this hymn Guru Nānak explains that without the *guru*'s protection one is like an abandoned and scattered corn which bears again and again body, filled with ashes.

jatu satu sañjamu sācu dr̥ḍāiā sāca sabadi rasa līṇā॥
merā guru haiālu sadā raṅgi līṇā॥
– *Ādi Granth*, p. 907

Abstinence, purity of mind, control over self and virtue are deep-rooted within him. He is filled with the flavour of *śabada.* His merciful *guru* remained ever deeply filled with the Lord's love.

Guru Nānak describes the state of love and essence of *śabada* experienced through the love of his *guru.*

dhadhai dharamu dhare dharamāpuri guṇakārī manu dhīrā॥
dhadhai dhūli paḍai mukhi masataki kañcana bhae manūrā॥
– Ibid., p. 930

Those who have developed love for God and reside in the garden of *dharma* are noble, steadfast and stabilized individuals. If one gets their feet's sand and applies to his body, head and face, he will get benefited. He appreciates all noble persons on the path of truth and advises us to keep them always high on head.

Guru Nānak advises us to follow those who are blessed with faith and are steadfast and stable on the path of *dharma* as they can transform the individuals. The dust of their feet is worth for one's forehead. One can understand oneself with the *guru*'s grace and live a life of hope without any attachment to the world.

bhabhai bhaujalu māragu bikhaḍā āsa nirāsā tarīe॥
guruparasādī āpo cīnhai jīvatiā iva marīe॥
– Ibid., p. 935

The path to the horrifying sea of this world is tricky. One should be free from hopes as well as despairs to cross over it. By *guru*'s grace one can realize oneself and the way to remain dead while yet alive.

Guru Nānak advises to follow one who is blessed with faith and is steadfast and stable on the path of *dharma* as he can transform the individual. Dust of his feet is worth for one's forehead. One can understand oneself with *guru*'s grace and live a life of hope without any attachments to hope.

(C) HOMAGE TO GURU

guri rākhe se ubare hori muṭhī dhaṅdhai ṭhagi ||
– *Ādi Granth*, p. 19

One who is saved by his *guru* progresses on spiritual path; others get drowned in the worldly entanglements.

nānaka beḍī saca kī tarīē gura vīcāri ||
iki āvahi iki jāvahī pūri bhare ahaṁkāri ||
– Ibid., p. 20

In the above two hymns, Guru Nānak pays tribute to the *guru* as a saviour of people from the turbulent world, full of conflicts and struggles. He advises us to approach a realized *guru*. *Guru* is the boat of truth and carries us across the seashore; those who are afflicted with ego shall continue to wander.

satiguru pūrā je milai pāīē ratanu bīcāru ||
manu dījai gura āpaṇe pāīē saraba piāru ||
mukati padārathu pāīē avagaṇa meṭaṇahāru ||
bhāī re gura binu giānu na hoi ||
pūchahu brahame nāradai bedabiāsai koi ||
....
saphalio birakhu harīāvalā chāva ghaṇerī hoi ||
....
sukhadātā dukha meṭaṇo satiguru asuru saṁghāru ||
bhavajalu bikhamu ḍarāvaṇo nā kaṅdhī nā pāru ||
nā beḍī nā tulahaḍā nā tisu vaṅjhu malāru ||
satiguru bhai kā bohithā nadari pāri utāru ||
– Ibid., p. 59

When individuals surrender their minds to the *guru*, they develop universal love. They get their evils removed and attain freedom. On the path of spirituality, one cannot attain wealth of spiritual progress without the *guru*. One may confirm this from gods Brahmā, Nārada and Vyāsa or who wrote the Vedas. A *guru* is a tree laden with fruits and remains evergreen providing dense shade. There is many kinds of wealth in the treasury of a *guru* from which we receive the heavenly *nāma*. The *guru* destroys the demon in us, removes pains and provides all of peace within.

> The horrifying world ocean is full of sufferings and difficult to cross over without any approachable shore. One has no boat, raft or boatman except the *guru* who only is the boat for crossing this terrible ocean. It is *his graceful glance that carries us across.*

In this hymn Guru Nānak explains that if we meet a true *guru* we get blessed with the power of discrimination. If one surrenders his mind to the *guru* he is blessed with universal love. There is no wisdom without the *guru*. This has also been confirmed by the writers of Vedas. A true *guru* is the only boat that can ferry one across the terrifying life ocean with his grace.

> *satigura kau bali jāīē* || *jitu miliē parama gati pāīē* ||
> *surinari munijana locade so satiguri dīā bujhāi jou* ||
> ....
> *nānaka satiguru aisā jāṇīē jo sabhasai lae milāi jīu* ||
> *satiguri miliē phalu pāiā* || *jini vicahu ahakaraṇu cukāiā* ||
> ....
> *satiguru miliā jāṇīē* || *jitu miliē nāmu vakhāṇīē* ||
> *satigura bājhu na pāio sabha thakī karama kamāi jīu* ||
> *hau satigura viṭahu ghumāiā* || *jini bhrami bhulā māragi pāiā* ||
> – *Ādi Granth*, pp. 71-72

> I appreciate the true *guru*. One can attain the high status on spiritual path by getting his protection. All the angels and silent sages seek him with ardent desire. Guru Nānak says that the Supreme Being made him to understand this that one should consider him as a true *guru* who unites all with the Supreme Being. One gets the fruits of his destiny and erases his ego from within after coming under the protection of the *guru*. It is he who teaches one as how to chant the true name. God cannot be found without the aid of a true *guru*. We get tired in performing religious rituals. I applaud my true *guru*. I was roaming in doubts and he has guided me in the right direction. With a graceful glance from him we get united with God.

In these lines Guru Nānak hails the true *guru* and reminds us that even the angels and men of silence in pursuit of truth seek for a true *guru* who can unite them with God. The *guru* drives out their egotism, teaches them to chant God's name and sets them on the right path.

nānaka manamukhi aṅdhu piāru ॥ *bājhu gurū ḍubā saṁsāru* ॥
....
nānaka gura binu nāhi pati pati viṇu pāri na pāi ॥
....
binu satigura mohu na tuṭaī sabhi thake karama kamāiā ॥
guramatī nāmu dhiāīē sukhi rajā jā tudhu bhāiā ॥
kulu udhāre āpaṇā dhaṅnu jaṇedī māiā ॥
sobhā surati suhāvaṇī jini hari setī citu lāiā ॥
– *Ādi Granth*, pp. 138-39

The individuals who act with their own will live in darkness and without an expert guide all get drowned. The *guru* is our protection and without his protection no one can reach the destination. He helps them to break their emotional attachments with the world. One gets tired performing religious ceremonies. But if one follows the teachings of the *guru* and concentrates on the name of the Lord, he acquires happiness and eternal peace by obeying His command.

This hymn explains, that the self-willed persons love darkness and declares that the whole world is drowned without a true *guru*. One can only be saved with the protection of a *guru*. No rituals can help a man in getting emancipation. Meditation with the guidance of a *guru* keeps one ever joyful as he surrenders himself to the will of God.

guramatī kālu na āvai neḍai jā hovai dāsanidāsā ॥
sacā sabadu sacu mani ghara hī māhi udāsā ॥
nānaka sataguru sevani āpaṇā se āsā te nirāsā ॥
– Ibid., p. 140

Fear of death does not come near to him who follows the teachings of the *guru* and serve him. One should serve them all (God's men) who serve the Lord. The *śabada* sprouts in their minds and they become detached to the outside world. They start living in themselves in their home within. Nānak says that those who come under the protection of a *guru* rise from all desires and become desireless.

In these lines Guru Nānak explains that those who come under the umbrella of teachings of the *guru* do not face death and consequent birth as they merge with the eternal.

satiguri tuṭhai pāīani aṅdari ratana bhaṅḍārā ॥
vinu gura kinai na ladhiā aṅdhe bhauki mue kūḍiārā ॥
– *Ādi Granth*, p. 141

It is at the pleasure of a true *guru* that we are blessed with the treasure of the diamonds deep within the self. One cannot find this treasure without the help of a *guru*. The blind men die barking uselessly.

In these lines Guru Nānak stresses that no one can realize the Self without the guidance of a Self-realized *guru*. Others who try get lost.

satiguru hoi daiālu ta saradhā pūrīe ॥
satiguru hoi daiālu na kabahūṅ jhūrīe ॥
satiguru hoi daiālu tā dukhu na jāṇīe ॥
satiguru hoi daiālu tā hari raṅgu māṇīe ॥
satiguru hoi daiālu tā jama kā ḍaru kehā ॥
satiguru hoi daiālu tā sada hī sukhu dehā ॥
satiguru hoi daiālu tā nava nidhi pāīe ॥
satiguru hoi daiālu ta saci samāīe ॥
– Ibid., p. 149

When a true *guru* showers his glance then all individual desires are fulfilled, you will never grieve, you will know no pain, you will enjoy the Lord's love. Then there is no reason to fear death. When the *guru* showers his mercy, the nine treasuries are obtained and one gets oneness with the True Lord.

This hymn is a real homage to the true *guru* with a counting of all the blessings from him.

kahu nānaka guri brahamu dikhāiā ॥
maratā jātā nadari na āiā ॥
– Ibid., p. 152

The *guru* has disclosed *Brahman* to me and now there remains no fear of anything like birth and death.

Guru Nānak declares that the true *guru* has shown him the *Brahman* and for him there is no difference between life and death.

satiguru milai su maraṇu dikhāe॥
maraṇa rahaṇa rasu aṅtari bhāe॥
garabu nivāri gaganapuru pāe॥
maraṇu likhāi āe nahī rahaṇā॥
hari japi jāpi rahaṇu hari saraṇā॥
satiguru milai ta dubidhā bhāgai॥
kamalu bigāsi manu hariprabha lāgai॥
jīvatu marai mahā rasu āgai॥
satiguri miliē saca saṅjami sūcā॥
gura kī pauḍī ūco ūcā॥
karami milai jamakā bhau mūcā॥
guri miliē mili aṅki samāiā॥
kari kirapā gharu mahalu dikhāiā॥
nānaka haumai māri milāiā॥

– *Ādi Granth*, p. 153

> The true *guru* shows the way as how to die. Remaining dead while alive brings joy from the deep within. When one overcomes egotism and false pride, he finds the tenth gate. Death is a must and no one can escape it. So one should utter the name of the true Lord, meditate upon Him and remain ever absorbed in Him. The *guru* makes duality disappear from individuals. The lotus blossoms forth and the mind gets attracted to God. One adopts truth, chastity and purity while serving the true *guru*. One climbs up and attains the highest position by treading the path of his *guru*.
>
> The fear of death runs away by the grace of God. By merging with the *guru*, we are attuned to the loving embrace of the Lord. The Lord with His mercy shows one the home of His living within the individual. When we overpower our egotism we get absorbed into the Lord.

In this hymn Guru Nānak explains as to how the *guru* reveals to us the merit of death. When we die to ourselves, we love to live. When we overpower our ego, we reach the realm of sky. When the true *guru* meets, and duality goes, one becomes pure and the lotus within blossoms. The adoption of the path of the *guru* leads one to climb to the higher regions of consciousness.

satigura viṭahu vāriā jitu miliē khasamu samāliā ||
jini kari upadesu giāna añjanu dīā inhī netrī jagatu nihāliā ||
khasamu choḍi dūjai lage ḍube se vaṇajāriā ||
satigurū hai bohithā viralai kinai vīcāriā ||
kari kirapā pāri utāriā ||

– *Ādi Granth*, p. 470

Guru Nānak says that he appreciates his *guru* to the highest esteem because by meeting him he came to desire for the Supreme Lord. He taught and gave him a soothing balm of spiritual wisdom and he started seeing the world through *guru*'s eyes. Those who leave their *guru* and get attached to duality suffer. Only a few can realize that the true *guru* is the boat and by his grace he carries one to the other shore.

In this hymn also Guru Nānak hails the true *guru*, who enables and increases one's urge for the company of the Lord, and provides spiritual wisdom for dealing with the world.

ai jī janami marai āvai phuni jāva binu gura gati nahī kāī ||
guramukhi prāṇī nāme rāte nāme gati pati pāī ||

– Ibid., p. 504

One takes birth and then dies, again and again; he continues to rotate in this way. Without the protection of a *guru* he cannot get free from this cycle. When those who are subject to death become lovers of God with the guidance of a *guru*, they get attuned to *nāma*, the Lord's name; they attain salvation by God's name.

Guru Nānak explains that there is no salvation without a *guru*. One is born and dies again and again, for there is no emancipation without a *guru*. But the God men are filled with God's name, and by that name, they attain honour and deliverance.

guru sāgaru ratanī bharapūre || *aṁmr̥tu santa cugahi nahī dūre* ||
hari rasu coga cugahi prabha bhāvai ||
saravara mahi haṁsu prānapati pāvai ||

– Ibid., p. 685

The *guru* is the ocean of spiritual wealth. The saints draw heavenly nectar and do not move to any distance. They enjoy the nectar and flavour of God and God also loves them. One finds God within the inner pool of the self who is the soul of all souls.

This is a beautiful description of a true *guru*. As a true *guru* is a treasure house of spiritual wealth, the seekers, like the birds of a pool, enjoy the company of God and never go away from Him. They enjoy His presence and get the return of love from Him.

tinā miliā guru āi jina kau līkhiā ||
aṁmṛtu hari kā nāu devai dīkhiā ||
cālahi satigura bhāi bhavahi na bhīkhiā ||
jākau mahalu hajūri dūje nivai kisu ||
– *Ādi Granth*, p. 729

The *guru* finds those souls who are predestined for spiritual progress. He teaches them and discloses the heavenly name of God. Individuals walking on the path of the true *guru* never get to wandering or begging from others. One who lives in the presence of the Lord need not bow to anyone else.

In this hymn, Guru Nānak says that the *guru* meets only those who have been chosen by God. The *guru* blesses them with the nectar, name of the Lord. Those who walk in the *guru*'s will do not wander hither and thither for bounty. Since they live always in the Lord's presence, they need not bow to anyone else.

guru dātā guru hivai gharu guru dīpaku tiha loi ||
amara padārathu nānakā mani māniē sukhu hoi ||
– Ibid., p. 137

The *guru* is giver. He is a cooling source for individuals. The *guru* is a torchlight to the three worlds. O Nānak! he is the everlasting and most valuable. One should put one's mind to have faith in him and thereby one is blessed with peace.

bhūle māragu jo dase tisa kai lāgau pāi ||
gura binu dātā ko nahī kīmati kahaṇu na jāi ||
sājanu dekhā tā gali milā sācu paṭhāio lekhu ||
mukhi dhimāṇai dhana khaḍī guramukhi ākhī dekhu ||
– Ibid., p. 1010

> Guru Nānak expresses that he will fall on the feet of one who shows him the way to Supreme Lord. Only a *guru* can bestow this knowledge upon him. One cannot assess and describe his value. "If I find the Supreme Lord I shall hug Him; I have dispatched a message to Him. I am His soul bride standing at the gate and wait with hope to see Him".

This is a soul's cry of Guru Nānak in his ecstasy.

> I know not what is to happen to me beyond this. O *guru*! I have strayed from thy path: Instruct me. I would pay my respects to him who leads me in the right path. Without the *guru* no one is my benefactor: I cannot know the whole worth of the *guru*. He expresses his eagerness to see Him and hug Him. I have sent Him a truthful request and am lost deep within me. I, like a bride, stand in wait for Him and if the *guru* blesses me, I will see Him with my own eyes.

(D) CONCLUSION

Role of a true *guru* at every step is explained in the Upaniṣads and hymns of Guru Nānak. One is advised to find a true *guru* and serve and follow him earnestly for spiritual progress by listening to scriptures from him, contemplating on their meaning and practise meditation under his guidance. The darkness of ignorance cannot be dispelled without a true guide. The Upaniṣads advise the seekers to find a guide who has learned the scriptures and has realized self within him. A *guru* is regarded as the spiritual father who raises one to the higher spiritual planes and is placed higher to the physical father who brings one down to this world. Guru Nānak also declares emphatically that without serving the true *guru* no one can attain *yoga*. God has placed Himself within the true *guru* who can lead the seeker to higher spiritual realms. It is through a true *guru* that one can see the divine self within oneself. Individual's mind is like a wild elephant roaming in the deep forests of this worldly life and the *guru* is the stick to control it.

Thus both the Upaniṣads and hymns of Guru Nānak teach that the path to liberation goes through a Self-realized preceptor.

GOD'S LOVE

It may not be out of place to say that love for God pervades in every religious and philosophical streams of thought. He is unseen, unheard, yet most cherished. The devotees abandon their homes and without any shelter go in His search and surrender themselves to Him completely. They wander without any direction in search of Him and see Him everywhere simultaneously. Sant Kabīr, Guru Nānak, Śrī Caitanya and Tulsīdās are some examples who frequently communicated their experiences in love with God and the ecstasy of union with Him.

Love is the dominant activity of the world. The Upaniṣads also recognize the joy of nature and life. The love of *eka sat* (one truth) is akin to an idealized human life. The upsurge of love of *Brahman*, "He desired, I will be many" is correlated to eternal Pure Consciousness, pure joy. He loves, bestows grace and out of His love He creates, sustains and merges into Himself the whole world process. His only activity is to love the world with its million manifestations and modes. It is His sheer grace and concern for the humanity that human beings are blessed with a vision and a path through their own living body for realizing Him.

The Upaniṣad's identity "That art Thou" (*Chāndogya Upaniṣad* 6.8.7) also suggests God's love for man and man's love for God. On account of man's love, which is the most precious gift of God, man stands at the doorstep of God. He arouses such a desire in the devotee that his bones burn of it. He creates such a strong yearning that the man himself forms His vision. His presence develops such an ecstasy in the devotee that he falls unconscious and when he reawakens he realizes that loving Him; he experiences His love for him. He feels like a poet and verses flow out of him. He finds the world a void without the reflection of His sun-like glory. He feels that God moulds His devotees the whole night when they are asleep as on potter's wheel into vessels for His love. When separated from Him, he seeks a face-to-face encounter with all his faith. His yearning is not a pining and a wasting away but an inspiring steadfast upsurge towards Him. He feels that separation cannot be endured, and this joy and sorrow both mingle in ecstasy.

According to the testimony of saints, the union with Him is an experience of His infinite love. It is an indescribable ecstasy which leaves the devotees senseless.

samāne vṛkṣe puruṣo nimagno 'nīśayā śocati muhyamānaḥ ।
juṣṭam yadā pasyatyanyamīśamasya mahimānamiti vītaśokah ॥
yadā paśyaḥ paśyate rukmavarṇaṁ kartāramīśam puruṣam brahmayonim ।
tadā vidvānpuṇya-pāpe vidhūya nirañjanaḥ paramaṁ sāmyam-upaiti ॥

– *Muṇḍaka Upaniṣad* 3.1.2-3

On the self-same tree, a person immersed (in the sorrows of the world) is deluded and grieves on account of his helplessness. When he sees the other, the Lord who is worshipped and his greatness, he becomes free from sorrow.

When a seer sees the creator of the golden hue, the Lord, the person, the source of *Brahman*, then being a knower, shaking off good and evil and free from stain, he attains supreme equality with the Lord.

PRAYER FOR THE VISION OF GOD

hiraṇmayena pātreṇa satyasyāpihitaṁ mukham ।
tattvaṁ pūṣannapāvṛṇu satyadharmāya dṛṣṭaye ॥
pūṣannekarṣe yama sūrya prājāpatya vyūha raśmīnsamūha ।
tejo yatte rūpaṁ kalyāṇulamaṁ tatte paśyāmi yo 'savasau puruṣaḥ, so 'hamasmi ॥
vāyuranilamamṛtamathedaṁ bhasmāntaṁ śarīram ।
auṁ krato smara kṛtaṁ smara krato smara kṛtaṁ smara ॥
agne naya supathā rāye asmānviśvāni deva vayunānai vidvān ।
yuyodhyasmajjuhurāṇameno bhūyiṣṭhāṁ te nama uktiṁ vidhema ॥

– *Īśa Upaniṣad* 15-18

The face of the truth is covered with a golden disc. Unveil it, O Pūṣan! so that I who love the truth may see it. O Pūṣan! the sole seer, O Controller! O sun! offspring of Prajāpati, spread forth your rays and gather up your radiant light that I may behold you of the loveliest form. Whosoever is that person (yonder) that also

I am. May this life enter into the immortal breath; then may this body end in ashes, O intelligent! what has been done, remember. O Agni! lead us, along the auspicious path to prosperity, O God! who knowest all our deeds, take away from us all our deceitful sins. We shall offer many prayers unto thee. . . .

These verses are the real cry of individual soul to have the experience of unity with the Supreme Soul.

ECSTASY OF REALIZATION OF BRAHMAN

bhidyate hṛdayagranthiśchidyante sarva-saṁśayāḥ ।
kṣīyante cāsya karmāṇi tasmindṛṣṭe parāvare ॥
– *Muṇḍaka Upaniṣad* 2.2.8

brahmaivedamamṛtaṁ purastādbrahma dakṣiṇataścottareṇa ।
– Ibid. 2.2.11

When He is seen who is both high and low, all the knots of heart are untied and doubts are dispelled and one's all deeds cease to bear fruit. One finds *Brahman* in his front, behind, right and left, i.e. all around him.

BLISS OF BRAHMAN

yuvā syātsādhuyuvādhyāyakaḥ । *āśiṣṭho dṛḍhiṣṭho. . . .*
te ye śataṁ prajāpaterānandāḥ sa eko brahmaṇa ānandaḥ ।
– *Taittirīya Upaniṣad* 2.8.1

Brahman is the blissful being of the highest value. In reaching Him one reaches at the highest fulfilment of feeling of nothing beyond this. Thus the love for God and love of God for His creation are mutual enjoyment of the individual soul and the Universal Soul.

GOD'S LOVE IN THE HYMNS OF GURU NĀNAK

The most dominant feature of the contents of hymns of Guru Nānak is his expression of love for God, his experiences of God's love, fire of separation and his urge for blessed vision and the ecstasy of union with God. Accordingly the selected verses are grouped nearly together for study as under even though some lines may convey varied, mixed expressions:

Expression of Love for God

koī ākhai bhūtanā ko kahai betālā ||
koī ākhai ādamī nānaku becārā ||
bhaiā divānā sāha kā nānaku baurānā ||
hau hari binu avaru na jānā ||
tau devānā jaṇīē jā bhai devānā hoi ||
ekī sāhiba bāharā dūjā avaru na jāṇai koi ||
tau devānā jāṇīē jā ekā kāra kamāi ||
hukamu pachāṇai khasama kā dūjī avara siāṇapa kāi ||
tau devānā jāṇīē jā sāhiba dhare piāru ||
maṅdā jāṇai āpa kau avaru bhalā saṁsāru ||

– *Ādi Granth*, p. 991

Some people called him a ghost; some said that he was afflicted with bad spirit. Some called him a mere helpless individual subject to death. Guru Nānak has become mad after the Supreme Father. He knew of no other than the Supreme Being. One is called insane who gets mad in the fear of the Lord. Since he looks for none else than the God, he works for the one Lord. Can there be any other wisdom than recognizing the true will of God? One who falls deeply in love with God gets mad and is known to be insane. He starts thinking himself to be useless and considers all others as useful.

In the above hymn, Guru Nānak describes his condition as a man, who cherishes the love of God above all worldly pleasures. He says that one who is in love with his Master with a single mind is mad indeed. He becomes out of step with the world and is forsaken as a lunatic in the world. Love of a man for God is spontaneous and makes him stranger to the world as he is ever absorbed in his beloved.

apune ṭhākura kī hau cerī ||
carana gahe jagajīvana prabha ke haumai māri niberī ||
pūrana parama joti paramesara prītama prāna hamāre ||
mohana mohi līā manu merā samajhasi sabadu bīcāre ||

– Ibid., p. 1197

I am a maid attending my Lord. I have sought protection at His feet and burnt my egotism. My Lord is the provider of life to

> the world and life of the world. I have recognized Him and my egotism has vanished from within. God is the perfect supreme light for me. He is my love and breathes in me. The enchanting Lord has fascinated my mind and I realize Him through *śabada*.

In this hymn Guru Nānak considers himself as a maidservant who knows no ego and devotes the self into the service of her master and remains happy with the fascinating qualities of her Master.

> *cakavī naina nīṅda nahi cāhai binu pira nīṅda na pāī*||
> *sūru carhai priu dekhai nainī nivi nivi lāgai pāī*||
> *pira bhāvai premu sakhāī*||
> *tisu binu ghaḍī nahī jagi jīvā aisī piāsa tisāī*||
> ....
> *cātr̥ku jala binu priu priu ṭerai bilapa karai bilalāī*||
> *ghanahara ghora dasau disi barasai binu jala piāsa na jāī*||
> – *Ādi Granth*, p. 1273

> The night bird does not wish for the sleep as it cannot go to sleep without its beloved. At the rise of the sun she can see her spouse and bows to touch his feet. She feels pleased with her spouse's love. She cannot stay for a moment without him. Such is her desire and thirst for him. In an individual the flower of love comes to bloom itself within the depth of the heart naturally. Such is the love for God which fills one with the desire to get ones light merged into the light of the Supreme Lord. The rain bird cries out for water. It weaps, cries and prays for water time and again. The thunder of clouds brings rain everywhere; even then its thirst is not satiated till it is able to catch the rain drops in its mouth.

In this hymn Guru Nānak describes his pangs of separation from the Lord. He describes that love for God sprouts forth intuitively like the rays of the sun.

> *hari binu kiu jīvā merī māī*||
> *jai jagadīsa terā jasu jācau mai hari binu rahanu na jāī*||
> *hari kī piāsa piāsī kāmani dekhau raini sabāī*||
> *srīdhara nātha merā manu līnā prabhu jānai pīra parāī*||
> *gaṇata sarīri pīra hai hari binu gura sabadī hari pāī*||
> *hohu daiāla kr̥pā kari hari jīu hari siu rahā samāī*||
> – Ibid., p. 1232

One cannot live without Hari (the essence God). So Guru Nānak advises to hail the one who is the Lord of the universe. Sing praises of that Lord without whom one cannot even survive. He says that he feels thirst for God; his soul bride stealingly looks towards God for all the night. His mind is one with his Lord. Only the God knows the pain of others. Guru Nānak says that he felt suffering of pain in his body without the Lord. He found the Lord through *śabada*. He prays to God to be kind and merciful to him so that he continues to remain one with Him.

Here Guru Nānak expresses that he cannot live without God. He recalls God as the only benefactor and one who knows all his pains.

mula kharīdī lālā golā merā nāu sabhāgā ||
gura kī bacanī hāṭi bikānā jitu lāiā titu lāgā ||
tere lāle kiā caturāī || *sāhiba kā hukamu na karaṇā jāī* ||
mā lālī piu lālā merā hau lāle kā jāiā ||
lālī nācai lālā gāvai bhagati karau terī rāiā ||
pīahi ta pāṇī āṇī mīrā khāhi ta pīsaṇa jāu ||
pakhā pherī paira malovā japata rahā terā nāu ||
lūṇaharāmī nānaku lālā bakhasihi tudhu vaḍiāī ||
ādi jugādi daiāpati dātā tudhu viṇu mukati na pāī ||
– *Ādi Granth*, p. 991

Guru Nānak felt blessed to be a slave of his Master, the Supreme Lord. He says that he sold himself for the word of *guru*; I get attuned to whatever he links me. One cannot do tricks with the Lord. My mother is a humble servant, my father is also His humble servant. I am the child of His humble servants who sing and dance for Him. We worship Him with love and devotion. I am ready to do any type of service to Him. I can work as waterman, grinder of grains, fan attendent, washer of feet, etc. I can be untrue to myself but I am your servant. I can utter your name continuously. You are bountiful and I beg your pardon. You had always been a giver of mercy and kindness from the beginning of the ages. I cannot get liberated without your mercy.

In this hymn Guru Nānak calls himself a slave who has sold himself to the *guru* for showing him the way to God. He says that he is the son of a slave mother and a slave father who also serve the same God. He is ready to serve Him in any way for His mercy and getting liberation.

> *yaka araja guphtama pesi to dara gāsa kuna karatāra* ||
> *hakā kabīra karīma tū be aiba paravaradagāra* ||
> *duniā mukāme phānī tahakīka dila dānī* ||
> *mama sara mūi ajarāīla giraphataha dila heci na dānī* ||
> *jana pisara padara birādarāṅ kasa nesa dasataṁgīra* ||
> *ākhira biaphatama kasa na dārada cūṅ savada takabīra* ||
> ....
> *mai devānā bhaiā atītu* || *kara kāsā darasana kī bhūkha* ||
> *mai dari māgau nītā nīta* || *tau darasana kī karau samāi* ||
>
> – *Ādi Granth*, p. 721

> I pray to you, O my Lord. Hear me. You are truthful, bountiful, a great giver. The world is shortlived and its inhibitors are subject to death. I have this knowledge surely in my mind. I am unaware that the death man has caught me by the hair. All my worldly relations like spouse, children, parents and siblings shall not be able to hold me back when I fall into the grip of death. No one will be of any help to me at the time of my last prayer. I roamed everywhere as a greedy person to plan for my greedy schemes. I never acted for good cause. I have described my position to you. With all my faults like being neglectful, without any shame, without any awe of God, I am your slave and lump of earth under the feet of your servants. I have become a hermit with begging bowl in my hands. I feel hunger for your blessing and vision. I wait at your door every time of the day, please bless me with your charity.

In this hymn Guru Nānak calls God as the true and only friend. All other worldly relations are false. The death is imminent and no one can help him in liberation. There is a soul's cry for the blessed vision of God.

> *morī ruṇa jhuṇa lāiā bhaiṇe sāvaṇu āiā* ||
> *tere muṅdha kaṭāre jevaḍā tini lobhī lobha lobhāiā* ||
> *tere darasana viṭahu khaṅnīē vaṅñā tere nāma viṭahu kurabāṇo* ||
> *jā tū tā mai māṇu kīā hai tudhu binu kehā merā māṇo* ||
> *cūḍā bhaṅnu palaṅgha siu muṅdhe saṇu bāhī saṇu bāhā* ||

....

jo saha kaṅṭhi na lagīā jalanu si bāhaḍīāhā ||
sabhi sahīā sahu rāvaṇi gaīā hau dādhī kai dari jāvā ||
– *Ādi Granth*, pp. 557-58

O sisters, the pleasant season of Sāwan has come. The peacocks are singing very sweetly. God's beautiful eyes are sparkling and charmful. These are attracting and inviting me who is His soul bride. I shall disintegrate all evil from me for His *darśana*. I appreciate His name. I cannot take pride in anything except Him.

Break your bangles by striking these against your bed. Strike your arms with the arms of your couch in agony. The arms which could not lie round the neck of the beloved suffer the agony of separation. My entire sister brides have left for enjoyment with the Supreme Lord, I find no other place to go.

This hymn is a beautiful depiction of his love for God. The reference to the worldly conjugal love is so beautifully described here. He compares himself with a bride waiting in agony for her Master who breaks her bangles on the bed and burns in anguish to embrace the neck of her husband Lord.

āvahu milahu sahelīho simarahu sirajaṇahāro ||
baīari nāmi sohāgaṇī sacu savāraṇahāro ||
gāvahu gītu na birahaḍā nānaka brahama bīcāro ||
– Ibid., p. 581

Come and assemble along each other, O brides of God; let us contemplate and remember our one Supreme Lord. A soul bride gets the favourite of the Lord through His true *nāma*; she is blessed with Truth. There is no need to mourn on separation, O Nānak, only concentrate on *Brahman*.

In this hymn Guru Nānak asks all his associates, calling them brides of the Lord, to come together and concentrate on *Brahman* for His blessed vision.

jālau aisī rīti jitu mai piārā vīsarai ||
nānaka sāī bhalī parīti jitu sāhiba setī pati rahai ||
– Ibid., p. 590

Do away all the practices of worship that take you away from the Supreme Being. O Nānak! my love for God is very great as it takes me near to Him.

Here Guru Nānak advises to give up all the rituals which mislead individuals and take one away from God.

jīu ḍaratu hai āpaṇā kai siu karī pukāra ॥
dūkha visāraṇu seviā sadā sadā dātāru ॥
sāhibu merā nīta navā sadā sadā dātāru ॥
anadinu sāhibu sevīē aṅti chaḍāe soi ॥
– *Ādi Granth*, p. 660

I feel frightened as to how can I put up a complaint against Him? I worship the One who redeems all my pains. He is the provider ever since. He ever lets me feel as if He is always new. Night and day I serve Him. He shall be my saviour always. O my companions! I always hear and listen to Him to get crossed to the other side of the world.

In these lines Guru Nānak explains that remembrance of God makes one forget all the pains of life. He advises to serve Him who shall save us at last. He discloses that by hearing and listening to Him he has crossed over to other side of life.

EXPERIENCE OF GOD'S LOVE IN THE HYMNS OF GURU NĀNAK

citai aṅdari sabhu ko vekhi nadarī heṭhi calāidā ॥
āpe de vaḍiāīā āpe hī karama karāidā ॥
vaḍahu vaḍā vaḍa medanī sire siri dhaṅdhai lāidā ॥
nadari upaṭhī je kare sulatānā ghāhu karāidā ॥
dari maṅgani bhikha na pāidā ॥
– Ibid., p. 472

All living beings are within His mind. He looks after them and moves them to act under His glance of grace. He himself is the cause of all glory and causes all individuals to work. The Supreme Being is the greatest of the great. The world created by him is also great and He puts everyone to his tasks. With a mere angry look he can convert the kings into blades of grass and make them beg. Even if they go for begging from one door to another they will not get anything.

In these lines Guru Nānak explains that God takes care of everyone and makes every thing move under His grace. He loves His creation and enjoys it. While everything moves in His love, with an angry glance He can transform everything to dust and no one can help for its restoration.

sāhibu hoi daiālu kirapā kare tā sāī kāra karāisī॥
so sevaku sevā kare jisano hukamu manāisī॥
hukami mannie hova paravāṇu tā khasamai kā mahalu pāisī॥
khasamai bhāvai so kare manahu cindiā so phalu pāisī॥
tā daragaha paidhā jāisī॥ – *Ādi Granth*, p. 471

Only those individuals can serve the true Lord to whom He showers His mercy to be able to obey His command. Such an individual obeys the order of His will and is accepted for realizing the residing place of God within him. Those who serve God for His pleasure get the desired mental bliss. They depart from this world, wearing the robes of His virtues and thus gets honour in His court.

Here Guru Nānak explains that it is He who causes everything to run according to His will. Those who serve Him by obeying His will are honoured in His court.

jā tisu bhāvā tadahī gāvā॥ *tā gāve kā phalu pāvā*॥
gāve kā phalu hoī॥ *jā āpe devai soī*॥
– Ibid., p. 599

I sing His praises when He is pleased and makes me sing for Him. I receive awards for singing his praises. The reward of my singing comes to me when He Himself gives it.

Guru Nānak explains that no one can sing God's praises without His mercy and grace. And He Himself rewards the individuals for their good deeds and on them showers His love and mercy.

tū guṇadātau niramalo bhāī niramalu nā manu hoi॥
hama aparādhī niraguṇe bhāī tujhahī te guṇu soi॥
mere prītamā tū karatā kari vekhu॥
hau pāpī pākhanḍīā bhāī mani tani nāma visekhu॥
– Ibid., pp. 636-37

You provide virtue to all, O faultless Lord, but my mind is faulty. I am a useless sinner and you provide all virtues to me also. O

> God, you are the creator of all and watch your creations. I am false and useless, bless my mind and body with your *nāma* to clean me from within.

This is a humble submission by Guru Nānak to God to bless his mind and body with virtues and His *nāma* to wash away his sins.

FIRE OF SEPARATION AND URGE FOR BLESSED VISION

> *cātr̥ka mīna jala hī te sukhu pāvahi sāriṅga sabadi suhāī* ||
> *raini babīhā bolio merī māī* ||
> *pria siu prīti na ulaṭai kabahū jo tai bhāvai sāī* ||
> *nīda gaī hamai tani thākī saca mati ridai samāī* ||
>
> – *Ādi Granth*, p. 1274

> The rain bird and fish both enjoy their association with water. The deer gets happy with the sound of music. The rain bird chirps in the night, O my mother. O my beloved! my love for you shall never end if You so desire. I do not sleep and my ego is eradicated; my heart is fully packed with truthfulness.

Guru Nānak says as the *cātaka* (rain bird) wails at night, so my sleep vanishes and ego runs out of him to be with God. If He so desires, his love for Him will not go out. This is an expression of pangs of separation.

> *jiu mīnā binu pāṇīē tiu sākatu marai piāsa* ||
> *tiu hari binu marīē re manā jo birathā jāvai sāsu* ||
>
> ....
>
> *tū prabha dātā dāni mati pūrā hama thāre bhekhārī jīu* ||
> *mai kiā māgau kichu thiru na rahāī hari dījai nāmu piārī jīu* ||
>
> – Ibid., p. 597

> Faithless individual dies of thirst as the fish dies when it is put out of water. O mind, you will also die as your breath goes waste without chanting God's name. O God, you are giver of all sorts of gifts. You are source of all understanding. I am only a beggar at your door. What can be begged from you? There is nothing which remains forever here. So O God, let me be blessed with your name.

Guru Nānak explains that his mind dies without the Lord, if he wastes even a single breath without Him. For those turned Godwards, the society of saints is the only pilgrimage. God is the beneficent and perfect wisdom and a person is a beggar at his door. Whatever one asks from Him shall not remain for ever, so one should ask to bless him with God's loved name.

hau pāpī patitu parama pākhaṁḍī tūṁ niramalu niraṁkārī ||
aṁmṛtu cākhi parama rasi rāte ṭhākura saraṇi tumārī ||
karatā tū mai māṇi nimāṇe || – *Ādi Granth*, p. 596

I am a cursed sinner and a big changer; you are without any fault and a formless Lord. It is only with your heavenly nectar that I get filled of your bliss. Let me be protected by my Lord. My Lord is the protector of the unprotected.

Guru Nānak says that his self is a great sinner and pretender, and as God is immaculate and formless, he seeks refuge in Him. He further prays that he is the servant of God's servants and there is no other one like God whom he can praise.

kiu simarī sivariā nahī jāi || *tapai hiāu jīaḍā bilalāi* ||
siraji savāre sācā soi || *tisu visariē caṅgā kiu hoi* ||
hikamati hukami na pāiā jāi || *kiukari sāci milau merī māi* ||
– Ibid., p. 661

How I can meditate on Him? He cannot be remembered in meditation. My body is burning and my soul is suffering in agony. Forgetting the true Lord who is the creator and preservator, one cannot remain happy. He cannot be attained by smart actions and orders. How can I find Him?

It is again a cry of soul to meet the Lord God.

jīvā terai nāi mani ānaṁdu hai jīu ||
sāco sācā nāu guṇa goviṁdu hai jīu ||
– Ibid., p. 688

I always remain with Your name and feel ecstasy. God's name is truth. He is the embodiment of glory and virtue.

Guru Nānak says that he lives by God's name only, which is glorious. He is the Lord of the universe.

iānaḍīe mānaḍā koi karehi ||
āpanaḍai ghari hari raṅgo kī na māṇehi ||

sahu neḍai dhana kaṁmalīe bāharu kiā dūḍhehi॥
bhai kiā dehi salāiā naiṇī bhāva kā kari sīgāro॥
tā sohāgaṇi jāṇīē lāgī jā sahu dhare piāro॥
– *Ādi Granth*, p. 722

O foolish and ignorant soul bride! what is there to be so proud of you? Why are you not enjoying the love of your Master who is within the home of yourself? He is so near to you. O foolish bride! why are you searching Him elsewhere? Adorn yourself with His fear in your eyes and your heart with love for Him. You will be accepted as a true devotee and faithful bride of the Master; you should imbibe deep love for the Supreme Being within you.

In this hymn, Guru Nānak expresses the earnest desire of the soul bride and advises that the Lord is within and very near. One has to be committed and devoted to enjoy His love.

sakhī sahelī garabi gahelī॥ *suṇi saha kī ika bāta suhelī*॥
jo mai bedana sā kisu ākhā māī॥
hari binu jīu na rahai kaṁse rākhā māī॥
hau dohāgaṇi kharī raṅñāṇī॥ *gaiā su jobanu dhana pachutāṇī*॥
tū dānā sāhibu siri merā॥ *khijamati karī janu baṅdā terā*॥
bhaṇati nānaku aṅdesā ehī॥ *binu darasana kaise ravau sanehī*॥
– Ibid., p. 990

O friends and companions full of pride within you! hear a love tale of the Supreme Being. I cannot share it with anyone else than you. I cannot live without my God husband who is so much loving. I cannot smooth myself. I am his depressed and estranged bride and feel totally miserable. I regret and repent for loss of my youth. He is my intelligent Lord who protects me. I am in His service as His faithful servant. I feel worried and suffer because I do not get His vision and without which I cannot enjoy Him.

This is an expression of pain of the soul bride to have a vision of the God Lord. Guru Nānak advises his soulmate to hear the blissful word of the Lord to find relief in pain.

hari binu kiu dhīrai manu merā॥
koṭi kalapa ke dūkha bināsana sācu dṛḍāi niberā॥
krodhu nivāri jale hau mamatā premu sadā nauraṅgī॥
– Ibid., p. 1232

Without the Lord one cannot find peace and comfort of mind. The guilt of sin of innumerable ages is cleared when the truth is implanted within and only then one is released from the rotation of being born again. When anger goes away, egotism and attachment get burnt away, then one is filled with His ever-fresh love.

Guru Nānak states that he cannot be comfortable without God. He hails Him as Lord of the universe and prays that he, the soul bride, wants to see Him throughout the night. He says that God has fully bewitched his heart, and He only knows his pain of separation. It is the word of the *guru* that leads one to attain Him. He asks for mercy to merge him with Him.

ECSTASY OF UNION WITH GOD

hama ghari sājana āe ॥ *sācai meli milāe* ॥
sahaji milāe hari mani bhāe pañca mile sukhu pāiā ॥
sāī vasatu parāpati hoī jisu setī manu lāiā ॥
anadinu melu bhaiā manu māniā ghara mandara sohāe ॥
....
āvahu mīta piāre ॥ *maṅgala gāvahu nāre* ॥
....
avuho sajanā hau dekhā darasanu terā rāma ॥
ghari āpanaḍai khaḍī takā mai mani cāu ghanerā rāma ॥
mani cāu ghanerā suṇi prabha merā mai terā bharavāsā ॥
darsanu dekhi bhaī nihakevala janama maraṇa dukhu nāsā ॥
– *Ādi Granth*, p. 764

Noble men have assembled in my house. I have the pleasure of unity with them by the grace of God; I feel very peaceful in their company. I have got the company of most desired companions. I am pleased to see them again and again at every time of the day or night. I find the true home within me very beautiful. The unstuck sound current of the *pañca śabada* (five primal sounds), is vibrating and resounding; so come beloved noble men and sing songs of joy, O sisters.

O Lord, come to me to enable me enjoy your blessed vision and holy look. I am standing at my door, waiting for you; I am yearning for your pleased visit with my faith and sincere believe in you.

In this hymn Guru Nānak expresses his joy of union with God and godly men. His soul companions and seekers of God have come to his place. They are the blessed people of God. He has met them through love and the Lord is pleased. Meeting the saints and blessed seekers, he is pleased. It was his desire to see them which has how been fulfilled. He feels associated with them eternally. The five unstuck strains of music ring within him. Come all sisters, mates and sing the songs of joy. Sing the wedding songs of truth that the Lord is pleased whose glory rings throughout the ages. The Lord comes into him and through His word, all his tasks are fulfilled. His body and mind are imbued with the nectar (word) and within him shines the jewel of love. True is your play, infinite, unfathomable Lord: who can reveal Thee without you yourself?

tere baṅke loiṇa daṅta rīsālā ॥ *sohaṇe naka jina laṁmaḍe vālā* ॥
kaṅcana kāiā suine kī ḍhālā ॥
sovaṅna ḍhālā kr̥sana mālā japahu tusī sahelīho ॥
jama duāri na hohu khaḍīā sikha suṇahu mahelīho ॥

– *Ādi Granth*, p. 567

Your eyes are sparkling; your teeth are shining; your nose is beautiful; your hair are flowing long; your body is golden and trendy; you are wearing Kr̥ṣṇa's string of beads. O blessed ones! concentrate on Him and if you ignore it you have to see the door of death again and again.

In this hymn, Guru Nānak, in the ecstasy of his vision of God, describes His beauty. Beauteous are the Lord's eyes. His teeth are sparkling. His gait is graceful and speech is very sweet. His youth is alluring like *koel* and He is absorbed in Himself. He is absorbed in His own majesty with measured steps of an elephant. Soul bride's love for the Lord flows like pure water of the Ganges and she feels proud in her love for such a Lord.

daiā dānu daiālu tū kari kari dekhaṇahāru ॥
daiā karahi prabha meli laihi khina mahi ḍhāhi usāri ॥
dānā tū bīnā tuhī dānā kai siri dānu ॥
dālada bhaṅjana dukha dalaṇa guramukhi giānu dhiānu ॥

– Ibid., p. 934

> Be merciful to me and let me be united with you O my Lord! In a blink of an eye things get destroyed and rebuilt by you. You are full of wisdom and watchful. You are the provider of all providers. You are the eraser of poverty and all sufferings. Only godly men can attain concentration and intelligence to contain you.

In this hymn, Guru Nānak prays that through *guru* there is complete surrender of mind before God and he has received immaculate name. He hails his *guru* who blessed him with the name. He cries in pain for the Lord's vision and asks whose skirt shall I hold? There is, nor there was, any one for him. He implores that God is the creator and supporter of all creations and embodiment of mercy, charity and compassion. He is the destroyer of poverty and pain; Nānak prays to Him to bless us with wisdom and contemplation and unite us with Him.

kari kirapā apanai ghari āiā || *tā mili sakhīā kāju racāiā* ||
khelu dekhi mani anadu bhaiā sahu vīāhaṇa āiā ||
gāvahu gāvahu kāmaṇī bibeka bīcāru ||
hamarai ghari āiā jagajīvanu bhatāru ||
....
bhanati nānaku sabhanā kā piru eko soi ||
jisa no nadari kare sā sohāgaṇi hoi ||

– *Ādi Granth*, p. 351

> He comes to my home by His own grace; my soul friends gather to attend my marriage with Him. I achieve complete bliss on watching all this play of God; my Master husband comes to be one with me. So call upon all my friends to sing songs of spiritual intelligence and happiness. My spouse who is the life of this world comes into my home. Nānak says that one God alone is the Master husband of all soul brides. His graceful glance makes them happy and blissful.

These lines express the ecstasy of Guru Nānak on being blessed by the grace of the Lord. He invites all his sister companions to witness and enjoy the moment.

jau tau prema khelaṇa kā cāu || *siru dhari talī galī merī āu* ||
itu māragi pairu dharījai || *siru dījai kāṇi na kījai* ||

– Ibid., p. 1412

> Those who wish to share the playful love with God should abandon all their mental dispositions and assemble before Him to tread on the path along with Him. One should forget all other worldly approaches to follow Him.

This is a very beautiful expression of Guru Nānak. If you seek to play the game of God's love then enter upon my path with your mind (head) upon your palm that is geared up fully. Once you set your foot on my way, then laydown your head and do not find the way out. Such is the glory and ecstasy of love of the Lord.

The Upaniṣads and hymns of Guru Nānak portray very vividly the human urge to have a vision of the Supreme Lord, individual soul's cry and pain of separation from Him and the ecstasy and fulfilment after beholding Him. This is not a one-sided love but individuals feel the reciprocation of His love by way of His grace and care for sustaining His creation. Man feels the pangs of separation from Him at the same time he enjoys the bounty of His care through fulfilment of one's needs right from his birth in a very natural way. Seers sing songs in pain of His separation and tread upon the difficult path of Self-realization to enjoy the union with Him. The Supreme Lord through His grace manifests Himself in those whom He chooses to be worthy. Thus the mutual love between man and the Supreme Lord forms an important subject matter of Upaniṣads as well as the hymns of Guru Nānak.

Nadar (Grace)

In spiritual and religious matters, grace is considered to be a gift bestowed upon the seeker. It may be either as a reward for following the commandments or by the mere whim or mercy. Thus the blessings bestowed remind and confirm the individual that the seeker is helpless to succeed on the progressive path of spiritual pursuits by his own efforts alone. Unless there is the element of the favour of the Supreme Lord one cannot succeed. Individual's efforts, combined with the blessings of supreme will of God, lead him on the progressive path of Self-realization.

The following verses of the Upaniṣads explain that without the grace of the Lord neither knowledge/learning, nor can self-efforts help individuals in Self-realization.

nāyamātmā pravacanena labhyo na medhayā na bahunā śrutena ।
yamevaiṣa vṛṇute tena labhyastasyaiṣa ātmā vivṛṇute tanuṁ svām ॥

– *Muṇḍaka Upaniṣad* 3.2.3

This Self cannot be attained by teaching only nor by intellectual power nor by much hearing. It is to be attained by the one whom (the Self) chooses. To such a one, the Self reveals its own nature.

. . . yadvai tatsukṛtaṁ । raso vai saḥ । rasaṁ hyevāyaṁ labdhvānandī bhavati । ko hyevānyātkaḥ prāṇyāt । yadeṣa ākāśa ānando na syāt eṣa hyevānandayāti । yadā hyevaiṣa etasminnadṛśye 'nātmye 'nirukte 'nilayane 'bhyaṁ pratiṣṭhāṁ vindate । atha so 'bhyaṁ gato bhavati, yadā hyevaiṣa etasminnudaramantaraṁ kurute । atha tasya bhayaṁ bhavati । tattveva bhayaṁ viduṣo 'manvanāsya . . .

– *Taittirīya Upaniṣad* 2.7.1

Verily, what that well made is the essence of existence. For, truly on getting the essence, one becomes blissful. For, who could live or breathe if there was not this bliss in the space? This verily is that which bestows bliss. For, when one finds fearlessness as support in Him who is invisible, bodiless, undefined, without support, then he reaches fearlessness. When however this (soul) makes in this one the smallest interval, then for him, there is fear. That verily is the fear of the knower, who does not reflect.

tadetaditi manyante 'nirdeśyaṁ paramaṁ sukham ।
kathaṁ nu tadvijānīyaṁ kimu bhāti vibhāti vā ॥

– *Kaṭha Upaniṣad* 2.2.14

This is that and thus they recognize the ineffable Supreme Bliss. How then I may come to know of this? Does it shine of itself or does it shine in reflection?

na tatra sūryo bhāti na candratārakaṁ nemā vidyuto bhānti, kuto 'yamagniḥ ।
tameva bhāntamanubhāti sarvaṁ tasya bhāsā sarvamidaṁ vibhāti ॥

– Ibid. 2.2.15

The sun shines not there, nor the moon and stars, these lightings shine not, where then could this fire be? Everything shines only after that shining light. His shining illuminates all in this world.

Guru Nānak also expresses similar thoughts in his hymns. He, time and again stresses that one cannot attain progress by self-efforts in spiritual pursuits without God's grace (*nadar*). He equally refers to the grace of a *guru* who lights the individual's path to self-realization.

nadari kare tā meli milāe ॥
guṇa saṁgrahi augaṇa sabadi jalāe ॥
....
prema prāeṇa prītama rāu ॥
nadari karetā būjhe nāu ॥

– *Ādi Granth*, p. 222

It is only with His grace that one is united with Him; the virtues come forth and vices are burnt away through *śabada*. The beloved God is pleased with true love only. It is due to His grace that one is able to acquire the word from *guru*.

In this hymn Guru Nānak explains that he who with the *guru*'s grace loves God, finds God residing within him. One cannot reach self without Lord's name. The Lord of love leans on the love of the devotees. It is the grace of God which leads one to know the essence of His name.

āpe mele bharamu cukāe ॥
gura parasādi parama padu pāe ॥

– Ibid., p. 223

The Lord unites individuals with Him by clearing their doubts and by the *guru*'s grace this position is acquired.

āpi upāe āpe dei ॥ *āpe duramati manahi karei* ॥
gura parasādi vasai mani āi ॥

– Ibid., p. 349

You Yourself created the world and You are the provider to all. You eradicate all mental and physical evils. You are found to reside in the individuals with the grace of *guru*.

Guru Nānak in the above two hymns explains that God Himself is the Lord who unites us with Himself by dispelling all our doubts.

With the *guru*'s grace this highest state of equipoise is attained.

guraparasādi jāṇai mihamānu ||
tā kichu daragaha pāvai mānu ||
– *Ādi Granth*, p. 350

One finds that he is a temporary visitor to this world with the grace of the *guru*. It is with this realization that one finds honour before the Supreme Being.

guri sacu kahiā aṁmṛtu lahiā mani tani sācu sukhāiā ||
āpe guramukhi āpe devai āpe aṁmṛtu pīāiā ||
– Ibid., p. 930

One is able to enjoy the heavenly drops; one attains both mental and physical peace. God Himself acts as *guramukha* and provides the pure drops of heavenly nature.

In the above two hymns, Guru Nānak explains the role of a *guru* and his grace for an individual to realize the Self.

sabha mahi varatai eko soi ||
jisa no kirapā kare tisu paragaṭu hoi ||
– Ibid., p. 931

Only one Lord dwells in all beings, but He manifests Himself to the one, only on whom He showers His grace.

lekhu na miṭaī he sakhī jo likhiā karatāri ||
āpe kāraṇu jini kīā kari kirapā pagu dhāri ||
karate hathi vaḍiāīā būjhahu gura bīcāri ||
likhiā pheri na sakīē jiu bhāvī tiu sāri ||
nadari terī sukhu pāiā nānaka sabadu vīcārī ||
– Ibid., p. 937

O my soul companions! the writ of the Lord cannot be overridden. He places his foot in the universe created by Him. All the virtues remain with God, this can be known from the *guru*. He cares for us in His own way. His graceful glance leads us to reflect on *śabada*.

Here Guru Nānak explains that the writ of God cannot be erased, it is only by His grace that He walks into some individuals. Reflecting on the *guru*'s word, one should know that all glory is in His hands and His writ cannot be challenged.

nāu bīju bakhasīsa bohala dunīā sagala daroga ||
nānaka nadarī karamu hoi jāvahi sagala vijoga ||
....
nānaka ihu jīu machulī jhīvaru tr̥sanā kālu ||
manūā aṅdhu na cetaī paḍai aciṅtā jālu ||
nānaka citu acetu hai ciṅtā badhā jāi ||
nadari kare je āpaṇī tā āpe lae milāi ||
– *Ādi Granth*, p. 955

If one considers the name of God as seed and His grace as sprouted crop, all around us will look unworthy. It is His graceful glance which can end all the pains of separation. Consider the soul to be a fish caught by the fisherman of death. One is ignorant of the fisherman who casts his net and drags one away. If the individual remains unconscious of this, he will go away from this world in painful condition. A graceful glance of the Lord can save him and unite him with the Supreme Being.

Here Guru Nānak explains that with the seed of name, and crop of grace the whole world seems an illusion. It is only when the Lord is merciful and He unites the Himself to Himself.

guraparasādī vidiā vīcārai paḍi paḍi pāvai mānu ||
āpā madhe āpu paragāsiā pāiā aṁmr̥tu nāmu ||
karatā tū merā jajamānu ||
ika dakhinā hau tai pahi māgau dehi āpaṇā nāmu ||
– Ibid., p. 1329

One should contemplate on spiritual knowledge, read it, study it and seek the *guru*'s grace. By knowledge of the word from the *guru*, one shall get spiritual progress and realize the Self within the self. O God! you are my only protector, please bless me with your name, I beg for it from you.

In these lines Guru Nānak explains that with the grace of the *guru* one dwells in wisdom and gathers glory and the Self within the self becomes manifest.

satiguru seve so sukhu pāe || *jisa no kirapā kare rajāī* ||
– Ibid., p. 1287

One who serves the *guru* attains peace within his mind. He experiences the graceful glance of the Supreme Being.

satiguru bheṭe so sukhu pāe || *hari kā nāmu manni vasāe* ||
nānaka nadari kare so pāe ||
āsa andese te nihakevalu haumai sabadi jalae ||
– *Ādi Granth*, pp. 467-68

To know the truth one has to approach the *guru*. He helps to instil the name of God within his heart. One finds the *guru* only with the grace of the merciful God; his all doubts get cleared and his egotism vanishes with the aid of *śabada*.

nadari karahi je āpaṇī tā nadarī satiguru pāiā ||
ehu jīu bahute janama bharammiā tā satiguri sabadu suṇāiā ||
....
sikhī sikhiā gura vīcāri || *nadarī karami laghāe pāri* ||
– Ibid., p. 465

The *guru* is found only if the merciful Lord shows His mercy. This soul roams through countless births until a true *guru* is found who instructs one into the *śabada*. I have been taught these teachings while contemplation upon the *guru*. By His Grace, He carries His servants across.

In the above two hymns, Guru Nānak explains that one finds peace if he finds a true *guru*. But one finds a true *guru* only with the grace of the Lord who instructs one to the *śabada* and by contemplating on the *guru*'s instructions one can find the way across.

nadari kare tā simariā jāi || *ātamā dravai rahai liva lāi* ||
ātamā parātamā eko karai || – Ibid., p. 661

One can remember the Supreme Being only if He showers His grace upon him; then he gets concentrated within; his mind melts and he remains merged in Him; his individual soul and the Universal Soul become one.

These lines explain that even if you find a *guru* and try to meditate, it is only God's grace that you may remember Him in meditation. One's mind gets softened and concentrated.

God loves His creation. He expresses His love and responds

through His grace (*nadar*) to the seekers who are on the right path of love and search for Him. The Upaniṣads declare that mere learning, practising virtue and austerities in life cannot bring Self-realization to a seeker. It is He who manifests Himself to one whom He chooses. Thus grace carries both His mercy as well as His will. The hymns of Guru Nānak also explain very vividly that if He wills (*nadar kare*) He manifests Himself into a seeker. With His grace, a seeker finds a true *guru*, and is able to concentrate and contemplate on Him. One cannot remember Him even in his meditation without His grace. He also explains that the writ of *prārabdha karma* cannot be erased; yet through His grace and mercy one gets care and relief.

5

Aim of Man's Life and Path of Liberation

STRUGGLES and sufferings in the worldly life make one tired and drowsy, at the same time experiences of splashes of cool breeze of God's love and grace keep him fresh and hopeful. Deeply in love and fear of God one tries to find a way as to how he should conduct himself to be happy in life and face death peacefully. He starts searching for the meaning of life and the true aim of his human form and path of liberation.

The concept of four *puruṣārtha*s – *dharma, artha, kāma* and *mokṣa* – accepts the necessity of pursuing all these four ends of human life with a principal goal of liberation from the cycle of birth and death.

Dharma stands for the well-being of individuals and the community as also of those who take on higher moral and spiritual order. It is therefore important that *dharma* regulates the pursuit of *artha* and *kāma*.

Artha is the accumulation of objects of enjoyment and means mainly in the form of wealth and other paraphernalia. For acquiring wealth and material possessions same principles should be adopted. Wrong and foul means should not be adopted for earning wealth nor should one grow greedy and begin hoarding. Indeed, *artha* is necessary to do good deeds like charity, i.e. *dharma*. Again it should be noted that man is instinctively drawn to the two *puruṣārtha*s of *kāma* and *artha*, but to be law abiding and charitable is not an instant tendency in all.

Kāma is the seeking of satisfaction of our desires of all sorts. One should not however come into conflict with other's interests nor should one come into conflict with his ultimate moral and spiritual well-being.

Mokṣa is the attainment of the *summum bonum* of life, the realization of divinity in man.

Aim of Man's Life according to Hymns of Guru Nānak

PERSONAL EXPERIENCE OF DIVINITY AND UNION WITH THE ULTIMATE TRUTH

According to Guru Nānak, the aim of life and human form is personal experience of divinity and union with the Ultimate Truth which is possible only in human life by practice under the guidance of a true *guru*. So one should not waste it and attain the goal while living a balanced life of virtue, devotion, attaining higher knowledge and practising *dharma*, adhering to the Divine Will.

suṇi mana mitra piāriā milu velā hai eha॥
jaba lagu jobani sāsu hai taba lagu ihu tanu deha॥
binu guṇa kāmi na āvaī ḍhahi ḍherī tanu kheha॥
mere mana lai lāhā ghari jāhi॥

– *Ādi Granth*, p. 20

Human life is a chance to meet the Supreme Being. This is the form for God-realization, let it be known to all. This body and its youth remain only till there is breath of life. Without good deeds it is worthless and shall get converted to dust. So one must utilize this opportunity to earn profit before he is called back.

In these lines Guru Nānak cautions individuals that human life is the time to unite with the Lord and reap some gains by practising virtues. Body remains till it is in bloom and one breathes. Otherwise it will go waste like dust returning to dust.

vaṇaju karahu vaṇajāriho vakharu lehu samāli॥
taisī vasatu visāhīē jaisī nibahai nāli॥
agai sāhu sujāṇu hai laisī vasatu samāli॥
bhāī re rāmu kahahu citu lāi॥
harijasu vakharu lai calahu sahu dekhai patīāi॥
jinā rāsi na sacu hai kiu tinā sukhu hoi॥
khoṭai vaṇaji vaṇaṁjiē manu tanu khoṭā hoi॥
phāhī phāthe miraga jiu dūkhu ghaṇo nita roi॥

– Ibid., pp. 22-23

Individuals should trade here with care and look after their

> accumulation of good deeds. One should invest his time in the actions which earn something which can be carried over with us. In the next world, the Supreme merchant of this creation will only accept your good deeds. O my sisters and brothers of my luck, utter God's name and concentrate your attention upon Him. Gather bundles of God's praises with you. The Supreme Being will look at them and approve them. One who does not accumulate the assets of truth cannot be peaceful. By trading in falsehoods here individual minds and bodies become false. They are bound to pain and sufferings like a deer fallen in a trap.

Guru Nānak advises mankind to trade and buy goods which may last with the individuals. The virtues and uttering of God's name will benefit them in the life after.

> *māṇasu janamu dulaṁbhu guramukhi pāiā*॥
> *manu tanu hoi culaṁbhu je satigura bhāiā*॥
> *calai janamu savāri vakharu sacu lai*॥
> *pati pāi darabāri satigura sabadi bhai*॥
> – *Ādi Granth*, p. 751

> It is very difficult to attain the human form; only the godly soul acquires it. If it pleases the true *guru*, individual's mind and body get the deep colour of devotional love in life. He departs from this world after proper utilization of human form and carries with him the profit of the True Name. Such a man is honoured in His *darbāra*, the royal court of the Lord through blessing of the *śabadu* and fear of God.

Guru Nānak declares that the human form is precious and only those who have turned Godwards attain it. Individual's body and mind feel a cooling effect with Lord's love and *guru*'s grace. One who is blessed with the *guru*'s word and God's fear is held high before the Supreme Being.

> *manamukhu lahari gharu taji vigūcai avarā ke ghara herai*॥
> *gṛha dharamu gavāe satiguru na bheṭai duramati ghūmana gherai*॥
> *disaṅtaru bhavai pāṭha paḍi thākā tṛsanā hoi vadherai*॥
> *kācī piṅḍī sabadu na cīnai udaru bharai jaise ḍhorai*॥
> *bābā aisī ravata ravai saṁniāsī*॥
> *gura kai sabadi eka liva lāgī terai nāmi rate tṛpatāsī*॥ – Ibid., p. 1012

> The self-willed persons in the fit of enthusiasm renounce their homes and get ruined and look towards other lands and houses. They avoid their duty towards their family and do not search for a *guru*. They get trapped in mental evils. They get tired roaming and studying religious books and their thirst for worldly things goes high. These mortals never practise *śabada*. They eat and their belly is like a beast. O wise man! a true renunciate lives his life; he develops love for God through the *śabada* and gets filled with His love; he remains ever satisfied and fulfilled.

Guru Nānak warns that those who abandon their homes, shirk their responsibilities of life and beg at the others doors, are caught in the whirlpool of an evil mind. They wander from land to land in vain. They do not reflect on the word within their fast dissolving body and thus waste their life.

> *so girahī jo nigrahu karai* || *japu tapu saṅjamu bhīkhiā karai* ||
> *puṅna dāna kā kare sarīru* || *so girahī gaṅgā kā nīru* ||
> ....
> *so audhūtī jo dhūpe āpu* || *bhikhiā bhojanu karai saṅtāpu* ||
> *auhaṭha paṭaṇa mahi bhīkhiā karai* || *so audhūtī siva puri caḍai* ||
> ....
> *so udāsī ji pāle udāsu* || *aradha uradha kare niraṅjana vāsu* ||
> ....
> *bolai gopīcaṅdu sati sarūpu* || *parama taṅta mahi rekha na rūpu* ||
> – *Ādi Granth*, p. 952

> One is a *gṛhasthī* who controls his desires, wish for concentration, practise restrains and remains disciplined. He offers his wealth for charitable purposes with his own body. Such a householder is as pure like the water of the Ganges. One can be called a detached *sādhu* who sheds away his deceptive nature. He asks for food of pain to be digested by him. Such a renunciate progresses on the path to the City of God. Lord embodies Truth. The Ultimate Truth is formless and shapeless.

Here Guru Nānak gives the definition of a householder and a *saṁnyāsī*. According to him, one who disciplines his sense desires and begs for God contemplation with austerity and self-control and gives charity, all through his body, is a pure householder like the water of Ganges. He only is the true *saṁnyāsī* who burns himself, begs for suffering and feeds himself on it.

saraba jīā siri lekhu dhurāhū binu lekhai nahī koī jīu ||
āpi alekhu kudarati kari dekhai hukami calāe soī jīu ||
mana re rāma japahu sukhu hoī ||
....
calatau ṭhāki rakhahu ghari apanai gura miliē iha mati hoī jīu ||
dekhi adr̥saṭu rahau bisamādī dukhu bisarai sukhu hoī jīu ||
pīvahu apiu parama sukhu pāīē nija ghari vāsā hoī jīu ||
janama maraṇa bhava bhañjanu gāīē punarapi janamu na hoī jīu ||
tatu nirañjanu joti sabāī sohaṁ bhedu na koī jīu ||

– *Ādi Granth*, pp. 598-99

Everyone is bound by the pre-written destiny. No one is there without the pre-written fortune. Only God Himself is beyond it. He created the creation by His creative power; He looks upon His creation and ensures that His command is being followed. One should utter the name of Rāma to be peaceful. Restrict your changing mind and keep it fixed within its own home; this teaching can be sought from the *guru*. When you see the Lord, you shall be astonished and overjoyed; you will forget the pains and shall be peaceful. With the pure drops of heavenly essence one will become blissful and reside ever in the home of himself. One should always sing the praise of God who destroys our all fears of rotating births. One will not take birth again. He is the light of all individuals. You will feel, I am He and He is me, there is no difference between us.

jisu jala nidhi kāraṇi tuma jagi āe so aṁmr̥tu gura pāhī jīu ||
choḍahu vesu bhekha caturāī dubidhā ihu phalu nāhī jīu ||
mana re thiru rahu matu kata jāhī jīu ||
bāhari ḍhūḍhata bahutu dukhu pāvahi ghari aṁmr̥tu ghaṭa māhī jīu ||
....
niramala nāmu japahu sada guramukhi antara kī gati tāhī jīu ||

– Ibid., p. 598

The *guru* has the knowledge of *nāma*, the name of the true Lord for which you have taken birth in this world. Leave behind all religious robes, different appearances and clever actions; you cannot get this as long as you are afflicted with duality. One should remain steady and should not roam hither and thither. If one tries to search God outside himself he is bound to experience the suffering and pain; the heavenly nectar is there within the home of one's own body. One should leave evil and attain virtue; sins will bring one to regret and repent later on. Since one is unable to distinct between the goodness and badness, he sinks into the worldly mud again and again. One should utter the pure *nāma* under the instructions of the *guru*, only then one gets freedom from life and death.

Guru Nānak reminds us in the above two hymns that no one is without the writ of the Lord except the God Himself who works through His own power. His writ runs over all. One should not be fickle-minded and should approach a true *guru* who can make one realize the essence that God and individual are one. Meeting with the *guru* one can hold one's flickering mind at its own place, i.e. self. The main aim of human form is to drink the Lord's nectar and gather the Supreme Bliss. Give up cleverness and garbs and abide in himself. No other tricks and costumes can work. One should know the difference between the good and the pleasant by following the instructions of a true *guru*.

nānaka sadā sohāgaṇī jina jotī joti samāi ||
jai ghari kīrati ākhīe karate kā hoi bīcāro ||
titu ghari gāvahu sohilā sivarahu sirajaṇahāro ||
– *Ādi Granth*, p. 157

O Nānak! the happy soul bride is one whose light merges into His Light. One should utter the name of the Lord in one's own house within. One should meditate wherein the praises of the Supreme are being sung.

Here Guru Nānak states the essence of the aim of human form. The soul bride whose individuality merges with the Universal Soul is ever happy and blessed. In whatever state of mind God dwells and His name is recited, one should attain that state. Meditate on Him and sing his praises.

jitu seviē sukhu paīē so sāhibu sadā samhāliē ||
jitu kītā pāīē āpaṇā sā ghāla burī kiu ghālīē ||

maṅdā mūli na kīcaī de laṁmī nadari nihālīe ||
jiu sāhiba nāli na harīe tevehā pāsā ḍhālīe ||
kichu lāhe upari ghalīe ||

– *Ādi Granth*, p. 474

Peace is gained by doing service to God; one should meditate and reside in the Supreme Being forever. One has to suffer for one's bad deeds so do not indulge in any evil; concentrate on time to come with long sight. So you play the card in such a way that you will not get away from your Lord. Your action should bring some good reward for you.

Here Guru Nānak advises to ingather and serve Him who is the source of permanent bliss. By doing good deeds, we can show our face to Him. One should strive for his real benefit.

raiṇi gavāī soi kai divasu gavāiā khāi ||
hīre jaisā janamu hai kauḍi badale jāi ||
....
anatā dhanu dharaṇī dhare anata na cāhiā jāi ||
anata kau cāhana jo gae se āe anata gavāi ||
....
karamā upari nibaḍai je locai sabhu koi ||
nānaka karaṇā jini kīā soī sāra karei ||

– Ibid., pp. 156-57

One wastes nights in sleep and days in eating. The precious human life is thus wasted in useless pursuits. All the worldly wealth is temporary and ought to be buried under the ground. One should not run after temporary gains which are of no use. One who dies with strong desires for these worldly things is bound to come again and again in this world. No one can accumulate wealth and carry it with him to the other world. One's fortune is the fruit of his accumulated past *karmas*. O Nānak! the Supreme Being who creates takes care of its creation also.

Guru Nānak warns against wasting the precious life in trifles and advises to know what is temporary and what is permanent. The deeds of this life affect one's destiny in the next life.

adhiātama karama kare tā sācā || *mukati bhedu kiā jāṇai kācā* ||

aisā jogī jugati bīcārai ।। *pañca māri sācu uridhārai* ।।
jisa kai aṅtari sācu vasāvai ।। *joga jugati kī kīmati pāvai* ।।
ravi sasi eko gr̥ha udiānai ।। *karaṇī kīrati karama samānai* ।।
eka sabada ika bhikhiā māgai ।। *giānu dhiānu jugati sacu jāgai* ।।

– *Ādi Granth*, p. 223

Those who act and live a spiritual life earn truth. Others who live a false life cannot understand the concept of individual's liberation. Those who walk on the way of contemplation of the Lord are *yogīs*. They overpower the five thieves of passion and imbue the name of true Lord in their hearts. Those who absorb the Lord deep within, they only can feel the value of the path of *yoga*. They feel the heat of the sun and coolness of the moon as one and the same. There is no difference of a house or forests for them. They praise God every day. They pray to Him for the wealth-providing faculty of *śabada*. They always are alert and awakened for getting the spiritual knowledge and thus practise meditation. They follow the right path in their life.

Here Guru Nānak explains that those who do works of the soul are only true whether they live in the house or woods. All wisdom, all meditation, for all ways of religion are to awaken to Truth.

khimā gahī bratu sīla saṅtokhaṁ ।। *rogu na biāpai nā jama dokhaṁ* ।।
mukata bhae prabha rūpa na rekhaṁ ।। *jogī kau kaisā ḍaru hoi* ।।
....
aiso dāsu milai sukhu hoī ।। *dukhu visarai pāvai sacu soī* ।।

– Ibid., pp. 223-24

To forgive others is a true fast, by one's good behaviour and self-contentment one can avoid pain and suffering in life and face death peacefully. By good actions one gets free for absorption into the Supreme Lord who has no form or feature. Thus a *karmayogī* gets no fears. If we meet such a godly man, we also get peace of mind. One forgets all pains when the true Lord is realized.

Guru Nānak explains that one who feels the presence of the Lord gets liberated from fear.

sevā eka na jānasi avare ।। *parapañca biādhi tiāgai kavare* ।।
bhāi milai sacu sācai sacu re ।।

aisā rāma bhagatu janu hoī॥ hariguṇa gāi milai malu dhoī॥
– *Ādi Granth*, p. 225

One who serves the one Lord forgets all others. He leaves all worldly arguments and gets away from all conflicts. It is only love and truth which matter to him on the path of the Truth. Such a Lord seeker is always humble. He sings the glorious praises of the Lord and washes off all his dirt and dust.

haṭhu kari marai na lekhai pāvai॥ vesa karai bahu bhasamala gāvai॥
nāmu bisāri bahuri pachutāvai॥ tūṅ mani hari jīu tūṅ mani sūkha॥
nāmu bisāri sahahi jama dūkha॥
– Ibid., p. 226

One who practises rigidity and dies stubborn is not approved by the Lord. He may wear various costumes and indulge in different religious looks. If one forgets the true *nāma* (the name of the Lord), he is bound to regret and repent in the last. If you believe in the Supreme Being you will remain in peace of mind and if you forget His *nāma* you shall experience pain and fear of death.

bolahi sācu mithiā nahī rāī॥ cālahi guramukhi hukami rajāī॥
....
nija ghari baisi sahaja gharu lahīe॥ hari rasi māte ihu sukhu kahīe॥
– Ibid., p. 227

Guramukhas do not utter any falsehood; they always speak the truth and live according to God's command. In this condition they always reside in the home of their own being within where they find eternal deep insight and peace. Only such one, who is filled with the Lord's essence, experiences this intuitive peace.

In the above three hymns Guru Nānak speaks of the deeds one should do to bring ones own mind under control and dwell in the home of his own being for intuitive peace.

so brahamaṇu jo biṅdai brahamu॥ japu tapu saṅjamu kamāvai karamu॥
sūla saṅtokha kā rakhai dharamu॥ baṅdhana toḍai hovai mukatu॥
soī brahamaṇu pūjaṇa jugatu॥ khatrī so ju karmā kā sūru॥
purina dāna kā karai sarīru॥ khetu pachāṇai bījai dānu॥
so khatrī daragaha paravāṇu॥
– Ibid., p. 1411

> One who knows *Brahman* should be taken as *Brahman*. He utters His name, devotes to meditation, practises austerity and indulges in good deeds. He faithfully observes *dharma*, practises humility and contentment. Such a man sheds his bondages and gets liberated. One should worship such a brāhmaṇa. He alone is kṣatriya who always performs heroic actions of goodness. He offers physical strength for good deeds. He remains firm in his duty and performs generous deeds. Kṣatriya of this type gets accepted before the Supreme Being.

In the above lines, Guru Nānak explains the qualities of a real brāhmaṇa and kṣatriya, worthy of respect. It is not by birth/caste but by the deeds performed which should determine the nature of caste/category.

NECESSITY OF HIGHER KNOWLEDGE

One should have the knowledge of what is real and what is unreal and choice between good and pleasant. Study of scriptures under the guidance of a *guru* is necessary for learning the essence to avoid entrapments in mere rituals and ceremonies.

> *āsā manasā baṅdhanī bhāī karama dharama baṅdhakārī* ||
> *pāpi puṅn jagu jāiā bhāī binasai nāmu visārī* ||
>
> – *Ādi Granth*, p. 635

> Hopes and desires entrap individuals in this world. Religious rituals and ceremonies bind one within religions. One's birth into this world is due to his good and bad deeds of previous life. One suffers and gets polluted if he forgets the name of the Lord.

Guru Nānak calls hopes and desires as chains for the soul. One shuttles between good and evil and is born and reborn and wastes life after life without the Lord's name.

> *dīvā balai aṅdherā jāi* || *beda pāṭha mati pāpā khāi* ||
> *ugavai sūru na jāpai caṅdu* || *jaha giāna pragāsu agiānu miṭaṅtu* ||
> *beda pāṭha saṁsāra kī kāra* || *paḍhi paḍhi paṅḍita karahi bīcāra* ||
> *binu būjhe sabha hoi khuāra* || *nānaka guramukhi utarasi pāri* ||
>
> – Ibid., p. 791

> When a lamp is lit, darkness runs away. By the study of Vedas evil mindedness is eliminated. As with the sunrise the moon becomes

> invisible, when one is spiritually awakened, his ignorance goes away. It is worldly to read the Vedas, the *paṇḍita*s go on reading and studying and then contemplating on these scriptures. But individuals do not try to understand their essence hence they get perverted. O Nānak! only the individuals with godly ways are carried across.

The study of Vedic scriptures lights the lamp of knowledge and dispels the darkness of ignorance. By understanding the essence of these sources of spiritual enlightenment God's men get illuminated.

> *aṁmṛtu nīru giāni mana majanu aṭhasaṭhi tīratha saṅgi gahe*॥
> *gura upadesi javāhara māṇaka sebe sikhu so khoji lahai*॥
> *gura samāni tīrathu nahī koi*॥ *saru saṅtokhu tāsu guru hoi*॥
> *guru darīāu sadā jalu niramalu miliā duramati mailu harai*॥
> *satiguri pāīē pūra nāvaṇu pasū paretahu deva karai*॥
>
> – *Ādi Granth*, pp. 1328-29

> One who gets spiritually awakened to the true *nāma* of the Lord gets benefits of visiting sixty-eight holy places in pilgrimage. The *guru*'s teaching is the real wealth; the seekers who serve their *guru* find this wealth. There is no sacred place equal to the *guru*. The *guru* shrouds the ocean of contentment. The *guru* is the stream of pure water; the water from this stream washes away the dirt and dust of evil-mindedness. The *guru* is a perfect cleansing spot wherein all sins are washed off and even the beasts and ghosts get transformed into gods. He is said to be the *guru* who is a Self-realized man and imbued with God's love in deep inside of his heart.

Guru Nānak emphasizes that for the fulfilment of individual's aim it is necessary to find a true *guru* who can well up the spiritual life within oneself and to enter the house of poise within.

> *guraparasādī vidiā vīcārai paḍi paḍi pāvai mānu*॥
> *āpā madhe āpu paragāsiā pāiā aṁmṛtu nāmu*॥
> ....
> *jatu satu cāvala daiā kaṇaka kari prāpati pātī dhānu*॥
> ....
> *āvatu kinai na rākhiā jāvatu kiu rākhiā jāi*॥
> *jisa te hoā soī paru jāṇai jā usa hī māhi samāi*॥

tū hai vāhu terī rajāi ॥
jo kichu karahi soī paru hoibā avaru na karaṇa jāi ॥
– *Ādi Granth*, p. 1329

One should contemplate spiritual knowledge under the guidance and grace of a *guru;* by higher knowledge one becomes blissful and obtains the true name of God. He Himself is revealed within the self. Guru Nānak prays to God for His blessings to attain virtues of truthfulness, self-discipline, generosity and contemplation. No one can stop anyone from coming to this world; similarly no one can hold back anyone from death. Only the Supreme Being, who is the source of all beings for their birth and merger, knows and understands His play. O Lord, you are great and your commandment is wonderful; whatever you do surely come to happen; nothing else can happen.

viṇu bhai paiē bhagati na hoī ॥ *sabadi rate sadā sukhu hoī* ॥
aisā giānu padārathu nāmu ॥ *guramukhi pāvasi rasi rasi mānu* ॥
giānu giānu kathai sabhu koī ॥ *kathi kathi bādu kare dukhu hoī* ॥
kathi kahaṇai te rahai na koī ॥ *binu rasa rāte mukati na hoī* ॥
giānu dhiānu sabhu gura te hoī ॥ *sācī rahata sācā mani soī* ॥
– Ibid., p. 831

Without developing fear for God, one cannot indulge in devotional worship. Peace is obtained only after one is filled with the *śabada.* The seekers who get the essence of God enjoy peace. Everyone gets curious to know about the spiritual wisdom and spiritual knowledge. They talk, discuss and argue with no end, but suffer. One cannot stop others from discussions and arguments but without getting the essence of God one cannot liberate. The *guru* is a source for all spiritual knowledge of concentration and meditation. One who leads a life of truthfulness, in him the Supreme Being resides. But without being filled with the subtle essence there is no liberation. Spiritual wisdom and meditation all come from the *guru*. Through the lifestyle of Truth, the True Lord comes to dwell in the mind.

In the above two hymns, Guru Nānak explains that one who by the grace of *guru* dwells upon Lord's wisdom gathers glory and within himself his Self becomes manifest. And he is blessed with the nectar name.

ROLE OF DEVOTION

It is necessary to cultivate love for Truth and *dharma,* i.e. love for the Supreme Father and the urge to know Him and the regulating rules for the well-being of an individual and the community that take one to higher moral and spiritual planes.

jīvadiā maru māri na pachotāīē ||
jhūṭhā ihu saṁsāru kini samajhāīē ||
saci na dhare piāru dhaṅdhai dhāīē ||
kāla burā khai kālu siri dunīāīē ||

....

kete kahahi vakhāṇa kahi kahi jāvaṇā ||
veda kahahi vakhiāṇa aṅtu na pāvaṇā ||
paḍiē nāhī bhedu būjhiē pāvaṇā ||
khaṭu darasana kai bhekhi kisai saci samāvaṇā ||
sacā purakhu alakhu sabadi suhāvaṇā ||
maṅne nāu bisaṅkha daragaha pāvaṇā ||

– *Ādi Granth,* pp. 147-48

One should die to the world when he is still alive to conquer death. One will not repent and regret for anything while leaving from this world. This world is not permanent but people do not understand it. They do not instill love for the truth and go on chasing the worldly affairs.

People love to talk and discuss. They leave this world talking and discussing. Even Vedas discuss and explain a lot but they cannot also determine His limits. It is not by the study of Vedas but by intuitive awareness that God's mystery is revealed to some individuals. Śāstras explain in six ways but only a few people could achieve absorption in Him through their means. God is beyond physical knowledge. The melody within us is very enchanting. He who believes in the infinite God gets approved by Him.

Guru Nānak stresses that we can win over death while alive. As Śāstras there are six schools of philosophy, yet rare is one who merges with truth by following them.

mātā mati pitā saṅtokhu || *satu bhāī kari ehu visekhu* ||
kahaṇā hai kichu kahaṇu na jāi || *tau kudarati kīmati nahī pāi* ||

sarama surati dui sasura bhae॥ *karaṇī kāmaṇi kari mana lae*॥
sāhā saṅjogu vīāhu vijogu॥ *sacu saṅtati kahu nānaka jogu*॥
– *Ādi Granth*, pp. 151-52

One should treat wisdom as mother and satisfaction as father and take truthfulness as brother. These virtues are best of your relations. Many have attempted to describe Him but no one could do so.

Let self-surrendering and quick understanding be your parents-in-law and noble deeds as your husband. One should consider union with the Supreme Lord as one's marriage date, and departure from this world as marriage. Nānak says that the Truth will be born out of this union.

Guru Nānak advises that let self-surrender and intuition be your parents-in-law and your good deeds be the husband. Let your union with the Holy be thy date of marriage and detachment from the world thy marriage. Thus your offspring will be Truth.

kiratu paiā naha meṭai koi॥ *kiā jāṇā kiā āgai hoi*॥
jo tisu bhāṇā soī huā॥ *avaru na karaṇai vālā dūā*॥
nā jāṇā karama kevaḍa terī dāti॥ *karamu dharamu tere nāma kī jāti*॥
– Ibid., pp. 153-54

It is explained that individual's past deeds cannot be removed. No one can know the tomorrow's happening; it is His pleasure to plan for tomorrow. He is the only doer and no one other than Him can do anything. One cannot exactly define *karma*. All our actions are contained in His name only.

Guru Nānak explains that the writ of *karma* cannot be erased as one has to bear the brunt. To him all the merits of works and religion are the essence of God's name.

nidhi sidhi niramala nāmu bīcāru॥
pūrana pūri rahiā bikhu māri॥ *trikuṭī chūṭī bimala majhāri*॥
....
hukami saṅjogī nijaghari jāu॥
garaba gataṁ sukha ātama dhiānā॥ *joti bhaī jotī māhi samānā*॥
– Ibid., pp. 220-21

All the *nidhis* and *siddhis*, spiritual powers, are contained in the name of God. The Supreme Being is spread throughout the creation. He is the destroyer of the power of *māyā*. With the Lord's command I am blessed to enter within the abode of myself. I feel intoxicated with His name and find perfect peace in concentration on Him. I have experienced the divinity within myself and absorption in Him.

Guru Nānak emphasizes again and again that he alone is in peace who sings Lord's praise. All the spiritual powers and miracles lie in dwelling on Lord's name. He discloses that to him with the *guru*'s word revealed to him, he has entered in the Self and enjoyed the real peace as he merged with equipoise.

terā nāmu karī canaṇāṭhīā je manu urasā hoi ||
karaṇī kuṅgū je ralai ghaṭa aṅtari pūjā hoi ||
pūjā kīcai nāmu dhiāīē binu nāvai pūja na hoi ||
bāhari deva pakhālīahi je manu dhovai koi ||
– *Ādi Granth*, p. 489

One should make His Name the sandalwood and one's mind the rubbing stone. One should make good deeds saffron and should perform devotional worship within the heart. Concentrate and contemplate on His name for devotional worship. There cannot be any worship without the holy name of the Supreme Being. Wash yourself from within as you wash idols from outside.

Guru Nānak says that the true worship is the contemplation of Lord's name. Without His name, there is no worship.

sacaḍā dūri na bhālīē ghaṭi ghaṭi sabadu pachāṇovā ||
sacu sabadu pachāṇahu dūri na jāṇahu jini eha racanā rācī ||
– Ibid., p. 581

The one, who is the creator and dissolver of the creation, alone knows His creative powers. One should not go far away in search of God; one should realize the *śabada* deep within the heart. By meditating His *nāma*, one becomes peaceful; one always incurs loss in forgetting His name.

Guru Nānak advises that there is no need to search for the Lord at far-off places. He is everywhere and in every heart. The need is to recognize the *śabada* in one's own self within.

bhau bhui pavitu pāṇī satu saṅtokhu baleda ॥
halu halemī hālī citu cetā vatra vakhata saṅjogu ॥
nāu bīju bakhasīsa bohala ḍunīā sagala daroga ॥
nānaka nadarī karamu hoi jāvahi sagala vijoga ॥
....
nānaka citu acetu hai ciṅtā badhā jāi ॥
nadari kare je āpaṇī tā āpe lae milāi ॥
– *Ādi Granth*, p. 955

One should make God's fear his field, treat purity of heart as water, his truthfulness and satisfaction bulls, humbleness the plough, awareness the plougher, remembrance preparation of the soil and unity with God the time to plant. Let the name of God be the seed, and His forgiving grace the crop. If one exercises this habit, all the worldly appearances shall seem illusions to him. Nānak says that a glance of mercy, God can end one's separation from Him to enjoy the Supreme Bliss.

Guru Nānak counts the virtues required to be cultivated for one's union with God. When the seed of name of God is added to a cultivated mind with these virtues, whole world visible before him will look like an illusion.

akhīṅ paraṇai je phirāṅ dekhāṅ sabhu ākāru ॥
puchā giānī paṅḍitāṅ puchāṅ beda bīcāra ॥
puchā devāṅ māṇasāṅ jodha karahi avatāra ॥
sidha samādhī sabhi suṇī jāi dekhāṅ darabāru ॥
agai sacā saci nāi nirabhau bhai viṇu sāru ॥
hora kacī mati kacu picu aṅdhiā aṅdhu bīcāru ॥
nānaka karamī baṅdagī nadari laṅghāe pāri ॥
– Ibid., pp. 1241-42

One may walk around with his fully open eyes and look all around the various forms of creation. He may ask spiritual teachers, religious scholars, those who explain the Vedas, gods, etc. or he may consult *siddhas* in *samādhi*, and visit the court of the Lord one will find that all forms of creation are Truth; God is fearless and has absolutely no fear. All other intellectualism is trivial and untrue; blind individuals indulge in blind contemplations. Nānak says by fruit of all virtues, the individuals come to concentrate upon God; His grace carries them across.

Guru Nānak explains unity of existence in all forms and the Truth is the ultimate cause and effect of the entire creation.

dūkhā te sukha ūpajahi sūkhī hovahi dūkha॥
jitu mukhi tū sālāhīahi titu mukhi kaisī bhūkha॥
nānaka mūrakhu eku tū avaru bhalā saisāru॥
jitu tani nāmu na ūpajai se tana hohi khuāra॥
– *Ādi Granth*, p. 1328

Pleasure originates from pain and out of pleasure pain is produced. That mouth which praises God does not feel hungry for anything else. O Nānak! you alone are foolish while all the rest of the world is good. That body in which the *nāma* does not grow up, that body becomes miserable.

Guru Nānak states that God's name is the jewel and His grace is the light for this world. One, whose mind is filled with God's name, gets illuminated with His light. His name is the cure for all ailments. Nothing can overweigh His name.

KARMA

ihu tanu dharatī bīju karamā karo salila āpāu sāriṅgapāṇī॥
manu kirasāṇu hari ridai jaṁmāi lai iu pāvasi padu nirabāṇī॥
....
bikhai bikāra dusaṭa kirakhā kare ina taji ātamai hoi dhiāī॥
japu tapu saṅjamu hohi jaba rākhe kamalu bigasai madhu āsramāī॥
bīsa sapatāharo bāsaro saṁgrahai tīni khoḍā nita kālu sārai॥
dasa aṭhāra mai aparaṁparo cīnai kahai nānaku iva eku tārai॥
– Ibid., p. 23

One should convert his body into a farm and the virtues as seeds to be sown in it. It should be irrigated with the God's name which controls the whole world. Convert your mind to be a farmer; the love for God shall grow in your heart and you shall acquire the state of equipoise. One should shed all badness, cruelty and falsehood; one should concentrate and meditate on God's name. When one gets protected within from all outside entanglements, the knots of heart are opened and the nectar flows out from within. Let the twenty-seven elements of one's body be brought under his control and throughout the three stages of consciousness remember death. See the infinite Lord in all the directions and all the variety of nature as one. Nānak says that in this way the Lord shall take you across.

Guru Nānak emphasizes to weed out the evil desires, abstain from sin, practise contemplation and austerity. Let the body gather all the twenty-seven *tattvas* abiding in it and remember the death in all three stages of life. Here he makes reference to the Sāṁkhya philosophy which specifies the body of twenty-seven *tattvas*: five subtle, five manifest, five *jñānendriyas*, five *karmendriyas*, five winds, mind and reason. When chanting, meditation and self-discipline portend one, the lotus blossoms and honey trickles.

amalu kari dharatī bīja sabado kari saca kī āba nita dehi pāṇī ||
hoi kirasāṇu imānu jaṁmāi lai bhisatu dojaku mūḍe eva jāṇī ||
matu jāṇasahi galī pāiā ||
māla kai māṇai rūpa kī sobhā itu bidhī janamu gavāiā ||
aiba tani cikaḍo ihu manu mīḍako kamala kī sāra nahi mūli pāī ||
....
khasama kī nadari dilahi pasiṅde jinī kari eku dhiāiā ||

– *Ādi Granth*, pp. 23-24

Treat your virtues like soil and sow the seed of *guru*'s word in it; water it with your truthfulness; your mind may work as farmer on it; from all this the faith will grow forth which will provide you knowledge of what is good and what is bad. Do not consider that you can attain God by mere words. Otherwise it will be a waste of your life in pursuit of material accumulations. Mind is a frog and body is mud. The mind does not listen and is attracted towards illusions. Those who meditate on God alone get the grace of the Lord and they become pleasing to Him.

Guru Nānak explains that with good actions as a farm, the word as seed, truth as water and mind as farmer, faith sprouts which brings forth the knowledge of all spiritual planes. One should not waste life in pride of wealth and beauty. Mind is a frog which does not know that it lives with the Lotus. One gets the grace of the Lord only through meditation.

japu tapu saṅjamu sādhīē tirathi kīcai vāsu ||
puṅna dāna caṅgiāīā binu sāce kiā tāsu ||
jehā rādhe tehā luṇai binu guṇa janamu viṇāsu ||

muṅdhe guṇa dāsī sukhu hoi ॥
avagaṇa tiāgi samāī guramati pūrā soi ॥
– *Ādi Granth*, p. 56

Merely chanting and meditating, practising self-control and self-restraint, residing and visiting holy places or to give donations and perform good deeds are not enough. Without the true Lord all these are of no use. As you sow, so shall you reap. If one does not acquire virtues, his life and human form go waste. One should acquire to be at peace in life. Abandon your evil actions and follow the teachings of the *guru;* it will help you to get merged with Him.

bhūlī phirai disaṅtari bhūlī gr̥hu taji jāi ॥
bhūlī ḍūṅgari thali caḍai bharamai manu ḍolāi ॥
dhurahu vichunī kiu milai garabi muṭhi bilalāi ॥
vichuḍiā guru melasī hari rasi nāma piāri ॥
....
akhara paḍi paḍi bhulīē bhekhī bahutu abhimānu ॥
tīratha nātā kiā kare mana mahi mailu gumānu ॥
– Ibid., pp. 60-61

An ignorant soul bride roams in distant places and her departure from her own place makes her stranger to her own home. She is afflicted with doubts and tries to go through the high mountains. Since she is separated from her own home within her she cannot meet the Supreme Being. Can she meet Him again, is the question before her and she feels her false pride and cries and moans. The *guru* helps such estranged souls and unites them with the Lord again reviving the love for God in them by true name of God. With too much reading of books over and again, people become crazy and feel proud of their religious knowledge. One is not benefited by taking bath at holy places of pilgrimages as long as the dirt and dust of falsehood do not get cleared.

Guru Nānak advises that right action and deeds are helpful only if these do not instill pride in individuals. The *guru* is the perfect guide and washes away the internal pride and filth, and unites separated individuals with the Lord.

sidaku sabūrī sādikā sabaru tosā malāikā ॥

dīdāru pūre pāisā thāu nāhī khāikā ||

....

phakaḍa jātī phakaḍu nāu || *sabhanā jīā ikā chāu* ||
āpahu je ko bhalā kahāe || *nānaka tāparu jāpai jā pati lekhai pāe* ||

– *Ādi Granth*, p. 83

The godly people live upon the food of their belief in God, self-satisfaction and forbearance. It is they only who get to the presence of the Absolute Being, there is no such chance for the gossiping individuals.

All types of self-pride due to social status or personal glory are of no use. There is only one Supreme Being who is the protector of all beings. One may call oneself good but it tentamounts to nothing, only those are good who are approved by God.

suine kai parabati guphā karī kai pāṇī paiāli ||
kai vici dharatī kai ākasī uradhi rahā siri bhāri ||
puru kari kāiā kapaḍu pahirā dhovā sadā kāri ||
bagā ratā pīalā kālā bedā karī pūkāra ||
hoi kucīlu rahā malu dhārī duramati mati vikāra ||
nā hau nā mai nā hau hovā nānaka sabadu vīcāri ||
vasatra pakhāli pakhāle kāiā āpe saṅjami hovai ||
aṅtari mailu lagī nahī jāṇai bāharahu mali mali dhovai ||

....

nāmu jape nāmo ārādhe nāme sukhi samāvai ||

– Ibid., p. 139

One may make his residing place in the mountains of gold or in the deepest waters; one may live on earth or in the sky; one may keep on standing on the head for years; one may cover himself with heavy clothes or abandon all clothes and keep them all clean; one may loudly utter all the Vedas; one may even remain dirty and filthy; these are only the imaginations of mind and the crop of the evil-mindedness. But if one dwells upon his *guru*'s word, all his ego will run out of him and he shall not feel the evil of I-ness.

Individuals wash and scrub their clothes and bodies and indulge in self-discipline also. But they remain unaware of the dirt and dust settled and stained their mind. They worry to clean their outside stains only. They look towards other's belongings to be their own assets and are subject to pain and egotism. Nānak says that godly individuals only utter *nāma* of the Supreme Being, contemplate on *nāma* and through *nāma* get absorption in Pure Bliss.

Guru Nānak describes that the various robes and means that people adopt to show off cannot benefit them for their spiritual uplift as the dirt and dust of doubt, pride and show off get increased. The only way to benefit individual is to chant God's name and meditate on it which in turn bring peace in life.

gṛhu banu samasari sahaji subhāi ।। *duramati gatu bhaī kīrati ṭhāi* ।।
saca pauḍī sācau mukhi nāuṅ ।। *satiguru sevi pāe nija thāu* ।।
mana cūre khaṭu darasana jāṇu ।। *saraba joti pūrana bhagavānu* ।।
–*Ādi Granth*, pp. 351-52

Whether resides at home or in the forest does not matter to one who remains in a balanced insight of calmness and steadiness. His bad thoughts go away and they are replaced with appericiations of the Lord. Chanting the name of the Supreme Being works as a ladder to spiritual progress. By serving the true *guru* one approaches to the inner being of the individual self. One takes control of mind with the knowledge of the six Śāstras and understands that the divine light of the Supreme Being perfectly pervades within him.

Guru Nānak explains the gist that all actions whether sitting at home or in the forest are the same for one who lives a balanced life of intuitive peace and poise. The knowledge of scriptures is the divine light and chanting the name of God works as stairs in spiritual progress. Service to the *guru* leads one to the innerself within him.

manu hālī kirasāṇī karaṇī saramu pāṇī tanu khetu ।।
nāmu bīju saṅtokhu suhāgā rakhu garībī vesu ।।
bhāu karama kari jaṁmasī se ghara bhāgaṭha dekhu ।।
....
hāṇu haṭu kari ārajā sacu nāmu kari vathu ।।
surati soca kari bhāṅḍasāla tisu vici tisano rakhu ।।
vaṇajāriā siu vaṇaju kari lai lāhā mana hasu ।।
suṇi sāsata saudāgarī satu ghoḍe lai calu ।।

kharacu bańnu caṅgiāīā matu mana jāṇahi kalu ॥
niraṁkāra kai desi jāhi tā sukhi lahahi mahalu ॥
lāi citu kari cākarī mańni nāmu kari kaṁmu ॥
bańnu badīā kari dhāvaṇī tāko ākhai dhańnu ॥
nānaka vekhai nadari kari caḍai cavagaṇa vańnu ॥

– *Ādi Granth*, pp. 595-96

One should consider thoughts a farmer, virtues as action on the field, humility as water and body as a farmhouse. Treat the name of the Merciful as seed, satisfaction as machine to cut and turn up the soil. Acting with love one will find that he is approaching near to the inner self. Illusionary power deceives the world and goes astray. All cannot understand this.

To make one's ever-reducing life a trading house to do a business of developing love for the Lord within oneself. Let one's concentration be the stores of the true name and interact with the godly people dealing with God's love. Earn your profit of *śabada* and enjoy the blessed state. Listen to scriptures. Take the truthfulness as horses for selling and accumulate virtues to spend while on the way back and do not postpone it to the other day of life. On reaching the domain of the Supreme Being who is formless, you will experience total peace in the palace of God. Concentrate and focus upon yourself within and deepen your love for the name of the Lord. Avoid sinful acts in life. Only then you will be considered as blessed. Then you will experience the graceful glance of the Supreme Being and then your honours will be multiplied four times before God.

Nānak advises to accumulate and carry with oneself the loads of merit without any delay till tomorrow to the land of formless God. God will glance him graciously and bless him with honour.

kiu marai mańdā kiu jīvai jugati ॥ *kańna paḍāi kiā khājai bhugati* ॥
āsati nāsati eko nāu ॥ *kauṇu su akharu jitu rahai hiāu* ॥
dhūpa chāva je samakari sahai ॥ *tā nānaku ākhai guru ko kahai* ॥
chia varatāre varatahi pūta ॥ *nā saṁsārī nā audhūta* ॥
niraṁkāri jo rahai samāi ॥ *kāhe bhīkhiā maṅgaṇi jāi* ॥

– Ibid., p. 953

How evil can be removed and how life is to be lived? There is no use to wear rings piercing ears or asking for food from others.

Being and non-being are names of the same truth. One should find that word can keep your heart in place. When one finds no difference in shining sun or its shade he reaches a place where the *guru* speaks to him. Those who follow the six systems of philosophy are neither materialistic nor renunciate, they adopt the mid-way life. But those who remain absorbed in God need not look towards other doors.

Guru Nānak says that mere learning of religious systems is not enough for the seekers; they have to practise regularly for remaining absorbed in the formless Lord.

na bhījai rāgī nādī bedi ।। *na bhījai suratī giānī jogi* ।।
na bhījai sogī kītai roji ।।
na bhijai rupīṅ mālīṅ raṅgi ।। *na bhījai tīrathi bhaviē naṅgi* ।।
na bhījai dātīṅ kītai puṅni ।। *na bhījai bāhari baiṭhiā suṅni* ।।
....
nānaka bhījai sācai nāi ।।
nava chia khaṭa kā kare bīcāru ।।
nisi dina ucarai bhāra aṭhāra ।।
tini bhi aṅtu na pāiā tohi ।।
nāma bihūṇa mukati kiu hoi ।।
nābhi vasata brahamai aṅtu na jāṇiā ।।
guramukhi nānaka nāmu pachāṇiā ।।
– *Ādi Granth*, p. 1237

One cannot win God's favour by instrumental or vocal music or the study of scriptures or feeling sad and depressed forever, beauty, wealth and pleasures, wandering naked at sacred shrines, giving donations in charity, living alone at secluded places, bravely facing death in the battlefield, wise actions, exerting in *yoga* or dusting the feet of people.

All these activities are accounted for the transformation of mental state of an individual. Nānak says that one can attain Him only by meditating upon His name.

One may go through nine grammars, six Śāstras and six divisions of the Vedas, or recite other scriptures like the *Mahābhārata* but will not be able to find His limits. Even Brahmā, who sat in a lotus that sprouted from the navel of Viṣṇu, could not find it. No one can be liberated without the *nāma* (name of the Lord).

Guru Nānak explains that God is not pleased by musical recitations of Vedas or other scriptures or going through many rituals, performing acts of wisdom and charity, by physical and mental sufferings or doing actions of bravery, etc. No doubt, all these acts are taken into account for spiritual progress but no one can be benefited without the *nāma*.

Aim of Man's Life according to Upaniṣads

One of the important disciplines for the knowledge of *Ātman* is the practice of ethical virtues. The *Kaṭha Upaniṣad* states that the sense organs are created with an inclination towards material pleasures and embodied souls are entangled in the rotation of coming and going, but calm sages turn the sense organs inward in order to attain freedom. It does not allow any compromise between the ideal of pleasure and the ideal of good. One who goes for the pleasant gets lost on the way. It does not mean mere mortification of flesh or sense organs. This is described in the *Kaṭha Upaniṣad* by an example. The individual body is like a chariot, senses are horses, intellect is the charioteer, the mind works as the reins, the sense objects are the roads and the embodied soul is the master of the chariot. The chariot can take the master to his destination only when the vehicle is well built, the driver knows the way, reins are sturdy, horses are completely held under control and the path is well determined. The knowledge of the *Ātman* is to be attained now and here and not elsewhere after death.

Liberation is not something which is created but is the realization of what has existed from eternity but has hitherto been concealed. All lives that appear on earth are initially pure by nature and have no bounds. He who knows the Self is liberated, as he realizes himself to be the very soul (*Ātman*). "He who knows the Supreme *Brahman* verily becomes *Brahman*." A liberated man is not given to inactivity. He sees action in non-action and non-action in action. Actions do not cling to him. Even when he performs actions through his body and senses he knows his inner Self to be actionless and detached. All his evil instincts are destroyed when he practises spiritual discipline. He sees all as Self.

The Vedānta teachers formulated the qualifications of the pupil entitled to study Vedānta. He must have attained purity of heart by freeing himself from sin, through avoidance of selfish and forbidden actions as well as by practice of daily devotions and obligatory duties, particular religious observances on special occasions and the customary penances prescribed by religion. Further he had to discriminate between the real and unreal and renounce the unreal. He had to cultivate inner calmness and control of senses, preserve the serenity of mind and organs after they had been controlled, acquire such virtues as forbearance and concentration and finally possess an intense yearning for liberation from the bondages of worldly life.

Knowledge is of two kinds. The first is derived from sense organs and corroborated by varied evidences based on the experiences of the sense organs. This is the form of knowledge that falls within the scope of physical sciences. The second however is transcendent and is realized through mental and spiritual discipline of *yoga*.

According to the doctrine of rebirth the desires are responsible for a person's embodiment. One takes birth in this world repeatedly, in a high or low embodiment, depending on the good or bad actions. The *Kaṭha Upaniṣad* states the doctrine of rebirth:

> Some lives enter the womb to be embodied as organic beings and some go into non-organic matter according to their work and according to their knowledge.

The seeker therefore resolves upon cutting the knot by turning away from the entire phenomenal existence of time, space and causality.

> *iha cedavedīdatha satyamasti na cedihāvedīnmahatī vinaṣṭiḥ* ।
> – *Kena Upaniṣad* 2.5

If a man knows *Ātman* here, he then attains the true goal of life. If he does not know it here, a great disadvantage awaits him. Having realized the self in every being, the wise relinquish the world and become immortal.

> *kurvanneveha karmāṇi jijīviṣecchatam samāḥ* ।

evaṁ tvayi nānyatheto 'sti na karma lipyate nare ||
– *Īśa Upaniṣad* 2

If a man wishes to live a hundred years on this earth, he should live performing virtuous actions. For one who cherishes such a desire and regard himself as a man (one who is identified with the body and conscious of his human duties and responsibilities) there is no other way by which he can keep work from clinging to him. (A person attached to his human body and desirous of enjoying on earth his full span of life should devote himself to religious duties and other unselfish actions, if not, he will engage in evil action.)

. . . sa mendro medhayā spr̥ṇotu amr̥tasya deva dhāraṇo bhūyāsam. . . |
– *Taittirīya Upaniṣad* 1.4.1

May, my body be competent to acquire knowledge. May, my tongue be exceedingly sweet. May, I hear abundantly with my ears. Thou (*oṁ*) art the sheath of *Brahman* concealed by worldly intelligence. Guard me for what I have learnt.

This is a prayer for acquiring retentiveness and for physical and moral health. A man who does not possess retentiveness of mind cannot acquire the knowledge of *Brahman*. Nor can he, who owing to sickness or some other cause, lack physical vigour. Nor he who suffers from want of food and clothing devote himself to the study of scriptures and acquire the knowledge of *Brahman*.

The present section shows the way to remove all such obstacles.

ahorātro vai prajāpati tasyahareva prāṇo rātrireva rayiḥ |
– *Praśna Upaniṣad* 1.13

Individuals who indulge in sexual activity during the day waste their self. But sexual enjoyment at night is chaste.

This kind of self-control is prescribed for the householder.

prāṇāgnaya evaitasminpure jāgrati gārhapatyo ha vā eṣo 'pāno . . . |
– Ibid. 4.3

Body is called the city of God. The fire of life alone remains awake in this city.

śreyaśca preyaśca manuṣyametastau saṁprarītya vivinakti dhīraḥ |
– *Kaṭha Upaniṣad* 1.2.2

Individuals get across both what is right and what is pleasing for them. A calm individual is able to examine and identify the difference. He prefers right over pleasing but the unwise chooses pleasing out of greediness and temptation.

avidyāyāmantare vartamānāḥ svayaṁ dhīrāḥ paṇḍitaṁ manyamānāḥ | – *Kaṭha Upaniṣad* 1.2.5

The unwise due to ignorance and considering them high adopt different twisting paths and go in round like a blind leading blinds.

naiṣā tarkeṇa matirāpaneyā proktānyenaiva sujñānāya preṣṭha |
– Ibid. 1.2.9

One cannot gain knowledge by arguments and reasoning. *Ātman* can be comprehended more easily when taught by another. . . .

yato vāco nivartante | *aprāpya manasā saha* | *ānandaṁ brahmaṇo vidvān* | *na bibheti kutaścaneti* | – *Taittirīya Upaniṣad* 2.9.1

He who knows the bliss of *Brahman*, whence words together with the mind turn away, unable to reach it. He is not afraid of anything whatsoever. He does not distress himself with the thought why did I not do what is good? Why did I do what is evil? Whosoever knows this regards both good and evil as *Ātman;* indeed he cherishes both as *Ātman*.

When *avidya* is destroyed, both good and evil like all other phenomenal categories merge in *Ātman*. Thus the knower of *Ātman* strips good and evil of their phenomenal nature and realizes them as *Ātman*. This realization makes good and evil powerless. Further it reveals their identity with *Ātman* and thus strengthens *Ātman*.

satyaṁ vada | *dharmaṁ cara* | *svādhyāyānmā pramadaḥ* |
– Ibid. 1.11.1

The teacher instructs: Be truthful. Act as per *dharma*. Study of Vedas should not be neglected. Do not neglect household duties. Start your home life with the blessings of the teacher. Offer him the desired gifts. Have the offspring and do not stop the progeny. Do not go away from truthfulness and *dharma*. Personal welfare and prosperity should not be neglected.

Duties towards the gods and manes should not be neglected. Mother, father, teacher and guest should be regarded as gods.

Perform only faultless actions and avoid faulty ones.

Brāhmaṇas superior to you should be comforted offering proper seats and respect. Whatever you give, give it with faith and according to your capacity with a humble approach and fear of God and compassion.

In case of any doubt about your actions do what a brāhmaṇa would have done or approach one for guidance who is competent and committed to good acts rather than performances. He should not be too strict but obeying to *dharma*.

trayo dharmaskandhā yajño 'dhyayanaṁ dānamiti | *prathamastapa eva . . .* – *Chāndogya Upaniṣad* 2.23.1

There are three divisions of *dharma*: sacrifice, study and charity form the first. Austerity is the second. Dwelling in the house of the teacher as *brahmacārī* mortifying the body is the third. All those who practise *dharma* attain the worlds of the virtuous. But who is established in *Brahman* obtains immortality.

tadya iha ramaṇīyacaraṇā abhyaśo ha yatte ramaṇīyāṁ yonimāpadyeran . . . – Ibid. 5.10.7

Those whose conduct here on earth has been good will quickly attain some good birth as brāhmaṇa, kṣatriya or vaiśya. But those whose conduct here has been evil will quickly attain some evil birth as a dog, pig or a *cāṇḍāla*.

According to the doctrine of *karma* and rebirth, the future of the embodied soul is determined by its present action and knowledge. By good actions it becomes good and by evil action it becomes evil. One can assume any body in the universe from that of a god to that of a plant.

yonimanye prapadyante śarīratvāya dehinahq |
– *Kaṭha Upaniṣad* 2.2.7

Some *jīvas* enter the womb for the purpose of new embodiment and some enter stationary objects according to their work and according to their knowledge.

yaccittastenaiṣa prāṇamāyāti prāṇastejasā yuktaḥ |
– *Praśna Upaniṣad* 3.10

Whatever, one is thinking at the time of death, with that one enters into *prāṇa*. *Prāṇa*, joined with fire together with the soul, leads to whatever world has been fashioned by thought.

maghavanmartyaṁ vā idaṁśarīramāttam mṛtyuna . . .
– *Chāndogya Upaniṣad* 8.12.1

This body is mortal, always held by death, It is the abode of the Self, which is immortal and incorporeal. The embodied Self is the victim of pleasure and pain. So long as one is identified with the body there is no cessation of pleasure and pain. But neither pleasure nor pain touches one who is not identified with the body.

taddhaitadbrahmā prajāpataya uvāca prajāpatirmanave manuh . . .
– Ibid. 8.15.1

He who after leaving the teacher's house has settled down into a householder's life and continued the study of the Vedas in a sacred spot and made others (his sons and pupils) virtuous; he who has withdrawn all the sense organs into the Self, he who has not given pain to any creature except as approved by the scriptures he conducts himself thus, all through his life, reaches the world of *Brahman* after death, and does not return, yea, does not return.

The Upaniṣads as well as the hymns of Guru Nānak call human body the city of God and this life as a chance to fulfil the ultimate aim of human form for liberation from the rotation of birth and death. They impress upon that man's life should be regulated by *dharma* meaning following principles of Divine Will for the welfare of self and humanity at large which enables one to achieve his real aim of life. One should pray for a healthy body, mind and enjoyment of material pursuits of *artha* and *kāma* to enable oneself to exercise *dharma* in his life. This aim can be realized by balanced combination of *karma*, knowledge and *bhakti*. The knowledge of difference between real and unreal, pleasant and good in this worldly life will develop love for the everlasting and permanent divine force behind all existence and will restrain one from falling into the clutches of worldly entrapments and pave the way for doing good deeds (*karma*) and exercising *dharma*. Thus the message "man know thyself" in the Upaniṣads and personal experience of divinity within oneself beyond the three states of consciousness (*turīya*) by Guru Nānak through right knowledge, *karma* and devotion should be the ultimate aim of human life.

Path of Liberation

Guru Nānak accepts the basic doctrine of the Upaniṣads that the end of life is release from the cycle of coming and going (*mokṣa*). The important features of the path of liberation in his hymns include Faith in His Existence (*manana*), listening to scriptures and word of the *guru* (*śravaṇa*) and disciplined meditation (*nididhyāsana*), experiencing divinity beyond the three states of consciousness, i.e. *turīya* state, and bliss of merger with Him.

PATH OF LIBERATION IN THE HYMNS OF GURU NĀNAK

FAITH

Guru Nānak's expression of faith is in line with the *Kaṭha Upaniṣad*'s (2.3.12) contents that He cannot be gained either by word or by mind or sight but by him who says "He is". Those, who believe He is, are in the sublime state.

maṅne kī gati kahī na jāi ||

. . . .

maṅnai surati hovai mani budhi ||

. . . .

maṅnai māragi ṭhāka na pāi ||

. . . .

maṅnai pāvahi mokha duāru ||

. . . .

aisā nāmu niraṅjanu hoi || *je ko maṅni jāṇai mani koi* ||

– *Ādi Granth*, p. 3

No one can describe the mental state of a man who has full faith in God. If one attempts to explain his state he will have to repent for his failure. There is no material of writing which can record his position. The faithful has deep insight, knowledge and understanding. The faithful experiences full knowledge of the universe, he never faces resistance and shall not have to go with the messenger of death. His path to spiritual progress shall never be obstructed and his departure from this world shall be honourable and easy. He does not believe in ritualistic approach and stands firm by *dharma*. A faithful finds the door to liberation. He uplifts and redeems all who get related to him. The faithful accompanies the *guru* to the other shore.

O Nānak! the man of belief never roams to beg anything from others. A man with belief in the existence of faultless pure Supreme Being can only understand his state of mind.

In the above lines Guru Nānak counts the bliss of a person who believes and has faith that there is God.

rāma nāmi manu bedhiā avaru ki karī vīcāru ||
sabada surati sukhu ūpajai prabha rātau sukha sāru ||
– *Ādi Granth*, p. 62

Mind is deeply struck through by the name of God. There is nothing to contemplate further. When one focuses his awareness on *śabada*, happiness springs forth. Superb peace is found when one gets attuned to God.

sabāhī sālāha jinī dhiāiā ikamani ||
seī pūre sāha vakhatai upari laḍi mue ||
dūjai bahute rāha mana kīā matī khiṇḍīā ||
bahutu pae asagāha gote khāhi na nikalahi ||
tījai muhī girāha bhukha tikhā dui bhaukīā ||
khādhā hoi suāha bhī khāṇe siu dosatī ||
cauthai āī ūṅghu akhī mīṭi pavāri gaiā ||
bhī uṭhi racionu vādu sai varihā kī piḍa badhī ||
sabhe velā vakhata sabhi je aṭhī bhau hoi ||
nānaka sahibu mani vasai sacā nāvaṇu hoi ||
– Ibid., pp. 145-46

One who remembers God at the dawn of the day, contemplates and concentrates on the name of the Lord gets best of benefits. Such an individual struggles at the right time of the day and dies to self. In the second part of the day attention of mind is diverted to other things of life and it falls into the deep pit of worldly affairs and becomes difficult to drag it out and place it on the right spot. In the third quarter of the day his attention diverts to food to be put into his mouth to satiate his hunger. He eats and when what is eaten converts into solid dust, he requires more food. In the fourth part of the day, he becomes sleepy. He closes his eyes and begins to dream. When he rises from slumber he again gets into arguments and controversies. One plans as if he will survive for 100 years. One should live in fear of God at all times of the day and at each moment of life so that he remains always attuned to the Supreme Being for his true cleansing bath from within.

In the above two hymns, Guru Nānak explains that if one has fear for the Lord day and night and remains attuned to Him, then all times are good for worship. If the True One comes into mind at any moment or part of the day one is cleansed. There is nothing more than the Lord's name being cherished by which one is focused on *śabada* and happiness wells up.

devatiā darasana kai tāī dūkha bhūkha tīratha kīe ||
jogī jatī jugati mahi rahate kari kari bhagave bhekha bhae ||
tau kārani sāhibā rangi rate ||
tere nāma anekā rūpa anantā kahaṇu na jāhī tere guṇa kete ||
dara ghara mahalā hasatī ghoḍe choḍi vilāiti desa gae ||
pīra pekāṁbara sālika sādika choḍī dunīā thāi pae ||
sāda sahaja sukha rasa kasa tajīale kāpaḍa choḍe camaḍa līe ||
dukhīe daradavanda dari terai nāmi rate daravesa bhae ||
khalaḍī khaparī lakaḍī camaḍī sikhā sūtu dhotī kīnhī ||
tūṅ sāhibu hau sāṅgī terā praṇavai nānaku jāti kaisī ||

– *Ādi Granth*, p. 358

Even the gods who cherished for the blessed vision of the Supreme Being had to bear painful conditions of being hungry and they went to religious places and lived a prescribed lifestyle. Others adapt to different colours and style of costumes and live in seclusion. For the sake of love of God they get drenched in His colour. He has many names and endless forms. No one can count His glorious virtues. His seekers leave behind their wealth and home, palaces, elephants, horses and native lands, and roam in other countries and places. Some renounce tasty foods, all comforts of life, happiness and pleasures and shed their clothes and start wearing skins. Some who suffer pain and are filled with your name have become beggars at your doors, others start dressing differently, they carry begging bowls, wooden sticks, sit on hides, convert their hair into tufts, wear different costumes for showing off their different looks but all these followers have no individuality other than you. You are the Master and all others are players in your hands.

In these lines Guru Nānak expresses the firmness and oneness of faith of all seekers including gods who go through various experiences in different guises, ways and means in search of Him. It is their strong desire and devotion with faith that keeps them on the way to search for Truth. Such true seekers of God have no individuality or class but only one goal in mind and all go and go for His realization.

kāiā kūḍi vigāḍi kāhe nāīē ।। *nātā so paravāṇu sacu kamāīē* ।।
jaba sāca andari hoi sācā tāmi sācā pāīē ।।
likhe bājhahu surati nāhī boli boli gavāiē ।।
jithai jāi bahīē bhalā kahīē surati sabadu likhāīē ।।
....
aṁmṛtu hari kā nāmu merai mani bhāiā ।।
nāmu mīṭhā manahi lāgā dūkhi ḍerā ḍhāhiā ।।
sūkhu mana mahi āi vasiā jāmi tai phuramāiā ।।
nadari tudhu aradāsi merī jini āpu upāiā ।।
....
vāri khasamu kaḍhāe kiratu kamāvaṇā ।।
maṅdā kisai na ākhi jhagaḍā pāvaṇā ।।
naha pāi jhagaḍa suāmi setī āpi āpu vañāvaṇā ।।
jisu nāli saṅgati kari sarīkī jāi kiā rūāvaṇā ।।
jo dei sahaṇā manahi kahaṇā ākhi nāhī vāvaṇā ।।
vārī khasamu kaḍhāē kiratu kamāvaṇā ।।
sabha upāīanu āpi āpe nadari kare ।।
kauḍā koi na māgai mīṭhā sabha māgai ।।
sabhu koi mīṭhā maṅgi dekhai khasama bhāvai so kare ।।
kichu puṅna dāna aneku karaṇī nāma tuli na samasare ।।
nānakā jina nāmu miliā karamu hoā dhuri kade ।।

– *Ādi Granth*, pp. 565-66

How to clean the body replete with falsehood? One must practise Truth for cleansing his body polluted by the dirt of false deeds to be acceptable to God. One can attain the pleasure of God when he develops love for Truth deep within the heart. One gets this understanding if he is pre-destined for it. Otherwise one wastes his life in arguments only. One may go or sit anywhere but he must always speak well and bear God's name in his consciousness. The Guru, the ambrosial name of Hari, is luring Nānak day and night. With the pleasure of His name within himself one forgets all his pains. He prays to Him and He bestows grace on him. Guru Nānak speaks what He makes him to speak.

The Supreme Being provides all the benefits to deserving individuals on the basis of their acts. It is useless to speak ill of others or argue about other's fate. Similarly one is advised to avoid arguing with God. By doing so one shall cause harm to himself. One must not challenge the One to whom he is bound to obey or he will repent in the end. One should be satisfied with whatsoever God provides him. One should make his mind understand that it is useless to complain against Him. The Lord gives everyone according to his share of deeds. Everyone begs for the sweets and no one desires for bitter things. Everyone may desire for the sweets; but one should understand that it is Will of the Lord as to what to be provided to him. Giving donations for charity or indulging in acts of any kind of ritual cannot equate with concentration upon the name of the Lord. One who imbibes the name of God in his heart is blessed.

In these lines Guru Nānak explains how to prepare one for developing faith in Him and live a meaningful life. One develops understanding of Him if it is pre-destined as a result of good *karmas*. The Lord gives us a turn of human birth, verily, as a fruit of our *karma*. One must accept what He gives and instructs one's mind not to grumble. No charity and no other deeds equal the contemplation of Lord's name.

bhāṅḍā dhoi baisi dhūpu devahu tau dūdhai kau jāvahu ॥
dūdhu karama phuni surati samāiṇu hoi nirāsa jamāvahu ॥
japahu ta eko nāmā ॥ *avari nirāphala kāmā* ॥
ihu manu īṭī hāthi karahu phuni netrau nīda na āvai ॥
rasanā nāmu japahu tab mathīē ina bidhi aṁmṛtu pāvahu ॥
manu saṁpaṭu jitu satasari nāvaṇu bhāvana pātī tṛpati kare ॥
pūjā prāṇa sevaku je seve inha bidhi sāhibu ravatu rahai ॥
kahade kahahi kahe kahi jāvahi tuma sari avaru na koī ॥
bhagatihīṇu nānaku janu jaṁpai hau sālāhī sācā soī ॥

– *Ādi Granth*, p. 728

> One should wash the vessel of this body, take a comfortable seat in mind and get ready to go for milk. One should clear his consciousness with his good actions and get oneself freed from desires. Your mind should be curdled. All other rituals are fruitless. One should use his mind as handle and then churn the curd without sleeping by chanting God's name, and then the curd will be shaken. Thus one can obtain the heavenly essence from within oneself. Let your mind be cleaned with water of truth and become a vessel to obtain the nectar. A humble servant of God who devotes earnestly to Him and offers his life in His service in this way remains ever absorbed in God. Some speakers go on speaking and speaking endlessly and depart from this world without getting the essence. These servants who lack in devotion should humbly pray and adhere to singing the praises of the Supreme Being.

In the above lines Guru Nānak explains as to how one should prepare him for serving the Supreme Being. He illustrates it by an example of fetching milk in a clean vessel, disinfecting it, and then fermenting it to curdle, churning it carefully to draw the butter from it. Similarly one has to perform acts to draw the essence from within for spiritual progress. Through a common example of getting butter out of milk he indicates the steps to the higher spiritual experience comparing every step of the process followed.

> *jogu na khiṅthā jāgu na ḍaṅḍa jogu na bhasama caḍāīē* ||
> *jogu na muṅdī mūṅḍi muḍāiē jogu na siṅī vāīē* ||
> ....
> *galī jogu na hoī* ||
> *eka dṛsaṭi kari samasari jāṇai jogī kahīē soī* ||
> *jogu na bāhari maḍī masāṇī jāgu na toḍī lāīē* ||
> *jogu na desi disaṅtari bhaviē jogu na tīrathi nāīē* ||
> ....
> *satiguru bheṭai tā sahasā tūṭai dhāvatu varaji rahāīē* ||
> *nijharu jharai sahaja dhuni lāgai ghara hī paracā pāīē* ||
> ....
> *nānaka jīvatiā mari rahīē aisā jogu kamāīē* ||
> *bāje bājhau siṅī bājai tau nirabhau padu pāīē* ||
> *aṅjana māhi niraṅjani rahīē joga jugati tau pāīē* ||
>
> – *Ādi Granth*, p. 730

> *Yoga* is not a patched gown. One cannot practise *yoga* by smearing one's body with ash or holding staff in hand or wearing earrings or shaving head or blowing of the conch. One cannot perform *yoga* by mere words. One who attains a position where he feels oneness in the all existence and see all creations as one deserves to be called a *yogī*. One cannot attain *yoga* by visits to shrines or by sitting in blankness or roaming in foreign lands or taking bath at sacred shrines. When one meets with the *guru* all his doubts go away and his roaming mind gets concentrated; pure essence rains down, heavenly music echoes and one gains wisdom deep within him.
>
> O Nānak! one should practise to die regarding worldly attractions while living an actual life here. One should realize the sound of the unstuck melody within himself to attain *yoga* position and remain untouched in the midst of the dirt of this world.

Guru Nānak explains that *yoga* is not the robes or to guise oneself. One also does not become a *yogī* by mere talks. One who acquires unity of all existence can be called a *yogī*. If one meets a perfect *guru* (one who has realized the Self), one's doubts are dispelled and outgoings of mind are ceased. And then oozes the nectar out of the spring of one's mind and experiences the melody of music within himself. If one gets rid of all worldly attachments and feels aloof from this world he is called a true *yogī*.

LISTENING TO SPIRITUAL DISCOURSES AND SCRIPTURES

> *suṇiē sidha pīra surinātha॥*
>
> ....
>
> *suṇiē īsaru barama iṅdu॥*
>
> ....
>
> *suṇiē satu saṅtokhu giānu॥*
>
> ....
>
> *suṇiē sarā guṇā ke gāha॥*
>
> ....
>
> *nānaka bhagatā sadā vigāsu॥ suṇiē dūkha pāpa kā nāsu॥*
>
> – *Ādi Granth*, pp. 2-3

> One gets ever blessed by listening to the *siddhas*, masters teaching higher experiences of *yoga* and spirit. By their talks one is freed

> from pain and suffering.
> By hearing about the gods and deities and persons who sing God's praises, teachers who explain the techniques of *yoga* and mystery of body, all religious scriptures, the devotees are forever in bliss.
>
> By listening to truth, contentment and spiritual wisdom, taking cleansing bath at the sacred places of pilgrimage, reading and reciting scriptures all get honours. One gathers the essence of meditation deep within oneself.
>
> By listening to the secrets of performing of virtues, the *seikhs*, theology experts, exponents of religion and persons of wisdom one's darkness of ignorance disappears.
>
> Nānak says that by listening to all these, pain and sin are cleared and the devotees feel His bliss forever.

These stanzas of *Japjī* explain the benefits of listening (*śravaṇa*) to spiritual discourses, scriptures and spiritual teachers.

EXPERIENCE BEYOND THE THREE STATES OF CONSCIOUSNESS, I.E. TURĪYA STATE

Guru Nānak often talks in his hymns to go beyond the three states of consciousness to experience the divinity of God.

> *ulaṭio kamalu brahamu bīcāri* ॥ *aṁmr̥ta dhāra gagani dasa duāri* ॥
> *tribhavaṇu bedhiā āpi murāri* ॥
> *re mana mere bharamu na kījaī* ॥ *mani maniē aṁmr̥tu rasu pījai* ॥
> *janamu jīti maraṇi manu māniā* ॥ *āpi muā manu mana te jāniā* ॥
> *najari bhaī gharu ghara te jāniā* ॥ – *Ādi Granth*, p. 153

> By virtue of concentration on the name of God, mind is turned upwards and one experiences the nectar oozing from the tenth door within the body at the top of the head. The presence of the Supreme Being is realized to be pervading everywhere. One should get away from all doubts and accept the truth. One enjoys the God's nectar. One must surrender mentally for a win over one's egotism and accept the truth of inevitable death. Once the I-ness is eradicated one feels the joy of company with the Lord. His inner vision is awakened and one starts his journey to the home of the Self.

In above lines Guru Nānak describes the path. He says that by reflecting on the Lord, the inverted lotus of mind turns upwards. And the rain of nectar pours in through the tenth door from the sky within.

> *janami marai trai guṇa hitakāru* || *cāre beda kathahi ākāru* ||
> *tīni avasathā kahahi vakhiānu* || *turīāvasathā satigura te hari jānu* ||
> *rāma bhagati gura sevā taraṇā* || *bāhuḍi janamu na hoi hai maraṇā* ||
> *cāri padāratha kahai sabhu koī* || *siṁmṛti sāsata paṅḍita mukhi soī* ||
> *binu gura arathu bīcāru na pāiā* || *mukati padārathu bhagati hari pāiā* ||
> – *Ādi Granth*, p. 154

> One in love with the attributes of *māya* comes in the grip of birth and death. The four Vedas describe the various forms of the Supreme Being. They explain the three attributes of consciousness. But the fourth state of union with the Lord called *turīya* can only be known from a true *guru*. Devotional worship of God and service to the *guru* help one swim to the other side of existence. Then one gets out of the bindings of being born again and again and facing death. Everyone talks about the four aims of life. The Smṛtis, Śāstras and *paṇḍita*s also explain the same. It is the true *guru* who can explain and make one understand the importance of these aims. Liberation can only be achieved by true devotion to the Almighty God.

Guru Nānak explains that the experience of *turīya* state can only be attained under the guidance of a self-realized *guru*. The service to the *guru* and devotional worship are a must for liberation.

> *eko saravaru kamala anūpa* || *sadā bigāsai paramala rūpa* ||
> *ūjala motī cūgahi haṁsa* || *saraba kalā jagadīsai aṁsa* ||
> *jo dīsai so upajai binasai* || *binu jala saravari kamalu na dīsai* ||
> *biralā būjhai pāvai bhedu* || *sākhā tīni kahai nita bedu* ||
> *nāda biṅda kī surati samāi* || *satiguru sevi paramapadu pāi* ||
> *mukato rātau raṅgi ravāṅtau* ||
> – Ibid., p. 352

> There is only one pool of water of Supreme Being and in it numerable beautiful lotuses bloom forth. One lotus blossoms continually and always stands with purity and fragrance. Saintly souls gather the valuable shines of *nāma* from this pool-like swans. They absorb the fragrance of the Almighty Master of the creation into them. Whatever is visible is mortal and comes

and goes. No one can find a lotus without a water pool. There are a very few wise persons who can realize this mystery. Even the Vedas explain the trinity of God. But who gets absorbed into the Supreme Being as Absolute One obtains the supreme spiritual bliss.

Guru Nānak explains that in the waters of God, saints like beautiful lotuses are ever in bloom and fragrance. The devotees like swans peck at the glamorous pearls of God's name. They imbibe in themselves the pure nectar from the Supreme Being and are blessed. Only a few people can know the mystery of this one in all. He who merges in the Universal Consciousness attains the highest state of bliss.

āsā manasā doū bināsata trihu guṇa āsa nirāma bhaī॥
turīāvasathā guramukhi pāīē saṅta sabhā kī oṭa lahī॥
giāna dhiāna sagale sabhi japa tapa jisu hari hiradai alakha abhevā॥
nānaka rāma nāmi manu rātā guramati pāe sahaja sevā॥

– *Ādi Granth*, p. 356

When all hopes and desires vanish from one's mind, he comes out of the control of the three qualities of *māyā*. Under the guidance and protection of assembly of saintly people, one attains *turīya* state of consciousness. One who gets deep into the love with the name of the Lord attains all knowledge, contemplation and concentration. Nānak says that when he was imbued with the Rāma *nāma* he found the Lord with ease.

Here again Guru Nānak declares that he has given up hope and desire and has risen above the three modes and become detached, and through the *guru* realized the highest *turīya* state.

utari avaghaṭi saravari nhāvai॥ *bakai na bolai hariguṇa gāvai*॥
jalu ākāsī suṅni samāvai॥ *rasu salu jholi mahā rasu pāvai*॥
aisā giānu sunahu abha more॥ *bharipuri dhāri rahiā sabha ṭhaure*॥
sacu bratu nemu na kālu saṅtāvai॥
....
gagani nivāsi samādhi lagāvai॥

– Ibid., p. 411

One should go deep inside within to take a bath in the cleansing pool inside the body. One should not speak or say anything except singing the songs of praise and glory of the Lord. One should remain merged in the Lord like evaporated water in the clouds. One should churn out the true pleasure to get the supreme essence. Lord is spread throughout and permeating all places. One, who is truthful, does not suffer the pain of fear of death. One burns all his anger and resides in the tenth gate with the support of the *guru*'s word and gets merged in the *samādhi* of deep meditation.

Guru Nānak explains the path and advises that one should bath deep within the pool of the Lord's name and should utter nothing but only the Lord's praise and should merge in the Lord like water in the atmosphere. He should then churn all true pleasures to procure the Lord's nectar. If one practises the discipline of Truth there is no pain of death for him. He through the *guru*'s word burns off all his wrath and lives ever in the sky of his mind wrapped in deep trance.

sabhi japa sabhi tapa sabha caturāī || *ujhaḍi bharamai rāhi na pāī* ||
binu būjhe ko thāi na pāī || *nāma bihūṇai māthe chāī* ||

– *Ādi Granth*, p. 412

All meditations, self restraints, tricky ways make one roam in darkness but one is unable to search the right path. In the absence of proper knowledge of the *nāma* one faces all sorts of ashes and dust around him.

Guru Nānak explains that all contemplation and cleverness lead one to astray and one cannot find the true path without knowledge.

kiā jaṅgalu ḍhūḍhī jāi mai ghari banu hariāvalā ||
saci ṭikai ghari āi sabadi utāvalā ||
jaha dekhā taha soi avaru na jāṇīe ||
gura kī kāra kamāi mahalu pachāṇīe ||
āpi milāvai sacu tā mani bhāvaī ||
calai sadā rajāi aṅki samāvaī ||

– Ibid., p. 420

One need not venture into the search of Him in the woodlands; one should try to find Him in his own green lands. The true *śabada* resides in my heart deep within. Wherever I look, I find Him there and I know no other one to be there. By serving the *guru*, I have found the palace of Supreme Being's presence within me. He absorbs us with Himself only when it pleases Him. One, who remains and acts according to His will, merges into His being.

Guru Nānak says that there is no need to go to forests in search of Him. See the bloom within our own self. The truth abides in our hearts through the *guru*'s word. Then wherever we see, we see the Lord alone and none else. When we walk in the *guru*'s way we realize Lord's presence. When the Lord Himself attunes us to His truth, we accept the fundamental moral principles/laws of God.

EXPERIENCING THE SOUND OF UNSTRUCK MELODY

bhugati giānu daiā bhaṅḍāraṇi ghaṭi ghaṭi vājahi nāda॥
āpi nāthu nāthī sabha jā kī ridhi sidhi avarā sāda॥
saṅjogu vijogu dui kāra calāvahi lekhe āvahi bhāga॥
— *Ādi Granth*, p. 6

Knowledge is the food for spiritual wisdom. Kindness is maid in attendance. The unstuck vibration of *nāda* in each and every heart is divinity within. He owns His created treasury and miracle power. All physical appearances are beaded into him like a garland. One merges with Him or separates from Him by His command. Individuals receive what is written in their fortune.

Guru Nānak explains that all creations are like beads on a string of the Supreme Being. In every heart there is melody of an unstruck sound current.

mudrā te ghaṭa bhītari mudrā kāṅiā kījai khiṅthātā॥
paṅca cele vasa kījahi rāvala ihu manu kījai ḍaṅḍātā॥
joga jugati iva pāvasitā॥
eku sabadu dūjā horu nāsati kaṅda mūli manu lāvasitā॥
– Ibid., p. 155

One should wear such hanging earings which may go deep within the heart. Use your body as gown to perform *yoga*. One should bring under control the five passions. O begging *yogī*! let your mind be a walking stick for support. This way you will find the way to *yoga*. One *śabada* shall remain forever, all else shall vanish. Let this be deep-rooted in your mind.

Guru Nānak advises that instead of piercing ears for rings a *yogī* should pierce his heart and control his five passions, i.e. lust, wrath, greed, attachment and ego. Let his mind be his stick to lean upon. Only then he will find the key to *yoga*. There is only one eternal *śabada*, the rest passes away. This should be the root and fruit of mind.

rāmi nāmi citu rāpai jā kā || *upajampi darasu kījai tā kā* ||
rāmu na japahu abhāgu tumārā || *jugi jugi dātā prabhu rāmu hamārā* ||
guramati rāmu japai janu pūrā || *titu ghaṭa anahata bāje tūrā* ||
....
jina kai hiradai hari hari soī || *tina kā darasu parasi sukhu hoī* ||

– *Ādi Granth*, p. 228

Whose consciousness gets imbued with the name of the Lord, he gets blessed with the vision of God in the pre-sunrise time. One is most unfortunate if one does not meditate on God. Our Lord is bountiful from the beginning of ages. One should follow the teachings of the *guru* and concentrate on the name of the Lord. This way within one's heart one will hear the vibrating unstuck melody. When the heart is filled with Hara-Hara (name of God) he attains peace with the blessed vision.

In these lines Guru Nānak explains that a perfect man, who dwells in the Lord, with the word of the *guru*, the music of the unstuck melody is heard within.

tāla madīre ghaṭa ke ghāṭa || *dolaka duṇīā vājahi vāja* ||
nāradu nācai kali kā bhāu || *jatī satī kaha rākhahi pāu* ||
nānaka nāma viṭahu kurabānu ||
....
jetā sabadu surati dhuni tetī jetā rūpu kāiā terī ||
tūṅ āpe rasanā āpe basanā avaru na dūjā kahahu māī ||

– Ibid., pp. 349-50

Desires are like ringing *ghuṅghrū* tied to one's ankles and world drum produces music to their tune. The men like Nārada dance to their tune in the Kali Yuga. It is difficult for the men of truth as to how he should place his feet in this world. Nānak appreciates only the name of the Almighty. O Lord! your melody is as vast as *śabada* is in mind. Your body is as the form of this universe.

This is a very beautiful expression of Guru Nānak. The desires clamour like the sound of a plate of brass when struck or ankle bells. The playful and mercurial mind dances to their tune. The world drum catches its tune. Men of truth find no place for their feet. Only the name of the Lord is the saviour. As much is the music in our minds that much is the sound of the Lord. As much is the form of the universe, that much is the body of God.

vājā mati pakhāvaju bhāu ॥ *hoi anandu sadā mani cāu* ॥
ehā bhagati eho tapa tāu ॥ *itu rangi nācahu rakhi rakhi pāu* ॥
pūre tāla jāṇai sālāha ॥ *horu nacaṇā khusīā mana māha* ॥

– *Ādi Granth*, p. 350

Let your intelligence be your instrument and your love for God your tambourine. You will feel blessed and overjoy in your mind. Do this exercise as this is the real devotion to God. So act in love with the Supreme Being with the beat of your heart and place your feet in rhythm. One should know that best dance and play is to praise the Lord. Other acts of performance lead to momentary enjoyment of mind.

Guru Nānak advises that let the awakened intellect and your love for God be the organ and tambourine to play with. You shall remain in bliss and ecstasy. This is the real devotion. You dance with your nimble feet to this tune with a true rhythm in God's praise.

gura kā sabadu manai mahi mudra khinthā khimā haḍhāvau ॥
jo kichu karai bhalā kari mānau sahaja hogu nidhi pāvau ॥
bābā jugatā jīu jugaha juga jogī parama tanta mahi jogam ॥
anmṛtu nāmu niranjana pāiā giāna kāiā rasa bhogam ॥

– Ibid., pp. 359-60

One should wear the *guru*'s word as earrings of the mind and tolerance as the gown. One should feel that whatever the Lord does is good for him; this way one can attain wealth of *sahaja-yoga*. One who acquires this status becomes a *yogī* forever. He remains evertuned to the word and enjoys *śabada* within. All his desires and conflicts vanish away. He experiences the sound of the unstuck melody at every moment of the time, day and night, and shall hear the unstuck melody of *nāda* within.

In these lines Guru Nānak advises that with the *guru*'s word in mind and with compassion submit yourself to the Lord's will, you will attain the *sahaja-yoga*, meaning the spontaneous concentration of mind. One who obtains the immaculate name gets attuned to the Lord and hears the melody of unstuck sound from within.

> *ghari rahu re mana mugadha iāne*॥
> *rāma japahu aṅtaragati dhiāne*॥
> *lālaca choḍi racahu aparaṁpari iu pāvahu mukati duārā he*॥
>
> – *Ādi Granth*, p. 1030

> One should remain in one's own home within oneself, always being attuned to God. One should meditate and concentrate upon the *guru*'s word from within. One should shed one's greed and with love contemplate on the Supreme Being. One shall be able to locate the path which leads to salvation.

Above lines are also an advice to go within to know the Self.

> *bhavajalu binu sabadai kiu tarīe*॥
> *nāma binā jagu rogi biāpiā dubidhā ḍubi ḍubi marīe*॥
> *guru devā gura alakha abhevā tribhavaṇa sojhī gura kī sevā*॥
> *āpe dāti karī guri dātai pāiā alakha abhevā*॥
> *manu rājā manu mana te māniā manasā manahi samāī*॥
>
> – Ibid., p. 1125

> One cannot cross the world ocean without realizing *śabada*. This world is engrossed in duality and individuals are drowning in it. The word of the *guru* is the key to the name of the Supreme Being. The *guru* is God; the *guru* is immeasurable and mystic. One can know and understand the mystery of all the three worlds by serving him. The beneficent *guru* gifts the word and unfolds the mystery of the true Lord. The mind is the king; it is satisfied through the mind itself and all its desires get reabsorbed within it.

Guru Nānak explains that without realization of *śabada* one cannot ferry across the sea of existence. Without the God's name the world seems afflicted with decease of duality. The *guru* leads the way to Him and unfolds His mystery before us.

> *hiradai nāmu saraba dhanu dhāraṇu guraparasādi paīe*॥
> *amara padāratha te kiratāratha sahaja dhiāni liva lāīe*॥

mana re rāma bhagati citu lāīē ||
guramukhi rāma nāmu japi hiradai sahaja setī ghari jāīē ||
– *Ādi Granth*, p. 1127

The word of the *guru* is very precious and key to all existence. One can imbue it deep within the heart only with the grace of the *guru*. One is filled with intuitive meditation and is able to focus on the Lord with love who imbues *guru*'s word which is everlasting. O mortals! fix your concentration on devotion to and meditation of God. Like God's lovers contemplate on Him within, you shall be able to return to your home within yourself with quick insight and ease.

sālagrāma bipa pūji manāvahu sukr̥tu tulasī mālā ||
rāma nāmu japi beḍā bāṅdhahu daiā karahu daiālā ||
kāhe kalarā siṅcahu janamu gavāvahu ||
kācī ḍhahagi divāla kāhe gacu lāvahu ||
kara harihaṭa māla ṭiṅḍa parovahu tisu bhītari manu jovahu ||
aṁmr̥tu siṅcahu bharahu kiāre tau mālī ke hovahu ||
– Ibid., p. 1171

One worships and believes in the stone gods and wear ceremonial dresses and rosary of beads, etc. which are of no use. One should build a boat of uttering the name of the Lord and pray. One wastes his life away in irrigating a barren alkaline soil. The mud wall crumbles and one tries to patch it with plaster. One should use his hands as containers stung on the moving chain in the well. Let his mind be yoked as a bull to draw heavenly water up from a well within. One should irrigate one's fields with this heavenly water. He shall be approved by Him who Himself is the biggest planter.

Guru Nānak advises that as the buckets stung to the chain and yoke pull out water from a well, let our hands be the bucket, and our mind a bull to get the ambrosial nectar to irrigate our fields. This should be the posture of offering prayers with the folded hands.

heko pādharu heku daru gura pauḍī nija thānu ||
rūḍau ṭhākuru nānakā sabhi sukha sācau nāmu ||
– Ibid., p. 1279

> There is one and only one way of leading to the final goal. The *guru* leads one like a staircase to reach that goal established within oneself. Our beloved God is very charming and one gets all comforts and peacefulness in Him.
>
> *cauthi upāe cāre bedā*॥ *khāṇī cāre bāṇī bhedā*॥
> *asaṭa dasā khaṭu tīni upāe*॥ *so būjhai jisu āpi bujhāe*॥
> *tīni samāvai cauthai vāsā*॥ *praṇavati nānaka hama tā ke dāsā*॥
> ....
> *khasaṭī khaṭu darasana prabha sāje*॥ *anahada sabadu nirālā vāje*॥
> *je prabha bhāvai tā mahali bulāvai*॥ *sabade bhede tau pati pāvai*॥
> – *Ādi Granth*, p. 839
>
> There are four Vedas, there are four sources of creation, there are different forms of speech. All these have been created by God Himself. He Himself is the creator of the eighteen Purāṇas, six Śāstras and the three modes of *māyā*. Only one to whom God causes this fact to understand can know it. One who gets control over the three attributes of *māyā* and enters into the fourth state of bliss, to him Guru Nānak prays to be a slave.
>
> God created six systems of *yoga*; we hear within us a melody of the unstuck word; it is at the pleasure of God that individual is called into his presence; by absorbing deep within the heart the word of the *guru* one gets glorified and experiences all these.

In this hymn Guru Nānak explains that all the scriptures were created by Him and He only knows the mystery as to whom He Himself reveals. Nānak prays to be His slave who goes beyond the three states of consciousness and abides in the fourth state of bliss. The Lord also created the six systems of *yoga*, i.e. Haṭha, Rāja, Bhakti, Jñāna, Kriyā and Karma and six principal systems of Hindu philosophy, Sāṁkhya, Yoga, Nyāya, Vaiśeṣika, Mīmāṁsā and Vedānta. Wonderful unstuck sound current of *śabada* vibrates itself. However if the Lord wills, only then he calls one to His presence.

> *caudasi cauthe thāvahi lahi pāvai*॥
> *rājasa tāmasa sata kāla samāvai*॥
> *sasīara kai ghari sūru samāvai*॥
> *joga jugati kī kīmati pāvai*॥

caudasi bhavana pātāla samāe ||
khaṅḍa brahamaṅḍa rahiā liva lāe ||
– *Ādi Granth*, p. 840

One who enters into the fourth state of consciousness, called *turīya*, gets control over time and three qualities (*guṇas*, operating modes of *māyā*) of *sattva, rajas* and *tamas*. He gets concentrated and his outgoing mind enters in its inward self. He alone knows the way of *yoga*. He gets attuned to the universe and all its parts.

This is part of a longer hymn, named Thitti, meaning lunar day. In this hymn Guru Nānak advises what a seeker should do and what he should not on the path of Self-realization. He concludes that one who enters into the fourth state of consciousness control over time and the other three *gunas*, *rajas* is influenced by the quality of passion or action. *Tamas guṇa* is influenced by the quality of darkness or inaction. *Sattva guṇa* means quality of goodness or purity. His outgoing mind enters in the Self and He only knows the way of *yoga*. He then becomes one with the fourteen regions and the underworld and is attuned to the universe and all its parts.

SPIRITUAL PLANES

ratī rutī thitī vāra, pavana pānī agnī pātāla |
tisu vici dharatī thāpi rakhī dharamasāla || (*Dharama Khaṅḍa*)
....
giāna khaṅḍa kā ākhahu karamu ||
kete pavaṇa pāṇi vaisaṅtura kete kāna mahesa || (*Giāna Khaṅḍa*)
....
sarama khaṅḍa kī bāṇī rūpu ||
tithai ghāḍati ghaḍīē bahutu anūpu || (*Sarama Khaṅḍa*)
....
karama khaṅḍa kī bāṇī joru ||
tithai horu na koī horu || (*Karama Khaṅḍa*)
....
saca khaṅḍi vasai niraṁkāru ||
kari kari vekhai nadari nihāla || (*Saca Khaṅḍa*)
– Ibid., pp. 7-8

Guru Nānak portrays the Path of Spiritual Progress of a seeker as under:

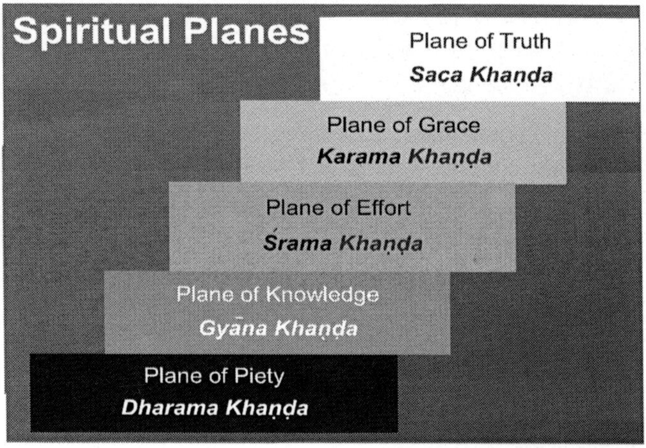

The path to spiritual progress is within the human frame. The spirit has to travel through these planes inwardly. As the spirit travels to higher regions the body becomes subtle and vanishes. When the spirit reaches the plane of truth, the formless soul merges with the formless Supreme Lord:

- *Dharama Khaṅḍa* (plane of piety). *Jīva*s are of diverse types, colours and names. They reap the fruit of their *karma*s. They are required to adopt real virtues in life and discriminate between the good and the pleasant.
- *Giāna Khaṅḍa* (plane of knowledge). Here, the seeker observes the vastness of universe and attains knowledge of various scriptures and sciences, and analyses his own position in the universal set-up and realizes his own potentialities. He tries to rise to higher planes and feels elated.
- *Sarama Khaṅḍa* (plane of effort). At this plane, the seeker sheds all his passions, vices and ego. His mind becomes pure and he becomes godly.
- *Karama Khaṅḍa* (plane of grace). At this stage, the seeker realizes that God is all powerful and His powers manifest themselves in him through His Grace. He is fully blossomed and resides here in ecstasy and glory.
- *Saca Khaṅḍa* (plane of truth). It is the abode of the formless who is infinite and the creator and master of infinite

creations. He controls the whole universe and directs it according to His will. He is the conscious power and sees and enjoys the sport of His creations conscientiously.

The seeker travelling through these spiritual planes of consciousness merges with the Universal Consciousness. *Dhātu milai phuni dhātu kau siphatī siphati samāi*. As the melted metal merges with another metal, the individual soul merges with the Universal Soul and gets one colour *jotī jota milāiē surtī surati saṅjogu*. When individual's light merges with the Light, his intuitive consciousness is joined with the Universal Intuitive Consciousness, one's cruelty and egotism depart and sorrows vanish and one feels the unity of all.

In the above part of the *Japjī*, Guru Nānak explains the stages of path to liberation.

MERGER WITH DIVINITY

> *dhātu milai phuni dhātu kau siphatī siphati samāi* ||
> *lālu gulālu gahabarā sacā raṅgu caḍāu* ||
> *sacu milai saṅtokhīā hari japi ekai bhāi* ||
>
> – *Ādi Granth*, p. 18
>
> As a metal which is melted merges with other melted metal, persons who utter the name of the Almighty God get merged into Him. They get to see a deep sight of red colour of truthfulness. Those fully-satisfied souls, who sing earnest prayers to God, experience union with Him.

These lines explain the position of individual souls after liberation. They merge with the Supreme Soul as a melted metal merges with another melted metal and thus get one colour.

> *jotī jota milāīē suratī surati saṅjogu* ||
> *hiṁsā haumai gatu gae nāhi sahasā sogu* ||
> *guramukhi jisu hari mani vasai tisu mele guru saṅjogu* ||
> *kāiā kāmaṇi je karī bhoge bhogaṇahāru* ||
> *tisu siu nehu na kījaī jo dīsai calaṇahāru* ||
>
> – Ibid., p. 21
>
> When individual's light merges into the Universal Light, individual awareness gets merged into the Universal

> Consciousness. One sheds his acts of cruelty and violence; I-ness departs, and doubts and sorrows vanish away. Such a *guramukha* experiences the abode of God within himself and merges in His union with the grace of his *guru*. If one surrenders one's body like a bride, the enjoyer will enjoy it. One should avoid love with the transient people other than the Supreme Being.

This is again an example of merger of the individual soul with the Universal Soul as the one light merges into another light.

PATH OF LIBERATION IN THE PRINCIPAL UPANIṢADS

One may wonder as to what path to follow in his endeavour to attain liberation. Should he follow the *karma-mārga* or take a route acquiring knowledge by *jñāna-mārga* or opt for the *bhakti-mārga* or practise the *yoga-mārga*? The Upaniṣads gave a clarion call to know the Self by means of higher knowledge.

Brahman is the highest reality. One who realizes *Brahman,* his self is merged in *turīya* as he goes beyond the notion of cause and effect, which is an inseparable part of *Ātman*. He is not born again as he has realized his identity with the causeless *turīya.*

The subject matter of the Upaniṣads is *Brahman* the Absolute, which transcends time, space and causality and cannot be comprehended by human thought or rendered in words. Human language and reasoning can describe and interpret sense-perceived phenomena, but *Brahman* is beyond their grasp.

The Vedānta teachers formulated the qualifications of a pupil entitled to study Vedānta. He must have attained the purity of heart by freeing himself from sins, through avoidance of selfish and forbidden actions as well as by the practice of daily devotions and obligatory duties, particular religious observances on special occasions and the customary penances prescribed by religion. Further he has to discriminate between the Real and the unreal, and renounce the unreal. He has to cultivate inner calmness and control of senses, preserve the serenity of mind and organs after they have been controlled, acquire such virtues as forbearance and concentration and finally possess an intense yearning for liberation from the bondages of worldly life.

The Upaniṣads abound in symbolic representations of *Brahman* and *Ātman*. Symbol is a visible sign of an invisible entity. Beginners with their restricted understanding need a symbol in order to contemplate on the Highest. In the minds of an unworthy, a symbol often degenerates into an idol which is worshipped. To worship a symbol as God is idolatry. But to worship God through a symbol is a legitimate means of divine communion. In the one case the Godhead is brought down to the level of a material object; in the other case the image itself is spiritualized.

KNOWLEDGE

śaunako ha vai mahāśālo 'ṅgirasaṁ vidhivadupasannaḥ papraccha |
kasminnu bhagavo vijñāte sarvamidaṁ vijñātaṁ bhavatīti ||3||
tasmai sa hovāca | *dve vidye veditavye iti ha sma yadbrahmavido*
vadanti para caivāparā ca ||4||
tatrāparā ṛgvedo yajurvedaḥ sāmavedo 'tharvavedaḥ śikṣā kalpo
vyākaranaṁ niruktaṁ chando jyotiṣamiti | *atha parā yayā*
tadakṣaramadhigamyate ||5||
yattadadreśyamagrāhyamagotramavarṇamacakṣuḥśrotraṁ
tadapāṇipādaṁ nityaṁ vibhuṁ sarvagataṁ susūkṣmaṁ
tadavyayaṁ yadbhūtayoniṁ paripaśyanti dhīrāḥ ||6||
– *Muṇḍaka Upaniṣad* 1.1.3-6

A householder named Śaunaka went to Aṅgirasa in a proper way and asked him about the knowledge by which one comes to know all. Aṅgirasa told him that one should obtain two kinds of knowledge called higher knowledge and lower knowledge. the knowledge of the *Ṛgveda*, the *Yajurveda*, the *Sāmaveda* and the *Atharvaveda* is lower knowledge and higher knowledge is that by which the the imperishable *Brahman* is attained. The wise beholds *Brahman* everywhere through higher knowledge. Otherwise *Brahman* cannot be seen or seized. *Brahman* has no root, or attributes, no eyes, ears, hands or feet; it is eternal and omnipresent, all-pervading and extremely subtle; it is imperishable and source of all beings.

avidyāyāmantare vartamānāḥ svayaṁ dhīrāḥ paṇḍitaṁ-manyamānāḥ | – Ibid. 1.2.8

The unwise men dwell in darkness, but wise in their conceit and puffed up with vain scholarship, wander about being afflicted by many ills like blind men led by the blind.

avidyāyāṁ bahudhā vartamānā vayaṁ kṛtārthā ityabhimanyanti bālāḥ ।
– *Muṇḍaka Upaniṣad* 1.2.9

Immersed in ignorance in various ways, people flatter themselves saying they have accomplished life's purpose. They who are performers of the *karma* do not know the Truth; owing to their attachment they fall from heaven, and miseries strike them when the fruit of their *karma* is exhausted.

tapaḥ śraddhe ye hyupavasantyaraṇye śāntā vidvāṁso bhaikṣacaryāṁ carantaḥ ।
– Ibid. 1.2.11

But those wise men of tranquil minds who live in the forest on alms, practising penances and contemplating their deities. They depart, freed from impurities by the path of the sun, to the place where that Immortal Person dwells whose nature is imperishable.

aṇoraṇīyānmahato mahīyān ātmāsya jantornihito guhāyām ।
– *Kaṭha Upaniṣad* 1.2.20

Ātman, smaller than the small, greater than the great, is hidden in the hearts of all living creations. A man who is free from desires beholds the majesty of the Self through the tranquillity of the senses and mind, and becomes free from the grief.

nāyamātmā pravacanena labhyo na medhayā na bahunā śrutena ।
– Ibid. 1.2.23

This *Ātman* cannot be attained by the study of Vedas or by intelligence or by much hearing of sacred books. It is attained by him alone whom it chooses. To such *Ātman* reveals its own form.

yaḥ pūrvaṁ tapaso jātamadbhyaḥ pūrvamajāyata ।
guhāṁ praviśya tiṣṭhantaṁ yo bhūtebhir vyapaśyte, etadvai tat ॥
– Ibid. 2.1.6

He verily knows *Brahman* who knows the first born . . . created prior to the waters and dwelling with the elements in the cave of the heart.

aṅguṣṭhamātraḥ puruṣo madhya ātmani tiṣṭhati ।

īśāno bhūtabhavyasya na tato vijugupsate, etadvai tat ||
– *Kaṭha Upaniṣad*, 2.1.12

The *Puruṣa* of the size of a thumb dwells in the body. He is the Lord of the past and the future. After knowing Him one does not conceal oneself any more.

yadvācānabhyuditaṁ yena vāgābhyudyate |
tadeva brahma tvaṁ viddhi nedaṁ yadidamupāsate ||
yanmanasā na manute yenāhurmano matam |
tadeva brahma tvaṁ viddhi nedaṁ yadidamupāsate ||
yaccakṣuṣa na paśyati yena caksmँṣi paśyati |
tadeva brahma tvaṁ viddhi nedaṁ yadidamupāsate ||
yacchrotreṇa na śṛṇoti yena śrotramidamँ śrutam |
tadeva brahma tvaṁ viddhi nedaṁ yadidamupāsate ||
yatprāṇeha na prāṇiti yena prāṇaḥ praṇīyate |
tadeva brahma tvaṁ viddhi nedaṃ yadidamupāsate ||
– *Kena Upaniṣad* 1.4-8, 2.1

That alone know as Brahman,
and not that which people here worship:
That which cannot be expressed by speech,
but by which speech is expressed
That which cannot be apprehended by mind but by which theysay,
mind is apprehended
That cannot be perceived by the eye, but by which eye is perceived
That cannot be heard by the year,
but by which the hearing is perceived
That which cannot be smelt by the
breath but which the breath smells as object.

The teacher said: if you think you know *Brahman* then surely you know but little of its form; you know only its form as conditioned by man or by the gods.

The forms of *Brahman* conditioned by the bodies and minds of men and gods are only insignificant manifestations of it in time and space. The gist is that *Brahman* free from all limitations is infinite, non-dual, sublime and eternal and therefore cannot be described, as well known by anyone. The rivers have their origin in the ocean and therefore are irresistibly drawn towards it. It is name and form that distinguish the river water from the water of ocean. After the destruction of the name and form, what remains is only the ocean. All things are only modifications of the Pure Being; the knowledge of the Pure Being makes all things known. Hence it has been rightly said that by the knowledge of One, all things become known.

A name is a mere word or sound. Through words one cannot know the nature of the Self. This is known only from a qualified teacher. The real Self which is beyond everything, cannot be denoted by words.

parīkṣya lokānkarmacitānbrāhmaṇo nirvedamāyānnastyakṛtaḥ kṛtena ।
tadvijñānārthaṁ sa gurumevābhigacchetsamitpāṇiḥ śrotriyaṁ brahmaniṣṭham ॥ – *Muṇḍaka Upaniṣad* 1.2.12

Let the seeker, after having examined all these worlds that are gained by works, acquire freedom from desires. Nothing that is eternal can be produced by what is not eternal. So he should understand that eternal. Let him approach a *guru* who is well-versed in the Vedas and always devoted to *Brahman*.

tasmai sa vidvānupasannāya samyak praśāntacittāya śamānvitāya ।
yenākṣaraṁ puruṣaṁ veda satyaṁ provāca tāṁ tattvato brahmavidyām ॥ – Ibid. 1.2.13

To that pupil who has dually approached him, whose mind is completely serene and whose senses are controlled, the wise teacher should indeed rightly impart the knowledge of *Brahman* through which one knows the immutable and true *Puruṣa*.

The duty of the preceptor is to help a qualified pupil who has duly approached him to cross the great ocean of ignorance.

KARMA

ātmānaṁ rathinaṁ viddhi, śarīraṁ rathameva tu ।
buddhiṁ tu sārathiṁ viddhi manaḥ pragrahameva ca ॥
indriyāṇi hayānāhurviṣayāṁsteṣu gocarān ।
ātmendriyamanoyuktaṁ bhoktetyāhurmanīṣiṇaḥ ॥
yastvavijñānavānbhavatyayuktena manasā sadā ।
tasyendriyāṇyavaśyāni duṣṭāśvā iva sāratheḥ ॥
– *Kaṭha Upaniṣad* 1.3.3-5

Know the *Ātman* to be the master of the chariot, the body the chariot, the *buddhi* the charioteer or driver and the mind the reins by which the intellect controls the senses. The senses are the horses; the objects are the roads. He who has the understanding of the driver of the chariot and controls the rein of his mind, he reaches the end of the journey, i.e. that Supreme abode of the all-pervading.

nāvirato duścaritānnāśānto nāsamāhitaḥ ।
nāśāntamānaso vāpi prajñānenainamāpnuyāt ॥
– *Kaṭha Upaniṣad* 1.2.24

Who has not first turned from wickedness, one who is not tranquil and subdued, whose mind is not at peace cannot attain *Ātman*. It is realized only through knowledge of Reality.

yadā sarve pramucyante kāmā ye 'sya hṛdi śritāḥ ।
atha martyo 'mṛto bhavatyatra brahma samaśnute ॥
– Ibid. 2.3.14

When all the desires that dwell in the heart fall away, then the mortal becomes immortal and attains *Brahman*.

agne naya supathā rāye asmānviśvāni deva vayunāni vidvān ।
yuyodhyasmajjuhurāṇameno bhūyiṣṭhāṁ te nama uktiṁ vidhema ॥
– *Īśa Upaniṣad* 18

O Fire (during Vedic time Fire was considered as an intermediary god through whom oblations to the other gods were made)! lead us by the good path for enjoyment of the fruit of our action. O God! you know all our deeds. Destroy our sin of deceit. We offer our salutations to you by words.

(At the time of death, the devotee cannot offer any other worship as his limbs become inert; he cannot prostrate himself hence the salutations by words alone.)

tasyai tapo damaḥ karmeti pratiṣṭhā vedāḥ sarvāṅgāni satyamāyatanam ॥
– *Kena Upaniṣad* 4.8

Austerities, self-restraint and sacrificial rites are its feet and Vedas are all its limbs. Truth is its abode.

The virtues mentioned in this verse are means for attainment of knowledge of *Brahman*. Austerity (*tapas*) is training in spiritual life for cleaning our soul of all that is sinful and imperfect. It is building up all that is good and holy.

> *kāmānyaḥ kāmayate manyamānaḥ sa kāmabhirjāyate tatra tatra* |
> *paryāptakāmasya kṛtātmanastu ihaiva sarve pravilīyanti kāmāḥ* ||
>
> – *Muṇḍaka Upaniṣad* 3.2.2

> He, who cherishes objects and desires them, is born again here or there through his desires. But for him whose desires are satisfied and who is established in the Self, all his desires vanish even here on earth.

This verse describes what is known as *karma-mukti* (gradual liberation). Those who worship *Saguṇa-Brahman* with whole soul devotion do not return to earth or go to any other lower plane. They dwell in *brahmaloka* absorbed in contemplation and attain final liberation at the end of the cycle when all merge in the Absolute.

MEDITATION

> *puramekādaśadvāramajasyāvakracetasaḥ* |
> *anuṣṭhāya na śocati vimuktaśca vimucyate, etadvai tat* ||
>
> – *Kaṭha Upaniṣad* 2.2.1

> There is the city with eleven gates belonging to the unborn *Ātman* of distorted consciousness. By ruling it one does not grieve; liberated from the bonds of ignorance, he becomes free.

Of the eleven gates nine are consisted of two eyes, two ears, two nostrils, mouth, anus and reproductive organ. Two others are navel and the opening at the top of the skull through which the liberated soul is said to escape death. When the soul controls the gates and lives in peace it is freed from sorrow. It is freedom which begins here (*jīvana-mukti*) and leads after death to complete release (*videha-mukti*).

> *eko vaśī sarvabhūtāntarātmā ekaṁ rūpaṁ bahudhā yaḥ karoti* |
> *tamātmasthaṁ ye'nupaśyanti dhīrāsteṣaṁ sukhaṁ śāsvataṁ netareṣām* ||
>
> – Ibid. 2.2.12

> That is to say the body with its eleven gates, there is one supreme ruler, the inmost Self of all beings, who makes His one form manifold. Eternal happiness belongs to the wise, who perceive Him within themselves, not to others.

yadidaṁ kiṁ ca jagatsarvaṁ prāṇa ejati niḥsṛtam ।
mahadbhayaṁ vajramudyataṁ ya etadviduramṛtāste bhavanti ।।
– *Kaṭha Upaniṣad* 2.3.2

Whatever there is – the whole universe – vibrates because it has gone forth from *Brahman*, which exists as its ground... That is to say that the source and sustaining power of the universe are *Brahman*. Evolution is not a mechanical process. It is controlled by *Brahman*.

na saṁdṛśe tiṣṭhati rūpamasya na cakṣuṣā paśyati kaścanainam ।
hṛdā manīṣī manasā 'bhiklṛpto ya etadviduramṛtāste bhavanti ।।
– Ibid. 2.3.9

His form is not an object of vision; no one beholds Him with the eye. One can know Him when He is revealed by the intellect free from doubt and by constant meditation.

We cannot form a visual image of God; we can apprehend Him by heart, by thought and mind.

aṅguṣṭhamātraḥ puruṣo 'ntarātmā sadā janānāṁ hṛdaye sanniviṣṭaḥ । . . .
– Ibid. 2.3.17

The *Puruṣa* not larger than a thumb, the inner self, always dwells in the hearts of men. Let a man separate him from his body with steadiness as one separates a tender stalk from a blade of grass. Let him know that the Self is as bright as the immortal.

yastu sarvāṇi bhūtānyātmanyevanupáśyati ।
sarvabhūteṣu cātmānaṁ tato na vijugupsate ।।
– *Īśa Upaniṣad* 6

The wise man beholds all beings in the Self and the Self in all beings, for that reason he does not hate anyone.

yasminsarvāṇi bhūtānyātmaivābhūdvijānataḥ ।
tatra ko mohaḥ koḥ śoka ekatvamanupaśyatuḥ ।।
– Ibid. 7

To the seer, all things have verily become the Self. What delusion or sorrow can there be for him who beholds that oneness?

When the unity is realized by an individual, he becomes liberated from sorrow; there remains no opposition between the One and the many.

hiraṇmayena pātreṇa satyasyāpihitaṁ mukham ।
tattvaṁ kūṣannapāvṛṇu satyadharmāya dṛṣṭaye ॥
– *Īśa Upaniṣad* 15

The door of the Truth is covered by a golden disc. Open it, O nourisher! so that I who have been worshipping the Truth may behold it.

athābdhyātmaṁ yadetadgacchatīva ca mano 'nena caita-dupasmaratyabhīkṣnaṁ saṅkalpaḥ ॥ – *Kena Upaniṣad* 4.5

The instruction about *Brahman* with regard to individual self: The mind as it were goes to *Brahman*. The seeker by means of the mind communes with it intimately again and again. This should be the volition of his mind.

While meditating on *Brahman*, the aspirant should think that his mind has attuned to luminous *Brahman* and is established in it. There is an analogy between the divine spirit, the cosmic world and the individual soul.

dhanurgṛhītvaupaniṣadaṁ mahāstraṁ śaraṁ hyapāsāniśtaṁ sandhayīta ।
āyamya tadbhāvagatena cetasā lakṣyaṁ tadevākṣaraṁ somya viddhi ॥
praṇavo dhanuḥ śaro hyātmā brahma tallakṣyamucyate ।
apramattena veddhavyaṁ śaravattanmayo bhavet ॥
– *Muṇḍaka Upaniṣad* 2.2.3-4

Take the Upaniṣads as a bow, the great weapon, and place upon it the arrow sharpened by meditation. Then having drawn it back with a mind directed to the thought of *Brahman*, strike that mark, that which is the imperishable.

Oṁ is the bow, *ātman* is the arrow, *Brahman* is said to be the mark. It is to be struck by an undistracted mind. Then *ātman* becomes one with *Brahman* as the arrow with the target. The fetters of the heart are broken, all doubts are resolved and all works cease to bear fruit when he is beheld who is both high and low.

na cakṣuṣā gṛhyate nāpi vācā nānyair devaistapasā karmaṇā vā ।
jñānaprasādena viśuddhasattvastatastu taṁ paśyate niṣkalaṁ dhyāyamānaḥ ॥
– Ibid. 3.1.8

> *Brahman* is not grasped by eye nor speech; nor by other senses or by penance or good works. A man becomes pure through serenity of intellect. Thereupon in meditation he beholds Him who is without parts.

> *yaḥ punaretantrimātreṇomityetenaivākṣareṇa paraṁ puruṣamabhidhyāyīta sa tejasi sūrye saṁpannaḥ* । *yathā pādodarastvacā vinirmucyata evaṁ ha vai sa pāpmanā vinirmuktaḥ sa sāmabhirunnīyate brahmalokaṁ sa etasmājjivaghanātparātparaṁ puriśayaṁ* । *puruṣamīkṣate* । *tadetau śloko bhavataḥ* ॥
>
> – *Praśna Upaniṣad* 5.5

> He who meditates on the highest person through this syllable *oṁ* consisting of three letters, becomes united with the effulgent sun as a snake is freed from its skin, even so he is freed from sin. He is led by the *Sāmaveda* verses to *brahmaloka*. From this which is the aggregate of all lives, he beholds the Supreme *Puruṣa* higher than the high and pervading all bodies.

The Upaniṣads prescribe the path to liberation through knowledge of *Brahman* and realization of oneness of the individual soul with the Universal Soul. For realization of this goal a balanced life of *karma*, knowledge, *yoga* and meditation is advised. When a seeker reaches his goal of Self-realization all his mental and physical knots are loosened and he realizes oneness with the Supreme Self and becomes immune to worldly pain and pleasure, and experiences the bliss in this life itself. Guru Nānak also identified the path to liberation through *manana* (faith in God), *śravaṇa* (repetition of *guru*'s word), *sunanā* (hearing to scriptures and *guru*'s words), *sahaja pāṭha* (spontaneous concentration of mind) for personal experience of divinity within oneself. He taught us to go beyond the tenth gate of the city of this body through *sahaja pāṭha* to achieve the fourth state of consciousness and hear the sound of unstuck melody within and experience the bliss of unity with the Supreme Being.

Personal Experience of Divinity

Contemplating the compassionate Lord one enjoys absolute bliss. All over and around us is the wonder of God. God can be described only as a greatest wonder. He has placed fire in ocean and water in the fire. This body is nothing but mud, that is to say clay built and full of water of life. *Karma, dharma, yoga* and meditation are the foundations of Truth. The seekers worshipping the Supreme Being with love and respect feel thirsty for His vision and they become tearful begging and imploring Him for His grace. In His love and affection their consciousness derives peace.

PERSONAL EXPERIENCE OF DIVINITY IN THE HYMNS OF GURU NĀNAK

> *ghara mahi gharu dikhāi dei so stiguru purakhu sujāṇu* ॥
> *pañca sabada dhunikāra dhuni taha bājai sabadu nīsāṇu* ॥
> *dīpa loa pātāla taha khaṇḍa maṇḍala hairānu* ॥
> *tāra ghora bājintra taha sāci takhati sulatānu* ॥
> *sukhamana kai ghari rāgu suni suni maṇḍali liva lāi* ॥
> *akatha kathā bīcārīē manasā manahi samāi* ॥
> *ulaṭi kamalu aṁmr̥ti bhariā ihu manu katahu na jāi* ॥
> *ajapā jāpu na vīsarai ādi jugādi samāi* ॥
> *sabhi sakhīā pañce mile guramukhi nija ghari vāsu* ॥
> *sabadu khoji ihu gharu lahai nānaku tā kā dāsu* ॥
>
> – *Ādi Granth,* p. 1291

A true *guru* is one who can lead his follower to the home within oneself. Where the orchestra of sweet melody of five sounds resonates. The distinguishing mark of *śabada,* which is vibrating gracefully is revealed there, wherefrom one can see the glory of all planets in the cosmos. There is the true throne of the Lord and the strings and the harps vibrate and resound. There one hears the melody of the music of the heart and experiences peace. There one can get lovingly tuned to His state of heavenly ecstasy and can enjoy the unspeakable word and one's strong mental wishes get eliminated. There the lotus of the heart is turned and gets filled with divine flow, thus the mind does not hanker hither or thither. There one is attuned to that speech which cannot be chanted and helps one to immerse in the Supreme Being. There my entire sister companions get blessed with the five primal sounds and always reside in their homes of the Self deep within them. Nānak opted to be the servant of that teacher who sought the *śabada* and found it within the Self, meaning the

Self-realized *guru*.

Guru Nānak in this hymn explains the gist of experience of divinity through the *sūrata-śabada-yoga*. All the five virtues, viz. truth, contentment, compassion, righteousness and patience, are imbibed by the five knowing faculties but one abides in the Self only through the grace of the *guru*. Only a Self-realized preceptor can show the true home within our home where orchestral melody of five sounds rings with the beat of the drum of the word.

aṁtari suṁnaṁ bāhari suṁnaṁ tribhavaṇa suṁnamasuṁnaṁ ||
cauthe suṁnai jo naru jāṇai tā kau pāpu na puṁnaṁ ||
ghaṭi ghaṭi suṁna kā jāṇai bheda || *ādi purakhu niraṁjana deu* ||
jo janu nāma niraṁjana rātā || *nānaka soī purakhu bidhātā* ||
suṁno suṁnu kahai sabhu koī || *anahata suṁnu kahā te hoī* ||
anahata suṁni rate se kaise || *jisa te upaje tisa hī jaise* ||
oi janami na marahi na āvahi jāhi ||
nānaka guramukhi manu samajhāhi ||

– *Ādi Granth*, p. 943

The Supreme Being is deep within us. He is at our outside as well. He fills totally all the three worlds. One who realizes Him in the fourth state of consciousness gets out of the domain of virtue or vice. One who knows the mystery of God who is spread throughout each and every heart comes to know the Supreme Being. A modest man, filled with the pure faultless name of God, is the manifestation of Supreme Being, who is the designer of this world. Everyone speaks of the unmanifest void but how can one find this absolute void? Who are they who are attuned to the absolute void? Such godly men are like the Lord from whom they have originated. They are not born; they do not die; they do not come and go. O Nānak! teach your mind this way.

Here Guru Nānak explains that there is void (God) within, outside and in between the within and outside us. One who goes beyond this, viz. the three states of consciousness and attains fourth (*turīya*), is not subject to virtue or vice. Such *guramukha*s are like God Himself from whom they have come and are the architects of destiny.

anahado anahadu vājai ruṇa jhuṇa kāre rāma ||

merā mano merā manu rātā lāla piāre rāma ||
anadinu rātā manu bairāgī suṅna maṅḍali gharu pāiā ||
ādi purakhu aparaṁparu piārā satiguri alakhu lakhāiā ||
āsaṇi baisaṇi thiru nārāiṇu titu manu rātā vīcāre ||
nānaka nāmi rate bairāgī anahada ruṇa jhuṇa kāre ||
titu agama titu agama pure kahu kitu bidhi jāīē rāma ||
sacu saṅjamo sāri guṇā gura sabadu kamāīē rāma ||
sacu sabadu kamāīē nija ghari jāīē pāīē guṇī nidhānā ||
– *Ādi Granth*, p. 436

Unstruck music rings within mind and he gets filled with the love for the Supreme Being. His mind gets detached and remains absorbed in the Lord all the time, day and night. He found his home in this heavenly void and resides in a state of desirelessness. He says that a true *guru* has disclosed to him the unseen Supreme Being. The Supreme Being has a permanent seat within his heart and does not move. His mind gets into reflective contemplation upon Him. The individuals who get detached from the world are filled with His Name, the unstruck music and heavenly vibrations within the Self. One can arrive at the city within oneself practising of truthfulness and austerity, by concentration upon God's virtues and His glory, and by practice with the word of the *guru*. Practice of the true word from *guru* brings one to the home of his own inner being and he attains the desired ability.

In these lines Guru Nānak talks about the experience of divinity in the *suṅna maṅḍala ghara* (void). The state of void is a state wherein one recognizes no such distinction as that of subject or object, or knower and known and the knowing, and even self-consciousness. He explains that unstruck music of bliss rings in his mind and he is imbued with God's love, practising the true word. His mind is attuned, night and day, to God and he abides in desirelessness.

joga sabadaṁ giāna sabadaṁ beda sabadaṁ ta brāhamaṇaha ||
khyatrī sabadaṁ sūra sabadaṁ sūdra sabadaṁ parākṛtaha ||
saraba sabadaṁ ta eka sabadaṁ jeko jānasi bheu ||
nānaka tāko dāsu hai soī niraṅjana deu ||
eka kṛsnaṁ ta sarabadevā deva devā ta ātamaha ||
ātamaṁ strī bāsva devasya je koī jānasi bheva ||

nānaka tāko dāsu hai soī nirañjana deva ॥

– *Ādi Granth*, p. 1353

> *Śabada* is *yoga*, spiritual wisdom and the Vedas for brāhmaṇas. *Śabada* is kṣatriya and his heroic bravery. *Śabada* is service to others for śūdras. *Śabada* is one for all who know His secret. There is one Lord who is divinity of all divinities and the divinity of the soul. If anyone knows the mystery of the soul and the omnipresent Lord, he is the divine pure Lord Himself. Nānak is the slave of that one who knows the secrets of the soul and the Supreme Lord.

This is a beautiful expression of Guru Nānak about the personal experience of divinity through *sūrata-śabada-yoga*. He declares that *śabada* is the way of all ways. It is Vedas' spiritual wisdom for the brāhmaṇas in pursuit of knowledge, heroic bravery for kṣatriyas in the battlefield, service to the others for śūdras.

gura mahalī ghari āpaṇai so bharapuri līṇā ॥
sevaku sevā tā kare saca sabadi patīṇā ॥
sabade patījai aṅku bhījai su mahalu mahalā aṅtare ॥
āpi karatā kare soī prabhu āpi aṅti niraṅtare ॥
gura sabadi melā tāṅ suhelā bājaṅta anahada bīṇā ॥
gura mahalī ghari āpaṇai so bharipuri līṇā ॥
kītā kīā sālāhīē kari vekhai sāī ॥ *tā kī kīmati nā pavai je lācai koī* ॥

– Ibid., p. 767

> One whom the word of the *guru* leads to enter into the self within, he gets merged in God who is spread throughout the creation. The creator God Himself does everything but He Himself stays forever the same and does not get reflected. If one is attuned to the *guru*'s word, he is at peace and then within him rings the unstuck melody. One cannot evaluate Him even if one tries his best. He alone can evaluate Him to whom He reveals Himself.

In the above lines there is a clear message of Guru Nānak that if one is attuned to the *guru*'s word, he is at peace and then experiences the ringing of unstuck melody within him.

sahaji milai miliā paravāṇu ॥ *nā tisu maraṇu na āvaṇu jāṇu* ॥
ṭhākura mahi dāsu dāsa mahi soi ॥ *jaha dekhā taha avaru na koi* ॥
....

so guru karau ji sācu dṛḍāvai॥ akathu kathāvai sabadi milāvai॥
....
tudhu binu dūjā mai ko nāhī॥ jiu tudhu bhāvai tiu rākhu rajāi॥
– *Ādi Granth*, p. 686

The union with the Lord is the true union which is attained through equipoise. Thereafter one does not come and go in incarnations. Then one resides in God and God in him. Wherever one looks he sees none other than God. So he should search for a *guru* who can implant the truth within him and lead him to speak the unspoken speech and show the path for merging into the *śabada*. O God, I am nothing without you, as you please, keep me under Your will.

These lines stress upon the need to find a true *guru* who leads one to the state of equipoise. After union with the Lord through *sahaja* (*sūrata-śabada-yoga*) one sees none other than God around him. God and He become One.

auhaṭhi hasata maḍī gharu chāiā dharaṇi gagana kala dhārī॥
guramukhi ketī sabadi udhārī santahu॥
....
sinī surati anāhadi vājai ghaṭi ghaṭi joti tumārī॥
parapañca beṇu tahī manu rākhiā brahama agani parajārī॥
pañca tatu mili ahinisi dīpaku niramala joti apārī॥
ravi sasi lauke ihu tanu kiṅgurī vājai sabadu nirārī॥
– Ibid., p. 907

God established His abode in the mansion of the heart of an individual. Both the earth and the sky are filled with His power. Word of the *guru* has saved many God-conscious men. Music of the unstuck sound current vibrates within. Every heart is illuminated with God's light whose flute's play ignites the fire.

Guru Nānak explains that a true *yogī* spreads the hand of his heart out of the tomb of his body and seeks the bounties from the Lord of earth and sky. The God-conscious beings have saved many through the word and they overpower their I-ness and mine-ness and start seeing the light of God in all around. They overwhelm their desires, and reflecting on the true word of the *guru* they hear the ringing of the unstuck melody within them.

pavana araṁbhu satigura mati velā || *sabadu gurū surati dhuni celā* ||
akatha kathā le rahau nirālā || *nānaka jugi jugi gura gopālā* ||
eku sabadu jitu kathā vīcārī || *guramukhi haumai agani nivārī* ||
– *Ādi Granth*, p. 943

The start of this creation came from air. The present age is to learn from a true *guru*. The word of the *guru* should be focused in one's consciousness then the melody shall follow. One should adhere to follow the unspeakable word and shed all attachments to the worldly pursuits. O Nānak! throughout the ages, *guru*'s word is God. One who contemplates on *guru*'s word extinguishes his fire of egotism.

In these lines Guru Nānak tells that the air is the beginning. The word is the *guru* and the mind attuned to the word is the disciple (like the sound and its waves). It is *guru*'s word through which one reflects on the Supreme Lord and quenches his inner fire.

nau sara subhara dasavai pūre || *taha anahata suṅna bajāvahi tūre* ||
sācai rāce dekhi hajūre || *ghaṭi ghaṭi sācu rahiā bharapūre* ||
gupatī bāṇī paragaṭu hoi || *nānaka parakhi lae sacu soi* ||
sahaja bhāi milīē sukhu hovai || *guramukhi jāgai nīda na sovai* ||
suna sabadu aparaṁpari dhārai || *kahate mukatu sabadi nisatārai* ||
gura kī dīkhiā se saci rāte || *nānaka āpu gavāi milaṇa nahī bhrāte* ||
– Ibid., pp. 943-44

By the practice of controlling the nine outflowing senses, one gets concentrated on the tenth aperture. It is in this place that one experiences the vibrations of the melody of unstuck sound current of the all-powerful God. One feels the presence of His being there. He penetrates and exists in every heart. It is here where the concealed word gets revealed and known to the seeker. One finds peace and love by meeting God through *sahaja*. A God-conscious man remains in His attendance and never sleeps or winks. He absorbs the limitless *śabada* deep within him. This concentration and contemplation makes one ever reside with the word. One emancipates himself and helps others to the same. O Nānak! without elimination of one's egotism and treachery, he cannot get adopted by Him. With the grace of the *guru* such individuals shed away all their doubts and remain ever absorbed in Him.

In these lines Guru Nānak explains the experience of divinity by filling up the breaches of all nine doors (outgoing senses) and arriving at the tenth door to experience the unstuck music within oneself and see the Lord who is all-permeating.

su sabada kā kahā vāsu aṭhīale jitu tarīe bhavajalu saṁsāro॥
trai sata aṅgula vāī kahīē tisu kahu kavanu adhāro॥
bolai khelai asathiru hovai kiukari alakhu lakhāe॥
suṇi suāmī sacu nānaku praṇavai apaṇe mana samajhāe॥
guramukhi sabade saci liva lāgai kari nadarī meli milāe॥
....
su sabada kau niraṅtari vāsu alakhaṁ jaha dekhā taha soī॥
pavana kā vāsā suna nivāsā akala kalā dhara soī॥
nadari kare sabadu ghaṭa mahi vasai vicahu bharamu gavāe॥
tanu manu niramalu niramala bāṇī nāmo maṅni vasāe॥
sabadi gurū bhavasāgaru tarīē ita uta eko jāṇai॥
cihanu varanu nahī chāiā māiā nānaka sabadu pachāṇai॥
traisata aṅgula vāī audhū suṅna sacu āhāro॥
guramukhi bolai tatu virolai cīnai alakha apāro॥

– *Ādi Granth*, p. 944

Which is the residing place for *śabada*? How shall we be carried over from this sea of the horrible world? The breathing out air goes up to the length of ten fingers. What supports this breathing? How can one keep steadiness and remain stable while he speaks and plays? How can one see the unseen? Guru Nānak explains that one should make his mind understand that the *guramukha* who gets lovingly attuned to the true *śabada* and the Supreme Being is united with the Lord by His graceful glance.

Śabada resides deep within the heart of each and every one. God cannot be seen; but in whatever direction one looks he finds Him there. The Supreme Being resides in the air. God has no attributes yet he is the source of all attributes. As and when He is pleased to bestow his graceful glace, *śabada* gets realized within the heart of individuals and all their doubts get vanished from within. One becomes pure both mentally and physically and faultless through the *guru*'s word. One should absorb God's name in his heart. The *śabada* is the *guru* which carries us to the other side of terrible sea of this world. One must know that there is one and only one God spread over everywhere. He is without any form or colour, shadow or illusion. Nānak says that one should attain the *śabada*. One should understand that the Supreme Being is the support of the outgoing air extended ten fingers beyond when breathing.

In these lines Guru Nānak answers the questions of the hermits and explains the experience of divinity realized through *śabada*.

sabadai kā nibeḍā suṇi tū audhū binu nāvai jogu na hoī॥
nāme rāte anadinu māte nāmai te sukhu hoī॥
nāmai hī te sabhu paragaṭu hovai nāme sojhī pāī॥
binu nāvai bhekha karahi bahutere sacai āpi khuāī॥
satigura te nāmu pāīē audhū joga jugati tā hoī॥
kari bīcāru mani dekhahu nānaka binu nāvai mukati na hoī॥
– *Ādi Granth*, p. 946

The essence of *śabada* is that there cannot be any *yoga* without the *guru*'s word. Those who get tuned to the *guru*'s word remain always excited and find peace within. It is only through the name that everything gets revealed and one understands *śabada*. Without the name, people tend to wear all sorts of religious costumes and get confused, as per the will of the Supreme Being. One gains name only from the true *guru*, before one adopts the way to find *yoga*. One should think deep and realize that without the name, there is no liberation.

Guru Nānak says that the essence of *sūrata śabada-yoga* is that there is no *yoga* without the true name which can be obtained from the true *guru* only.

nā sati dukhīā nā sati sukhīā nā sati pāṇī janta phirahi॥
nā sati mūṅḍa muḍāī kesī nā sati paḍiā desa phirahi॥
....
jisu hathi sidhi devai je soī jisano dei tisu āi milai॥
nānaka tā kau milai vaḍāī jisu ghaṭa bhītari sabadu ravai॥
sabhi ghaṭa mere hau sabhanā aṅdari jisahi khuāī tisu kauṇu kahai॥
jisahi dikhālā vaṭaḍī tisahi bhulāvai kauṇu॥

jisahi bhulāī paṅdha siri tisahi dikhāvai kauṇu ||

– *Ādi Granth*, p. 952

One cannot gain the Ultimate Truth by physical sufferings or getting excited in comforts. One cannot find Truth by roaming like animals or living in water. One cannot find Truth by shaving his head, studying religious books or roaming in other lands, etc. All spiritual progress comes from Him whom He chooses for it through His graceful glance only. O Nānak! who is filled with *śabada* gets blessed with all glory of spiritual perfection. God makes all realize that all individual hearts are His and He abides in all hearts. A confused individual is unable to understand it. No one can confuse that individual to whom He Himself shows the way. One cannot show the path to that individual whom He confuses ever since the beginning.

This is a wonderful revelation of Guru Nānak. Glory of perfect bliss comes only through *śabada* and He Himself makes one realize it within the Self.

sabadu vasāe bharamu cukāe sadā sevaku dinu rāti ||
ūpari gaganu gagana pari gorakhu tā kā agamu gurū puni vāsī ||
gura bacanī bāhari ghari eko nānaku bhaiā udāsī ||

– Ibid., p. 992

One who is consistent all the day and night in the practice of *śabada* within, all his doubts are vanished. The Lord is above the sky of mind and beyond, and protects His creation but He is not accessible without the *guru*'s word who always abides there.

pavaṇai pāṇī aganī jīu pāiā ||
dehī nagarī nau daravāje so dasavā gupatu rahātā hai ||
cāri nadī aganī asarālā || *koī guramukhi būjhai sabadi nirālā* ||
....
aṅtari premu parāpati darasanu || *gurabāṇī siu prīti su parasanu* ||
ahinisi niramala joti sabāī ghaṭi dīpaku guramukhi jātā he ||
bhojana giānu mahārasu mīṭhā || *jini cākhiā tini darasanu dīṭhā* ||
darasanu dekhi mile bairāgī manu manasā māri samātā he ||

– Ibid., pp. 1031-32

Above lines explain that the body consists of air, water and fire, and God has placed the soul therein. The body is like a village.

It has nine outward doors and its tenth door is not visible. It has four dangerous rivers filled with fire. The God-conscious individuals understand it and remain unattached from these four vices through *śabada*.

One, who is filled with love for God, gets the experience of His presence and *darśana*. One, who is in deep love for the *guru*'s word experiences His presence every moment of the day and night. Such an individual's heart gets illuminated by His light. This spiritual experience is a sweet essence and one gets blessed and overjoyed. Whosoever tastes it gets blessed with the vision of the Supreme Being. When one is blessed with His vision, the individual gets unattached with the world and realizes His presence. After all the desires of one's mind get exhausted, one is absorbed into the Almighty.

Guru Nānak explains that God has made life to throb in a body of air, water and fire. There are nine gates to the township of this body. He kept the tenth gate hidden within the mind. There are four dreadful rivers of fire: greed, wrath, infatuation and worldly attachments. God-conscious men are rare, who are detached from these and realize *śabada*. Such people are blessed with the vision of the Lord.

kāiā nagaru nagara gaḍa aṅdari ।। *sācā vāsā puri gaganaṅdari* ।।
usathiru thānu sadā nirmāilu āpe āpu upāidā ।।
aṅdari koṭa chaje haṭa nale ।। *āpe levai vasatu samāle* ।।
bajara kapāṭa jaḍe jaḍi jāṇai gura sabadī kholāidā ।।
bhītari koṭa guphā ghara jāī ।। *nau gharu thāpe hukami rajāī* ।।
dasavai purakhu alekhu apārī āpe alakhu lakhāidā ।।
....
akathī kathau cihanu nahī koī pūri rahiā mani bhāidā ।।
pasarī kiraṇi joti ujiālā ।। *kari kari dekhai āpi daiālā* ।।
anahada ruṇajhuṇakāru sada dhuni nirabhau kai ghari vāidā ।।
anahadu vājai bhramu bhau bhājai ।। *sagala biāpi rahiā prabhu chājai* ।।

– *Ādi Granth*, pp. 1033-34

The body is like a village and deep within it is a fort. The Supreme Being resides deep within this body village. God is at the tenth gate within this body. He resides permanently here in the heart of individuals by His own will.

There are a large number of covered lanes and by-lanes in it. The trade of mind and heart goes on. God Himself sells and purchases the items and takes care of the soul. The tenth gate bears protective heavy door and is locked from within. This get opened with the word of the *guru*. There is one inner cave within this fortress which is the residing place of the Self. All these gates exist and work according to the will of God. Supreme Being resides at the tenth gate. He cannot be known or seen but He reveals Himself.

Guru Nānak describes the state which is indescribable. There is no mark there but the presence of the Supreme Being experienced here is most pleasing. The radiance of the light divine is spread in full and the unstuck sweet melodious sound echoes non-stop. This is the residing place of the Supreme Being who is fearless. With the hearing of this unstuck sound resounding within, all individual doubts and fears run away. God is omnipresent and protects all individuals.

Guru Nānak explains in detail the experience of divinity in human fort of nine gates and the tenth gate of deliverance in this hymn.

tū purakhu alekha agaṁma nirālā॥
sata saṁtokhi sabadi ati sītalu sahaja bhāi liva lāiā॥
trai varatāi cauthai ghari vāsā॥ kāla bikāla kīe ika grāsā॥
niramala joti saraba jagajīvanu guri anahada sabadi dikhāiā॥
ūtama jana saṁta bhale hari piāre॥ hari rasa māte pāri utāre॥
nānaka reṇa saṁta jana saṅgati hari gura parasādī pāiā॥

– *Ādi Granth*, p. 1038

The Supreme Being cannot be seen. The primal Lord cannot be accessed. He is true and content. He can be realized through *śabada* which is cool and soothing. One gets lovingly attuned to Him through it. Three states of consciousness are experienced by individuals, but one has to obliterate these states to enter into the fourth where the Supreme Being resides. Death and birth are His food. His light illuminates the whole world. One is led by a true *guru* to this light. All individuals who are filled with His love are loved by God too. Such people remain excited with the pure love of God and cross the sea of life. Nānak declares himself to be the servant of such assembly of godly people.

In these lines Guru Nānak explains that the world moves and has its being within the three modes and three states of consciousness while the Lord abides in the fourth state of consciousness of Absolute Bliss.

dehī nagarī ūtama thānā ॥ *pañca loka vasahi paradhānā* ॥
ūpari ekaṁkāru nirālamu suñña samādhi lagāiā ॥
dehī nagarī nau daravāje ॥ *siri siri karaṇaihārai sāje* ॥
dasavai purakhu atītu nirālā āpe alakhu lakhāiā ॥
purakhu alekhu sace dīvānā ॥ *hukami calāe sacu nīsānā* ॥
nānaka khāji lahahu gharu apanā hari ātama rāma nāmu pāiā ॥
....
āpi pachāṇai sabadu vīcārā ॥
sacai mahali nivāsu nirantari āvaṇa jāṇu cukāiā ॥
nā manu calai na pauṇu uḍāvai ॥ *jogī sabadu anāhalu vāvai* ॥
pañca sabada jhuṇakāru nirālamu prabhi āpe vāi suṇāiā ॥
bhau bairāgā sahaji samātā ॥ *haumai tiāgī anahadi rātā* ॥
– *Ādi Granth*, pp. 1039-40

Noble people and lovers of God always live in the sublime place of their body. They feel the presence of the Supreme Being always there with them lovingly absorbed in the profound primal state of *samādhi*. The body is like a village with nine gates. These have been designed by the Supreme Being for each and every one. The Supreme Being dwells at the tenth gate and remains detached and no one can be equal to Him. The Supreme Lord, who cannot be otherwise known, reveals Himself to such individuals. The primal Lord cannot be held responsible for anything; yet He controls all His creations. His *hukam* is the final command and stamp of Truth. O Nānak! one should search and find Him in his own home and he shall realize His presence there.

Who goes deep into own self and contemplates the *śabada*, he realizes His presence in the abode of the Self within his own body. Then the individual's cycle of coming and going to this world ends. His mind gets stabilized and he is not affected by the flow of desire. Such a *yogī* hears the vibrations of unstuck melody of *śabada*. God plays the pure music of *pañca śabada* (the five primal sounds). Such a person lives in the fear of God and remains unattached to the world and gets deeply merged into the Supreme Lord. When all egotism goes away he is filled with the unstuck sound current.

In these lines Guru Nānak advocates the policy of "know thyself" to attain the pure bliss of life. When one does the deeds of soul night and day, deep within him burns the pure light of God. He enjoys the nectar essence of the word and his tongue emits the sweet notes of a flute. One should know this state through the word of the *guru* and get filled with the Lord's name.

tārā caḍiā laṁmā kiu nadari nihāliā rāma ||
sevaka pūra karaṁmā satiguri sabadi dikhālia rāma ||
gura sabadi dikhālia sacu samāliā ahinisi dekhi bīcāriā ||
dhāvata paṅca rahe gharu jāṇiā kāmu krodhu bikhu māriā ||
aṅtari joti bhaī gura sākhī cīne rāma karaṁmā ||
nānaka haumai māri patīṇe tārā caḍiā laṁmā ||
– *Ādi Granth*, pp. 1110-11

The metre of awareness rises across the sky. One cannot assess it with his eyes. This happens when a true *guru* unfolds the mystery of *śabada* to the seeker who is virtuous and deserving. When the *guru* instructs the seeker with his word, one dwells upon Supreme Being all the time of the day and finds the glory of God and contemplates upon Him. The five restless desires come under control and he gets the knowledge of the dwelling place of his own self. All his sexual desires, ill temperament and falsehood are conquered. He gets illuminated by the teachings of the *guru*; he looks to the plays of God. O Nānak! one gets satisfied after elimination of his ego, and his metre of vision shoots across the sky.

Here Guru Nānak expresses the state of experience of revelations of *śabada* in individual. One's restless desires are restrained and one comes to know his own heart and beholds the play of *karma* with his extended faculty of awareness.

merā mano merā manu rātā rāma piāre rāma ||
sacu sāhibo ādi purakhu apaṁparo dhāre rāma ||
agama agocaru apara apārā pārabrahamu paradhāno ||
ādi jugādī hai bhī hosī avaru jhūṭhā sabhu māno ||

karama dharama kī sāra na jāṇai surati mukati kiu pāīē॥
nānaka guramukhi sabadi pachāṇai ahinisi nāmu dhiāīē॥
– *Ādi Granth*, p. 437

O Friends! My mind is drenched in the love of my glorious Master. God is the Supreme Being, He is infinite and support of the earth. He cannot be measured, He cannot be approached, He is without limits of time and space, and cannot be compared. He is the Supreme Lord and above all. He is from the beginning, throughout the ages, now and evermore; one should know that everything other than Him is false. One has to develop love and appreciation for His understanding to gain *dharma*, faith, clarity of vision for awareness and salvation. O Nānak! the godly man remains tuned to *śabada* at every moment of the day and night. He concentrates upon the true name of God.

In these lines Guru Nānak expresses the experience of ecstasy of being attuned to the Lord. He says that he does not know the way of the works, nor as to how one attains the salvation. He knows only the Lord's word through the *guru* and dwells upon His name. He has realized that Lord's name is his only true companion and that I-ness or other attachments will not accompany beyond and he has trampled it all under his feet.

sidha samādhi karahi nita jhagarā duhu locana kiā herai॥
aṅtari joti sabadu dhuni jāgai satiguru jhagaru niberai॥
suri nara nātha beaṅta ajonī sācai mahuli apārā॥
nānaka sahaji mile jagajīvana nadari karahu nisatārā॥
– Ibid., p. 489

The *siddhas* remain in conflict in *samādhi*. They cannot see anything with the two eyes. They should know that the divine light is within all hearts, and melody of *śabada* is heard if the *guru* showers his grace. The Supreme Being is the master of all angels and men, infinite and unborn, His mansion cannot be compared. One gets merged with the Lord through *sahaja* and grace of God.

In these lines Guru Nānak says that one cannot see anything beyond this world with one's eyes. When the inner self opens and the sound of *śabada* is revealed with the grace of the *guru* all conflicts of mind are settled.

> *ējī japu tapu saṅjamu sacu adhāra* ||
> *hari hari nāmu dehi sukhu paīē terī bhagati bhare bhaṅḍāra* ||
> *suna samādhi rahahi liva lāge ekā ekī sabadu bīcāra* ||
> *jala thalu dharaṇi gaganu taha nāhī āpe āpu kiā karatāra* ||
> *nā tadi māiā maganu na chāiā nā sūraja caṅda na joti apāra* ||
> *saraba dṛsaṭi locana abha aṅtari ekā nadari su tribhavaṇa sāra* ||
> – *Ādi Granth*, pp. 503-04

> *bhagati prema ārādhitaṁ sacu piāsa parama hitaṁ* ||
> *bilalāpa bilala binaṁtīā sukha bhāi cita hitaṁ* ||
> – Ibid., p. 505

Uttering God's name, deep concentration and contemplation, self-restraint and truthfulness are foundations of truth. One finds peace with the blessed name of the Supreme Being. Devotion and faith are the real wealth. When gets absorbed in *samādhi*, mind gets concentrated with love for the one God and one focuses on *śabada* only. In that state one is not aware of one's surroundings. One feels the existence of only one God who created all beings. There is no incitement from illusions of *māyā* and one is not aware of any shadow or the shine of any sun or moon. Eyes within mind see all the three worlds. The seekers love and adore the almighty. They feel thirsty and hungry for the Almighty with unlimited love.They with tears in their eyes seek and approach God for His love and care and their hearts thus rest peacefully.

In these lines Guru Nānak explains the experience of state of devotional worship.

> *āvahu milahu sahelīho sacaḍā nāmu laehāṅ* ||
> *rovaha birahā tanakā āpaṇā sāhibu saṁmhālehāṅ* ||
> *sāhibu samhāliha paṅthu nihāliha asā bhi othai jāṇā* ||
> *jisa kā kiā tina hī līā hoā tisai kā bhāṇā* ||
> *jo tini kari pāiā su āgai āiā asī ki hukamu karehā* ||
> *āvahu milahu sahelīho sacaḍā nāmu laehā* ||
> *maraṇu na maṅdā lokā ākhīe je mari jāṇai aisā koi* ||
> *sevihu sāhibu saṁmrathu āpaṇā paṅthu suhelā āgai hoi* ||
> *paṅthi suhelai jāvahu tāṅ phalu pāvahu āgai milai vaḍāī* ||
> *bheṭai siu jāvahu saci samāvahu tāṅ pati lekhai pāī* ||

mahalī jāi pāvahu khasamai bhāvahu raṅga siu ralīā māṇai॥
– Ibid., p. 579

Guru Nānak invites all his godly friends and says: come and get together and contemplate upon the holy name. We may weep for our separation from Him in mind. Let us remember Him and be watchful for the path we shall have to follow to be there with Him. It is His will to create and also destroy that works, and everything happens according to His will only. We cannot command Him, whatever He does it has to happen. He repeats his call to all his godly friends to assemble and contemplate on the name of God. Fear of death will run away if we learn how to die while living this life. With service to the Lord our path in this world will become easy. Walk upon this road to find peace and get awards for our service. Offer ourself to Him, we shall be getting merged with the Supreme Being and we will be honoured for serving Him. We will find His presence and if it pleases Him we shall get all love and blessings from Him.

jīvā terai nāi mani ānandu hai jīu॥
sāco sācā nāu guṇa govindu hai jīu॥
gura giānu apārā sirajaṇahārā jini sirajī tini goī॥
– *Ādi Granth*, p. 688

My mind is excited in living by your name and I feel total peace within my mind. Your name is true; you are glorified. My *guru* opened before me the excellent spiritual knowledge which leads me to your presence.

In the above two hymns, Guru Nānak calls all his sister companions to come on the path of *sūrata śabada*. Imbued with tender and pure love they are invited to dwell on the true name for God's bliss and experience the joy of living by His name. He also appreciates the *guru* who led him on this path to the Supreme Lord.

jinī sakhī sahu rābiā tina pūchaugī jāe॥
pāi lagau benatī karau leugī panthu batāe॥
hukamu pachāṇai nānakā bhau candanu lāvai॥
guṇa kāmaṇa kāmaṇi karai tau piāre kau pāvai॥
jo dili miliā su mili rahiā miliā kahīe re soī॥
je bahuterā locīe vātī melu na hoī॥

dhātu milai phuni dhātu kau liva livai kau dhāvai ||
– *Ādi Granth*, p. 725

> I will consult with my other godly friends about their experience of enjoying the presence of God I will implore them most humbly to lead me to that path. O Nānak! individuals who surrender to the will of God and are always fearful develop fragrance which pleases the Lord. A bride with virtue and pleasant behaviour becomes dear to her husband. She heartly unites herself with her beloved and remains ever involved with him thus enjoying the perfect union with him. She may long for him much but by mere words she cannot meet him unless she melts into him as a metal.

These lines express a rare feeling of bliss and ecstasy, which only a saint like Guru Nānak can experience when one's individual consciousness melts into the Universal Consciousness as the merging of two molten metals.

raiṇi aṅdhārī niramala joti || *nāma binā jhūṭhe kucala kachoti* ||
bedu pukārai bhagati saroti || *suṇi suṇi mānai vekhai joti* ||
sāsatra simṛti nāmu dṛḍāmaṁ || *guramukhi sāṅti ūtamā karamaṁ* ||
– Ibid., p. 831

> Life is like a dark night and divinity is pure and shining. One who does not adhere to *nāma* should be considered as dirty, untruthful and not worth mingling. The Vedas are the source of preaching devotion and worship of Him. By listening to God and believing scriptures and men of wisdom, one realizes the divine light within the self. Śāstras and Smṛtis put the seed of the *nāma* within. The spiritually inclined people live in peace and tranquillity by doing good deeds with purity of mind.

Here Guru Nānak says that the creator Lord Himself makes us worship Him. The Vedas commend the song of the loving adoration of God, but those who hear and believe alone see the divine light. Śāstras and Smṛtis too emphasize on the discipline of the name and he who does this sublime deed by the *guru*'s grace abides in peace.

surati sabadu sākhī merī siṅī bājai loku suṇe ||
patu jholī maṅgaṇa kai tāī bhīkhiā nāmu paḍe ||
....

sidha sādhika aru jogī jaṅgama pīra purasa bahutere ||
je tina milā ta kīrati ākhā tā manu seva kare ||
kāgadu lūṇu rahai ghṛta saṅge pāṇī kamalu rahai ||
aise bhagata milahi jana nānaka tina jamu kiā karai ||
....
praṇavati nānaku āgamu suṇāe || *gura cele kī sandhi milāe* ||
dīkhiā dārū bhojanu khāi || *chia darasana kī sojhī pāi* ||

– *Ādi Granth*, pp. 877-78

I live with the word of the *guru* and hear the sound of unstuck melody of music within me. The *guru*'s word is wrapped in my consciousness, I sing to this tune. I make my body the begging bowl and ingather the Lord's name. Whenever I happen to meet *siddhas*, *yoga* teachers, roaming saints and noble men, I utter the glory of God before them while I keep myself concentrated within me. A piece of paper or a lump of salt treated with ghee is not affected by water and the lotus is not affected by the slit of water; so I remain within me without any fear. O Nānak! even death cannot touch such devotees.

Nānak prays and shares the mysterious secret of the Supreme Being. Both the *guru* and his follower are one in spirit. Individuals who enjoy this spiritual union and medicate themselves with the teachings of the *guru* get the wisdom of the six Śāstras.

Guru Nānak says that he sings to the tune of the sound of the unstuck melody which rings in his consciousness. He makes his body a bowl to beg from the Lord and ingather His name. One who remains absorbed in the *śabada* remains unaffected by *māya* as paper and salt treated with ghee remain untouched by water.

khaṭu maṭu dehī manu bairāgī || *surati sabadu dhuni antari jāgī* ||
vāje anahadu merā manu līṇā || *gura bacanī saci nāmi patīṇā* ||
prāṇī rāma bhagati sukhu pāīe ||
guramukha hari hari mīṭhā lāgai hari hari nāmi samaīe ||
....
binu gura sabada na sojhī pāi ||
anahada sabadu vajai dinu rāti || *avigata kī gati guramukhi jātī* ||
tau jānī jo sabadi pachānī || *eko ravi rahiā nirabānī* ||
suna samādhi sahaja manu rātā || *taji hau lābhā eko jātā* ||

– Ibid., pp. 903-04

> The detached mind dwells in a body of six *cakras*. The melody of the word rings deep within. My mind is attuned to hear this unstuck sound of bliss. From the *guru*'s word my mind takes pleasure in the true name. A man should understand that one gains bliss only by dedication to the Supreme Lord. Then the name of God seems sweet to him and one is absorbed in it.
>
> One cannot understand the *śabada* without the *guru*'s word. The vibration of unstuck sound current of the *śabada* continues day and night. The godly people understand this state only when they realize the *śabada* within themselves. The one Lord is residing everywhere and surrounding everything. My mind is deeply absorbed within the state of deepest *samādhi*. By shedding all I-ness and greediness I have realized the existence of only one Lord.

In these lines Guru Nānak explains that the body of six *cakras*: *mūlādhāra* (above the organ of base of the spine), *svādhiṣṭhāna* (at the root of reproductive organ), *maṇipūra* (in the naval region), *anāhata* (in the heart), *viśuddhi* (in the throat), *ājñā* (between the eyebrows) is the seat of the detached conscious mind. The unstuck melody of the sound resonates within. If the unstuck melody of the word rings within day and night, then the state of deathlessness is known by the grace of the *guru*. The Lord is revealed when one realizes the word and then one sees the Lord of *nirvāṇa* pervade all over. One then enters the seedless trance and one's mind is imbued with equipoise.

> *khasamai kai darabāri ḍhāḍhī vasiā* ॥
> *sacā khasamu kalāṇi kamalu vigasiā* ॥
> *khasamahu pūrā pāi manahu rahasiā* ॥
> *dusamana kaḍhe māri sajaṇa sarasiā* ॥
> *sacā satiguru sevani sacā māragu dasiā* ॥
> *sacā sabadu bīcāri kālu vidhausiā* ॥
> *ḍhāḍhī kathe akathu sabadi savāriā* ॥
> *nānaka guṇa gahi rāsi hari jīu mile piāriā* ॥
>
> – *Ādi Granth*, pp. 148-49

> I am a bard who sings God's praises in the presence of God. While me singing praises of the Lord the lotus within my heart has blossomed forth. With the mercy of that perfect Lord, I am

imbued with happiness and remain ever in ecstasy. He has wiped out all my evil foes from within so my Lord, friend is happy with me. I served the true *guru* who has shown me the true path. Reflecting on the true word of the *guru*, I have conquered over the fear of death. Then the bard speaks the unspoken speech of the Lord. By holding to the *śabada* within, he is met with his cherished friend with all the love.

saṅta janā kau mili rahai dhanu dhanu jasu gāe ||
ādi purakhu aparaṁparā guramukhi hari pāe ||
naṭūē sāṅgu baṇāiā bājī saṁsārā ||
khiṇu palu bājī dekhīē ujharata nahī bārā ||
haumai caupaḍi khelaṇā jhūṭhe ahaṁkārā ||
sabhu jagu hārai so jiṇai gura sabadu vīcārā ||
jiu aṅdhulai hathi ṭohaṇī harināmu hamārai ||
rāma nāmu hari ṭeka hai nisi dauta savārai ||
jiu tūṅ rākhahi tiu rahā hari nāma adhārā ||
aṅti sakhāī pāiā jana mukati duārā ||
janama maraṇa dukha meṭiā japi nāmu murāre ||
nānaka nāmu na vīsarai pūrā guru tāre ||

– *Ādi Granth*, p. 422

Guru Nānak invites all his society of saints to join together to sing the praises of one Lord. So that they all can gain approach to the Supreme Being who is without any limits of time and space. The world is a stage and the play of the life has to be acted upon. As one sees the show for a moment and forgets the same next moment, life passes away. We play here the game on the chessboard of the Self with ego and illusion as dices. The whole world loses here except the one who resides with the word of the *guru*. As the blind man depends upon his staff for moving forward which he holds tight, individuals who dwell upon *guru*'s word get help from it. The name of God is the support for the men who move on the path of God. As He keeps us, we live with His only support. His name remains the only comfort in the end and the gate to emancipation is found by the humble servants. The recitation and meditation of His name removes the fear of pain of birth and death. Individuals who do not forget the name of God are saved with the grace of the *guru*.

In these lines Guru Nānak explains that life is a game of chess on the board of ego. He advises all the saintly people to join and sing the praises of God. As the stick in hand helps the blind man while walking let us take the stick of the word with us to proceed on the path of bliss.

pūrā satiguru sevi pūrā pāiā ||
pūrai karami dhiāi pūrā sabadu maṁni vasāiā ||
pūrai giāni dhiāni mailu cukāiā ||
hari sari tīrathi jāṇi manūā nāiā ||
sabadi marai manu māri dhaṁnu jaṇedī māiā ||
dari sacai saciāru sacā āiā ||
puchi na sakai koi jāṁ khasamai bhāiā ||
– *Ādi Granth*, p. 1286

I served the true *guru* and could find the Supreme Being. I attained the Almighty God by performing virtue and meditation upon the word of the *guru*. I absorbed the *śabada* in my mind deep within me. All my filth has been washed away by concentration and meditation. Now the Supreme Being is my most pious place for pilgrimage and worship. I continue to clean my mind in His company. One who controls his mind and gets absorbed into *śabada* is the most blessed soul. His mother who gave birth to him is also blessed. No one is there to argue with such an individual who becomes pleasing to God.

In these lines of Guru Nānak we find his personal experience of divinity at a glance.

PERSONAL EXPERIENCE OF DIVINITY IN THE PRINCIPAL UPANIṢADS

The contents of the personal experience of divinity in the hymns of Guru Nānak can be traced in the following verses of the Upaniṣads.

puruṣa evedaṁ viśvaṁ karma tapo brahma parāmṛtam |
etadyo veda nihitaṁ guhāyaṁ so 'vidyāgranthiṁ vikiratīha somya ||
– *Muṇḍaka Upaniṣad* 2.1.10

O my good friend! he who knows this *Brahman*, the supreme and immortal hidden in the cave of the heart, cuts asunder even here the knot of ignorance.

One who knows that which is set in the secret place of the heart cuts asunder the knot of ignorance.

aviḥsaṁnihitaṁ guhācarannāma mahatpadamatraitatsamarpitam ।
ejat prāṇannimiṣacca yadetajjānatha sadasadvareṇyaṁ paraṁ
vijñānādyadvariṣṭhaṁ prajānām ॥
yadarcimadyadaṇubhyo 'ṇu ca yasmँillokā mihitā lokinaśca ।
tadetadakṣaraṁ brahma prāṇastadu vāṅmanaḥ tadetsatyaṁ
tadamṛtaṁ tadveddhavyaṁ somya viddhi ॥
– *Muṇḍaka Upaniṣad* 2.2.1-2

The radiant *Brahman* dwells in the cave of the heart and is known to move there. It is a great support of all for in it is centred everything that moves, breathes and blinks that alone is to be struck. Strike it my good friend. What is luminous, what is subtler than the subtle, in which, all the worlds are centred is to be known.

hiraṇmaye pare kośe virajaṁ brahma niṣkalam ।
tacchubhraṁ jyotiṣāṁ jyotistadyadātmavido viduḥ ॥
na tatra sūryo bhāti na candratārakaṁ nemā vidyuto bhānti kuto
'yamagniḥ ।
tameva bhāntamanubhāti sarvaṁ tasya bhāsā sarvamidaṁ vibhāti ॥
– Ibid. 2.2.9-10

There the stainless and indivisible *Brahman* shines in the highest golden sheath. It is pure. It is the light of lights. It is that which they know, who knows self. The sun does not shine there, nor the moon and stars, nor these lightnings, not to speak of this fire. When He shines everything shines after Him, by His light everything is lighted.

The sheath referred to here is *buddhi* (intellect). *Brahman* is most vividly manifest in the *buddhi* which is described as golden because it is endowed with reason and knowledge and therefore superior to other organs.

yadā paśyaḥ paśyate rukmavarnaṁ kartāramīśam puruṣaṁ
brahmayonim ।
tadā vidvānpuṇyapāpe vidhūya nirañjanaḥ paramaṁ sāmyamupaiti ॥
– Ibid. 3.1.3

When the seer beholds the self-luminous creator, the Lord, then

> he shakes off good and evil, becomes stainless and reaches the supreme unity.

When the seer sees the creator of the golden hue, the Lord, he then being a knower shakes off good and evil and free from stain, he attains the Supreme equality with the Lord.

> *satyena labhyastapasā hyeṣa ātmā samyagjñānena brahmacaryeṇa nityam* |
> *antaḥśarīre jyotirmayo hi śubhro yaṁ paśyanti yatayaḥ kṣīṇadoṣāḥ* ||
>
> – *Muṇḍaka Upaniṣad* 3.1.5
>
> This *Ātman* resplendent and pure, whom the sinless seeker beholds, residing within the body is attained by unceasing practice of truthfulness, austerity, right knowledge and continence.

This self within the body of the nature of light and pure is attainable by truth, by austerity, by right knowledge, by constant practice of chastity.

> *bṛhacca taddivyamacintyarūpaṁ sūkṣmācca tatsūkṣmataraṁ vibhāti* |
> *dūrātsudūre tadihāntike ca paśyatsvihaiva nihitaṁ guhāyām* ||
>
> – Ibid. 3.1.7
>
> *Brahman* shines forth vast, self-luminous, inconceivable, subtler than the subtle. He is far beyond what is far, yet here very near at hand. Verily He is seen here dwelling in the cave of the heart of conscious beings.

Vast, divine of unthinkable form, it shines forth farther than the far yet near at hand, set down in the secret place of the heart as such even here it is seen by the intelligent.

> *saṁprāpyainamṛṣayo jñānatṛptāḥ kṛtātmāno vītarāgāḥ praśāntāḥ* |
> *te savagaṁ sarvataḥ prāpya dhīrā yuktātmānaḥ sarvamevāviśanti* ||
>
> – Ibid. 3.2.5
>
> Having realized *Ātman*, the seers become satisfied with that knowledge. Their souls are established in the Supreme Self, they are free from passions and they are tranquil in mind. Such calm souls, ever devoted to self, behold everywhere the omnipresent *Brahman* and in the end enter into it.

Having attained Him, the seers are satisfied with their knowledge and are the perfect souls free from passion, and tranquil, having attained the omnipresent self on all sides. Those wise concentrated minds enter into the all Self.

yathā nadyaḥ syandamānāḥ samudre 'staṁ gacchanti nāmarūpe vihāya।
tathā vidvānnāmarūpādvimuktaḥ parātparaṁ puruṣamupaiti divyam॥

– *Muṇḍaka Upaniṣad* 3.2.8

As flowing rivers disappear in the sea, losing their names and forms, so the wise man, freed from name and form, attains *Puruṣa* who is greater than the great.

Just as the flowing rivers disappear in the ocean casting off name and shape, even so the knower freed from name and form attains the Divine Person.

nāntaḥprajñaṁ na bahiṣprajñaṁ nobhayataḥ prajñaṁ na prajñānaghanaṁ na prajñaṁ nāprajñam।
adṛṣṭamavyavahāryamagrāhyamalakṣaṇamacintyamavyapadeśyamekātmapratyayasāraṁ prapañcopaśamaṁ śāntaṁ śvamadvaitaṁ caturthaṁ manyate sa ātmā sa vijñeyaḥ॥

– *Māṇḍūkya Upaniṣad* 7

Turīya is not that which is conscious of the inner (subjective) world, nor that which is conscious of the outer (objective) world, nor that which is conscious of both, nor that which is a mass of consciousness. It is not simple consciousness nor unconsciousness. It is unperceived, unrelated, incomprehensible, uninferable, unthinkable and indescribable. It is cessation of all phenomena. It is all peace, all bliss and non-dual. This is what is known as the fourth (*turīya*). This is *Ātman* and this is to be realized.

In *turīya* there is a permanent union with *Brahman*.

amātraścaturtho 'vyavahāryaḥ prapañcopaśamaḥ śivo 'dvaita evamaṁkāra ātmaiva saṁviśatyātmanātmānaṁ ya evaṁ veda ya evaṁ veda॥ – Ibid. 12

The fourth (*turīya*) is without parts and without relationship. It is cessation of phenomena. It is all good and non-dual. The *oṁ*

> is verily *Ātman*. He who knows this merges his self in *Ātman*.
>
> The fourth state is that which has no elements, which cannot be spoken of, into which the world is resolved, non-dual. Thus the word *oṁ* is the very self.

Oṁ uttered through sounds points, by contrast, to the soundless *oṁ*. All sounds must some time or other merge in silence or soundlessness. This soundless *oṁ* is same as *turīya*. Those who realized *Brahman*, the Highest Reality, merge the self in *turīya* because they have transcended the notion of cause and effect, which inheres in the third quarter of *Ātman*. They are not born again, because they have realized their identity with the causeless *turīya*[1] (adapted from Śaṅkarācārya's commentary).

> *sa ya eṣo 'ntarhṛdaya ākāśaḥ । tasminnayaṁ puruṣo manomayaḥ ।*
>
> – *Taittirīya Upaniṣad* 1.6.1
>
> There is a space (*ākāśa*) within the heart; in it lies the Person (*Puruṣa*) consisting of mind (*manomaya*), immortal and luminous. The space which is within the heart, therein is the person consisting of mind, immortality and resplendent.

We are taught to look at God as one residing in one's own heart. Other view is that brain is the seat of the soul. The diseases of the heart are most fatal whereas psychical affections such as fear, sorrow and joy cause an immediate disturbance to the heart. The heart is the first part to be formed in the embryo.

> *oṁ brahmavidāpnoti param । tadeṣā 'bhyuktā । satyaṁ jñānamanantaṁ brahma । yo veda nihitaṁ guhāyāṁ parame ।*
>
> – Ibid. 2.1.1
>
> One who knows *Brahman* which is Reality, Knowledge and Infinity, hidden in the cave of the heart and is highest in *ākāśa* – he, being one with the omniscient *Brahman*, enjoys simultaneously all desires.
>
> *. . . sa yaścāyaṁ puruṣe । yaścāsāvāditye । sa ekaḥ । sa ya evaṁvit । asmāllokātpretya ।* – Ibid. 2.8.1
>
> This is the enquiry regarding the bliss of *Brahman* and explains

---

[1] Swami Nikhilananda, 2008, *The Upanishads*, p. 167.

> He, who is here in man and in the yonder sun both are one. He who knows this, after dying to (withdrawing from) this world, attains the self which consists of food, the mind, intellect, vital breath and attains the self which consists of bliss.

This refers to the *Saguṇa-Brahman*, who according to the Vedas, dwells in the sun and is the embodiment of the bliss directly experienced by the illuminated sage free from desires. He does not see any difference between his own physical body and that of the *virāṭ*, which is the aggregate of all physical bodies. He loses attachment to his individual self and attains to that Being in whom the physical universe takes its rise, has his being and in the end attains dissolution. He also realizes that the self-consisting of food is none else than the self-consisting of vital breath. Thus passing to higher and higher selves he gives up attachment to lower ones, until he finally attains the fearless *Brahman* which is beyond the visible and invisible.

> *atha yadidamasminbrahmapure daharaṁ puṇḍarīkaṁ veśma daharo 'sminnantarākāśastasminyadantastadanveṣṭavyaṁ tadvāva vijijñasitavyamiti* ||
> – *Chāndogya Upaniṣad* 8.1.1

> There is a city of *Brahman*, an abode, the small lotus of the heart, within it is a small *ākāśa*. Now what exists within that small *ākāśa*, that is to be sought after, that is what one should desire to understand.

The heart is compared to a royal palace. Its shape is that of the lotus bud. Though *Brahman* pervades the entire body, its presence is felt especially in the heart. The word *ākāśa* (space) denotes *Brahman*, because the latter is like the *ākāśa*, incorporeal, subtle and all-pervading.

Both the Upaniṣads and the hymns of Guru Nānak explain that the mansion of the Supreme Lord is within the cave of human heart. The Supreme Lord has established the tenth gate within the human body (aperture at the top of the head) as escape route for seekers of higher levels of consciousness to experience the bliss of unity with Him. The Upaniṣads explain that after realizing *Ātman*, the seeker becomes free from passions and achieves perfect tranquillity of mind. He beholds the self-luminous creator, sheds all his virtues and vices and sees Himself in everything around him. One experiences the pleasant melody of unstuck sounds within oneself and the seeker loses all his identity as all the rivers lose their names and forms once they merge into the sea.

Guru Nānak also explains that the seeker of God travels through the spiritual planes of *dharama, giāna, sarama* and *karama khaṅḍa*s to experience divinity of *saca khaṅḍa* in the fourth state of consciousness (*turīya*) and becomes free from all vices and virtues. The hard and heavy doors of the tenth gate are opened with the word of the *guru* and the seeker hears the vibrations of unstuck sounds and a melody of *pañca śabada*s (five primal sounds). The *pañca śabada*s, echo (resound) and re-echo (resonate) within oneself. Individual soul merges with the Universal Soul as molten metals merge each other.

6

Conclusion

LIFE is shrouded in the mystery of time and space. Among all the uncertainties of life there are certain physical and experiential realities known to all. These are not new, but have to be repeatedly visited and endorsed afresh, generations after generations, to keep pace with the changing priorities of life. These can safely be called the torchbearers for individuals who endeavour to know the meaning of life and struggle towards fulfilment of ultimate aim in life:

(a) Everyone comes naked to this world and goes naked from this world. Nothing is covered or concealed from God.

(b) Inevitable death waits at the end of life's journey. One may travel fumbling, jumping, enjoying, crying, experiencing unions or separations, all pains or pleasures of worldly existence, love or hate it, but the momentum of death clock is not affected.

(c) None of the worldly relations can last longer to accompany one beyond the lifespan. Each relation lives and dies its own death. Unions and separations are like the meeting of travellers in motion on the same road.

(d) One cannot carry any of his worldly possessions or accumulations along with him and has to leave all instantly at the call of death without any resistance.

One, who remembers all these physically experiential realities of life at every moment and tries to get best for himself out of the fleeting moments of his precious life by searching within for all his actions, can avoid undesirable involvement with the world. Human life is considered to be precious for it is this frame which carries the highest level of consciousness as compared to other forms of life. There are various kinds of human beings in this world. Some take birth, and act as sinners or men of virtue with a hope to live here comfortably as long as they can. In spite of their sufferings and pain in life their jest to live a long life along with the kith and kin that they consider to be their own never dies. They just act as tools for enforcement of Divine Will for continuity and expansion of His creation. Others may, while living a worldly life, engage in sciences of matter and energy in pursuit of making this world more comfortable by their perceived and experimented innovations in physics, medical and all types of other sciences. They work hard for it without minding for the transitory character of all creation and dream of unveiling the mask of the Ultimate Reality and search for physical cosmic laws with cherished vision to create a robot of human form and exercise control over creation. Whatever may be their aspirations, goal or vision, in fact they act as technicians of the Divine Will for maintenance and beautification of His creation. These men live in the realms of duty, action and knowledge.

However, the Divine Will seems in favour of a plan for redemptions of all humanity at large and sends reminders that human life is shortlived and the free will to live and expand the awareness to sustain the worldly comforts or knowledge is limited. Some blessed few who live evertuned to the Ultimate Reality receive and interpret the Divine Will. These are the men of God with a mission, sent for creating of awareness among the human beings who get entangled in the worldly life and get entrapped in duality and forget their real form. These men live in unoccupied awareness in Pure Consciousness. Their consciousness is not occupied by cognition, thought, cognition-related and created experience, senses or their retrieval. They live with the illuminating principle of experience which is shared in common by all forms of knowledge by self in oneness with *Brahman* that is the subtle essence in which all the things have their existence. They take the form of human beings, live an apparent life of human beings, receive the sound currents of Divine Will and transmit to a chosen few (seekers) for fulfilment of their assigned mission. They live in the realms of ecstasy, power and abode of truth. In one of his hymns Guru Nānak says, "O Lalo! as I receive the word of God, so do I utter its content (*jaisī mai āvai khasama kī bāṇī, taisaḍā karī giānu ve lālo – Ādi Granth,* p. 722)". We may find such rare blessed human forms in every age who are the source of spiritual illumination. This is true of all incarnations, saints and seers and preachers of truth known or unknown who rose above the glamour of worldly life.

Religious leaders and preachers who claim to be the custodians of faith may argue over the meanings of the verses of Upaniṣads or hymns of Guru Nānak here and there and may not reach at a common platform of understanding, yet they cannot deny the common basic ideas of supreme knowledge experienced by all great sages and seers which are expressed in the Upaniṣads and in the hymns of Guru Nānak. My efforts are to express the deep sense rather than giving word to word rendering of comparisons as I believe the saints and sages generally choose simple language for expressing their thoughts rather than the coded or metaphysical terms of subtleties or very high learned words. There are near repetitions of same ideas time and again in the different hymns of Guru Nānak selected for study, the purpose of selection of all the verses from different hymns serves to impress on the instructions repeated time and again by Guru Nānak in broken pieces to address all sorts of seekers at different times and places.

Both the Upaniṣads and the hymns of Guru Nānak direct and carry a message: "Man, Know Thy Self". The philosophy of life in the hymns of Guru Nānak cannot be attributed to confine to any religion or founding separate identity of any new sect. It is true for all, anywhere and at all times. The philosophy does not oppose any school of thought, religion or interpretations of scriptures and carry a uniqueness of methods for explaining the various concepts held true for all times. Preachers of religions may advocate and make individuals dependent on priests, temples or idols, blind faith, dogmas but independence of thought and clarity of vision are necessary for self-enlightenment.

Both Guru Nānak and the Upaniṣads stress on inner realization as compared to blind faith, rigidity of traditions, dogmatic and ritual approach to follow sectarian prophets and preachers. One must be logical and practise reason in life and adopt a way of contemplation and meditation to achieve one's goal of Self-realization. While one may commune with the divine force through symbols or idol but to worship a symbol or idol as God may not be of any help for enlightenment. While godhead cannot be brought down to the level of a material object, one may reach godhead by appreciating and adoring all His creation.

The Upaniṣads probably contain the highest of philosophy of life, and sometimes seem diversified or contrary in their meaning to a lay man. A single *mantra* may carry wisdom worth scribing a book of hundreds of pages for its explanation to a man of ordinary intelligence. A lay or average man cannot absorb the essence of their teachings without an adept guide. They are only meant for a select few who are fit and worthy to absorb the instructions. S. Radhakrishnan writes:

> In the quietude of forest hermitages the Upaniṣad thinkers pondered on the problems of the deepest concern and communicated their knowledge to fit pupils near them. The seers adopt a certain reticence in communicating the truth. They wish to be satisfied that their pupils are spiritually and not carnally minded. Upaniṣads became a name for a mystery, a secret (*rahasyam*), communicated only to a tested few. When the question of man's final destiny was raised, Yājñavalkya took his pupil aside and whispered to him the Truth.[1]

The *Chāndogya Upaniṣad* lays down that the principle of *Brahman* may be taught by a father to his son or to a trusted pupil and not to anyone even if the later may offer the vast lands surrounded by the waters and filled with all sorts of treasures. It is said that the teacher communicated the secret knowledge only after repeated entreaty and severe testing of the seeker. Thus the secret knowledge given by the seers and sages was limited to a very few deserving and intelligent persons.

On the other hand, the hymns of Guru Nānak are Songs of Life for the masses and share with them the highest knowledge in a simple way. Guru Nānak accepted the basic doctrines of

---

[1] Radhakrishnan, 2012, *The Principal Upanishads*, p. 19.

knowledge of seers and sages of the Upaniṣads and elaborated and explained to the common man their most essential parts by rejecting the pseudo knowledge of priests and, conflicts and controversies of the existing schools of religious thoughts. Guru Nānak cautions time and again as not to say anyone bad and understand the real words and not to argue with fools. He deeply felt a need to bring the real knowledge down to the masses to save them from the clutches of orthodox religious priests and preachers. Gopal Singh describes various cults of Hinduism at the time of Guru Nānak and concludes:

> Nānak was thus not only a *bhakta* (a detached devotee) of God, but a man deeply involved with the affairs of the world. Not only a great poet, musician and philosopher but also a social and political rebel, an integrator of warring creeds and the creator of a New Man in the New World supported by God that not only punishes and rewards, but reclaims and redeems both man and society.[2]

In his hymns Guru Nānak considers himself to be a bard who is assigned to sing Lord's praises in His Court and his personal experience of divinity through repetition of His Name. He explains that he became a wandering recluse in search of men of God. He made tiring efforts to achieve this goal. He underwent various austerities like those being practised by various *yogīs* at least for some time in his early life. He calls himself Nānak Śayara (Nānak the poet). He describes his sister's pain of separation on his departure from family in pursuit of Ultimate Truth. He ridicules the doctor who was called to feel his pulse for finding his ailment who could not know his real pain for searching the truth or his love for God. Guru Nānak placed true love for God above all religions. All his verses explain his human nature and urge for godly life and love for men of God. In fact, hymns of Guru Nānak are a unique song of divine life as they explain the real experience of life lived in Pure Consciousness and a message for better worldliness through Universal Love.

Selected materials from the hymns of Guru Nānak establish

---

[2] Gopal Singh, 2005, *Sri Guru Granth Sahib*, p. xxxix.

that he had a very sound knowledge of the contents of existing Vedic literature, appreciated it and had deep love for the philosophy of life explained in the Upaniṣads. He expressed unity of all existence in Pure Consciousness and advocated for better worldliness. He placed love for God and godly life above all religions. The Upaniṣads constitute the knowledge section of Vedas and are called Vedānta, i.e. the end of the Vedas or final purport of Vedas. Guru Nānak describes beautifully the scene of intellectual wrestlers coming together, fully prepared to fight with each other forgetting that this play is also the play of the same one Lord who is the master of all and writes the inscription of His Will on every forehead: *dovai taraphā upāi iku varatia* (*Ādi Granth*, p. 1280). Thus he advises to follow one path or system whichsoever glorifies and adores the One Lord and teaches unity of all existence in Pure Consciousness. He explains that One Power is the source of all speech, hearing, mind and breath for all existence and advises the priests not to create any strife over the meaning of word *oṁ* as it contains the essence of all the three worlds, meaning the three states of consciousness. He further explains that the three stages of consciousness do not bring any spiritual change, one who knows the fourth, i.e. *turīya*, goes beyond the cycle of virtue and vice.

A large number of hymns of Guru Nānak express the knowledge and message of Upaniṣads in a more simplified, vivid and common poetic language form for the common masses.

Spiritual Unity and Solidarity in All Existence

> *yastu sarvāṇi bhūtānyātmanyevānupaśyati* |
> *sarvabhūteṣu cātmānaṁ tato na vijugupsate* ||
> – *Īśa Upanisad* 6

One who sees all beings in his own self and his own self in all beings he does not feel any revulsion by reason of such a view. Meaning, the wise man looks upon all beings in the Self and the Self in all beings; that is the reason that he does not hate anyone.

Guru Nānak writes:

> *sabha mahi joti joti hai soi* ||

tisa kai cānaṇi sabha mahi cānaṇu hoi ||
– *Ādi Granth*, p. 663

There is one same divine light within everyone. It is that light which shines within everyone.

akula niraṁjana siu manu māniā . . .
– Ibid., p. 1127

Pleased with the vision of the perfectly pure Lord who does not have any ancestor, one's mind becomes calm and quite by his own mind and he knows only the Lord within and without and sees God in everything around him.

kāla bikāla sabadi bhae nāsu || *rahai atītu jāṇai sabhu tisa kā* ||
– Ibid., p. 832

By realizing the *śabada* one conquers death and one gets detached from everything as he feels that everything belongs to Him. He surrenders his body and mind to Him who is the real owner of it. He does not take birth and die anymore. He is absorbed in Truth and merges with the Supreme Being.

dekhi adr̥saṭu rahahu bisamādī . . .
...
tatu niraṁjanu joti sabāī sohaṁ bhedu na koī jīu ||
– Ibid., p. 599

Seeing the unseen Lord one is amazed, delighted, forgets all pain and is at peace. We are all His essence and His light is within all of us. There is no difference between us and Him. One feels I am He and He is me.

Balanced Combination of Rituals and Meditation: Ignorance and Knowledge

andhaṁ tamaḥ praviśanti ye 'vidyāmupāsate |
tato bhūya iva te tamo ya u vidyāyām̐ ratāḥ ||
– *Īśa Upaniṣad* 9

andhaṁ tamaḥ praviśanti ye 'saṁbhutimupāsate |
tato bhūya iva te tamo ya u saṁbhūtyam̐ ratāḥ ||
– Ibid. 12

Life of the world leads to one and life of the meditation to another; Those who are devoted to ignorance (rituals), they enter into blind darkness; but they who engage in knowledge (of a deity) alone, enter into a greater darkness. They say one thing is obtained from knowledge, another they say from ignorance. He who knows that both knowledge and ignorance should be pursued together overcomes death through ignorance and obtains mortality through knowledge. One thing is obtained from the worship of the manifested, another from the worship of the unmanifested. . . .

Guru Nānak writes:

giāna hīṇaṁ agiāna pūjā॥

....

gura binu giānu dharama binu dhiānu॥

– *Ādi Granth*, p. 1412

Without a *guru* there is no spiritual wisdom and without faith there is no meditation.

Without the spiritual enlightenment the people worship ignorance. They grope in darkness because of their love for duality.

tīrathu tapu daiā datu dānu॥ *je ko pāvai tila kā mānu*॥
suṇiā maṅniā mani kītā bhāu॥ *aṅtargati tīrathi mali nāu*॥
sabhi guṇa tere mai nāhī koi॥ *viṇu guṇa kīte bhagati na hoi*॥

– Ibid., p. 4

Outer performances like pilgrimages, austerity, compassion and charity bring iota of merit and relief. One has to go within with all love and devotion for real benefit.

Who Is the Real Agent in the Individual?

oṁ keneṣitaṁ patati preṣitaṁ manaḥ kena prāṇaḥ prathamaḥ praiti yuktaḥ।
keneṣitām vācamimāṁ vadanti caksuḥ śrotraṁ ka u devo yunakti॥
srotrasya śrotraṁ manaso mano yadvāco ha vācaṁ sa u prāṇasya prāṇaḥ।

cakṣuṣaścakṣuratimucya dhīrāḥ pretyāsmāllokādamṛtā bhavanti ||

– *Kena Upaniṣad* 1.1-2

At whose behest mind light on the object, men utter speech, eyes are prompted to see and ears to hear? It is that which is, the ear of the ear, mind of the mind, speech of the speech, breath of the breath, eye of the eye. The wise men giving up the wrong notions of their self-sufficiency renounce the world (sense organs) and attain immortality.

Guru Nānak expresses the similar thoughts (*kudarati disai kudarati suṇīe* . . .) in his hymns (*Ādi Granth*, p. 464) wherein he says that it is His power by which we see and hear, fear and feel awareness of happiness. Thus the creator is all powerful.

That Alone Know as Brahman

yadvācānabhyuditaṁ yena vāgabhyudyate ||

. . . .

tad eva brahma tvam viddhi nedaṁ yadidamupāsate ||

– *Kena Upaniṣad*, 1.5, 9

One should know Brahman *as that*
which is not expressed by speech but by which speech is expressed
which does not think by mind but by
which they say mind is thought
which does not see by the eye, but by which one sees
which does not hear by the ear, but by which the ear is heard
which does not breathe by breath but by which breath is drawn
and not that which people here adore.

In the above verses, the gods who are worshipped by the ignorant people living in darkness are compared with the knowledge of *Brahman*. He is the source of all speech, sight, thought, sound and breathe. Behind or before all perception and cognition is Pure Consciousness.

Guru Nānak says:

. . . *je jāṇasi brahmaṁ karmaṁ* || *sabhi phokaṭa nisacau karamaṁ* ||

– *Ādi Granth*, p. 470

Rosary round the neck, sacred mark on the forehead are not the signs/symbols of one's love for God. If you know the true nature of *Brahman*, all these beliefs and rituals are in vain.

Brahman Is beyond All Perceptions

aśabdamasparśamarūpam avyayaṁ tathā 'rasaṁ
nityamagandhavaccha yat ।
anādyanantaṁ mahataḥ paraṁ dhruvaṁ nicāyya
tanmṛtyumukhātpramucyate ॥
– *Kaṭha Upaniṣad* 1.3.15

He who becomes aware of or identify that which is without sound, touch, form, decay or taste, eternal, without smell, beginning, end, beyond the great and unchangeable, is freed from the jaws of death.

anyatra dharmādanyatrādharmādanyatrāsmātkṛtākṛtāt ।
anyatra bhūtācca bhavyācca yattatpaśyasi tadvada ॥
– Ibid. 1.2.14

Naciketā said: "That which you see as neither this nor that, as neither effect nor cause, as neither past nor future, tell me that".

sarve vedā yatpadamāmananti tapāṁsi sarvāṇi ca yadvadanti ।
yadicchanto brahmacaryaṁ caranti tatte padaṁ saṁgraheṇa bravīmyomityetat ॥
– Ibid. 1.2.15

Yama said: "That word (or place) which all the Vedas record, which all penances proclaim, which men desire when they live as religious students, that word I tell you briefly, it is *oṁ*".

edaddhyevākṣaraṁ brahma etaddhyevākṣaraṁ param ।
etaddhyevākṣaraṁ jñātvā yo yadicchati tasya tat ॥
– Ibid. 1.2.16

That everlasting or indestructible syllable means *Brahman*,that syllable means the highest *Brahman*; he who knows that syllable (*auṁ*), whatever he desires, is his.

edadālambanaṁ śreṣṭhametadālambanaṁ param ।
etadālambanaṁ jñātvā brahmaloke mahīyate ॥
– Ibid. 1.2.17

This is the best support, this is the highest support; he who knows that support is magnified in the world of *Brahman*.

na saṁdṛśe tiṣṭhati rūpamasya na cakṣusā paśyati kaścanainam ।
hṛdā manīṣī manasā 'bhikṛlpto ya etadviduramṛtāste bhavanti ।।
– *Kaṭha Upaniṣad* 2.3.9

His form is not an object of vision, no one beholds Him with eyes. One can know Him when He is revealed by intellect free from doubt and constant meditation.

In the above verses *Brahman* is described as unimaginable and inexpressible, neither this nor that, neither effect nor cause, neither past nor future. It is to say that nothing can be said about *Brahman*. *Brahman* is identified with the word *oṁ* or *auṁ*, recited in meditation. This syllable is the focus of all the Vedas. *Oṁ* is not a word but rather a rise and fall of the pitch of the voice in speaking, more like music than speech. It is the foundational sound of the world since it contains all other sounds.

Guru Nānak says:

oṁkāri śabadi udhre ।।
onama akhara suṇahu bīcārū ।।
onama akharu tribhavaṇa sāru ।।
– *Ādi Granth*, pp. 929-30

Oṁkāra is He who created Brahmā. *Oṁkāra* is that who created the mountains and the *yugas* and Vedas. Hear the message of the creator of this universe who is not perishable, through the word *oṁkāra* or *oṁkāra* which is the essence of three states of consciousness.

alakha apāra agaṁma agocara . . . .
– Ibid., p. 597

He cannot be known, He is beyond any limitation of time and space, cannot be approached and perceived. He is not subject to death or *karma*. He has no form or colour or features, He reveals Himself through *śabada*.

Two Kinds of Knowledge Are to Be Known the Higher as well as Lower

dve vidye veditavye, iti ha sma yadbrahmavido vadanti parā caivāparā ca ||
tatrāpara ṛgvedo yajurvedaḥ sāmavedo 'tharvavedaḥ śikṣā kalpo vyākaraṇaṁ niruktaṁ chando jyotiṣaniti |
atha parā yayā tadakṣaramadhigamyate ||

– *Muṇḍaka Upaniṣad* 1.1.4-5

The knowledge of the *Ṛgveda*, the *Yajurveda*, the *Sāmaveda*, the *Atharvaveda*, phonetics, rituals, grammar, etymology, metrics and astrology is the lower knowledge. And higher knowledge is that by which the imperishable *Brahman* is apprehended.

Guru Nānak says:

cāre veda hoe saciāra || *paḍahi guṇahi tinha cāra vīcāra* ||
bhāu bhagati kari nīcu sadāe || *tau nānaka mokhaṁtara pāe* ||

– *Ādi Granth*, p. 470

Knowledge of Vedas and other scriptures instills the discrimination faculty between the merit and demerit but for emancipation one has to go deep within for higher knowledge with loving adoration.

guraparasādī vidiā vīcārai . . .

– Ibid., p. 1329

One who by the grace of *guru* contemplates spiritual knowledge, reads and studies it, gathers glory. But it is only the higher spiritual knowledge that the Self is revealed within the self, and one is blessed with the ambrosia of *nāma*.

Brahman Is Both the Efficient and Material Cause of the Creation

yattadadreśyamagrāhyamagotramavarṇamacakṣuḥśrotraṁ tadapāṇipādaṁ nityaṁ vibhuṁ sarvagataṁ susūkṣmaṁ tadavyayaṁ yadbhūta-yoniṁ paripaśyanti dhīrāḥ ||

– *Muṇḍaka Upaniṣad* 1.1.6

Brahman, which the wise regard imperishable and as the source of all beings, is that which cannot be seen, nor seized, which has no family and no caste, no eyes or ears, no hands or feet. He is eternal, the omnipresent and infinite.

yathorṇanābhiḥ sṛjate gṛhṇate ca yathā pṛthivyāmoṣadhayaḥ saṁbhavanti ।
yathā sataḥ puruṣatkeśalomāni tathākṣaratsaṁbhavatīha viśvam ॥
– *Muṇḍaka Upaniṣad* 1.1.7

As a spider brings forth and draws in its thread, the herbs grow on earth, the hair grow on the head and the body of the living person, similarly from the imperishable the universe arises here.

Guru Nānak says:

āpīnhai āpu sāji āpu pachāṇiā ॥
....
na tisu bāpu na māi kini tū jāiā ॥
nā tisu rūpu na rekha varana sabāiā ॥
– *Ādi Granth*, p. 1279

He Himself created Himself. He Himself understands Himself. . . . There is no equal to Him. He has no father, no mother, who gave birth to Him. He has no form or feature. He transcends all creations.

Nature of Liberation

saṁprāpyainamṛṣayo jñānatṛptāḥ kṛtatmāno vītarāgāḥ praśāntāḥ ।
te sarvagaṁ sarvataḥ prāpya dhīrā yuktātmānaḥ sarvamevāviśanti ॥
– *Muṇḍaka Upaniṣad* 3.2.5

After realization of *Ātman*, the seers become satisfied with that knowledge. Their souls are established in the Supreme Self, they get free from passions, and they become peaceful in mind. Such calm souls, who get ever devoted to the Self, see everywhere the omnipresent *Brahman* and enter into it in the end.

dekhi adṛsaṭu rahau bisamādī ...
....

tatu nirañjanu joti sabāī sohaṁ bhedu na koī jīu ||
– *Ādi Granth*, p. 599

Seeing the unseen Lord one is amazed, delighted, forgets all pains and is at peace. We are all His essence and His light is within all of us. One realizes that there is no difference between the individual soul and the Universal Soul.

sa yo ha vai tatparamaṁ brahma veda brahmaiva bhavati nāsyābrahmavitkule bhavati | – *Muṇḍaka Upaniṣad* 3.2.9

He who knows the Supreme *Brahman* verily becomes *Brahman* himself.

Guru Nānak says:

satiguru sevahi se paravāṇu jinha joti joti milāī ||
so sāhibu so sevaka tehā jisu bhāṇā maṅni vasāī ||
– *Ādi Granth*, p. 1287

One who serves a true *guru* becomes acceptable to Him and is led to merger of one's light into His Light. He enshrines the will of the Lord within him and becomes just like his Lord and the Master.

Turīya: Fourth Stage of Consciousness; Significance of Syllable Auṁ

sarvaṁ hyetadbrahmāyamātmā brahma so 'yamātmā catuṣpat |
– *Māṇḍūkya Upaniṣad* 2

All this is verily *Brahman*. The self is *Brahman*. The same self has four quarters.

amātraścaturtho 'vyavahāryaḥ prapañcopaśamaḥ śivo 'dvaita evamoṁkāra ātmaiva, saṁviśatyātmanātmānaṁ ya evaṁ veda ya evaṁ veda || – Ibid. 12

The fourth (*turīya* state) has no elements; it cannot be spoken of, into which the world is resolved, benign, non-dual. Thus the syllable *auṁ* is the very self. He who knows it thus enters the Self with his self.

Guru Nānak says:

janami marai trai guṇa hitakāru ||

....

tīni avasathā kahahi vakhiānu ||
turīāvasathā satigura te hari jānu ||
– *Ādi Granth*, p. 154

One who remains in the three states of consciousness is subject to birth and death, which are described in scriptures but the forth state of *turīya*, which is a state of union with the Lord, can be known only from a true *guru*.

That Form from which the Origin, Continuance and Dissolution of the World Come Is Īśvara

taṁ hovāca | *yato vā imāni bhūtāni jāyante* | *yena jātāni jīvanti* |
yatprayantyabhisaṁviśanti | *tadvijijñāsasva* | *tadbrahmeti* |
– *Taittirīya Upaniṣad* 3.1.1

That verily, from which these beings are born, that by which, when born they live, that into which when departing they enter. That is *Brahman*.

Guru Nānak explains:

anhata sunni rate se kaise ||
– *Ādi Granth*, p. 943

What kind are they who are enraptured in the state of endless void. Yet they are alike the one from whom they have sprouted. They are beyond life and death and they do not come and go.

nānaka tākau milai vaḍāī āpu pachāṇai saraba jīā ||
sācau upajai sāci samāvai sāce sūce eka maiā ||
– Ibid., p. 940

Blessed with great vision one realizes himself in all beings. He comes forth from Truth and merges into Truth again.

Seeking Brahman-Knowledge from a Teacher

tānha sa ṛṣiruvāca bhūya eva tapasā brahmacaryeṇa śraddhyā saṁvatsaraṁ saṁvatsyatha yathākāmaṁ pṛśnānpṛcchat yadi vijñāsyāmaḥ sarvaṁ ha vo vakṣyāma iti ||

– *Praśna Upaniṣad* 1.2

To them that seer said: "Live with me another year with austerity, chastity and faith. Then ask us questions according to your desire and if we know, we shall tell you all that".

This explains the limits and the hard path set for the seekers who wished to attain higher knowledge of the Upaniṣads from a seer.

True Nature of Brahman Is Pure Consciousness

The various mental functions are only classification of different kinds of perception, conception, intuition as well as feeling and will.

yadetat hṛdayaṁ manaścaitat | *saṁjñānamājñānaṁ vijñānaṁ prajñānaṁ medhā dṛṣṭirdhṛtirmatirmanīṣā jūtiḥ smṛtiḥ saṁkalpaḥ kraturasuḥ kāmo vaśa iti sarvāṇyevaitāni prajñānasya nāma-dheyāni bhavanti* || – *Aitareya Upaniṣad* 3.1.2

That which is the heart and this mind that is consciousness, perception, discrimination, intelligence, wisdom, insight, steadfastness, thought, thoughtfulness, impulse, memory, conception, purpose, life, desire, control, all these indeed are names of the consciousness. One having realized oneness with the Pure Consciousness soars from this world having obtained all desires and becomes immortal.

Guru Nānak explains:

tārā caḍiā laṁmā kiu nadari nihāliā rāma . . .

– *Ādi Granth*, pp. 1110-11

These lines explain the experience, ecstasy and joy of revelations of *śabada* in individual. The consciousness metre shoots up to the sky and experiences oneness with the Pure Consciousness. With this experience of unity of all existence in Pure Consciousness one's passions come under control and one beholds and reflects only on the Supreme Lord everywhere.

Teaching the World of Brahman

idaṁ vāva tajjyeṣṭhāya putrāya pitā brahma prabrūyātpraṇāyyāya vāntevasine ||

nānyasmai kasmaicana yadyapyasmā imāmadbhiḥ parigṛhītāṁ
dhanasya pūrṇaṁ dadyād etadeva tato bhūya ityetadeva tato
bhūya iti ||
– *Chāndogya Upaniṣad* 3.11.5-6

A father may teach this *Brahman* to his eldest son or to a worthy pupil and to none else, even if one offers him the whole of this earth encompassed by water and filled with treasure.

This again shows as to how the higher knowledge of *Brahman* was limited to a few and common masses were actually at the mercy of priestly class for higher knowledge.

na ha vā asmā udeti na nimlocati sakṛddivā haivāsmai bhavati
ya etāmevaṁ brahmopaniṣadaṁ veda ||
– Ibid., 3.11.3

For one who knows the doctrine of *Brahman*, the sun neither rises nor sets. For him it is day for ever.

Meaning that the knower becomes one with *Brahman* not conditioned by time as marked by the rising and setting of the sun.

Guru Nānak explains:

jaise harahaṭa kī mālā ṭiṅḍa lagata hai ika . . . ||
....
suratī kai māragi cali kai ulaṭī nadari pragāsī ||
– *Ādi Granth*, p. 1329

As the buckets rotate, hung on a chain of the wheel, one being emptied and the other filled, so is the play of God. Such is His glory. By following the way of keen and quick internal awareness one feels detached from the world and gets enlightened. One comes from Him and by surrendering to Him, one is approved whether a householder or a renunciate.

āgai dekhau ḍau jalai pāchai hario aṅgurū ||
jisa te upajai tisa te binasai ghaṭi ghaṭi sacu bharapūri ||
– Ibid., p. 20

I see burning woods before me, and behind me I find green plants sprouting again, all these are destined to merge in Him from whence they come from. The true Lord is pervading in each and every heart.

āpe suratā āpe karata . . . ||

....

pūre gura te sācu kamāvai gati miti sabade pāī ||

– *Ādi Granth*, p. 940

By His command we take birth, by His command we go back and merge in His absorption. Through the grace of the *guru*, one practises Truth and knows the Lord's extent through word.

The Primal Sound Resonates Deep Within

sa ya etamevaṁ vidvānādityaṁ brahmetyupāste 'bhyāso
ha yadenaṁ sādhavo ghoṣā ā ca gaccheyurupa ca nimreḍeran-
nimreḍeran || – *Chāndogya Upaniṣad* 3.19.4

He who knowing this meditation on the sun as *Brahman*, pleasant sounds will quickly approach him and continue to delight him. Yes, it will continue to delight him.

Guru Nānak explains:

ghara mahi gharu dikhāi dai so satiguru purakha sujāṇu ||
pañca sabada dhunikāra dhuni taha bājai sabadu nīsāṇu ||

– *Ādi Granth*, p. 1291

One who shows our true home within the home of the self is the true *guru*. The primal five sounds resonate and resound within. The insignia of *śabada* is revealed there which is vibrating gloriously within.

Everything Flows from the Self

ātmataḥ prāṇa ātmata āśātmataḥ smara ātmata ākāśah
ātmatasteja ātmata āpa ātmata āvirbhāvatirobhāvātmao 'nnam-
ātmatobalamātmatovijñānamātmato dhyānamātmataścittam-
ātmataḥ saṁkalpa ātmato mana ātmato vāgātmato nāmātmato
mantrā ātmataḥ karmāṇyātmata evedaṁ sarvamiti ||

– *Chāndogya Upaniṣad* 7.26.1

Life breath springs from the Self; hope, memory, ether, heat, water, appearances and disappearances, food, strength, understanding, meditation, thought, determination, mind, speech, name, sacred hymns, sacred works all spring from the Self.

Guru Nānak explains:

āpīnhai āpu sāji āpu pachāṇiā ||

....

sacai takhati nivāsu hora āvaṇa jāṇiā ||

– *Ādi Granth*, p. 1291

He Himself created Himself. He spread his canopy without any pillars. He is the creator of the sun and the moon, night and day, sacred shrines and scriptures.

Guru Nānak explains in many of his other verses that everything flows from the Lord, exists in Him and merges back in Him.

Theoretical Unknowability of Brahman

na dṛṣṭerdraṣṭāraṁ paśyerna śruteḥ śrotāraṁ śṛṇuyānna matermantāraṁ manvīthā na vijñātervijñātāraṁ vijānīyā eṣa ta ātmā sarvāntar oto 'nyadārtaṁ . . .

– *Bṛhadāraṇyaka Upaniṣad* 3.4.2

One cannot see the seer of seeing, one cannot hear the hearer of hearing; one cannot think the thinker of thinking; one cannot know the knower of knowing. He is yourself which is within all. Everything else, but this, is perishable.

Guru Nānak explains:

ohu vekhai onā nadari na āvai bahutā ehu viḍāṇu

– *Ādi Granth*, p. 7

He is the seer and cannot be seen. This is very strange. He runs the show according to His Will.

Thus while reading the hymns of Guru Nānak we experience unity of spiritual knowledge of the philosophy of life in a very vivid, easy to understand, touching the hearts and simplified philosophy of life as taught by the sages and seers of the Upaniṣads.

Hymns of Guru Nānak contain many aspects of philosophy

of life as well as many theological concepts traceable from the Upaniṣads. Selected extracts from the hymns of Guru Nānak and principal Upaniṣads are arranged as nearly as possible under the relevant head of study in the preceding Chapters 1-5 with notes and brief conclusions.

The Truth

The Upaniṣads and hymns of Guru Nānak define the attributes to identify the Ultimate Truth in a most similar way. The *Chāndogya Upaniṣad* 8.3.4-5 explains that the enlightened serene being rises from the physical body and attains the Highest Light and reaches a state which is his own true form. This is the Self. It is immortal and fearless. This is *Brahman* and of this *Brahman*, the name is *satyam*, the Truth. The name *satyam* consists of three syllables: *sat*, *ti* and *yam*. That which is *sat* signifies the immortal; and that which is *ti* is the mortal and *yam* binds them both. Since the syllable binds both, it is called *yam*. He who knows this goes everyday in deep sleep to heaven, i.e. *Brahman* is dwelling in the heart. In the beginning, the *Chāndogya Upaniṣad* 6.2.1-3 explains that this universe was being (*sat*) alone, one only without a second. Some say that in the beginning this was non-being (*asat*) alone, one only without a second; and from that non-being, being was born. But how could being be born from non-being? So there was Being alone that existed in the beginning one only without a second. Being or *Brahman* thought "may I be many, may I grow forth. It created water . . ." the purpose of this text is not to show the order of creation but to emphasize that all things are produced from One Being alone. All have roots in the Being or Truth (*Chāndogya Upaniṣad* 6.8.1-7). Individual soul is fastened to this Truth. Imperishable *Brahman* is known only by knowing the Self, which cannot be seen or seized otherwise. It has no roots or attributes; it is eternal, omnipresent, omniscient and extremely subtle; it is imperishable and source of all beings.

Guru Nānak also explains in the opening lines of the *Japjī* known as the *mūla mantra* that there is *one oṁkāra* (manifested as well as unmanifested *Brahman*). His name is Truth. He is the creator. He is without any fear or enmity. He is self-existent and without any birth or death. He was Truth in the beginning, at present and shall ever be Truth in the future. Guru Nānak did not establish any separate identity or attributes of the Ultimate Truth or reality or *Brahman* other than the Upaniṣadic description.

Cosmogony or Origin of Creation

The contents of the Nāsadīya Sūkta of the *Ṛgveda* X.129 and the hymns of creation by Guru Nānak *arabada narabada dhaundhūkārā* (*Ādi Granth*, p. 1035) in Chapter 2 explicitly show similar thoughts regarding the pre-creation state of void or non-being, transformation of non-being into being. Both explain the Divine Will to expand and stress that no one can tell as to how and when there was transformation of non-being into being as the birth of all gods came after Him. Thus the Upaniṣads and hymns of Guru Nānak both do not support the theory of evolution or automatic development of creation without any intelligent cause at the back of helm of all creations. There is a common belief that there is One Supreme Being who is both the material and efficient causes of creation. He created Himself out of Himself.

Identity between Individual Soul and Universal Soul

The Upaniṣads establish oneness of the individual self and *Brahman* in most illustrative ways as described in the selected materials from the Upaniṣads and hymns of Guru Nānak in Chapter 2. The four *mahāvākyas* – *prajñānam brahma, ayam ātma brahma, tat tvam asi* and *aham brahmāsmi* – carry a universal message of oneness of the individual soul and the Universal Soul as the essence of burning cannot be different from fire, or waves of the agitated sea cannot be different from the sea. However there are different views as to what is the relationship of the individual soul with the Universal Soul held by Dvaita, Advaita and Viśiṣṭādvaita schools of thought as already discussed.

Guru Nānak avoids controversies and beliefs held by these schools and explains simplified Upaniṣadic view saying that *sāgara mahi būṅda būṅda mahi sāgara* (*Ādi Granth*, p. 878). The relation between the individual soul and the Universal Soul is like a drop in the ocean and ocean in a drop. As the night is in the day and the day is in the night (*dina mahi raiṇi raiṇi mahi dinīaru* – *Ādi Granth*, p. 878), as a female is born from the sperm of a male and a male is born from a female (*purakha mahi nāri nāri mahi purakhā* – ibid.), such is the relation of the individual soul with the Universal Soul. *ātama mahi rāmu rāma mahi ātamu* (ibid., p. 1153) can be realized through the teachings of a *guru*. That very cosmic Universal Soul dwells in every heart. It is hidden in every heart (*sabhanī ghaṭī sahu vasai* – ibid., p. 1412). Only one soul wanders through all three worlds (*eko havaru bhavai tihu loi* – ibid., p. 930) and He Himself assumes all sorts of forms. He explains: *jetā sabadu surati dhuni tetī jetā rūpu kāiā terī* (ibid., p. 350). His body is as vast as the stretch of all existence. There is nothing other than or outside Him. He is the tongue that tastes, the nose that smells and the eye that sees.

Individual Soul and Body

Selected materials from the Upaniṣads and the hymns of Guru Nānak in Chapter 2 illustrate vividly the relationship between the individual soul and human body. Both show a very close similarity of concepts of soul and human body. A human body is called a city with a fort within it which is called the dwelling place of the Lord within the human body. The concept of nine doors is also similar with the tenth gate (aperture at the top) in the human body to be an escape route for the soul to the higher level of consciousness for a personal experience of divinity. Both describe the transitory nature of body very vividly and advise to make use of it for salvation. Both describe that the nature of soul as immaculate meaning perfectly pure, faultless and clean.

Mutual Relationship between God, Man and the World

The materials selected from the Upaniṣads and the hymns of Guru Nānak in Chapter 3 portray the mutual relationship between God, man and the world (*Īśvara, jīva* and *jagat*). According to the *Muṇḍaka Upaniṣad* 2.1.1 many kinds of beings issue forth and return thereto from *Brahman* as sparks come from the blazing fire. the *Chāndogya Upaniṣad* 6.8.2 also explains that all individuals are fastened with the string of *prāṇa*. Man's very existence depends on Him. Guru Nānak compares human life as a bucket of water tied with a string in the deep well (*ḍolu badhā kasi jevarī ākāsi patālā* – *Ādi*

Granth, p. 228) which is lowered and raised continuously. He says both body and soul are His *jīu piṅḍu sabhu terai pāsī* (ibid., p. 25). He is near, He is far away and He is in between the body. All are the brides of the Husband Lord who enjoys His creation (*sabhe kaṅta sahelīā sagalīā karahi sīgāru* – ibid., p. 54). As a dairy farmer (*jiu gāī kau goilī rākhahi kari sārā* – ibid., p. 228) watches over and protects his cows, so does the Lord cherish and protect us day and night. Thus the Upaniṣads and Guru Nānak share a common belief that man is an *aṁśa* of God and has no separate identity of its existence outside Him. Man is a separated soul, enshrined in a body, and the ultimate peace lies in reunion with Him.

According to the *Īśa Upaniṣad* 1, whatever moves in this world is enveloped by God. World does not stand apart from God but is pervaded by Him. The *Muṇḍaka Upaniṣad* 2.2.5 explains that heaven, earth and space in between and mind with all its sense organs are woven in Him. The *Bṛhadāraṇyaka Upaniṣad* 2.1.20 explains that as the spider moves along the thread and as sparks come from fire, all worlds, all divinities and all beings come forth from Him. Nothing exists outside Him. Guru Nānak also says that *sace tere khaṅḍa sace brahamaṅḍa* ... (*Ādi Granth*, p. 463). The one Lord is the creator and the king of the world. He created all worlds, solar systems, realms. Since these are created by the True Lord as such all His creations are also true. He is the creator of the world of *māyā* with all its colours and spices. After creation He Himself takes care of it. He commands all His creation and no one can command Him. He yokes everyone into his service and feeds all, but remains unattached. When He withdraws His power, the whole existence crumbles down.

The Upaniṣads advocate living a life of action in this world with the ultimate aim of life as to get out of cycle of birth and death. the *Īśa Upaniṣad* 2 wishes a man to live a life of hundred years without binding oneself with the world. The *Taittirīya Upaniṣad* 1.2.1-3 advises a pupil after completion of his studies to live a life of virtue, not to neglect the householder's life, not to cut off the line of progeny, not to neglect personal welfare and prosperity. The *Muṇḍaka Upaniṣad* 3.2.6 explains that the real meaning of Vedānta is to get the knowledge of self, live a life of virtue and get liberation from the cycle of birth and death.

The hymns of Guru Nānak also advise a man to escape from the mud of desires and attachments as all these lead to create anxiety and pain of fear of losing them (*tr̥sanā māiā mohaṇī suta baṅdhapa ghara nārī*. . . – *Ādi Granth*, p. 61). Our stay in this world is only a transit camp (*mukāmu kari ghari baisaṇa nita calaṇai kī dhokha* – ibid., p. 64) and more we get involved in it, the more will be the feeling of agony for losing it. Man moves through many forms of life: *kete rukha birakha hama cīne kete pasū upāe* ǁ ... (ibid., p. 156) (may be trees, animal life, crawling worms or winged birds). We are in this world for a short time as a shepherd is in the field. He gave a clarion call to mankind to wake up and realize the truth. Man will go back from this world in the form in which he had come to this world (*jiu āiā tiu jāvahi baure jiu* – ibid., p. 906). So he advises man not to waste the life in pleasures of mind and body but to build up virtues for himself which he can carry with him. He ridicules that the sign of success or prosperity is not the accumulation of grain (*udo sāhai kiā nīsāni toṭi na āvai aṅnī* – ibid., p. 1412) and worldly pleasures or having a number of children or women around you as there is no end to such desires. When one's body falls nothing shall go with. This world is a fortress (*kāgada koṭu ihu jaghu hai* ... ibid., p. 1274) of paper cleverly coloured and formed. A puff of wind or a drop of water can make it fall flat. He concludes: *raji na koī jīviā, pahuci na caliā koī* – ibid. p. 1412 (no one can live long enough to fulfil all his worldly wishes in his lifetime). Only the wise man who cherishes God in his consciousness lives eternally and is honoured.

Divine Will, Fear of God and Free Will

Selected materials in Chapter 3 explain the concepts of Divine Will, fear in life and free will in the Upaniṣads and in the hymns of Guru Nānak. The *Kaṭha Upaniṣad* 2.3.2-3 explains that in the whole world, whatsoever exists here springs from and moves in life in great fear like a thunderbolt. The whole universe vibrates as it has come forth from *Brahman* which exists as its ground. Like a poised thunderbolt, *Brahman* is a great terror. Due to fear of Him, the fire burns, sun gives heat and other gods run for work. The *Taittirīya Upaniṣad* 2.7.1 also explains that because of the fear of *Brahman* the wind blows and the sun rises and other gods run for maintaining the cosmic order.

Vedic texts refer to *ṛta* as order of the universe or Truth. *Ṛta* is the Divine Law which governs the world. It implies the physical order of the universe and the moral law pervading over this world. The dawn breaks out in the morning according to *ṛta,* the sun is bright due to *ṛta*. The year is a wheel of *ṛta* with twelve spokes (months). The river's play obeys the rule of *ṛta*. *Ṛta* is the cosmic order and the moral universal order. It commands positive action. The *Chāndogya Upaniṣad* 7.4.1-3 explains that will is greater than mind, for when a man wills, then he thinks in his mind, then he utters speech and employs speech in the recital of a name. The sacred hymns are included in a name. One who meditates on will as *Brahman* will reach as far as his will reaches.

Guru Nānak expresses similar thoughts: the concept of fear for God and Divine Law regulating and governing the creation in his hymns (*bhai vici pavaṇu vahai sada vāu*… – *Ādi Granth*, p. 464). In the fear of God the wind blows, thousands of rivers flow, fire is forced to labour. Earth is crushed under its fear and clouds move in the sky. In His fear the sun shines, moon reflects and they travel millions of miles endlessly and *dharma* stands at His door (*siri dhari calīe sahīe bhāru* – ibid., p. 151). One should place the fear of God on his head and bear that weight. One should place the fear of God within the home of heart (*ḍari dharu ghari ḍara ḍari ḍaru jāi* – ibid., p. 151). With this fear of God in one's heart all other fears shall run away. One will be able to follow the right path and exercise his free will to achieve the goal of life. Living with the worldly fears the mind gets confused as emotions surround him. One should live a fearless life by practising only God's fear. We come across very frequently the references to the supremacy of Divine Will and fear of God in the hymns of Guru Nānak. He says that God has placed the inscription of His fear on every head, and only the True Lord Himself is fearless. His concept of *Hukama* or Divine Will is comparable with the stern and permanent laws (*ṛta*) of *prakṛti*. He advises mankind to know, recognize and follow the Divine Will and develop a fear for it. Once the fear of God's will is adopted it will make one fearless of all fears of the world which are unreal. One will develop a free will for life to follow the desired aim of his life (*hukme āvai hukme jāvai hukme rahai samāī* – *Ādi Granth*, p. 940). It is only by His command that we come and go and merge in absorption (*sabhe suratī joga sabhi sabhe purāṇa . . . hukami calāe āpaṇai karamī vahai kolāma* – ibid., p. 124).

The Upaniṣads and the hymns of Guru Nānak both share a vision that all intuitiveness, understanding, *yoga*, Vedas, songs of spiritual wisdom, intellect and enlightenments come into being and exist according to the Divine Will.

Haume (I-ness)

The concluding conversation between Yājñavalkya and Maitreyī about the duality or two forms of reality and the absolute Self in the *Bṛhadāraṇyaka Upaniṣad* 2.4.14 explains that where there is duality, there one smells another, sees another, hears another, speaks another, thinks and understands another. Whereas when everything has become the Self, one cannot smell, see, hear, speak and understand anything other than Him. This is the blissful state of mind. The duality or I-ness takes one away from the Reality. The *Īśa Upaniṣad* 6-7 explains that the wise man sees all beings in the self, and self in all beings; that is why he does not hate anyone. To the seer all things have verily become the Self, what delusion or sorrow can there be for him who beholds that Oneness? The *Kaṭha Upaniṣad* 2.2.12-13 describes that there is one Supreme ruler in the inmost self of all beings who makes His one form manifold. Among all non-eternal objects, there is only One who is the eternal Reality. There is only one truly conscious entity among all conscious objects. One who perceives Him within oneself, he is wise and ever happy.

Guru Nānak very emphatically declares that *haumai karatiā naha sukhu hoī* || *manamati jhūṭhī sacā soī* || – *Ādi Granth*, p. 222 (I-ness takes individual away from God). When the seed of I-ness sprouts in an individual, ego develops in him and he falls into the trap of *māyā*. Acting in egotism peace cannot be obtained. The Lord cannot be seen, as such cannot be described. Only *guramukha* can realize Him with intuitive ease. One has to surrender one's mind in devotional worship. Egotism binds people in bondage (*haumai baṅdhana baṅdhi bhavāvai* – *Ādi Granth*, p. 27) and causes them to wander around all lost. In duality and evil mindedness, one acts blindly (*dubidhā duramati adhulī kāra* – ibid., p. 1190) and only a true *guru* can dispel his darkness. Guru Nānak preaches that all creations are but the God himself (*haumai karī tāṅ tū nahī tū hovahi hau nāhi* – ibid., p. 1092). There is nothing other than Him. Where there is I-ness, there is no God and where there is God there cannot be I-ness. The soul bride, under the influence of duality, is blind and deaf. The all-powerful Lord is within the home of one's own heart; one is not able to enjoy His presence due to evil of dual feeling. The self-willed *manamukha* wanders and is lost in darkness (*hau vici āiā hau vici gaiā, hau vici jaṁmiā hau vici muā* – ibid., p. 466). One who comes, goes and lives in I-ness cannot find the gate to liberation. Such persons cannot absorb the essence of reality and get burnt to ashes in duality (*guramukhi hovai su giānu tatu bīcārai haumai sabadi jalāe* – ibid., p. 946). By raising oneself above the three qualities of *māyā*, one should go within and take refuge in *śabada* so that he is able to control the mind and realize the Self which is nothing other than the God Himself. Desire is overcome only when the mind is filled with *nāma hau muā mai māriā pavaṇu vahai darīāu* – ibid., p. 1091. Thus a man who does not realize the self dies in egotism and roams in the cycle of birth and death.

World Struggle and Suffering in the World

The *Muṇḍaka Upaniṣad* 3.2.2 explains that one who entertains desires is born again here on account of his desires. But one who has his desires fully satisfied and is a perfect soul, all his desires vanish here on earth. Obviously one may satisfy oneself by fulfilment of desire or by elimination of desire by Self-realization.

Nānaka dukhiā sabhu saṁsārū (ibid., p. 954) are the household words for all who happen to study the hymns of Guru Nānak. Guru Nānak explains *dukha vici jaṁmaṇu, dukhi maraṇu, dukhi varataṇu sāṁsāri* (ibid., p. 1240) (one takes birth in pain, lives in pain and dies in pain due to worldly attachments). There are countless festivities and celebrations on birth of a child in the family forgetting that one who comes has to leave this world. God has given *dukhu vichoḍā iku dukha bhūkha* (*Ādi Granth*, p. 1256) (union and separation, pain and pleasure together) and one should remain detached. None of the worldly relations and accumulations can last long always with one in life and life after. The separation from our loved ones, poverty and hunger, not getting what one desires, getting what one does not desire, the physical and mental pain due to decease and fear of death all there all these cause great pain. Man is free from pain and gets rejuvenation only in the company of true Lord. True relationship which is established by uniting oneself with Him is the only relation which will last longer than life. All other worldly relations are false, temporary and will fall down on the way of life causing great pain. When one is inspired with praises for the Lord, the mind and body blossom and get refreshed. *kañcana kāiā niramala haṁsu jisu mahi nāmu nirañjana aṁsu, dukha roga sabhi gaiā gavāi, nānaka chūṭasi sācai nai* (ibid., p. 1256).

> man gets a golden body and the soul swan is stainless and pure. A tiny particle of immaculate *nāma* is within, all pain, suffering and disease are eradicated.

One may love an innumerable number of persons or relations (*lakha siu prīti hovai lakha jīvaṇu kiā khusīā* – ibid., p. 1243), but should not forget that all shall be separated one or the other day. Then what is the pleasure of these entanglements with relations and accumulations when these cannot be carried along with you and fear of their separation may cause further pain. He wonders that we own and love the transitory relations of the world (*suta kañcana siu hetu vadhāiā, sabhu kichu apanā iku rāmu parāiā* – ibid., p. 1342) but forget God who is the ultimate relation of all creations.

The historical/mythical events from the hymns of Guru Nānak described in Chapter 3 make a very interesting reading to conclude as to how the well-known heroes of their times were enticed by their ego, false honour, anger, lust; wish to grab other's share and pre-destined deeds and suffered agony and pain in life. These also explain Guru Nānak's sound knowledge of Hindu scriptures and belief in the *karma* theory.

Role of a Guru

A true *guru* is the dispeller of darkness of ignorance. His role in the spiritual progress and spiritual illumination of an individual is very crucial and important. That is why sometimes he is placed above the personal deity because it is he who shows the path and makes one feel the presence of one's deity. He is considered to be more revered to one's own father as father brings one down to this perishable world but a true *guru* uplifts one to the higher regions of spirituality and shows the path for unity with the Ultimate Reality. When one comes across such a *guru* who has realized the self, one is advised to follow him, serve him and hail him.

The role of a teacher is highlightened at every step in the Upaniṣads. Selected verses from the Upaniṣads and the hymns of Guru Nānak are placed in Chapter 4 explaining the role of a *guru*. The *Muṇḍaka Upaniṣad* 1.2.12-13 advises that one should search for a teacher who is learned in scriptures and established in *Brahman*. The knowing teacher should teach the knowledge about *Brahman* to one who approaches him in due form, whose mind is consistent and who has attained peace. In the *Praśna Upaniṣad* 6.8 a teacher is saluted and hailed as above one's father who takes his pupils to the other shore of ignorance. The teacher who teaches about the truth is a spiritual father as compared to the physical father. The *Kaṭha Upaniṣad* 1.2.8 establishes that taught by an inferior man, He (*Brahman*) cannot be truly understood as He is thought of many ways. He can be known from a teacher who knows Him as himself, meaning a Self-realized preceptor. The *Chāndogya Upaniṣad* 6.14.1-2 explains through a parable of man with a bandage on eyes and left in the forest who cries for help to lead him on the way. Someone comes and removes his bandage of ignorance and shows him the way. Guru Nānak in his hymn *bana mahi bhuli je phirā binu gura būjha na pāu* (*Ādi Granth*, p. 57) expresses nearly the similar disposition.

Guru Nānak time and again stresses in his hymns that there is no salvation without a true *guru*. On finding a true *guru*, one should serve him and run fast to follow and worship him. He hails and pays high tributes to a true *guru*. Accordingly the selected material from his hymns is classified into three parts describing vividly the need for a true *guru*, serving a true *guru*, homage by Guru Nānak to a true *guru*.

Guru Nānak emphasizes that there is no other way than to go through a self-realized *guru* for God-realization (*horu kitai bhagati na hovaī binu satigura ke upadesa* – *Ādi Granth*, p. 22). God (*Brahman*) cannot be found without the protection of a *guru* (*gura saraṇi na āīe, brahamu na pāīe*). He warns that there may be many preachers trading in the knowledge of learning but all are not Self-realized (*sabhi guṇavantī ākhīahi mai guṇu nāhī koi* – ibid., p. 56). A true *guru* helps in cleansing the inner self and to free oneself from the three modes. The Lord has placed His self within the true *guru* and He speaks and reveals His self through the *guru* (*satigura vici āpu rakhionu kari paragaṭu ākhi suṇāiā* – ibid., p. 466). One cannot find love without a *guru* and unite with *śabada* to experience inner joy. One acquires *nāma* (the name of God) from a true *guru* and the way of *yoga* to remain ever absorbed in truth (*pūre gura te nāmu pāīā jāī, joga jugati saci rahai samāi* – ibid., p. 941). Without serving a true *guru* one cannot attain *yoga* and without following the path of a *guru* no one is liberated (*binu satigura seve jogu na hoī, binu satigura bheṭe mukati na koī* – ibid., p. 946). The mind is an elephant like in the forest of life and the *guru* is the stick to control it. By meeting a true *guru*, darkness is dispelled, egotism is eradicated and the way to emancipation is paved (*satiguru milai andherā jāi, nānaka haumai meṭi samāi* – ibid., p. 939).

Guru Nānak advises that the essence and style of life should be to run fast and follow and worship a true *guru*. A true *guru* converts the counterfeit into genuine ones (*satigura pichai bhaji pāvahi ehā karaṇī sāru* – ibid., p. 143). One should serve the *guru* fearlessly to dispel his all doubts. Always hail, hail the one who shows us the way, one who teaches about the *śabada* and unites one with the Lord. One may perform hundreds of rituals but without a true *guru* he remains in all-darkness. One cannot see the path without a *guru*. He declares that he with the grace of the *guru* obtained the sublime essence of Lord (*guraparasādī hari rasu pāiā, nāmu padāratha navanidhi pāī* – ibid., p. 352). He further says that he bowed down again and again and fell at the feet of his true *guru*; it is through his true *guru* that he saw the Divine Self within (*nivi nivi pai lagau gura apune, ātama rāmu nihāriā* – *Ādi Granth*, p. 353). One who serves the *guru* comes to know God. His pains vanish and he realizes *śabada* within himself (*gura seve so ṭhākura jānai* – ibid., p. 416). Guru Nānak talks frequently about the grace of the his *guru*. He says that only those can serve a *guru* to whom the *guru* himself inspires to do so. One should offer one's head to the *guru* for emancipation (*gura kī sevā so kare jisa āpi karāe, nānaka siru de chūṭīe* – ibid., p. 427).

Guru Nānak applauds a true *guru* who makes angels out of men without any delay (*balihārī gura āpaṇe diuhāḍī sadavāra, jini māṇasa te devate kīe karata nā lagī vāra* – ibid., p. 462). He laments that self-willed *manamukha* loves the darkness and the world is drowning without a *guru*. He pays high tributes to a true *guru*. If a *guru* is pleased and merciful one's all desires are fulfilled, he will never grieve and always enjoy the Lord's love (*kahu nānaka guri brahamu dikhāiā* – ibid., p. 152). Nānak says that a true *guru* has revealed *Brahman* and now there is nothing like birth and death for him. The *guru* has shown him how to die while living and overcoming his ego, he has found the tenth gate. He hails the *guru* who enables one's urge for the company of the Lord, provides spiritual wisdom for dealing with the world. Thus Guru Nānak declares that the path to emancipation goes through a true *guru*. All the above abstracts from the hymns of Guru Nānak point towards the fact that he Nānak had the blessings of a true *guru*.

God's Love

Man has a natural tendency to be attracted to someone unknown, unseen and abodeless recluse (a hermit who lives alone and avoids other people) every time or in the hour of extreme joy or agony. There is a common gesture of raising or folding of hands, look towards the sky in awe, fall flat on the ground or prostrate in respect when gravitated and pulled from within self. Whatever may be the action or momentum of awareness aroused in the individual one feels the urge to know Him, to see Him and to be close to Him. With awareness concentrated, one's bones burn, one wants nothing else but Him to be at his side. Verses flow out of him describing his suffering of pangs of his love for Him. In the ecstasy of His love one imagines His form and clutches to that form to enjoy union with Him. I feel this is nothing but an idealized love of human life for God.

The Upaniṣads also recognize this idealized love for *eka sat* (one truth). God also loves His creation. It is His Will to be many out of sheer love and joy that He extends His Self like an agitated sea; He creates, sustains and calls back His waves at His Will. "You are that" is the soul cry of the Upaniṣads identifying oneness or union as the ultimate goal. Perhaps it is His love for His creation that He created a path within the human body to revert to Him. Whenever a strong love and unbearable agony of departure from Him is experienced, one's awareness shoots upward, gets concentrated and pierces through the sky of one's mind making him senseless to the worldly region and experiencing the joy of union with the truth in the higher regions of consciousness. The *Muṇḍaka Upaniṣad* 3.1.2-3 describes the relationship of the Universal Soul and the individual soul. When a seer sees the creator of the golden hue, he becomes free from sorrow and union of the agitated wave with the sea experiences total calmness and tranquillity. In the *Īśa Upaniṣad* 15-18, there is a prayer for the vision of God. I feel it is the sheer mutual God's love that sustains the whole creation by its playful nature.

This mutual God's Love is the essence of the hymns of Guru Nānak. I feel wonderstruck at the echo of Guru Nānak's hymn: *tārā caḍiā laṁmā kiu nadari nihāliā rāma* (*Ādi Granth*, p. 110). The metre of consciousness rises rapidly across the sky to have a vision of the Lord. How can it be seen? Momentum of love can only be experienced, not seen. The selected materials from his hymns in Chapter 4 describe his expression of love towards God, his experience of God's love for him, fire of separation and urge for the blessed vision and experience of the ecstasy of union with God. He explains – *koī ākhai bhūtanā* . . . (– ibid., p. 991) that after seeing his condition some call him a ghost or a demon-stricken person, other's call him a helpless mortal. He concludes that only one who falls in love with God is known to be insane as his worldly appearances and behaviour change. He calls himself to be a handmaiden of Lord and he is restless like the *cakavī* who longs for its love and cannot sleep. He explains that God is the only love and benefactor of him; all other relations are false. He calls all his sister companions on the spiritual path as His brides and advises them to shed all the rituals and come together to enjoy the blessed vision of their Lord.

Guru Nānak explains that the Lord has immense love for His creation: *citai aṅdari sabhu ko vekhi nadari heṭhi calāidā* (*Ādi Granth*, p. 472) He sees and moves all His creations under His glance of grace and all remain within His mind. God loves His creation and enjoys it. God causes everyone to run according to His will: *mere prītamā tū karatā kari vekhu* . . . (ibid., p. 636) (O my God! you create and see your creation). He gives a vivid picture of his suffering due to separation from Him. He feels like a fish out of water: *hari binu kiu dhīrai manu merā* . . . (ibid., p. 1232). He exclaims that he cannot be comfortable in this world without Him. God has completely bewitched him and he prays to his *guru* to unite him with the Lord. But all these mutual love and pangs of suffering are not in vain. He expresses also the joy of his experiences of moments of union with the Lord: *hama ghari sājana āe* . . . (ibid., p. 764)

Guru Nānak expresses his joy at the sight of his companions and godly people assembled around him for communion with the Lord. He asks them to join him for experiencing the unstuck sound current of the *pañca-śabda*. Moments of union with God and godly men enthrall Guru Nānak. In the moments of ecstasy he forms a vision of Lord: *tere baṅke loiṇā daṅta rīsālā* . . . (ibid., p. 567) He explains that Lord's eyes are beautiful, His teeth are sparkling, His gait is very graceful and voice very sweet. His youth is alluring and He is absorbed in Himself. *Kari kirapā apanai ghari āiā* (ibid., p. 351): He explains beautifully that when by His grace He comes to his home, then his mind becomes blessed and his marriage with the Lord is celebrated with songs of joy. He advises his spiritual companions: *jau tau prema khelaṇa kā cāu, siru dhari talī galī merī āu* (ibid., p. 1412). If they want to play the game of love with the Lord then they have to enter his path (*sahaja-yoga*), with their head on their palm (surrender their mind) and be ready to lay down head (shed all ego) on this path.

Nadar (Grace)

I consider grace as another way of God to express His love for man. God is merciful and loves his creation and showers His favours and wills to control and facilitate man's spiritual progress. It reminds a man that he cannot tread and succeed on the way of spiritual progress without His bounty. The Upaniṣads teach that much of learning, physical efforts, good *karma* and austerities alone cannot succeed in realizing the Self by an individual. It is He who bestows His grace upon deserving seekers for His bliss. The selected materials in Chapter 4 explain this in detail. The *Muṇḍaka Upaniṣad* 3.2.3 teaches that self is attained by one whom (the Self) chooses. The *Taittirīya Upaniṣad* 2.7.1 teaches that by realizing the essence of all existence one becomes blissful. It is by His grace that one realizes this truth and finds a fearless support in Him. In fact, grace is another expression of Divine Mercy as well as Divine Will.

Similarly Guru Nānak also reminds again and again through his hymns that *sabha mahi varatai eko soi, jisa no kirapā kare tisu paragaṭu hoi* (*Ādi Granth*, p. 931) (only one Lord permeates in all beings but He manifests to only one, whom He bestows His grace). *Nadari kare tā mali milāe* (ibid., p. 222) (with his glance of grace, He unites one in His union). *Nadari kare tā . . . būjhe nāu* (when the Lord puts forth His grace one knows the essence of Name). *Gura parasādi vasai mani āi* (ibid., p. 349) and *gura parasādi parama pada pāe* (ibid., p. 223) (with *guru*'s grace highest state of mind is established, and the Lord unites one with Himself by dispelling all doubts and with the grace of *guru* the supreme state is obtained. Guru Nānak explains that one finds a true *guru* by the grace of Lord who shows one the path of union with the Lord. *Sikhī sikhiā gura vīcāri, nadarī karami laghāe pāri* (ibid., p. 465) (a true *guru* is found when the merciful God shows His mercy. Who can instruct one to the *śabada*). *Nadari kare tā simariā jai . . .* (ibid., p. 661) (one remembers God in meditation if the Lord Himself bestows His grace).

Aim of Life

What is the purpose of this life? Everything around me is transitory and I have also to leave this world at His call and leave all my worldly accumulations and relations behind. How should I behave in life in order to be at peace during my life and prepare myself to the journey beyond life? How long I have to bear the pangs of birth and death? Can I be liberated from this cycle of coming and going? The Upaniṣads and the hymns of Guru Nānak explain and point towards the sign posts and direction to be followed by all humanity at large for their final goal of emancipation. The purpose of this life is stated to be *dharma*, i.e. a life to be lived according to the Divine Will, follow the rules for the well-being of the individual self and community which regulate the life for higher spiritual and moral order. One has to exhaust the burden of accumulated *karmas*, shed all the bondages of this material world to enjoy the unity with the Ultimate Reality and finish the cycle of coming and going in this world. One must remember that his stay in this world is limited and he has to leave behind everything which he considers as his own, it will help one to live a life of detachment. He must utilize this life and wish to exhaust all his accumulated *karmas* due to which he has taken birth and avoid all further bondages with this world. The way to find peace in this world is to develop love for the everlasting and permanent Divine Force behind all existence and Self-realization rather than entrapping oneself in the short-lived worldly relations. One should seek the company of Self-realized beings who can help one to rise to higher spiritual regions rather than rising to pure worldly fortunes of name, fame and possessions. One can be liberated from birth and death by realizing the Self while living in this world and experience unity with the Ultimate Reality. The Upaniṣads and the hymns of Guru Nānak both advise to aim at realization of Self while living; individual liberation paves the way for union with the Ultimate Truth. Liberation is not treated to be a creation of anything outside the body by way of action, speech or indulgence in rituals, but realization of something within the body which is considered to be the abode of the Supreme Lord. Again liberation is not inactivity or negligence of household duties, or shirking responsibilities of worldly affairs but to see action in non-action and non-action in action. One need not cling to actions performed by his body for discharging his duties but remain actionless and unattached by practising spiritual discipline.

Study materials from the Upaniṣads and the hymns of Guru Nānak in Chapter 5 provide a vivid description of the aim of man's life. The *Īśa Upaniṣad* 2 lays down that a man should wish to live hundred years of life and should live it performing actions. The *Kena Upaniṣad* 2.5 states that a man should cherish to know the self in the life itself as the true goal of one's life. The *Taittirīya Upaniṣad* 1.4.1 directs to possess and pray for a healthy body and mind for acquiring higher knowledge as sickness of body and lack of physical vigour may hamper the spiritual progress. One should not suffer from want of food and clothing to be able to devote fully to the study of scriptures and acquire knowledge of *Brahman*. The *Praśna Upaniṣad* 1.13 advises the kinds of control prescribed for a householder. The *Kaṭha Upaniṣad* 1.2.2 asks to develop a faculty for discrimination between the good and pleasant and preference of selection of good over pleasant by the wise. The *Chāndogya Upaniṣad* 8.12.1 explains that the embodied soul is the victim of pleasures and pain. So long as one is identified with the body, there is no end to pleasure or pain. Thus a man should aim at a healthy body and mind fit to receive higher knowledge, attain both lower and higher knowledge from the scriptures and Self-realized Beings, live a life of action without getting bondage with his actions or worldly relations and possessions, develop urge for Self-realization, aim at a state of *jīvan-mukti* while living and develop a strong desire for personal experience of divinity with an aim for liberation from the cycle of birth and death or *jīvan-mukta*.

Guru Nānak in his hymns repeats time and again that the aim of human form is to have personal experience of divinity for his final emancipation and unity with the Lord. One should not waste time in arguments and strife but act to achieve his goal of unity with the Ultimate Reality. This is possible only in human form which one gets by virtue of his good deeds. *Suni mana mitra piāriā milu velā hai* (*Ādi Granth*, p. 20) (there is no need to abandon home, shirk responsibilities and beg at others doors in search of the Lord). Reflect on word deep within your body. Develop love for one God. One who disciplines one's sensual desires, cherishes deep within for contemplation, exercises self-control and develops love for God is on the right path. Guru Nānak explains that preordained destiny looms over all heads. God himself is only without any destiny and His writ runs over all (*saraba jīā siri lekhu dhurāhū* – *Ādi Granth*, p. 598). One should restraint one's fickle mind and live a life without any fear other than His fear. According to Guru Nānak one needs to develop the qualities of a brāhmaṇa as one who knows *Brahman*, maintains his *dharma* with faith, humility and contentment breaking all his bonds and is liberated; as a kṣatriya as one who is a hero of good deeds, understands duty and plants a seed of generosity rather than feeling elated by mere virtue of their birth in a particular caste (*so brahamin, jo bindai braham... khatarī so jo karama kā sūra*).

Guru Nānak lays emphasis on for aiming at acquiring higher knowledge also. *Dīvā balai andherā jāi, beda pāṭha mati pāpā khāi* (ibid., p. 791) (study of the Vedas destroys sinful intellect; spiritual wisdom dispels ignorance). He advises us to find a true *guru* who can well up the life of spirit from within oneself and lead to the house of equipoise. *Aṁmṛtu nīru giāni mana majanu... guraparasādī vidiā vīcārai* (ibid., pp. 1328-29) (one needs to contemplate on spiritual knowledge with the grace of a *guru*). But mere spiritual knowledge is not enough. *Giānu giānu kathai sabhu koī, kathi kathi bādu kare dukhu hoī . . . binu rasa rāte mukati na hoī* (ibid., p. 831).

Everyone asks about spiritual wisdom and knowledge; they talk and talk, argue and suffer. No one can stop them from arguments. But no one can attain liberation without imbuing the subtle essence of the Lord. Guru Nānak therefore advises that one should aim to develop love for Truth and not only read scriptures but understand the mystery revealed therein. One should aim to develop modesty, humility and intuitive understanding. No one knows what will happen next, the writ of *karma* has to be accepted. When the seed of God's name is added to a cultivated mind all world will look false. So shed out all evil, cruelty and falsehood and leaving all vices, let one's soul contemplate and meditate on the name of God.

It is clear that Guru Nānak was a champion or a protagonist of Bhakti tradition of religion of saints. His philosophy and aim of life revolve around union of the individual soul with the Universal

Soul by developing love and devotion for the one Supreme Lord. Contemporary saints of his period, Śrī Vallabhācārya (1481–1533), Caitanya Mahāprabhu (1486–1534), Sant Kabīr (1440–1518) also preached, in their own way, that love for God is not only a means of liberation but it is an end in itself. Puṣṭi-Mārga, meaning the path of grace, of Vallabhācārya taught worship of the idol of child form of Lord Kṛṣṇa as a living child with tender love to earn God's grace. Caitanya Mahāprabhu was an ecstatic worshipper of Lord Kṛṣṇa as an incarnation of Viṣṇu. He gave "Hare Kṛṣṇa" *mantra* and worshipped Śrī Kṛṣṇa along with Rādhā Rānī. Sant Kabīr taught *sahaja-patha* (the natural way) for oneness with God. All these saints taught to aim to develop love for their deity and seek grace for final emancipation.

Guru Nānak with his poetic excellence describes the individual's aim of life and journey to higher regions in a most picturesque manner: *vaṇjāriā siu vaṇaju kara lai lāhā mana hasu* (*Ādi Granth,* p. 595) and advises that trade should be listening to scriptures, take truth as horses to be sold, accumulate virtues for one's travelling expenses, and not to postpone anything for tomorrow. When you gain access to the land of formless Lord, you will experience peace and His presence. One should remain absorbed in the formless Lord and aim at developing harmony with the Divine Will to attain everlasting peace.

Path of Liberation

The Upaniṣads describe *Brahman* as the ground and support of all existence. Path of liberation is prescribed as knowledge of *Brahman* by the realization of *Ātman*–individual self through balanced combination of *karma, knowledge, yoga* and meditation. For that one has to cultivate inner calmness, control over senses and sense organs, attain serenity and tranquillity of mind. One should practise virtue as humility, forbearance, charity and avoid forbidden actions. One should have an intense yearning for liberation from the bondages of worldly life and cycle of birth and death. One should approach a self-realized guide who can lead one to the higher knowledge of *Brahman* and lead to the higher spiritual regions for experiencing the glory of the Self.

The *Muṇḍaka Upaniṣad* 3.2.2 explains that one is born again and again here and there through his desires. But for one whose desires are satisfied and is established in the Self, all his desires vanish here while on earth. This explains the way to *karma-mukti* (gradual liberation). But those who worship the *Saguṇa-Brahman* with whole soul devotion do not return to earth or go to lower plane. They live ever absorbed in contemplation and attain final liberation at the end of the cycle when they merge in the absolute. The *Kaṭha Upaniṣad* 1.2.24 explains that one has to abandon wickedness, be tranquil, subdued and at peace of mind. It further explains (KaUp. 1.3.3-5) that one should know *Ātman* to be the master of the chariot; the body is the chariot, the *buddhi* is the charioteer and the mind its reins; the senses are horses; are the objects are the roads and the mind is the enjoyer. Unless there is full control over the body and senses one cannot enjoy a smooth ride to the higher regions.

The *Muṇḍaka Upaniṣad* 1.2.8-9 explains that the performers of *karma*, owing to their attachments, fall from heaven, when their *karma* is consumed. They do not know the truth. It also explains two kinds of knowledge which one must know. Thus the Upaniṣads stress upon higher knowledge for knowing the Supreme Lord. The *Kena Upaniṣad* 1.5-9, 2.1 explains that you know that which cannot be expressed by speech but by which speech is expressed, which cannot be apprehended by mind but by which mind is apprehended, cannot be perceived by eye, by which eye is perceived, cannot be heard by the ear but by which hearing is perceived, which cannot be smelt by breath but which breath smells as object. The *Muṇḍaka Upaniṣad* 1.2.12 therefore advises that eternal cannot be produced by one which is not eternal. So that eternal should be known. Let one approach a *guru* who is well versed in the Vedas and always devoted to the *Brahman*.

But the *Kaṭha Upaniṣad* 1.2.23 restricts that one cannot know *Ātman* by study of Vedas or by intelligence or by all hearing of sacred books only. One can attain it only if it chooses one to reveal its own form. Thus the element of divine grace is a must.

With acquiring adequate *karma* and knowledge, the Upaniṣads prescribe *yoga* and meditation a culminating path to liberation. The *Kaṭha Upaniṣad* 2.3.9 explains that the form of *Brahman* is not an object of vision. No one can behold Him with an eye. One can know Him when He is revealed by intellect free from doubt and by constant meditation. The *Muṇḍaka Upaniṣad* 3.1.8 also explains that *Brahman* cannot be seen by eye, nor expressed by speech, nor other senses, nor by self-punishment/good works. A man becomes pure by calmness of intellect; one can behold Him in meditation. The *Kena Upaniṣad* 4.5 says that through meditation the seeker communes with *Brahman* intimately again and again. The *Praśna Upaniṣad* 5.5 tells that one who meditates on the highest person through this syllable *auṁ* consisting of three letters becomes united with the effulgent sun. As a snake is freed from its skin, he is freed from his sin. The *Kaṭha Upaniṣad* 2.3.17 explains that *Puruṣa* dwells always in the hearts of men, the inner self. It is not larger than a thumb, let a man separate Him from the body with steadiness as one separates a tender stem from a blade of grass. One should know that the Self is bright and immortal.

In the hymns of Guru Nānak also we find basically the doctrine of *karma*, importance of higher knowledge, role of a *guru*, and ultimate experiential knowledge of self by chanting God's name, concentration and contemplation, going beyond the three states of consciousness in meditation to achieve the fourth state of *turīya* for the liberation of the individual self. He also compares the body with a city of eleven gates and an abode of the Lord.

The detailed materials selected from his hymns in Chapter 5 establish many close and elaborated concepts and commonalities to the path of liberation by personal experience of divinity as explained in the Upaniṣads and the hymns of Guru Nānak.

Guru Nānak expresses that one should have faith in the existence of God (*manana*); listen to scriptures and exercise repetition of the *guru*'s word (*śravaṇa*); disciplined meditation for personal experience of divinity by going beyond the tenth gate of the city of this body for achieving the *turīya* state of consciousness; hearing the sound of unstuck melody within for bliss of merger with Him. The selected material has accordingly been arranged under these heads.

Four stanzas of *Japjī* (*pauṛīs* 12-15) describe the sublime state of the faithful concluding that no pen, paper or subscribe can record the state of the faithful who get intuitive awareness and intelligence by faith. *Maṅne kī gati kahī na jāi* (*Ādi Granth*, p. 31). With faith one is focused on *śabada* and happiness wells up. It is oneness of faith of all seekers, spiritual leaders, prophets and seers that they left behind all the pleasures of life, travelled to foreign lands bearing all the sufferings for becoming acceptable to Him. *Devatiā darasana kai tāī dūkha bhūkha tīratha kīe* (ibid., p. 358). There is a piece of advice: *bhāṅḍā dhoi baisi dhūpu devahu tau dūdhai kau jāvahu* (ibid., p. 728). As one washes and disinfects the vessel before gathering milk in it, one should get the milk of good deeds and put conscious mind as ferment and be disinterested from the world to allow curdling.

Four stanzas of the *Japjī* (*pauṛī*s 8-11) explain the benefits of listening (*śravaṇa*) of spiritual discourses, scriptures and spiritual teachers (*suṇie sidha pīra surināthа* – ibid., p. 2). By listening to *siddhas*, spiritual teachers and yogic masters, the seekers attain bliss. Sufferings and sins get destroyed by listening to them.

Guru Nānak explains the path to higher spiritual regions beyond the three states of consciousness that is the *turīya* state: *ulaṭio kamalu barahamu bīcāri, aṁmr̥ta dhāra gagani dasa duāri* (ibid., p. 153) that the reverted heart lotus gets upturned through deep contemplation of God. Pure nectar oozes down from the self within the individual. When one's mind gets surrendered to the word of the *guru*, it absorbs the essence of that pure nectar. One's intuitive awareness is awakened and one gets the knowledge of one's own home which is within the individual. *Janami marai trai guṇa hitakaru, cāre beda kathahi ākārui tīn avasathā kahahi vakhiānu, turīāvasathā satigura tehari jānu* (ibid., p. 154) (one who remains in the three states of consciousness remains in rotation of coming and going. The scriptures describe and explain the three stages of consciousness, but one can learn about the fourth state of union with God, i.e. *turīya*, from a true *guru* only). *Sabhi japa, sabhi tapa sabha caturāī* (ibid., p. 412) (all rituals and sacrifices and tricks make one to wander aimlessly). *Kiā jaṅgalu ḍhūḍhī jāi . . .* (ibid., p. 420) (there is no benefit to go to forests or wild lands when one can realize the Self within his own home which is the abode of God by serving a true *guru* and realize the mansion of Lord's presence within oneself who blends us with Himself when it pleases Him).

Guru Nānak speaks of experiencing the melody of unstuck sounds in many of his hymns. *Pauṛī* 29 of *Japjī* explains: "*. . . ghaṭi ghaṭi vājahi nāda .... saṅjogu vijogu dui kāra calāvahi lakhe āvahi bhāga*" (ibid., p. 6). In every heart there is vibration of a sound current of *nāda*. But it is by His will that one experiences union with or separation from Him. We get what is written for us in our fate. He advises: *paṅca cele vasa kījahi rāvala ihu manu kījai ḍaṅḍātā...eku sabadu dūjā horu nāsati kaṅda mūli mana lāvasitā* (ibid., p. 155) (pierce deep within your body, make your five passions your disciples under control. There is only one *śabada*, everything else is just passing. This should be the fruit and root of mind). *Guramati rāmu japai jana pūrā, titu ghaṭa anahata bāje tūrā* (ibid., p. 228). In these lines Guru Nānak explains that perfect man who dwells in Lord through the *guru*'s word experiences the music of unstuck melody in his abode within himself.

Guru Nānak further says:

> *jo kichu karai bhalā kari manau, sahaja joga nidhi pāvau* ||
> ....
> *sagalī joti hamārī saṁmiā nānā varana anekaṁ* ||
> *kahu nānaka suṇi bharathari jogī pārabrahama liva ekaṁ* ||
>
> – Ibid., pp. 359-60

Whatever God gives one should think that as to be good, by this one will acquire the wealth of *sahaja-yoga*. A renunciate remains always united with the essence of the Supreme Being in all the ages. He gets the name of the true Lord and sits in his yogic posture in the city of the Supreme Being and sheds all wishes and contradictions. The vibrations of unstuck melody within oneself rings out day and night and one experiences the sound current of *nāda*. So submit yourself with compassion to the Lord's will with the *guru*'s word in your mind, you will attain *sahaja-yoga*, meaning spontaneous concentration of mind. You will get attuned to the Lord and hear the melody of unstruck sound within. *Heko pādharu heku daru gura pauḍī nija thānu, ruḍau ṭhākuru nānakā sabhi sukha sācau nāmu* (ibid., p. 1279) (there is only one door leading to the path of ultimate goal and the *guru* assists as a ladder to reach one's own self). *Tīni samāvai cauthai vāsā, praṇavati nānaka hama tā ke dāsā* (*Ādi Granth*, p. 839) (Nānak prays to be his slave to one who has come out of the three states of consciousness and resides ever in the fourth state (*tūrīya*). *Anahada sabadu nirālā vāje . . . sabade bhede tau pati pāvai* (ibid., p. 839) (the unstuck sound current of *śabada* vibrates itself ... one who gets deeply inflicted with *śabada* obtains this honour).

Thus hymns of Guru Nānak explain the path of Self-realization through *sahaja-yoga* up to *turīya* state of consciousness and beyond. However *turīyatīta*, a state beyond *turīya* in meditation practises, is not referred to in the principal Upaniṣads. *Turīya* state is the fourth state as the witness state to the earlier three states of consciousness and a spiritual aspirant has yet to realize himself beyond this state – as the non-dual *Brahman* – described as *turīyatīta*.

Guru Nānak portrays the journey of spiritual consciousness through five spiritual planes as discussed in Chapter 5. These five planes, comparable with the *pañca kośa* (five sheaths) of *Ātman* explained in the *Taittirīya Upaniṣad*, are as follows:

1. *Annamaya Kośa* (plane of matter) or *dharma khaṇḍa* denotes the material frame of human beings of different types, colours and names meaning physical existence of body and its needs.
2. *Prāṇamaya Kośa* (plane of life) or *jñāna khaṇḍa* denotes the force working behind the various organs and senses through which we perceive the urge to know the external world around us.
3. *Manomaya Kośa* (mental plane) or *śrama khaṇḍa* denotes the effort of a man to develop skill for knowing the world around him and shed all his passions and vices or ego and aim at godly way in life.
4. *Vijñānamaya Kośa* (plane of self-consciousness reason) or *karma khaṇḍa* denotes developing extrasensory perceptions through higher knowledge and attainment of spiritual powers through grace of the Lord. The seeker is fully blossomed.

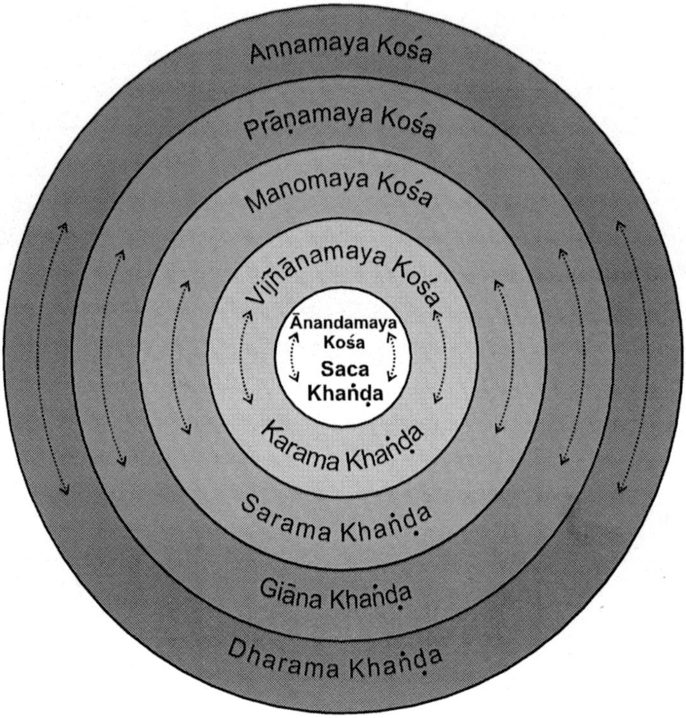

5. *Ānandamaya Kośa* (plane of non-dual bliss) or *saca khaṇḍa* denotes the plane of Truth which is called abode of the Formless, infinite and creator of all creations. Herein the knower, the known and the knowledge become fused in a transcendental unity.

The seeker travelling through all these stages can reach the deep within him and enjoy the unity with the Ultimate Truth. Each stage is an integral part of the whole journey and when the individual consciousness gets merged with the Universal Consciousness, one attains the Supreme Bliss.

Personal Experience of Divinity

We live a life of wonder with wonder all around us. Contemplating deep within us upon this wonder must also be a wonderful experience. What is that personal experience of divinity that pulls us from within to the higher regions of consciousness to see, hear, taste, feel and realize which cannot be experienced by our senses and sense organs? There are many references in the Upaniṣads and hymns of Guru Nānak, to the home of the Lord in the deep cave of the heart, to the tenth gate of human body and *turīya* – a state of consciousness experienced after the three states of consciousness, i.e. awake, sleep and deep sleep – are obliterated and the unstruck melody of sound resounding within oneself. These references point towards a common path to the goal of self-realization and emancipation as well as the personal experiences of divinity.

According to Sant Kabīr who was a contemporary of Guru Nānak,

> spiritual experience cannot be described. Can a mute person explain the taste of sugar? Realization seals the lips of the devotee; bliss of realization can be understood only by one who achieves the selfsame knowledge. – *Kabīr Sākhī Saṁgraha* 76.1-2

> The moment the soul realizes itself, sorrow and happiness disappear and the dispute and debate end. The inner heart shines with enlightenment. One sees God everywhere . . . as the bridal procession loses its glamour the moment the bride and bridegroom meet, so the words become insipid after realization.
> – Ibid. 77.5-7

The materials selected in Chapter 5 from principal Upaniṣads and hymns of Guru Nānak provide glimpses of personal experience of divinity disclosed by the sages and seers of Upaniṣads and Guru Nānak.

The *Muṇḍaka Upaniṣad* 3.1.5 explains that by one's hard practice of truthfulness a sinless seeker beholds *Ātman* residing within his body. *Brahman* shines forth (MU 3.1.7) vast, self-luminous; inconceivable is seen here dwelling in the cave of the heart of conscious beings. The radiant *Brahman* (MU 2.2.1-2) dwells in the cave of the heart and is known to move there. It is a great support of all, for in it is centred everything that moves, breathes and blinks; that alone is to be struck. He who knows this *Brahman* (MU 2.1.10), which is the supreme and eternal, hidden in the cave of the heart, unfolds every knot of one's ignorance. When the seer beholds the self-luminous creator (MU 3.1.3), the Lord, then one becomes free from good and evil. One becomes stainless and reaches the supreme unity having realized *Ātman* (MU 3.2.5), the seers become satisfied with the knowledge. Their souls are established in the Supreme Self, they are free from passions and tranquil in mind. Such calm souls ever devoted to self behold everywhere the omnipresent *Brahman* and in the end enter into it. As flowing rivers disappear in the sea (MU 3.2.8) losing their identity of name, the enlightened man is freed from his identity and attains *Puruṣa* who is the greatest. The *Taittirīya Upaniṣad* (1.6.1) explains: "within the heart lies the person (*Puruṣa*) consisting of mind (*manomaya*)". One who knows *Brahman* and being one with the omniscient *Brahman*, enjoys simultaneously all desires (TU 2.1.3). To an enquiry to the bliss of *Brahman*; He who is here in man and yonder sun both are one. He, who knows this, attains the Self which consists of bliss (TU 2.8.1).

The *Māṇḍūkya Upaniṣad* explains the word/sound of *oṁ* and the *turīya* state of consciousness. The *turīya* is neither simple consciousness nor is it unconsciousness. It is unperceived, unrelated, incomprehensive, uninferable, unthinkable and indescribable. It is all peace, all bliss and non-dual. This is known as the fourth (*turīya*). This is *Ātman* and this is to be realized (MU 7). In *turīya* there is a permanent union with *Brahman*. The forth state of consciousness is *turīya*. It is cessation of all phenomena, it is all good and non-dual. The *auṁ* is verily *Ātman*, one who knows this merges his self in *Ātman* (MU 12). Thus those who realize *Brahman*, the highest reality, merge the self in *turīya*, because they transcend the notion of cause and effect which inheres in the third quarter of *Ātman*. They are not born again because they have realized their identity with the causeless *turīya*. Thus the Upaniṣads describe that the *turīya* state of consciousness is a state of all bliss and cessation of all duality.

Guru Nānak also explained in his hymns that the Absolute Lord is deep within us. *Aṅtara suṅnam, bāhari suṅnam, tribhavaṇa suṅnamasuṅnaṁ, cauthe suṅnai jo nara jāṇai tā kou pāpu na puṅnaṁ* (*Ādi Granth*, p. 943) (He is outside as well inside and in between. He fills all the three worlds totally. But one who attains the Supreme Lord in the fourth state of consciousness becomes free from all virtue or vice). *Nau sara subhara dasavai pūre, taha anahata suṅna bajāvahi tūre* (ibid., p. 943) (one who practises and controls his nine outflowing doors, he is able to proceed further towards the tenth gate. There one experiences the unstruck melody vibrating and resounding within the self. There one beholds the presence of the Supreme Being and gets absorbed in Him. In another hymn: *kāiā nagaru nagara gaḍa aṅdari, sācā vāsā puri gaganaṅdari* (ibid., p. 1033), he explains that the true Lord resides deep within this body village. The true Lord is within the tenth gate. The tenth gate is guarded with strong heavy lid closed and locked from within. These are opened through the word of the *guru*. Within the fort there is a cave which is the residing place of the Self. These nine gates are established by God's will and direction. It is here that the Supreme Being who is beyond any knowledge resides; He who cannot be seen with the eyes reveals Himself. *Dehī nagarī ūtama thānā . . . āpi pachāṇai sabadu vīcārā, sacai mahali nivāsu niraṅtari āvaṇa jāṇu cukaiā* (ibid., p. 1039) (one who realizes his own self, concentrates upon the *śabada*, he reaches out deep within the true palace of God's presence. There is no further birth or death for him. His mind gets stabilized and winds of his desires come under his control. Such a *yogī* hears the vibrations of unstruck sounds current of *śabada*. God plays the pure music of *pañca-śabda* (five primal sounds). In the fear of Lord and in detachment one intuitively merges into the Lord. This is a clear message of Guru Nānak: "Man know Thyself". One beholds the play of *karma* when one is illuminated by *guru*'s teachings. The consciousness shoots up the sky with the grace of *guru* and one experiences the revelations of *śabada* within one self. One's restless desires are restrained and one comes to know one's own heart and see the play of *karma*.

Guru Nānak preaches *sahaja-patha* – *sahaja-yoga* or *sūrata-śabada-yoga*. He explains his experience of divinity that through the *sūrata-śabada-yoga* all the five virtues, viz. truth, contentment, compassion, righteousness and patience, are imbibed by the five knowing faculties but one abides in the Self only through the grace of a *guru*. Guru Nānak again and again refers to the Guru's word

(Name of the Lord), his love for the name and unstuck melody of five primal sounds experienced by him in his hymns. For him by repeating the word of the *guru* (name of God) internally, one gets concentrated within. Deep concentration and meditation at tenth door reveal the *śabada* within and one gets attuned to the higher levels of consciousness and hears the sweet unstuck melody of *śabada*.

Sant Kabīr also shared the same experience through the Natural Path at *sahaja-patha* described by him as, "that easily takes you straight to Lord and gives you conquest over all passions" (Kohli 1969: 76, 1-2). He explains that:

> The adventure of the divine love is very strange. The door that leads to it is in the forehead and it is no easy path. Those who describe the adventure have not reached the end and those who reach there, become silent. – Ibid.: 53, 7-8

Guru Nānak sums up his experience of divinity and explains in one of his hymns: *ghara mahi ghasu dikhāi dei so satiguru purakhu sujāṇu* II *pañca sabada dhunikāra dhuni taha bājai sabadu nisāṇu* II (*Ādi Granth*, p. 1291) (One who leads us to our home within the home of the individual self is true *guru*. The *pañca-śabda*, the primal five sounds echo loudly (resound) and re-echo (resonate) within.) The heart lotus gets turned upside down and is filled with pure nectar. Then the mind does not wander hither and thither.

The *Chāndogya Upaniṣad* (3.19.4) also explains that he who, meditates on the sun (inner self) as *Brahman*–pleasant sounds will quickly approach him and continue to delight him, yea, will continue to delight him. Guru Nānak explains and discloses *śabada guru, sūrata dhuna celā* one has to focus one's consciousness on *śabada* and the melody follows. *Pūrā satiguru sevi pūrā pāiā, pūrai karami dhiāi pūrā sabadu manna vasāiā* (ibid., p. 1286). (By service to the perfect *guru* he realized all powerful Supreme Being deep within himself. By doing virtuous deeds and meditation he acquires the *śabada* resounding within him.) With the knowledge and contemplation of the *śabada* all his dirt and dust vanish. Thus he finds the Supreme Being as his most pious resort for visiting.

The Upaniṣads and Guru Nānak teach that the whole world moves under the Divine Law and we should develop a living harmony with the Divine Will by living a virtuous life. In the words of Guru Nānak, God abides in the hearts of all; there is no heart without God. But she is the God's bride to whom with the grace of *guru*, God reveals Himself. No one can live so long to fulfil all his desires. The life goes on at its own pace. The mortals try to hold it back but death takes it away without any individual's agreement. So one should not be anxious about dying or hope of living, *maraṇai kī ciṅtā nahī jīvaṇa kī nahī āsa* ।। *tu saraba jīā paratipālahī lekhai sāsa girāsa* ।। (*Ādi Granth*, p. 20). Lord is fond of and careful for all His beings and keeps the account of all our respirations and every small mouthful piece of food.

****

Message

There is a message for claimants and custodians of legacy of Guru Nānak to shun off all preachers and practices advocating separation, for any institutionalized religion, on the basis of philosophy of life of Guru Nānak from the universal approach of Upaniṣadic philosophy being attributed to Sikhism and Hinduism. Both are above the boundary walls of any institute of religions and for the benefit of all mankind at large. Any argument and strife for using the highest knowledge revealed by the sages, seers and Guru Nānak for the separation and division of society and caging it into religions rather than absorbing its essence for better living of mankind is sheer ignorance.

The aspirants of unveiling the mask of Ultimate Reality and cosmic laws by searching for the God element and dreamers of creating a robot of human form are the technicians of Divine Will to add to the wonder of this wonderful creation for the betterment of human life. The revelations in the hymns of creation in Nāsadīya Sūkta and *arbada narbada dhauṅdhūkārā* (ibid., p. 1035) still hold good for humanity. Divine Force reveals itself to one whom it chooses.

In the present fast worldly life of competitions and turmoil, seekers on the path of liberation should waste no time in religious conflicts, arguments, pseudo rituals and penances and develop harmony with Divine Will and live a life of righteousness, acquire knowledge, pursue for prosperity of health, wealth and accumulations necessary for their security in life and their spiritual advancement. They should not live a sordid life but seek pleasure of senses and human love to enjoy life but should not be lost in the smoke of these worldly aspirations. Let the experiential realities of life not be forgotten in the crazy run for unreal attractions. With a balanced life of action one should approach an apt guide to tread upon spiritual path for his ultimate goal of liberation and find everlasting abode of happiness.

Revelations at a Glance

Hymns of Guru Nānak are a fearless and bold expression of his experiential Universal Truth based on real experiences of life lived in Pure Consciousness. His philosophy of life is Upaniṣadic in origination and portrays his sound knowledge of existing Vedic literature. In his hymns there is a vivid description of:

1. the self or essence of man – *Ātman*;
2. the Self or essence of the creation – *Brahman* or *Oṁkāra*; and
3. the relation between *Ātman* and *Paramātman*.

These three components constitute a major part of the teachings of the Upaniṣads as well as the hymns of Guru Nānak. He gave a clear message: "Man Know Thyself". His concepts of Truth, cosmogony or origin of creation, identity between the individual soul and the Universal Soul, the individual soul and body, mutual relationship between God, man and the world, supremacy of Divine Will, fear of God, curse of duality, struggle and suffering in the world due to *karma*, God's love and grace are all in consonance with the Upaniṣadic philosophy of life. However, Guru Nānak with his transcendental exposition, sharp skill and argumentative capability and common poetic language further enriched, explained, simplified, modernized and expressed various theological concepts for the use and understanding of a common man. He elaborated and explained the most essential parts of philosophy of life to the masses by rejecting and condemning pseudo knowledge of the priests and preachers of his times. Thus he brought the wisdom of the philosophy of life from the clutches of the highly learned brāhmaṇas, sages and seers down to the common man through simplicity of expression, thought and action. He preached that recourse to spirituality does not mean to forget or neglect one's worldly duties and advocated that bookish knowledge of the sacred books or religious scriptures is not enough for personal experience of divinity and like the Upaniṣads, he stressed the need for deep meditation to realize the Self within.

- Guru Nānak's exuberance of love and search for God and godly people was not confined to any religion, religious institution or founding separate identity of any new religious sect. Like the Upaniṣads, his hymns express both unity of all existence and unity of all knowledge in Pure Consciousness and declare that the fountain source of all knowledge, all scriptures, all intuitive experiences is One. Guru Nānak expresses that the conflicts and controversies amongst various schools of philosophy are also His creation and teacher of all teachers of systems and doctrines is only One Lord. He gave a message of universal love, developing living harmony with the Divine Will, accept the writ of predestined *karma* with pleasure and patience as what cannot be cured must be endured, live a practical virtuous life, not to waste a single moment of precious human life in conflicts and strife and remain always attuned to God to enjoy his love, mercy and grace along with godly people around you. The way to find peace in this world is to develop love for the everlasting and permanent Divine Force behind all existence. Thus his message of Universal Love for better worldliness is beyond all religions or religious institutions or religious thoughts, true for all mankind at large and is not subject to change with time, space or community.

- Guru Nānak was a protagonist of Bhakti tradition of religion of saints and stressed more on Bhakti or Devotion to God rather than observing rituals, hard penances, austerities or blind faith. The hymns of Guru Nānak and the Upaniṣads, both, explain that the real aim of human life is to attain liberation from the repeated coming and going in incarnations which can be attained only in human form. With adequate *karma* and knowledge, both instructs the need of a disciplined meditation for personal experience of divinity with God's grace, as a culminating path to liberation by going beyond the tenth gate of the city of this body for achieving the *turīya* state (and beyond) of consciousness. Both emphasize the intense yearning desire for liberation from the bondages of worldly life and advise to approach a Self-realized guide who can lead the individual to the higher levels of consciousness. However, Guru Nānak teaches the *sahaja-patha* or *sūrata-śabada-yoga,* meaning the natural path that easily takes one straight to the Lord by spontaneous concentration of mind, making one conquest over all passions by constant repetition of the *guru*'s word (name of the Lord), and by disciplined concentration and constant meditation, which draw the aspiring soul upward to the higher spiritual realms for personal experience of divinity and merger of the individual soul with the Universal Soul.

* * *

Bibliography

Chopra, Madhu, 2006, *Upaniṣadoṅ ke Svara*, New Delhi: Satyam Publishing House.

Duggal, K.S., 1980, *Sikh Gurus: Their Lives & Teachings*, Delhi: Vikas.

Gupta, M.G., 2012, *Nanak: The Saint* (first published, M.G. Publishers, Agra 1990), Noida: Harper Collins Publishers.

Hume, Robert Earnet, 1921, *The Thirteen Upanishads*, translated from Sanskrit with an Outline of the Philosophy of Upaniṣads, London: Oxford University Press.

John, Davidson, 2003, *A Treasury of Mystic Terms*, vol. 1: *Universe of Spirituality*, Beas: Science of Soul Research Center, Radhasoami Satsang.

Joshi, L.M., 2000, *Sikhism*, Patiala: Panjabi University.

Kabīr Sākhī Saṁgraha, Allahabad: Belvedere Printing Works.

Kapoor, Subodh, 2002a, *Encyclopedia of Vedic Philosophy: The Age, Religion, Literature, Pantheon, Philosophy, Traditions and Teachers of the Vedas*, vol. 8, Delhi: Cosmo Publications.

———, 2002b, *Encyclopedia of Vedanta Philosophy*, Delhi: Cosmo Publications

Kohli, S.S., 1969, *Philosophy of Guru Nanak*, Chandigarh: Publication Bureau, Panjab University.

———, 1997, *Travels of Guru Nanak*, Chandigarh: Publication Bureau, Panjab University.

Komal, Harnek Singh, 2007, *Bhai Gurdas di Pehli Vaar: Sahitak Prepakh* (Punjabi), Amritsar: Ruhi Prakashan.

Macauliffe, Max Arthur, 2009, *The Sikh Religion: Its Gurus, Sacred Writings and Authors*, Amritsar: Satvic Media.

Nikhilananda, Swami, 2008, *The Upanishads*, Kolkata: Advaita Ashrama.

Pruthy, R., 2004, *Sikhism and Indian Civilization* (Cultural and Civilization Series), New Delhi: Discovery Publishing House.

Puri, J.R., 2004, *Guru Nanak: His Mystic Teachings*, Beas: Radha Soami Satsang Sabha.

Radhakrishnan, S., 2012, *The Principal Upanishads*, Noida: Harper Collins.

Rahlan, O.P., 1992, *Encyclopedia of Sikhism, Religion and Culture*, vol. 2, New Delhi: Anmol Publications.

Ranganathananda, Swami, 2006, *The Charm and Power of the Upanishads*, Kolkata: Advaita Ashrama.

Sagoo, Harbans Kaur, 1992, *Guru Nanak and Indian Society*, New Delhi: Deep and Deep.

Sen, Pritam, 1995, *God's Love in Upanishads*, Bombay: Bharatiya Vidya Bhawan.

Shiromani Gurdwara Parbandhak Committee, 1951, *Sri Guru Granth Sahib* (Hindi), Amritsar.

———, 2009, *Sikh Rehit Mryada*, Amritsar: Dharam Prachar Committee.

Singh, Daljit, 1979, *Sikhism: A Comparative Study of Its Theology and Mysticism*, New Delhi: Sterling Publishers.

Singh, Gopal, 2005, *Sri Guru Granth Sahib* (English version), New Delhi: Allied Publishers.

Singh, Harbans and Lal Mani Joshi, 1996, *An Introduction to Indian Religions*, 2nd edn, Patiala: Publication Bureau, Punjabi University.

Singh, Jodh, 1981, *Sikh Dharam kī Rūparekhā*, Varanasi: Sahityakar Prakashan.

———, 2010, *Guru Nanak Bani* (Punjabi), 6th edn, Delhi: National Book Trust.

Singh, Kehar, 2009, *Guru: Dispeller of Darkness*, 2nd edn, Tarn Taran: Association of Radha Swami Dera Baba Bagga Singh.

Singh, Khuswant, 1969, *Japji: Guru Nanak Quincentenary Celebrations*, published by Capt. Anant Singh, editor *The Punjab Mail*, Chandigarh.

Singh, Sahib, 2011, *Bara Mah Tukhari te Majh* (Punjabi), 14th edn, Amritsar: Singh Brothers.

Singh, Tarn, 1996, *Guru Nanak Bani Prakash*, parts 1-2, Patiala: Punjabi University.

Tiwari, Vishwanath, 1991, *Krantikari Guru Nanak*, Chandigarh: Publication Bureau, Panjab University.

Trumpp, Ernest, 1970, *Adi Granth or the Holy Scripture of Sikhs*, New Delhi: Oriental Publishers.

Index